Baptists in Israel

The Letters of Paul and Marjorie Rowden
1952–1957

Rebecca Rowden

Fields Publishing
Nashville, Tennessee

Printed in the United States of America

Library of Congress Control Number 2010928816
ISBN: 978-1-57843-075-8

published by

Fields Publishing, Inc.
8120 Sawyer Brown Road, Suite 108 • Nashville, Tennessee 37221
615-662-1344
e-mail: tfields@fieldspublishing.com

To Robin and Paige
and
In memory of Ric

CONTENTS

INTRODUCTION

Rummaging through closets in the Atlanta homes of my grandparents, I came across boxes of onion-thin overseas airmail letters. Carefully opening the fragile pages, I discovered that the letters were written by my parents, Paul and Marjorie Rowden, and contained an account of our sojourn in Israel. In March 1952, our family of four traveled by freighter to Israel and over the next five years, we lived in Nazareth, Jerusalem and Haifa. My parents served as members of the Baptist Convention in Israel. My father became the administrator of the Nazareth Baptist School and both parents taught classes. They were active in the Nazareth Baptist Church and oversaw the administration of the George W. Truett Children's Home for a year. The family moved to Jerusalem where my parents attended *ulpanim*, Hebrew language classes, and assisted with the Jerusalem Baptist Church. Our last years in Israel, we lived in the port city of Haifa.

My parents chronicled their observations of the culture, the land and its people, their struggle to learn Arabic and Hebrew and their desire to express their faith in an ancient land sacred to many world religions. The letters were informal and intended for family and close friends. An occasional newsletter was sent to the church that helped to sponsor them, the Cascade Baptist Church in Atlanta, Georgia. In one letter, my father—writing to a friend in America who was considering overseas Christian mission service, cautioned, "There are some things that only experience can teach…One never hears about the problems of adjustment of a new worker to language, people, new diseases, living conditions. …There is that wearing care of work that tries to rob a worker of his spirituality. There are those differences of opinion among fellow workers, and sometimes conflicts of personalities. There are the disappointments of months and even years of work that seem so fruitless. However, if this is what the Lord wants for you in spite of all the above things, there is a joy and satisfaction that is most rewarding."[1]

My parents are deceased. Blessed be their memory. After several years of research, and as a contribution to the history of Baptists in the Middle East,

I am publishing some of the letters with historical context and supplemental documentation from unpublished documents, personal interviews, mission magazine articles, books and minutes of the Southern Baptist Convention Foreign Mission Board. The chapters are organized by stations where Baptists lived and worked; including Nazareth, Jerusalem, Haifa, Tel Aviv and Petah Tikva. Baptist activity in Jordan, Lebanon and the Gaza Strip is occasionally referenced. The American Friends Service Committee (Quakers), the Edinburgh Medical Mission Society Hospital in Nazareth and the U.S. State Department in Tel Aviv and Jerusalem are addressed to the extent that their staff interacted with members of the Baptist Convention in Israel. The major political and historical events that shaped and redefined the landscape in Palestine-Israel serve as a backdrop.

When Paul and Marjorie Rowden arrived in Israel in March 1952, there were two small Baptist congregations—one in Jerusalem and one in Nazareth. Around 300 children attended the Nazareth Baptist School. Donations from Baptists in the United States had enabled the Nazareth and Jerusalem Baptist Churches to be constructed and provided for the administration of the Nazareth Baptist School. Donations also provided tuition for several young Arab Palestinians from Nazareth to travel to America and further their education with the goal of returning to help in the Baptist church and school. Inland from Tel Aviv, on the Plain of Sharon in Petah Tikva, Baptists planned to build a communal farming center. The center would be one in which the members and their children could live each day within the unique experience of Christian fellowship, constituted around an indigenous Baptist church in Israel. The settlement would also serve the need for a centrally located meeting place for conferences, retreats and camps.[2] The plan, however, was still in the proposal stage.

The Baptist mission members met formally once a year. They elected officers and committee chairmen, adopted a budget, submitted reports to the Foreign Mission Board of the Southern Baptist Convention in Richmond, Virginia and made plans for the upcoming year. On a day-to-day basis, however, interactions with each other were very informal and plans changed daily. Members left for the United States on furlough, or due to illness, leaving gaps that had to be filled. New members were often given responsibilities immediately upon arrival and had to postpone language study or get it "on the run." Budget fluctuations hampered progress and families lived together until separate residences could be obtained. Occasional conflict among members called for consensus or resolution. To overcome cultural isolation, they socialized with other Americans and with English-speaking friends. Laughter relieved stress. They met weekly to pray for God's guidance. They cared for each other's children and the children in the Baptist sponsored Children's Home. They rallied in support when someone fell ill and acted, by and large, as an extended family. In March 1952, the members of the Baptist Convention in Israel were: Dwight and Emma Baker and Elmo and Hannah Scoggin, stationed in Nazareth, with Robert and Margaret Lindsey, Eunice Fenderson and Tom and Mary Helen Francis, stationed in Jerusalem.

American Southern Baptists had deeply instilled ideas of religious freedom that sometimes clashed with the historical and political realities governing religious communities in the Middle East. Coming from a culture where Protestants represented a significant portion of the general population, they found living in a land where Christians were an insignificant minority, not to mention despised by some extremists, to be a new and challenging experience. They developed ecumenical relations with other Christian groups, successfully worked through administrative issues with the Israeli Ministry of Religious Affairs and generally lived in harmony with people of other faiths or those with no faith.

The intent of the book is to document more than one family's account. It is a partial history of Baptists—those from America—as well as national Baptists—who lived and worshiped in the land of the Bible during the first fifty-seven years of the twentieth century. I have chosen to end the historical account in late 1957 due to the fact that my family returned to America and the correspondence ended. However, in the Epilogue, I discuss some of the ongoing Baptist ministries in Israel.

A wide variety of letters written by my parents, Paul and Marjorie Rowden, have been selected for publication in this book. The letters are primarily addressed to my grandparents—the Paul Rowden Sr.'s and the Byron H. Coles—in Atlanta—sometimes written by Paul, sometimes by Marjorie, and often addressed to "Folks," meaning it was circulated among all four grandparents. Paul usually signed his letters "S" for "Sonny," the nickname his parents had given him. Marjorie's letters sometimes included the name of her brother "Bill" or "Billy."

My parents readily admitted to having much to learn about the Middle East. They wrote openly and honestly from their hearts. If any statements in their letters appear to the reader to be offensive or insensitive in any manner, an apology is most humbly extended.

—Rebecca Rowden

1

BAPTISTS IN NAZARETH
1911–1952

In 1911, Shukri Musa, a Palestinian Arab, began a Baptist ministry in Nazareth. Palestine was then part of the vast Ottoman Empire. Musa was born in 1870 in the town of Safed—a small town in Galilee, in northern Palestine. The Musa family members were communicants in the Greek Catholic Church. In 1908, Musa left his family for two years and traveled to America, in order to work and improve the family's fortune. He and his nephew made a living traveling around Texas on horseback selling merchandise from farm to farm.[1] Musa became interested in Southern Baptist denominational worship, attended services, converted to the Baptist faith and was baptized. Dr. George W. Truett, pastor of the First Baptist Church of Dallas, Texas, ordained him as a minister. Rev. Musa returned to Palestine in 1910 determined to begin his ministry.[2] He carried with him a little portable organ that was to provide the music for his new church.[3] Baptist churches in Southern Illinois, who affiliated with the Southern Baptist Convention in 1910, supported Rev. Musa. The Illinois churches encouraged the Foreign Mission Board (FMB) of the Southern Baptist Convention to take over the support of the ministry, but uncertainties of World War I hindered the board from making any plans for Baptist missions in Palestine.[4] In 1920, however, the FMB took over the support of the well-established stations at Rasheya in Syria and Nazareth in Palestine.[5]

Shukri Musa's wife, Munira, was a very educated woman. Her father, Youssef Badr, attended the Syrian Protestant College, later called the American University of Beirut, in Lebanon. He also attended a Protestant theological seminary in Abeih in Mount Lebanon. In 1890, Youssef Badr was installed as the first Arab pastor of the National Evangelical Church of Beirut.[6] Munira attended the British Syrian Training College in Beirut. In

10

her book, *Teta, Mother and Me, Three Generations of Arab Women,* author Jean Said Makdisi wrote of her grandmother:

> At the British Syrian Training College, my grandmother [Munira], a daughter of the people, from one of the most ancient civilizations, bearer of a complex and long history, met with Englishwomen bringing with them, from their own complex background, an altogether alien notion of reality and history. It was the interaction between these Englishwomen and girls like my grandmother that caused a deceptively quiet but enormously important cultural upheaval, from which many of my mother's and then my generation of middle-class, urban women emerged… Gradually [Munira] was transformed from a provincial girl from the hinterland to a young woman from the increasingly sophisticated port city of Beirut, with its ancient Mediterranean cultural inheritance and its openness to the world.[7]

Upon his return to Palestine, Shukri Musa decided to take his ministry to Nazareth, known as the hometown of Jesus. When Musa moved to Nazareth, he found that it was a backward country town under the rule of the Turks. The government demanded exorbitant taxes and practically all of the officers governing the land were foreigners who cared little or nothing for the well being of the people. Justice was almost unknown and bribery was the rule rather than the exception.[8] In *Questing in Galilee,* Velora Hanna writes, "[Munira Musa's] heart ached at the poverty, the ignorance, and the neglected [babies] and abused women surrounding her. She became an advisor on sanitation, hygiene and childcare…She pitted her education, her refinement, and all of God's Word against [local] superstitions, being always careful to neither offend nor insult…"[9] She witnessed in her home with small groups of women who gathered to study the Bible and sew. She also started a ministry for children.

Moslems, Catholics and members of the Eastern Orthodox churches in Nazareth were suspicious when Shukri Musa moved into their community with his Protestant beliefs. Nonetheless he was able to rent a house for his family and a room for the beginning of his church.[10] The multi-lingual and multi-ethnic Christian groups that historically have roots in Palestine include the Eastern Orthodox, Oriental Orthodox and Catholic families. In their book, *Who Are the Christians in the Middle East?* authors Betty Jane and J. Martin Bailey state:

> The Eastern churches did not experience the sixteenth-century Reformation that resulted in the great diversity of Protestant churches in the West; nor were they impacted by the religious fervor and mission movements of these churches until the early nineteenth century when missionaries became active in the Middle East. Those who responded to the biblical teaching of the missionaries became known as *injiliyyeh* (pronounced in-jee-lee-ah), an Arabic term sometimes translated as "evangelists" and derived from the word for gospel or evangel. Some of these *injiliyyeh* were adherents of the historic Eastern churches who were impressed by the testimonies, personal devotion and daily example of the men and women who had left their homelands to express their faith. The Protestants of the Middle East therefore became known as "Evangelicals," which does not refer to a conservative theology as it does in the West, but to their response to the gospel.[11]

Evangelical groups that brought their protestant beliefs and programs to Palestine were a threat to the established Eastern churches. However, some church members—primarily the young people—gravitated from the Greek Orthodox or Catholic churches to Protestant churches, where they read and studied the Bible firsthand, participated in outreach activities and developed a personal prayer life with God. The Protestant doctrines and religious practices stood in contrast to the Eastern Church services steeped with ancient liturgies performed by priests on behalf of the communicants. Some Nazareth residents attended both Protestant and Eastern Church services, mixing the familiar and traditional religious rituals with the new Protestant expressions of worship.

In 1914, the Ottoman Empire entered World War I on the side of Germany against Britain, France, Russia and America. When war began, Shukri Musa was conscripted into the Ottoman army leaving his wife, Munira, to raise the children and pay the rent. A Turkish Moslem officer and his wife moved into a part of the Musa's home, as was the custom in wartime. Shukri Musa was sent to Baghdad. Munira befriended the Turkish officer's wife and she in turn, influenced her husband to show kindness to Mrs. Musa and her children. Finally, through the influence of the Turkish officer, Shukri Musa was brought back to Nazareth.[12] The war ended in 1918. Britain and France divided the Arab world. The countries that are now Syria and Lebanon became French mandates, while Iraq, Palestine and Transjordan came under British mandate.

The Anglicans, a branch of the Protestant church led by the Archbishop of Canterbury, had a presence in Nazareth prior to World War I. They built Christ Church in Nazareth, dedicated by King Edward VII in 1862. Anglican missionaries of the British Church Missionary Society established the Episcopal Christ School in 1851. The school was held in the church and later expanded to parts of St. Margaret's Guest Hospice on a hill above Nazareth.[13] The Edinburgh Medical Mission Society Hospital in Nazareth provided medical services to the Arab population during the British Mandate. With British rule in Palestine, English was frequently taught and became a second language for some Palestinians.

In 1923, Shukri Musa reported that four people were baptized into the Baptist faith. The average attendance at the weekly women's meeting held by Munira Musa was eighty-five and the Sunday school hour had a large attendance of boys and girls.[14]

National Baptist pastors and laymen asked the Foreign Mission Board (FMB) for missionaries to help support the ministries. "March 6, 1923, was a momentous day in the lives of four Southern Baptists who landed in Jaffa," wrote Mrs. J. Washington Watts, "for we had come [from America] as a fulfillment of the long-deferred hopes of faithful native workers to lay the foundation for a Baptist program in Palestine and Syria."[15] The FMB appointed Rev. James Washington (Wash) Watts and his wife, Mattie Leila (Reid) Watts, and Dr. and Mrs. F.B. Pearson as the FMB's first missionaries to Palestine and Syria. The area referred to as "Palestine-Syria," included land that is today Jordan, Syria, Lebanon, Israel and the Gaza Strip. Within a few months, the Pearsons had to return home due to illness. The Watts moved to Jerusalem and began studying Hebrew.[16] Rev. Watts traveled over a wide area and reported, "My mind runs unto the verse:

> Behold, how good and how pleasant it is for brethren to dwell together in unity! Like the dew of Hermon, that cometh down upon the mountains of Zion. Psalm 133:1, 3a."[17]

According to Watts, the verse reflected the breadth of the Syrian-Palestinian field that lay from Mt. Hermon to Mt. Zion. "When we go a journeying about the field, the route lies from Jerusalem to Nazareth to Damascus, circling around to those churches at the foot of Mt. Hermon, then out to Beirut, and back to Nazareth and Jerusalem."[18] The Watts were not given any promises of money to be invested in the work. Their budget covered little more than their salaries. They were advised to view the land, the conditions within it, the opportunities and needs, and to form opinions—before making any recommendations to the FMB concerning the establishment of Baptist work.[19] Rev. Wash Watts traveled sometimes around Palestine-Syria by donkey until friends in America purchased a car and sent it to Jerusalem for his use.[20]

The year 1924 was providential for the national Baptists in Nazareth. A group of Baptists from America visited the Holy Land, saw the work that Rev. and Mrs. Musa were doing, and returned home to begin seeking greater financial support for Baptist efforts in that land. The party included Dr. George W. Truett, pastor of the First Baptist Church of Dallas, Texas, and Dr. L. R. Scarborough, from Southwestern Baptist Seminary in Fort Worth, Texas. Both men had been influential in Rev. Musa's theological study of the Baptist faith when Musa was in Texas. As a result of that visit, and the subsequent campaign for donations for the work in Palestine, Mr. and Mrs. George W. Bottoms of Texarkana, generously gave ten thousand dollars to build the Nazareth Baptist Church.[21] Wash Watts and Shukri Musa participated in the long months of bargaining—Middle Eastern fashion, for the price of the lot—finally agreed upon. But tangles in the registration of the land were found in the Land Office, heritages of the Turkish regime. It took eight months to complete the process before Baptists officially secured title to the property.[22] Construction of the church was then begun.

As time allowed, there was outreach work in the surrounding villages, especially in Cana and Tur'an. Pastor Musa wrote, "The harvest is ripe, but the laborers are few. I am indeed bothered. Surely we need at least three workers in these villages."[23] In 1926, the Nazareth Baptist Church was dedicated. The dedication was lead by Rev. Musa, who had long worked for its establishment. Along with the dedication, Rev. Musa hosted the first Baptist worker's conference in Palestine-Syria. Attending the conference from Lebanon were Rev. Sa'eed Jureidini,[24] Rev. Najeeb Dawood [David], and Rev. Najeeb Khalaf. Rev. Wash Watts came from Jerusalem for the conference.[25] Rev. Sa'eed Jureidini, a natural and powerful evangelist from Beirut, led the services during the week.[26] Rev. Jureidini had been ordained in 1895 by the Baptist pastor of the Third Baptist Church of St. Louis, Missouri. He was influential in starting Baptist work in Beirut

and the surrounding area. Crowds filled the church for the dedication.[27]
Rev. Watts reported:

> During the same week [of the dedication,] a conference of our
> Baptist workers was organized. This gave an opportunity for an
> approach to many problems. We tried to create a vision of our
> work as a whole, hearing reports from each station and learning
> how to face our common as well as individual problems. We tried
> to define clearly our relations to each other, relations between
> Jewish and Arab workers, between native workers and mission-
> aries, between all workers on the field and our brotherhood in the
> homeland. And we felt our brotherhood in Christ more closely
> knit by these efforts.[28]

Shukri Musa ministered in Nazareth and the Galilee area from 1911
until his untimely death in 1928.[29] For the next few years the church was
under the capable leadership of Munira Musa, who with the help of a deacon, Elias Taballage, kept the church and its programs together. Elias Taballage took charge of the preaching services, while Munira Musa carried
on her Bible study among the women.[30] Rev. Saʿeed Jureidini traveled from
Beirut to preach on occasion. In early March 1929, the Watts returned to
America and were not able to return to Palestine due to health problems.[31]
Due to the Great Depression that had spread across America, funding for
missions as a whole was decreased.

In 1930, Rev. Louis Hanna,[32] a nephew of Shukri Musa, became the new
pastor of the Nazareth Baptist Church. He met his American wife, Velora
Griffin, while he was studying at Howard Payne College in Texas. Hanna
completed his studies at Southwestern Baptist Theological Seminary in Ft.
Worth, Texas. Under the leadership of Rev. Louis Hanna, the work grew
again and the church members began witnessing in surrounding villages.
They also opened a small school.[33]

Rev. Roswell E. Owens and his wife, Doreen, were appointed as Southern Baptist missionaries to Palestine in 1929 and moved to Nazareth in the
summer of 1931. They stayed in Nazareth for a year helping with the
Nazareth Baptist Church.[34] In 1932, the Owens moved to Haifa, to minister to former members of the Nazareth Baptist Church who had moved to
Haifa to work in the growing port city and to provide Bible study at the invitation of those interested in the gospel. Rev. Hanna continued as pastor of
the church in Nazareth.

An American Presbyterian toured Palestine in 1935, saw the work being done by the little Baptist community and expressed the desire to finance construction of a parsonage beside the Nazareth Baptist Church. The second floor was to be used as the pastor's home and the lower floor was constructed in order to provide a location for church classes, meetings and a day school.[35] Due to this generosity, the much-needed building was constructed. Soon thereafter, Munira Musa was persuaded by her adult children to move from Nazareth to be closer to family. Munira Musa was greatly respected by all who knew her. She had become known as "the 'lady of ladies,' *sit al-sittat.*"[36]

In 1936, the FMB appointed Dr. Leo Eddleman to Palestine. He was born in Morgantown, Mississippi and graduated from Mississippi College. After finishing his doctorate at Southern Baptist Theological Seminary, Louisville, Kentucky in 1935, he traveled to Palestine. He spent eighteen months in Jerusalem studying Hebrew at the Hebrew University and serving as pastor of the Jerusalem Baptist Church.[37] He returned to America temporarily to marry Sarah Fox, whom he had met before leaving for Palestine, and who had completed a degree at the Women's Missionary Union Training School in Louisville, Kentucky. In 1939, Dr. Eddleman became the pastor of the Nazareth Baptist Church allowing the local pastor, Rev. Louis Hanna, to take a much needed furlough. An uprising by Palestinian Arabs began in 1936 and continued through 1939. The Palestinian Arabs were frustrated with the increase in Jewish immigration to Palestine and with British rule. Due to the fighting and riots, curfews were imposed. The curfews limited the programs of the church. Dr. Eddleman's contribution to the church in Nazareth, however, was significant, despite the fact that the Palestinian riots of 1936–1939 were at their height. He stated that the reason he learned Arabic so quickly and could preach in Arabic was due to the nightly curfew. There was nothing to do but stay inside from sunset to sunrise and the long evenings provided ample time for language study.[38] As World War II loomed on the horizon, the Eddlemans left Palestine in 1941 and did not return.[39]

Kate Ellen Gruver was appointed by the FMB in 1938 to serve in Palestine.[40] She worked among Arab women and children in Nazareth. By 1941, however, due to World War II, all the missionaries were advised to leave the region. During World War II, the British Government requisitioned the Baptist property in Nazareth.[41] Miss Gruver returned to Palestine in 1944 and lived in Jerusalem.[42]

Rev. Henry Hagood and his wife Julia were appointed to serve in Nazareth and arrived in 1945. They moved to Jerusalem during the summer in order to attend Arab language classes. In the late fall of 1945 they moved to Nazareth where Rev. Hagood became the pastor of the Nazareth Baptist Church.[43] But tragically, in January 1946, he became ill and suddenly died. He was buried in the Church of Scotland cemetery overlooking the Sea of Galilee. When Rev. Hagood died, leaving Julia Hagood with a young son, Julia decided to stay in Nazareth and take in children who were either orphaned or whose family could not care for them. The FMB approved her plan and provided a small budget. The Children's Home was called, the "George W. Truett Children's Home."[44] The first child accepted into the Children's Home was Rhadia, an Arab girl whose mother had died. Rhadia's father, Jameel Said Shurrush, also known as Abu George (father of George—the eldest son), was caring for several older children. When Abu George and his sister Zebedie brought the tiny baby to the Nazareth Baptist Church for services, Julia Hagood looked after the child. Abu George asked if Julia would help care for Rhadia on his behalf, so he could work. She agreed. Abu George worked at the Baptist compound in Nazareth and could visit with his daughter as time allowed.

Kate Ellen Gruver and Elizabeth Lee volunteered to move to Nazareth to help with the Children's Home. Kate Ellen Gruver took care of the business, finances and record keeping. Julia Hagood and Elizabeth Lee took care of the children and supervised the kitchen.[45] Local residents were also hired to help. Elizabeth Lee had served for years as the Matron, (supervisor of nurses) at the Scots Hospital in Tiberias.[46] She attended the American University in Beirut, Lebanon and received nursing training in Palestine. When she heard about the Children's Home, she applied to the FMB to work in Nazareth and was appointed to do so. Elizabeth Lee, an American, had served in Palestine for over a decade, and during that time, she had seen the need for work with unwanted children, young girls and women.[47] About a year later, however, the FMB instructed the missionaries to stop taking in children. It was phasing out the Baptist-run orphanage.[48] The Children's Home in Nazareth had taken in 20 children and thereafter stopped taking any more.[49]

In early 1947, Julia Hagood left Nazareth to attend language school in Jerusalem. At an Arabic language class, she met Finlay Graham, a Scotsman, who had served in the Middle East in the Royal Air Force during World War II. With blessings from friends and mission workers, they married in September 1947. The FMB appointed Finlay Graham as a Southern Baptist missionary and the couple moved first to Transjordan and then to Lebanon to work with Arab national Baptists. Kate Ellen Gruver and Elizabeth Lee continued to administer the Children's Home in Nazareth.[50] They also administered a small school. The school was primarily for the children in the Children's Home, but then took additional students to accommodate children whose parents wanted a school with a Christian atmosphere. Local teachers were employed. However, the school did not last long.

On November 29, 1947, the General Assembly of the United Nations adopted a resolution calling for the partition of Palestine into a Jewish and an Arab State and for the internationalization of Jerusalem. Following the adoption of the resolution, the British left Palestine. On May 14, 1948, Israel proclaimed itself a State. Arab armies in countries surrounding Israel attacked. On November 30, 1948 a ceasefire was agreed upon and went into effect on April 3, 1949. "Jerusalem was divided with barbed-wire fences and minefields and rows of windowless structures."[51] Israel was a state unrecognized by the Arab world. Palestinian Arabs, uprooted from their homes, had expected that they would soon return home after the fighting. Instead they became refugees living in camps in Jordan, Syria, Lebanon, and the Gaza Strip. Those Arabs who stayed within the Israeli partition were grouped into Arab towns—with Nazareth as the largest. Palestinian Arabs living in Israel were unsure of their status in a Jewish state. Threat of war between Israel and the surrounding Arab countries was constant and border skirmishes frequent.

The Nazareth Baptist School had been disrupted and eventually stopped due to the 1948 war. Yusef Qupti, a Palestinian teacher, kept the keys to the school in hopes it could open again. Anna Cowan, a teacher in Missouri, heard Elizabeth Lee speak at a conference and became interested in mission work in Palestine. She was appointed by the FMB and arrived in Nazareth soon after the Arab-Jewish war. She assisted with relief work and was asked to serve as the headmistress of the Baptist school. The FMB provided funds for the school and its administration. During Anna Cowan's tenure, secondary school classes were added.[52]

The Arab population of Nazareth doubled in 1948 and the Nazareth Baptist Church was packed with people seeking shelter. In 1949, Kate Ellen Gruver wrote:

> The people [in Nazareth] had not resisted and had made no defense preparations, and they had immediately and unconditionally surrendered the city upon the entrance of the Jews. Of course military government was set up immediately. Everything was closed; for a few days people were

confined to their homes. The Government has made arrangements for food supplies to come into Nazareth. The authorities have approved our children's home.[53]

Baptists worked alongside the United Nations Relief and Works Agency (UNRWA) for Palestine Refugees in the Near East. The Nazareth Baptist Church opened its doors to the Arab refugees coming in from all over the area. UNRWA furnished milk, vitamins and the medicines for the children, the Quakers provided clothing, and the Red Cross gave them food for their soup kitchen. The church became a distribution center for supplies and rations. The Baptist mission members and national workers provided labor. "Every day at noon," according to Kate Ellen Gruver, "500 children sitting back to back on the church floor got a hot meal; every afternoon 1,200 children from newborn babes to teenagers got vitamins and milk; and more than 26,000 persons in Galilee received one or more pieces of clothing."[54] Because of the war, many refugees did not have proper clothing. The Baptist Relief Center in New Orleans sent 500 bales of clothing to Nazareth. The Israeli government allowed the shipment to come in free of duty and waived all port fees. Elizabeth Lee played a primary role in managing the distribution. She worked out a record system, "that was so clear and comprehensive, it was adopted by the United Nations International Children's Emergency Fund for its own official use and put into [effect] in all its centers in the country."[55]

Although the women mission members were active with work in the Children's Home and Nazareth Baptist School, there was no minister for the church. "The lack of any Baptist minister has been keenly felt by our Nazareth Mission and the entire community," wrote Kate Ellen Gruver.[56] The women of the mission stationed in Nazareth were faced with the problem of either closing the church doors entirely or trying somehow to continue with some sort of worship service. "In the past it has been utterly impossible for a woman to speak in any kind of meeting," Gruver wrote, "especially a religious one, where men were present. Men [from] other missions and one or two Arab Christians graciously preached for us on Sunday mornings. [Robert] L. Lindsey, Baptist minister of the Jerusalem Baptist Church, added a monthly trip to Nazareth to his already overwhelming schedule in order that at least one service a month should be under Baptist leadership." But the invasion of Western ways and attitudes had affected even Nazareth and so the women led Wednesday evening Bible study and the Sunday evening service became an informal song service with a short devotional talk by Anna Cowan. In addition, they carried on a small mission service in Cana."[57]

The Nazareth Baptist School was expanding. "The standard of education, high quality of teaching and Christian spirit has rapidly made it the outstanding school in the town," wrote Miss Gruver. "The seventh [grade] class was added, but the government is requiring an additional eighth [grade] class next year as well. Bible is the most important subject taught and full emphasis is given to it in every class. Hebrew classes are begun in the fourth [grade] class and English, taught from kindergarten with American textbooks, gives the school an added uniqueness. Except for the language classes, the studies are in Arabic."[58] The Nazareth community petitioned the FMB to open a qualified secondary school for the boys and girls of the town who, with limited educational resources, found it impossible to complete their secondary education. Word came that a new couple had been appointed by the FMB to work in Nazareth. Miss Gruver wrote, "The coming of our pastor-teacher couple will enable us to open this additional section of our school next September."[59]

In June of 1950, Rev. Dwight Baker, his wife, Emma, and their two small sons, Bron and Bill, arrived in Nazareth. The FMB appointed them to the Baptist Convention in Israel. Dwight Baker, born in Bolivar, Missouri, was a graduate of Baylor University in Waco, Texas. He was ordained to the Christian ministry in 1944. In 1945, while attending Southwestern Baptist Theological Seminary in Fort Worth, Texas, his theological studies were interrupted for service as Chaplain in the 82nd Airborne Division in Germany.[60] Emma Weatherly (Baker), born in Narrows, Virginia, attended Mars Hill Junior College and Blue Mountain College receiving her B.A. in 1943. She was a 1944 graduate of the New Orleans Baptist Theological Seminary, obtaining a Bachelor of Christian Training and a Master of Christian Training. From 1944–1945 she served at the Toledano Mission in New Orleans.[61] Dwight Baker completed his Th.M degree at Southwestern Baptist Theological Seminary in 1949. From 1949–1950, he served as pastor of the First Baptist Church in Miami, Texas. Soon after the Bakers arrived in Nazareth, Kate Ellen Gruver, Elizabeth Lee and Anna Cowan returned to the United States. Anna Cowan was reappointed a few years later to work in a Baptist school in Jordan. Elmo and Hannah Scoggin, appointed to the Baptist Convention in Israel, had been studying Hebrew in Jerusalem. They moved to Nazareth to administer the Children's Home.

Dwight Baker began serving as both pastor of the Nazareth Baptist Church and administrator of the Nazareth Baptist School—while starting to learn Arabic."[62] The Nazareth Baptist Church had declined without a full time pastor. Many church members fled during the 1948 war. Although the Nazareth Baptist Church had been in existence for almost forty years, there were few members who remained. It was clear to Rev. Baker that he should find and train new leadership while seeking revival of the congregation.[63] The Israeli parliament was confronted with a decision as to how the minority religious communities would be governed within the framework of a Jewish State. In 1952, the population in Israel was approximately 1,606,000. Slightly more than 89 percent were Jews. The non-Jewish population numbered 176,000, of whom 120,000 were Muslim, 40,000—Christian Arabs, 16,000—Druse, and the remainder, non-Arab Christians.[64] Israel's Proclamation of Independence stated:

> The State of Israel…will be based on the principles of liberty, justice and peace as conceived by the Prophets of Israel; will uphold the full social and political equality of all its citizens, without distinction of religion, race or sex; will guarantee freedom of religion, conscience, education and culture; will safeguard the Holy Places of all religions…

Despite the Proclamation, Dwight Baker found that an obstacle in seeking new members and leadership in the Nazareth Baptist Church was the continued acceptance, by the varied religious groups, of the *millet* system. The *millet* community accepts the position that one is born into his religion and must never leave it. Muslim dynasties had through the centuries, reinforced the subordinate status of Christians and Jews through the *millet* system, whereby a ranking religious leader—recognized and tolerated by the government—was responsible for the internal working and governing of the minority religious group.[65] The minority religious leaders governed their own religious groups regarding matters such as marriage, divorce, death, burial and inheritance.

The Israeli government created a Ministry of Religious Affairs and within that department, the Christian Desk was set up to oversee the various Christian communities. Religious groups continued to control personal law, although an overlapping system of civil courts was also created. Dwight Baker wrote:

> In the Middle East, the struggle for religious rights has been within the framework of minority religious commu-

nities fighting for the right to govern their group and organizing their lives according to their own traditions. To
the Western mind, religious freedom has a chiefly personal
application. It seeks the right to worship and propagate
one's faith with no interference from the state. In the Middle East an individual is the "national" of his religion and
the "citizen" of his state; in the West, he is the citizen as well
as the national of his political state and religion is regarded
solely as a matter of conscience—not an affair of state.[66]

"The religious sterility here is the result of the millet system," said Baker.
It is a relic of the feudal system of the Middle Ages. Like the dukes and
barons in their day, the church hierarchy has inherited its property and its
populations. It wants to keep things as they are."[67] Dwight Baker believed
that the only way of getting people to leave old traditions was to teach,
preach and practice the true concept of individual liberty.[68] "If spiritual leaders had to attract their people here on a religious basis, rather than inherit-
ing them as organized communities, it might shake things up…Christians
in the Holy Land could have the opportunity to bear witness to their faith
in a way [that] would make a bridge between Arab and Jew in the Middle
East. But what we need is a real shaking up, a complete change of heart and
spirit, the sort of thing the [Biblical] prophets…asked for."[69]

Baptists preferred to use the word, "Believer" rather than "Christian," to
distinguish those who chose to align themselves with the evangelical teachings of the gospel. If you so believed, then you could make an outward profession of belief in Jesus. This was called "a profession of faith." For many,
this was the last step. For a few, who dared to go against the wishes of family and friends, there was the act of baptism, symbolizing rebirth into a new
life following the teachings of Jesus. Dwight Baker found that the Arab culture was quite different from America. "It was a slow eastern culture. There
wasn't very much response to the Christian Gospel. It was a little discouraging, for I was very *gung ho*."[70] Of his first years on the field he said, "I suf-
fered a strong dose of culture shock,"[71] and, "I was wearing too many hats."[72]
With the arrival of Paul and Marjorie Rowden in March 1952, Dwight Baker
was anticipating help with the administration of the church and school in
Nazareth.

2
PAUL AND MARJORIE ROWDEN

Paul Dennis Rowden Jr. and Marjorie Ann Cole, both born in 1924, grew up in the southwestern part of Atlanta, Georgia, off of Cascade Avenue. Their homes were almost an equal walking distance from the church they both attended from childhood—Cascade Baptist Church.[1] At church, Paul and Marjorie worshiped, socialized and were married. It was there that Paul Dennis Rowden Jr. was ordained as a minister. I was their first child.

In the early part of the twentieth century, my grandparents gravitated to Atlanta from rural parts of Georgia. One grandfather worked in the furniture wholesale distributing business and the other as a clerk for the Central of Georgia railroad company. They married, put down roots, and raised their children. When my father, an only child, joined Cascade Baptist Church at age nine, his parents joined the church as well and all became staunch members. My paternal grandfather, Paul Dennis Rowden Sr., served for many years as a deacon and superintendent of the Sunday school program. Mary Evelyn Strong Rowden, my paternal grandmother, played the piano and sang in the choir.

At age nine, at a tent revival, my mother felt God calling her to make a profession of faith. Revivals were held yearly at the Cascade Baptist Church as well as across the South—often outdoors in the summer—under open-air tents. Hand-held fans were passed out to the crowds—especially on nights when there was no breeze. Visiting preachers came to town and as the crowd gathered, there was singing of hymns, powerful preaching and soul-searching, professions of faith, repentance and renewal. The Sunday following the revival, my mother made a profession of faith in her home church, Cascade Baptist Church.

Byron Hunt Cole, my maternal grandfather, and a Methodist, did not feel the need for a Baptist immersion and therefore did not join Cascade Baptist. He kept his church membership at the little Methodist Church near his family home on Finchersville Road outside of Jackson, Georgia. In Atlanta, he became active in the Masons—Cascade Lodge No. 94 F&AM where he was a member for many years. He did, however, attended Cascade Baptist Church on special occasions.

Cascade Baptist Church was a member of the Southern Baptist Convention. The Convention was organized in Augusta, Georgia in 1845. "The central purpose of the denomination's 'sacred effort' was reflected in the major actions of the constituting convention: the establishing of mission boards for home and foreign missions."[2] Baptist churches that wanted to participate could share in the cooperative Christian effort. In 1888, thirty-two women delegates from ten southern states organized the Woman's Missionary Union (WMU). The WMU became the primary fundraiser in support of missions and provided churches with mission literature for all ages. They elected officers who attended regional, state, and national WMU conferences. The Woman's Missionary Union remains the largest Protestant woman's missionary society in America.[3] Alma Kelly Cole, my maternal grandmother, had a strong presence as a member and later President (1937–1939), of the Cascade Baptist Church WMU, where the ladies studied the Bible, learned about missions and raised money in support. During her years as President, she was given a gold WMU pin. It became a priceless possession and she moved it regularly from one dress to another so that it could always be prominently displayed. In the center of the emblem on the pin is a Bible, opened at 1 Corinthians 3:9—"Laborers together with God," the permanent WMU watchword. Above the open Bible is a lighted torch, a symbol of Jesus who said, "I am the light of the world. Whoever follows me will never walk in darkness, but will have the light of life." (John 8:12). The globe signifies that there is no boundary for the spread of the gospel and calls believers to their responsibility to share God's word with all people.[4]

From childhood Paul and Marjorie were members of church youth mission groups. As a boy, Paul took an interest in the geography of countries where mission work was ongoing and tacked maps of the world on the wall in his room. During his teenage years he subscribed to Baptist mission magazines and worked in the Atlanta City Missions Program.

Paul and Marjorie were fifteen years of age the summer of 1939 when Atlanta hosted the 6th Baptist World Alliance, a gathering of Baptists from all parts of the world, who met every five years. It was the first time the Alliance had met in the South—"the world center of Baptist population."[5] The Atlanta Crackers, the local baseball team, scheduled their games on the road for a week so that the Ponce de Leon Ball Park could be used for the event.[6]

The *Atlanta Constitution* reported that approximately a third of the more than 12,000,000 Baptists in the world were Negroes, most of them living in the southern states.[7] "Many in the Baptist World Alliance had serious reservations about holding the 1939 Congress in Atlanta. A committee worked to see that segregation laws were not enforced, seating was integrated and African Americans were involved in the planning and on the program."[8] Dr. Louie Newton, a "prominent Baptist preacher, denominational leader, and the pastor of Druid Hills Baptist Church in Atlanta," was on the planning committee.[9] He said, "It is possible that the cooperation of the races in this undertaking set a record for harmony between the races for the entire nation."[10]

"[One] hundred and twenty-five thousand Atlantans of all faiths lined the downtown streets to welcome Baptists travelers from five continents and sixty nations who formed a mile-long procession marching to the strains of Onward Christian Soldiers."[11] World-renowned Baptist preachers spoke to crowds of over 50,000. Dr. George W. Truett, pastor of the First Baptist Church of Dallas, Texas, and President of the Baptist World Alliance, welcomed his Baptist brothers and sisters from around the encircling globe to "this beautiful, forward looking, and nobly hospitable city of Atlanta."[12] In his main address, Dr. Truett spoke of basic Baptist principals when he said, "Religion is a matter of personal relationship between the soul and God, and nothing extraneous may properly intrude here—no ecclesiastical or civil order, no church, nor ordinance, nor sacrament, no preacher, nor priest may dare to stand between the individual soul and Christ."[13]

A letter to the Alliance from President Franklin D. Roosevelt urged Baptists to "hold high their peculiar heritage" of religious liberty and employ that heritage so that "justice may be maintained and extended among men and nations."[14] Rabbi David Marx, on behalf of The Temple on Peachtree Road, also spoke to the crowd welcoming the Baptist men and women from all over the world saying, "May their deliberations be laden with blessings to our common humanity and to the honor of our Universal Father."[15] Cheers came when Dr. L. K. Williams, president of the National Baptist Convention,[16] the nation's oldest and largest African American religious convention exclaimed, "We gather here today, many races and many nations but under the cohesive principle of 'One Lord, One Faith, One Baptism, One God and Father of All.'"[17]

In 1939, Atlanta was also the host for a more dazzling gathering. Marjorie and her cousin, Frances Kelly from Rome, Georgia, walked all the way from Cascade Avenue to Loew's Grand Theatre on the corner of Peachtree and Forsyth Streets in downtown Atlanta, to see the movie stars in town for the premier of the movie, *Gone with the Wind*. When she saw the celebrities, Marjorie became so excited that she dropped her camera and consequently missed the photo opportunity. The next day, the girls rode the trolley to the theater, sat through the movie twice and cried and cried.

Dinner was served around noon, and *supper* meant the evening meal. Southern cuisine included: grits, scrambled eggs, biscuits with gravy, pancakes with syrup and bacon—cornbread, fried chicken, sliced tomatoes, ham, mashed potatoes, squash, black eyed peas, rice, corn-on-the-cob, coleslaw, chicken pot pie, creamed corn, candied yams, creamed spinach, green peas and carrots, green beans, barbecued beef and pork, cakes and pies of every kind—and, as my paternal grandfather always said, following a big family meal, "That was some fine eating." Folks drank massive amounts of sweetened tea, milk, buttermilk and of course, most consumed Coca-Cola. After all, Atlanta was the city where the Coca-Cola Company was born.

During the nineteen forties, in homes across Atlanta, the radio brought the evening news, music and entertainment. It was the fifties before most folks bought their first black and white television. When the weather was good, families gathered on screened-in porches—where they talked and greeted their neighbors. Groceries could be delivered to the door. No one had air conditioning. Big bands were popular and Paul and Marjorie could "cut a rug" as they danced the Jitterbug. They were seventeen years old in 1941, when President Franklin Roosevelt announced the bombing of Pearl Harbor by the Japanese.

Marjorie attended Atlanta's Girls High, went one year to the Georgia College for Women in Milledgeville, Georgia and then graduated from Agnes Scott College—riding the trolley daily from her home in southwest Atlanta to the campus in Decatur and back. Money was tight but my grandfather was determined that his son and daughter receive a good education. The first night at college in Milledgeville, Marjorie opened her suitcase to find a note from her father that said:

> You have now reached a turning point in your life. We have tried to teach you right from wrong and are now looking forward with much hope and anticipation to the development of a beautiful and consistent life. Make friends of everyone possible but be careful of them. Never lose sight of the fact that holding the hand of Jesus day by day is to ensure the most happiness on earth and

eternal life hereafter. We are no further from you than the telephone. The challenge is yours.[18]

Paul went to Joel Chandler Harris Grammar School and graduated from Atlanta's Boys High and Emory University. In Boys High, Paul was a member of the Bible Club sponsored by his Latin teacher, L. P. Wilson. At age sixteen Paul and Marjorie began dating and continued to date through college years. They were both members of the "Buddy Class," a large group of Cascade Baptist young people who formed a coed Sunday school class and planned many social events. Dedicated adult leaders at the church provided support and spiritual counseling to the young people and were available day and night to listen and advise.

Paul entered Emory University in Atlanta as an undergraduate. One day he walked into the Emory University library and found a book about Robert Moffat (1795–1883), a Scottish pioneer missionary to South Africa. In a sermon given years later, Paul recalled that Moffat wrote, "I have stood this morning and seen the smoke rising from a thousand [African] villages where Jesus Christ has never been preached."[19] He read about a missionary to China—Hudson Taylor and the China Inland Missions, [20] and said, "I marveled at the leading of the Lord in this man's life. I reasoned, what God could do for him, He could do for others. My appetite was whetted for mission biography, and I read the lives of other great missionaries. I began to feel that the Lord was calling me into full-time work as a minister and perhaps as a missionary."[21]

America's role in World War II was in full swing and Paul signed up for the U.S. Naval Reserve V-12 program at Emory University. The V-12 was an officer-training program—a partnership between the U.S. Navy and 131 American Colleges and Universities. "[It] was distinctly a college program designed to give [U.S. Navy] officer candidates the requisite and minimum education necessary…and to give it on an accelerated schedule."[22] Paul entered the pre-medical program. After three years of undergraduate study he asked to be placed on active military duty and attended the U.S. Naval Training Command in Great Lakes, Illinois. Largely due to his pre-medical undergraduate studies, he served as a U.S. Naval Hospital Corpsman stationed in Charleston, San Diego and Pensacola. During long nights on the hospital ward, as the patients slept, Paul would read books and write letters home. While on leave one weekend he attended a missionary conference sponsored by the Moody Church in Chicago. He wrote home elated, saying, "I sat with, talked with, ate with, listened to and sang with missionaries from every part of the world…I heard talks and testimonies about Africa, China, Central America and every land…my heart was thrilled."[23] Although he enjoyed seeing new parts of the country, he longed for the war to be over so he could go home. Commuting by train with other soldiers he wrote to his parents:

> Well I am passing through some of the most beautiful country I've ever seen. We just left Salt Lake City and now I can see snow covered mountains…my, this is beautiful country—but none like the red hills of Georgia.[24]

Paul kept up a correspondence with Marjorie in Atlanta who completed her college education and was working at a bank. On August 6th and 9th 1945, atomic bombs were dropped on Hiroshima and Nagasaki and war in the Pacific came to an end. In mid-August, Marjorie rode the South Bound Pullman from Atlanta to Pensacola, Florida to visit Paul at the Naval Hospital. Paul's father gave Marjorie a small wrapped box and instructed her to deliver it to Paul. The box contained an engagement ring that Paul had selected earlier. When he proposed marriage at dinner that evening, Marjorie accepted, and the ring was placed on her finger. They were 21 years of age. Paul received an honorable discharge on December 27, 1945. He returned to Atlanta and completed his undergraduate degree at Emory University. On June 8, 1946 Paul and Marjorie married in a ceremony at the Cascade Baptist Church surrounded by family and friends.

I was born in 1948, a redhead, and named "Rebecca," but called "Becky." My sister, Robin came along in 1951. We were the first grandchildren in both families and much pampered by adoring grandparents. My father pursued a Bachelor of Divinity degree at New Orleans Baptist Theological Seminary, located then in the Garden District of New Orleans. Every morning before classes, he rose early, sat in his rocking chair, read his Bible and prayed. He loved to rock and our home was never without rockers. If I awoke early and found him rocking, he simply picked me up, sat me in his lap and continued rocking and reading. My father was soft-spoken—a gentle and humble man. My mother was outgoing, laughed a lot, and said whatever was on her mind. She loved being around people and easily made new friends.

During seminary days, my father sought a job for much needed financial support and was invited to become pastor of two small rural churches in south Alabama—Durant Chapel in the Crossroads community and Stapleton Baptist Church, formerly a mission of the First Baptist Church in Bay Minette. Neither church could support a full time preacher so they alternated weeks. My father rode by bus from New Orleans to Alabama and back again every weekend for church services, until my grandfather made a down payment on a car. He gave it to Paul who was able to make small monthly payments towards its purchase with his salary as pastor. The family then traveled with him on weekends.

As their time at the seminary came to a close, Paul and Marjorie resolutely completed an application to be appointed by the Foreign Mission Board of the Southern Baptist Convention in Richmond, Virginia, to serve in an overseas mission. The application required them to write essays regarding their spiritual development and to articulate their religious beliefs. The process included interviews, medical exams, psychiatric evaluations and intensive background checks. There was endless waiting as the processing took time. Paul was almost disqualified as an applicant for missions because of a history of asthma and bronchitis during childhood. The FMB Personnel Department required "strong bodies and stable personalities to match the rigors of service overseas" in addition to educational requirements—and a demonstration that the applicant had a "successful experience in the ministry."[25]

The FMB looked for applicants with certain personal qualities—health, spirituality, maturity, flexibility and love—"the absolutely indispensable missionary quality."[26] In *Global Mission*, author Winston Crawley writes:

> The missionary candidate was entirely human—neither superman nor sub-par. Neither the halo concept, with its glow of exalted spirituality and success, nor the martyr figure, with its shadow of heroic suffering, gave a true picture of qualities sought in a missionary. The typical missionary had a normal human quota of weaknesses and strengths, failures and successes, hardships and joys. The selection process sought to evaluate a real person in relation to some real situation of need and opportunity overseas and match them appropriately.[27]

Paul and Marjorie began a discussion with the FMB as to where they might best serve. On his application to the FMB, Paul requested to be sent to India, with Africa and Japan as alternatives.[28] In 1947, India gained freedom from Britain's colonial rule. A report of the FMB in January 1951 stated, "We were much disappointed that the government of

India rejected the application for missionary visas for three missionary couples. Our impression is to wait for a time and then reopen the question of entering India."[29] Although Protestant missionaries were stationed in India, the FMB considered the country closed for new missionaries, at least for a while. Then a call for help came from Rev. Dwight Baker serving with the Baptist Convention in Nazareth, Israel. Rev. Baker wrote the FMB asking for help with the administration of the Nazareth Baptist School and Church. Samuel E. Maddox, Secretary of the FMB, forwarded Dwight's letter to Paul and Marjorie.[30] The Rowdens talked with Dr. Wash Watts, who was on the faculty of the New Orleans Baptist Theological Seminary. Dr. & Mrs. Watts had been Baptist missionaries sent by the FMB to Palestine (1923–1928) and Dr. Watts, along with local pastor, Rev. Shukri Musa, had been instrumental in obtaining the land upon which the Nazareth Baptist Church was built. The Watts shared information about the Baptist mission in Nazareth. Paul and Marjorie corresponded with Dwight and Emma Baker, prayed for guidance, and then accepted the call to go to Nazareth. On October 9, 1951, at the commissioning ceremony for newly appointed missionaries in Richmond, Virginia, Paul and Marjorie were appointed to serve in Israel. They were twenty-seven years of age.

At the same commissioning ceremony, Alta Lee Grimes Lovegren from Cedartown, Georgia and her husband, Dr. Lloyd August Lovegren, son of missionaries to China, were appointed to Jordan. Dr. Lovegren had a medical degree. Dr. and Mrs. Lovegren were to be stationed at the Baptist hospital in Ajloun, Jordan following a year of Arabic language study in Beirut,

Dr. Loyd August Lovegren and wife, Alta Lee Grimes Lovegren, c. 1952.

Lebanon. The Rowdens and Lovegrens talked about the events in their lives that led them to missions and were featured in an article in the *Christian Index*, the newspaper of the Georgia Baptist Convention.[31] Although the two couples would live within close proximity of each other, one couple in Israel, the other in Jordan, the conflict in the Middle East would serve to block all but rare communication.

In 1951, Baptist missionaries were required to serve five-year-terms followed by a year of furlough. The Rowdens began crating up their furnishings, clothing, canned goods and medical supplies—everything they thought they might need. The *Atlanta Constitution* carried a picture of the family and announced that on Sunday, December 2, 1951, the Cascade Baptist Church would honor the couple at a "Paul and Marjorie Day" service.[32] My grandparents said good-by to their son, daughter and two granddaughters, (Becky, almost four, and Robin— nine months old), whom they would not see again until summer of 1956.

In February 1952, the family traveled by train from Atlanta to New York City and then boarded the *S.S. Exilona*, of the American Export Lines. The freighter carried seven passengers. The Rowden family made up four of the passengers. The remaining three passengers were Jew-

Paul and Marjorie Rowden are pictured with daughters Robin and Becky in Atlanta, Georgia, December 1951.

ish—also headed to Israel. One was a survivor of the Holocaust—the other two, Zionists. The freighter was scheduled to unload cargo in Turkey and then head to Haifa, the port city in Israel.

In January 1952, the *Flying Enterprise*, a 6,711-ton ship, cracked open in a gale in the stormy Atlantic making headline news. The *Atlanta Constitution* carried the headline story for days. Fifty-one passengers and crewmen—one of them dead—were evacuated. The captain, Henrik Kurt Carlsen, stayed aboard the battered and listing steamer, "determined to bring his vessel to port or see her go down."[33] Finally, the captain abandoned the ship, swam to a nearby lifeboat and was hauled onto a British tug as the *Flying Enterprise* sank into the cold waters.[34] In his State-of-the-Union message to Congress in January 1952, President Harry S. Truman praised Captain Carlsen, "who dared the ancient perils of navigation to uphold the traditions and character...of men who place principles ahead of life itself. The year 1952 is a very crucial year," he said. "We have the great responsibility of saving the basic moral and spiritual values of our civilization..."[35] A few weeks later, the freighter carrying the Rowdens headed out into the stormy Atlantic Ocean.

3

LETTERS

FEBRUARY–MARCH 1952

The first three letters were written as Paul and Marjorie Rowden traveled to Israel on a freighter, the S.S. Exilona, of the American Export Line.

Letter to:
Mr. & Mrs. Paul D. Rowden Sr.
1712 Westhaven Dr. SW
Atlanta, Georgia

Paul Rowden
S.S. Exilona, Pier F
Jersey City, N.J.

Thursday, February 21, 1952

Dear folks:

Just a line about 10 a.m.—nothing new about us, or the boat. We have very fine quarters. There is only one other couple, and a single lady besides us on the boat. We have very good meals and more than we can ever eat...The Lord has been so good to us in so many ways. He has not failed in one good thing! We have a private bath, 2 closets, about 15 drawers...Evidently there must be a stevedore shortage in N.J. and N.Y. because of the difficulty in loading. We were to sail Monday, 18th as you remember, and didn't. Then Wednesday, 20th and didn't. We are told that it may be tomorrow before we sail now. Anyway, we are as well off here as in a Hotel, and not paying for the food as well.

We woke up with it snowing this morning. Becky and I, after breakfast, went out on deck to see it, and watch them loading the boat. We are straight across the Hudson River from N. York City and last night it was beautiful—every building lighted up.

Our room is the best on the boat as far as location, and we have two nice portholes to look out of. Becky keeps her head glued to the window one half the time. She takes to every change just fine.

We have steam heat, plenty of ventilation. About a day after we leave here we will be in the South Atlantic, which everyone says, is delightful. Hope I can mail this now. We could sail today but I doubt it. Truly in every way God has gone before us, and is with us. Call the Coles and give them the gist of this letter.

Love,
S

Letter to:
Mr. & Mrs. B.H. Cole
1546 Richland Rd. SW
Atlanta, Ga.

Marjorie Rowden
S.S. *Exilona*

Sat. 6 p.m. March 1, 1952

Dearest Mother, Daddy and Billy,

Well, I haven't written since Monday 5 days ago. There really hasn't been too much to write about. The weather has been pretty stormy and we couldn't do much except try to keep ourselves in an upright position. The wind blew so hard and the water was so rough that for three nights and two days we were never completely straight up. At night we had to strap ourselves in bed to keep from falling out. In the daytime we put both children on one bed. I packed them all around with pillows to keep them from falling when the ship rocked back and forth…

Yesterday the weather cleared up and today it is beautiful. This morning

Becky and I ran and played out on deck…for about an hour…We have been seeing nothing but water for 9 days today! But, tonight at 10 p.m. we pass Gibraltar and they say we can easily see the lights of Europe and Africa at the same time…

The Lord has been so good to us on our trip. We have certainly felt his presence. We have all been perfectly well, not sick in anyway. Mr. [Charles A.] Cowen fell last week and has been in bed very ill up until today. Miss Cohn (a single lady) also fell and hurt her knee. And yet none of us have hurt ourselves at all—neither of the children have fallen. And for 2 days even the crew had trouble standing up. It was never dangerous, but it was awfully uncomfortable. Two mornings we all had boiled eggs for breakfast because that's all they could cook. The Lord can certainly be real to you in a time like that…

We have come to know most of the officers on board ship now and they're real nice…Mr. Cowen is a very grand old man and while he was sick he entertained himself by telling stories to Becky and she listened on and on. Robin can almost pull herself up now. She has been practicing…

Thurs 3:30 P.M.
March 6

Dear Folks:

…We are running along the southern coast of Turkey now and it is beautiful, very mountainous. We will arrive during the night sometime tonight but the captain said we'd wait and dock around 5 a.m. in the morning since Iskenderun has a poorly lighted harbor and a rocky one too. He said we could go ashore—we'll probably be there 3-5 days. Both Antioch and Tarsus (cities of Paul's time)[1] are within 50 miles of Iskenderun…

Tuesday night after I wrote you I went [to] visit Miss Cohn, the single Jewish lady on board and talked with her a long time. She's a very nice person and I've enjoyed being on deck with her a lot. She came to America in 1939 just before Hitler made a quick massacre of all the Jews. She lost everything she had and has never heard from her family there since. She is a graduate nurse and is now employed in the Cancer Memorial Hospital in New York City. She doesn't speak English too well and I have to listen [closely] to

35

understand her but she certainly has a lot to tell. She shudders when she talks about Germany. It was her family's home for generations. She is going to Israel to visit a cousin and then she's going to come back to America through Europe, but she isn't going to Germany. She said she couldn't stand it.

Mr. and Mrs. Cowen came in and spent the whole morning with us. They are very lovely people. He is a very cultured and educated man. He has been a noted Zionist lecturer in the U.S. for many years. He is a former Theological Professor in a Jewish Seminary. They are planning to stay in Israel for one year. She is a public school teacher in Newark, New Jersey.

I hope I can be smart enough to get up at 5 in the morning to see us dock in Iskenderun. It will be wonderful to put our feet on solid ground again.

Marjorie

On March 13, 1952, twenty-one days after departing New York Harbor, the S.S. Exilona arrived in the ancient port of Jaffa—just down the coast from Tel Aviv, Israel. Passengers were required to disembark in Jaffa while the freighter went on to the port of Haifa to unload freight. The Rowdens were met by the four men of the Baptist mission: Dwight Baker, Elmo Scoggin, Tom Francis and Robert (Bob) Lindsey and driven to Nazareth. The Nazareth Baptist Church and School were set back behind a high stonewall on a narrow road running through the heart of town. Between the church and school, an open area was used as a playground. The Baptist compound was just down the road from the public well, known as Mary's well fed by an underground spring. Rev. Dwight Baker, his wife Emma, sons Bron and Bill and daughter Carol, lived in the parsonage quarters above the school next to the church. Up the hill from Mary's well in a residential area was the George W. Truett Children's Home located in a house rented by the Baptists.

Aerogramme To:
Mr. & Mrs. B. H. Cole
1546 Richland Rd. S.W.
Atlanta, Georgia U.S.A.

Mrs. Paul Rowden
Baptist Mission
Nazareth, Israel

Friday, March 14, 1952

Dearest folks:

…Well, we arrived here in Nazareth yesterday about 2 pm. We were met in Tel Aviv by all 4 men missionaries here. We arrived in Tel Aviv Wed about 4 pm, but had to stay on board until Thurs morn[ing]. There is no dock at Tel Aviv so we had to go ashore in a little tugboat and boy what a rough ride. But as we stepped out of the boat all 4 men were right there and they looked better than Santa Claus. They helped us through all the process, customs…and by noon we were on our way in the station wagon to Nazareth.

Emma Baker had a wonderful dinner waiting for us. We have 2 large rooms and a private bath here with them…All our cargo stayed on ship and will come off next week in Haifa. These two rooms are large enough for us to make an efficiency apartment out of and then do all our own cooking…

The floors are beautiful tile. Besides the Bakers and their three children there are two Jewish young people living here [in the Baptist Compound] helping in the house for their tuition and also one Russian boy.[2] Emma has an Arab woman who comes from 9 am to 7 pm and also another one who does the wash and another one who does the ironing. Still she seems to have her hands full constantly. Paul went to prayer meeting last nite [at the Nazareth Baptist Church] with Dwight [Baker] and they had 60 people there. He is going to preach for Dwight Sunday night. It is now 2:30 and Emma and I are fixing to go up to visit the Truett Children's Home and meet Hannah Scoggin. Elmo Scoggin (her husband) is a fine fellow. The [Children's Home has] 20 children from 3 to 8 years [of age]. They are not taking any more.

7 pm. Well, Emma and I went to 4 o'clock tea at Hannah's. We had such a nice time meeting her and her Arab workers. The orphanage looks just like the pictures and is lovely on the inside. Hannah is a vivacious person—

they have no children of their own and she and Elmo just love these 20 orphans. The whole place is very artistically arranged and the children are orderly and well-behaved. Each child has a cute little bed and each has a job to do. They have an Australian woman as matron, an Arab woman as cook, and two Arab girls as helpers, also a full time man to care for yard, marketing...

The food situation is not good at all and it is hard to get enough. We are anxious for our canned goods to arrive from Haifa next week. We're eating off the Bakers right now. Poor Emma has to feed 5 in her family, 4 in ours, 3 boarding students and two to three helpers every meal...

Much, Much love,

Marjorie

Aerogramme To:
Mr. & Mrs. Paul Rowden Sr.

Nazareth Baptist Church, (L) and a two-story building (R) with Nazareth Baptist School on lower floor and residence of Dwight and Emma Baker on the second floor. Nazareth, Israel c. 1951

1712 Westhaven Dr. S.W.
Atlanta, GA. USA

Paul Rowden
Baptist Mission
Nazareth, Israel

Monday, March 17, 1952

Dear Mother and Dad:

Well I know our letters have been spotty and in a hurry. I'm sure that you understand. The matter of moving and settling down several [thousand] miles across the sea is tremendous…

The High School [secondary school] is below us in several rooms and in some church rooms. The grammar school [primary school] is about a block away in rented quarters. We have approximately 300 students and the enrollment is limited only by space and grades. We could have a 1000 if we had room for them. As to our permanent living space—we don't know…Our boat, the *S.S. Exilona*—arrives in Haifa today, and this week we will go to Haifa and see about getting our goods here…

I preached last night at the church from Acts 2:21-24 through an interpreter into Arabic and did very well. Elmo Scoggin…preached for the morning hour. We had around 80-100 at both services. I had my first Arabic lesson this morning…Grammar and syntax will be hard.

We ate dinner yesterday at Fuad [Farah's] home. His folks invited the Bakers and us… [We] had a real Arab spread, and mighty good. See if you can get [Fuad Farah] on the phone at Glenn Dorm, Georgia Tech University, and tell him we enjoyed it.[3]

Nazareth is a beautiful place—quite old though. But the early mornings and late afternoons are indescribable in their beauty. It is cool yet, but warming up gradually…Listen, get 2 bottles of—no get 5 bottles of Chloromycetin capsules, 50 mg-100 [capsules] to bottles and send them airmail to us. There is no duty on medicine, and this is unavailable here, and we did not bring enough for an emergency if all of us got sick. Airmail will reach us in at least 10 days. Wrap it very, very good. Send me a bill. I must have a bill to give the [FMB], because it pays 1/2 our drugs…

By the way, get Dr. Stegar to give you 200 pills of trasentin with phenobarbital and send airmail. These pills are excellent for the stomach when this new food—or rather way the food is prepared—doesn't set too well. One gradually gets use to it. Tell Stegar his stuff is a gold mine to us out here.[4]

Lots of love,

S

Aerogramme To:
Mr. & Mrs. P. D. Rowden Sr.
1712 Westhaven Dr. S.W.
Atlanta, Ga. U.S.A.

Marjorie Rowden
Baptist Mission
Nazareth, Israel

Tuesday, March 18, 1952

Dear Folks,

Well, the children and I left home one month ago today—in some ways it seems ages ago and in some ways it doesn't seem like a month. We will have been in Nazareth one week, day after tomorrow. The Bakers have been so nice to us and I don't know what we'd do without them. They have been here almost 2 years and can speak Arabic fairly well—also they know how to cook and eat this Arabic food—they are breaking us in on it gradually.

Yesterday we had an Arab dish called "*malfouf mashe*,"[5] which is cabbage stuffed with rice and meat and spices. It was very good. We will be glad when our freight comes however so we can open up a good ole can of "pork and beans."

…Becky and Robin are both asleep and Paul is sitting here opening Arab grammar books trying to learn this language. He has private lessons 4 days a week and I have them only once on Saturday afternoon. Paul is doing real well already and should learn it far quicker than I. Becky is going to nursery school every morning from 8 to 12 and she will learn Arabic real fast

Nazareth c. 1952

that way. The nursery is in the church right next door and there is a wall around it and our house, so I can watch her from my window. She hasn't seemed half as amazed at the difference in language as I thought she would. She will learn it far better than we ever will. Bill and Bron [Baker] already know a great deal of Arabic. As soon as our freight gets here from Haifa we will make some pictures of the place, the children, and Dwight and Emma and send them to all of you.

Nazareth is a quaint place. You see tourists riding or walking through here all the time. You see everything in the way of dress from modern American clothes to long draped robes and turbans. One day, 3 camels passed in front of the house—Becky nearly had a fit. Large herds of goats with several shepherd-like men pass by regularly. Nazareth is a group of about nine hills with the city spread out all over it—therefore you're always walking up hill or down hill one or the other.

…We are going to Haifa tomorrow to get some food at the scrip stores there. I think Paul explained to you that they are something like [CARE boxes]; only certificates are sent rather than actual food. All our woolen clothes have certainly come in handy because these houses are really cold—otherwise they are nice. This house is very nice with nine large rooms up-stairs…Well, I must close. You can pass this on to mother if you like.

Much love –

Marjorie and all

41

In January 1952, a month before the Rowdens set sail to Israel, the Atlanta Constitution *ran a story of three Arab Christian Rotary exchange students from Nazareth, spending their holidays together in Atlanta. Suhail Mu'ammar was studying at Baylor University located in Waco, Texas. Fuad Farah was at Georgia Tech and Butrus Kawar was attending the University of Georgia. The Arab students found the celebration of Christmas in Atlanta more glamorous than in Nazareth, where Christmas was spent reverently. The Rowdens had an opportunity to meet Fuad Farah and talk with him prior to leaving Atlanta. The parents of the young men issued invitations for the Rowdens to visit in their homes in Nazareth.*

Aerogramme To:
Mr. & Mrs. B.H. Cole & Bill
1546 Richland Rd. S.W.
Atlanta, Ga.

Mrs. Paul Rowden
Baptist Mission
Nazareth, Israel

Children play on seesaw at the Nazareth Baptist School. The school (L) and the Nazareth Baptist Church (R) are in the background. c. 1952.

March 19, 8 a.m.

Dearest Mother, Daddy and Bill,

…Saturday night Mr. and Mrs. Mu'mar [Mu'ammar] came to visit us. Their son, Suhail, is the one at Baylor [University]. Mr. Mu'mar owns a cigarette factory here… They were both very nice and he spoke English pretty good. Yesterday morning we had church at 11 a.m. Elmo Scoggins preached… and then Sunday School was not until 2 p.m. and then church last nite at 6:30. Paul preached last nite and did real good through an interpreter, of course.

Yesterday at noon we had dinner with Fuad Farrah's [Farah] family. Mr. Farrah and [his] sons came for us (on foot) and we walked to their home about 3 blocks (not any actual blocks here, however)…We took the stroller, [for Robin] but the streets were so rough we couldn't use it. We walked up hill most of the way…Fuad's picture was all over the place and they asked a million questions about him. His mother said she wished she had my eyes and when we asked her why, she said, "Because they have seen Fuad such a short time ago." They are all very picturesque in their speech. She spoke no English at all but Mr. Farah spoke a little and Fuad's older sister and younger brother spoke real well in English.

We sat and talked until almost 2 pm before they took us to the table. The food was very good, but very different! —Also very highly seasoned. We had a cabbage dish and stuffed cabbage with rice and ground meat. We had another rice dish with macaroni mixed with it, and another two dishes with several things like cauliflower, okra…in it. None of the vegetables taste like American vegetables however. Then we had cornstarch pudding with fresh almonds on top, oranges (just peeled and ate them) and home made cookies. Then we went back to the living room and an hour later we had *strong* coffee and cookies. It was a very interesting experience. Fuad's brother told me I had to eat everything on my plate, but I just couldn't. I hope I didn't insult them. The mother did not eat with us, nor was she even seen except when we arrived and when we left. That's the custom.

All my love,

Marjorie.

❧

Letter to:
Rowdens
1712 Westhaven Dr. SW
Atlanta, Ga. USA

Paul Rowden
Nazareth, Israel

March 23, 1952

Dear Mother and Dad,

…The work is going so very good here. Dwight Baker has done a splendid job with God's help. In a few minutes I'm going to speak at the Y.M.C.A. here in Nazareth. They have afternoon devotional services on Sunday. They have just organized a Rotary Club here in Nazareth, which Elmo, Dwight, and I attend on Monday night. In April, there are 20 holidays for the school and in that time we have our Mission meeting, probably here in Nazareth. The Lindsey's, Francises, Scoggins, Bakers and Rowdens make up the mission. We have hopes of a couple being appointed in April for our work here in Israel. We need about 8 more couples.

Monday, noon, March 24

We had a good day yesterday. I spoke at the YMCA at 4 pm, and at 6:30 we had our evening service. I have just finished an Arabic lesson, and *gradually* am picking up words and phrases. Just after the lesson I walked to the shopping district in Nazareth. So interesting. Winding streets, very narrow, cobble stone, small shops, donkeys, camels, etc. I found two nice pharmacies—no sodas, but really a drugstore. Nazareth has at least 8 doctors, and Dr. [Doris] Wilson and Dr. [William] Bathgate are at the Edinburgh Medical Mission Hospital. Very nice to our mission here. Then Haifa is only an hour's drive—for specialists if needed.

I just sent off a cablegram for Marjorie to her mother. It costs only about $2.00 and it is the quickest way of communication for you or us. Give our regards to all at church…

Love,

S

Letter to:
Mr. & Mrs. Paul D. Rowden
1712 Westhaven Dr. SW
Atlanta, Ga. USA

Near East Mission of the Southern Baptist Convention U.S.A.
Paul Rowden
Post Office Box 20
Nazareth, Israel

March 25, 1952

Dear Mother and Dad,

…Mr. Wilbur Chase, the American Consul in Haifa had dinner with us today. A young man, and very nice. Came over just to check on the Americans in Nazareth and to pay us a visit.[6]

Our boat, the *S.S. Exilona* is unloading in Haifa finally, and Thursday, Dwight and I will go over and try to make arrangements to clear our stuff. We have not gotten it yet, but we have been getting along nicely, using the Bakers' things.

…The electricity just went off so I'm writing from the light of an Aladdin lamp. Gives good light. Good thing I bought two at King Hardware…

Love,
S

Mr. & Mrs. B. H. Cole
1546 Richland Rd. SW
Atlanta, Ga. USA

Near East Mission of the Southern Baptist Convention U.S.A.
Marjorie Rowden
Post Office Box 20

Nazareth, Israel

March 26, 1952

Dearest Folks:

I'm writing this today, but there's no telling when you might receive it. A friend of Dwight's is leaving here in a few weeks for America and we are writing a letter to the [Foreign Mission] Board, the Rowdens and to you and he will mail them in the States for us. Therefore they will not be censored. There's really no special reason for doing this since we can say most anything in the regular mail. The main thing that is difficult to pass the censors is money dealings, so that is why Paul has written the Board…this way. We have asked the Board to send our check to Mr. Rowden [Sr.] instead of to us and then as we need money we can ask for it…

If we can buy our food at the Scrip Stores (with Scrip Certificates sent from the States) and also get food occasionally in [CARE] Packages then we won't have need for much money here. Besides there is absolutely no food available in the local stores. I don't know how the people live unless they buy through the black market. We are all rationed out what little is available and then the cost is terrific. Paul spoke at the YMCA Sunday afternoon and the next day he met a man who owned a store and who had heard him speak so he (out of kindness) sold him 2 cans of applesauce and a box of matches…

The Bakers have a huge store of canned food that they have gotten from Care, Scrip stores, etc. and also have a lovely vegetable garden…Emma also is very good at using whatever Arab food she can get such as some vegetables and stuff we never heard of…Every morning she calls the little store where they get their rations and asks what they have available…and she gets whatever it is. Yesterday all they had was oranges, cauliflower and brown flour. And I mean that was all! The oranges so far have been very plentiful and they are delicious—large and juicy and very few seeds…The people eat lots of bread and that keeps them looking good. Nobody looks undernourished. They must eat something…

Hannah Scoggin is flying home to the United States tomorrow. She is going on a sick leave to get treatment for arthritis. Her home is in Charleston, S.C. She is taking one of the little orphan girls—8 years old—with her and she and Elmo are going to adopt her legally if all goes as they plan. My! But I wish you could see them while they're there. Hannah is a wonderful person. She is Jewish, you know, but Elmo is not.[7] This little girl is half Jewish, and half British so she's just perfect for them…The rest of the children are Arab, I think. They are all cute as pie. Poor Elmo will have all 19 [children] on his hands until Hannah comes back in about 3 months…He has about 5 or 6 good helpers up at the Home to help him so they should do O.K.

Let me know if and when you receive this but just say "received your long letter written on March 26" and that's all. Don't say, "received letter mailed in States." Well, I guess I can say anything else I want to in another regular letter so I'll close now. Write often.

Much, much love,

Marjorie

Aerogramme To:
P.D. Rowdens
1712 W. Haven Dr. S.W.
Atlanta, Ga. U.S.A.

Rowden
P.O.B. 20
Baptist Mission
Nazareth, Israel

March 29, 1952
Sun. 3:30 p.m.

Dearest Folks:

…Honestly, you just can't imagine how complicated life is here with babies! I spend half my day sterilizing every drop of water we use—boiling cups, spoons, bottles, everything that the children use at all. And when you have to borrow somebody else's kitchen to do it in it takes even more time. Besides the Bakers family of 5 there are 3 older children boarding here and going to school and one girl who works from 9 to 7 and a man who does odd jobs. That makes 14 of us trying to use one kitchen! We almost stand in line at the stove and refrigerator. We don't dare drink this water without boiling it ourselves, so you can imagine how careful we have to be with the children…Emma does a wonderful job of running this big ole house with all the people in it.

Everything is so slow here…These first months of adjustment and getting settled are always hard on new missionaries, but God has been so good to us…Must close.

Much love,
Marjorie

4

LIFE IN ISRAEL 1952

The Law of Return was enacted in 1950. It gave every Jew who settled in Israel the automatic right to become a citizen. Tom Segev, author of *1949—The First Israelis*, states, "They came like a tidal wave: in the first six months of Independence 100,000 immigrants arrived. In 1949, over 250,000. As a result, the population of Israel increased by 50 percent…One out of three Israelis was therefore a newcomer and a stranger."[1] When Paul and Marjorie Rowden arrived in Israel in March 1952, approximately 687,000 immigrants had reached Israel's shores. Most were survivors of Nazi extermination camps in Europe and members of entire [Jewish] communities that emigrated to Israel from the Arab countries in Asia and North Africa.[2]

Dwight Baker traveled from Nazareth to Haifa on occasion and would go down to the port and watch the ships come in from different countries in Europe. He said, "I watched especially the old Jews as they would come down the gangplank and fall down on their face and kiss the soil when they touched it with tears and weeping and great joy."[3] The Jewish Agency for Israel reported that the majority of the Jewish immigrants who arrived in Israel in 1951–1952 were members of oriental communities. Their figures showed that 9,500 came from Morocco, Tunisia and Algiers; 3,800 from Libya; 1,350 from Egypt; 5,800 from Iran; 1,000 from Iraq; 650 from Turkey; 6,800 from Rumania, 650 from Bulgaria; 160 from Poland and 170 from the U.S.[4]

In a report to the FMB, Robert (Bob) Lindsey, pastor of the Jerusalem Baptist Church wrote, "It is generally admitted by the [Israeli] Government that with the rate of immigrations remaining so high, it is impossible to keep up the industrial and agricultural development necessary for the growth of the population. Inflation and the necessity of floating loans abroad present critical problems for the young state. Little villages of prefabricated wood and aluminum houses are springing up all over the countryside. Yet the winter rains have found more than 60,000 people still in tents."[5] Many villages and towns in Israel were suffering with typhoid epidemics and the public was advised to boil drinking water for 20 minutes to render it free from typhoid contamination.[6]

Throughout Israel the economy was weak. An austerity program was initiated, "which included strict price controls, rationing of food and services, raw materials and foreign currency…The austerity regulations were copied principally from the rationing methods which had been enforced in Britain during World War II."[7] The austerity policy led to black marketeering and profiteering. In October 1951, the United States approved a 65 million dollar grant to help alleviate the difficult situation. However, in 1952, inflation was more than 60 percent.[8] *Kibbutzim* or communal farming communities were established everywhere absorbing many Jewish newcomers, but the farming communities could not produce enough food to meet the demand.

Those who had relatives in America often relied on food packages sent through the mail. In the years following World War II, Americans packaged food, medicine and baby supplies and sent them as CARE packages to parts of the world where there were shortages, including Israel.[9] However, the "[Israeli government] decided what food could be imported from abroad, in what quantities and at what prices."[10] Another source of food distribution came from a program called "Scrip". The Israeli government reached an agreement with a commercial company in America whereby money sent to *Scrip to Israel*, in New York City, would provide the recipient in Israel with a *Scrip* certificate. The certificates could be exchanged for a standard choice of food at designated scrip stores, which were better stocked than the local markets. The Baptist Convention members received both CARE boxes and Scrip certificates from family and friends in America and the additional food greatly contributed to their diet in the early fifties. As Paul and Marjorie adjusted to Middle Eastern cuisine, and as food became more plentiful, they relied less on American processed foods.

Censorship of mail, a holdover from the Defense Emergency Regulations during the British Mandate, remained in effect. In 1948, the State of Israel adopted most of the British Mandate legislation word for word. "The new government thus found itself effortlessly in possession of a formidable apparatus of emergency powers that could be attributed to the law-abiding British."[11] When Americans wanted to bypass Israeli censorship, they gave letters to friends who were traveling back to America or abroad to mail once they were outside of the country. The Israeli censors looked primarily for monetary exchanges and if there was a question, appeared at the owner's residence or business. The Baptist Convention in Israel received funds for salary and operational costs regularly from the FMB administrative offices in Richmond, Virginia. Church groups in America sent donations. The treasurer of the Baptist Mission in Israel had the burdensome duty of regularly providing explanations of financial transactions to the Israeli Censorship Offices. There was no postal service between Israel and the surrounding Arab countries. If mission members in Lebanon or Jordan wanted to write to a fellow Baptist in Israel, or vice versa, the letter was mailed back to America to a relative or friend, who repackaged it in a new envelope, and mailed it out to the recipient. Thus the letter would appear to have come from America.

Immigration brought such a large number of children to the country that primary education grew quickly. Israel's compulsory education law applied to all children from five to fourteen. Elementary education was free, but secondary schools had to charge comparatively high tuition fees. Arab government schools had a registration of over 27,000, and 5,000 children attended Christian mission sponsored schools. The rise in the percentage of Arab school attendance, as compared with the British Mandatory period, was notable. Before 1948 it had been 45 percent. In 1951-52, it increased to 90 percent.[12] The Nazareth Baptist School was filled to capacity and its secondary school was expanding—adding an additional grade each year with the goal of providing education through the twelfth grade class.

Few immigrants understood or spoke Hebrew. Modern Hebrew language classes, called, "*ulpanim*" were offered everywhere. Almost no one owned a car. There were about five or six cars in all of Nazareth in 1952, and the Baptist mission owned two of them. Those who had a vehicle were expected to be generous in providing transportation for others, especially to transport people to a hospital. Israeli soldiers on break from duty lined roads hitching rides to and from their homes. News was available only through newspapers, radio and word of mouth. The *Voice of America* provided news from the United States. Some people had telephones but overseas calls were expensive and rarely possible. Baptist mission families living in Israel looked to each other and to God for support and comfort in uncertain times.

Before 1948, Baptist missionaries in Palestine were part of the vast Palestine-Syria Near East Mission. Following the 1948 war, however, the borders of Israel were closed and neither Israel nor the bordering Arab countries allowed crossings. Between Israel and Jordan were border areas called "no-man's land," that served as demilitarized zones and no one was allowed to enter that area. Signs were posted along the barbed wire informing people that there was "danger." Jerusalem was a divided city with the more modern West Jerusalem located in Israel. East Jerusalem, with its ancient city walls, was located in Jordan. The only crossing point between West Jerusalem and East Jerusalem was the Mandelbaum Gate, so named because the gate was next to a house that had belonged to a Dr. Mandelbaum. It was not really a gate but a passageway between barbed wire and entanglements and was monitored on each side. Whoever crossed had to be "released" by one side and "received" by the other. There were a few exceptions for crossing the border between West and East Jerusalem. Foreign diplomats and embassy staff could travel across as representatives of their countries. Christians with passports and other credentials could apply for special tourist visas to cross from Israel to East Jerusalem in Jordan to attend services at Easter and Christmas in Holy places.

In April 1952, the *Jerusalem Post* reported that on Good Friday, before Easter Sunday, the borders between the old and new Jerusalem opened and allowed processions of "Italian, Spanish, Arab, English and French monks, nuns, priests and laity" to wind its way through the narrow streets of the Old City in Jordan "to the site of Calvary in the Church of the Holy Sepulcher."[13] The patriarchs for the western and eastern Christian churches conducted ceremonies in Latin and Ancient Greek.[14] Christians also gathered at the Garden Tomb, the site of a rock-hewn tomb believed to be the place, or very like the place, where the body of Jesus was taken following his crucifixion.[15] Baptist mission members Bob and Margaret Lindsey and Dwight Baker traveled across the border to Jordan in April 1952, to the Old City of Jerusalem and participated in an Easter Service.

Although Baptists from America living in Israel could apply for visas to cross over into Jordan at Easter and Christmas, Baptist Americans in Jordan and Lebanon did not generally cross into Israel. Moreover, the Arabs with whom they worked would not have understood why the Americans would have wanted to travel to Israel, or to even associate with anyone who chose to live in Israel. Palestinian families had been uprooted and severed. Israel was the enemy. Identification with Arabs both in Israel and in the surrounding Arab countries required that mission members be sensitive to external political realities. "The friend of my enemy is my enemy," is a saying clearly demonstrating how many Arabs feel toward Israel's supporters. "To Arabs, Israel is the enemy because Israel exists today on what Arabs consider to be stolen Arab land."[16] There was little opportunity for Baptist mission members in Israel and those in the surrounding Arab countries to visit unless they happened to meet in East Jerusalem. Baptist Americans ministering in the Middle East struggled to understand the complexity of the Arab-Jewish world in all its ramifications.

In April 1952, the members of the Baptist Convention in Israel met in Nazareth for their annual meeting. At the yearly meeting, decisions were made as to who would work in the various stations. Bob Lindsey, the pastor of the Jerusalem Baptist Church, would soon be leaving for the United States with his family, for two years of furlough, to work on his doctorate at the Southern Baptist Theological Seminary in Louisville, Kentucky. Dwight Baker, who since 1950 had served as pastor of the Nazareth Baptist Church and administered the Nazareth Baptist School, had not been given an opportunity to focus on Arabic language study. With the arrival of the Rowdens, Dwight could turn over some of the responsibilities of the work in Nazareth and set-aside time for language study. Elmo Scoggin, whose wife Hannah was on medical leave in the United States, was the only mission member, other than Bob Lindsey, who could speak Hebrew, and therefore would be moving from Nazareth to Jerusalem to be pastor of the Jerusalem Baptist Church. This left the new mission members—Paul and Marjorie Rowden—with the challenging responsibility of administering the Nazareth Baptist School, the Nazareth Baptist Church and the Children's Home.

Temporary housing for Israeli immigrants set up in rows beside Sea of Galilee near Tiberias, c. 1952.

The other members of the Baptist mission were Miss Eunice Fenderson and Tom and Mary Helen Francis. Miss Fenderson, an elderly lady, lived in Jerusalem at the Baptist mission house. She worked with small groups of women who met to sew and have Bible study. The women provided care for the poor and sick. Six months prior to the arrival of the Rowdens, Tom and Mary Helen Francis had arrived in Jerusalem for Hebrew language study. Tom had a background both in the ministry and in agriculture, and was appointed by the FMB specifically to oversee construction of buildings and agricultural production on undeveloped land in Petah Tikva, near Tel Aviv. The property was to be a Baptist center for believers who wanted to live and work together.

5
LETTERS
APRIL–JUNE 1952

Aerogramme To:
Mr. & Mrs. B. H. Cole
1546 Richland Rd. S.W.
Atlanta, GA U.S.A.

Mrs. Paul Rowden
Baptist Mission
Nazareth, Israel

April 13, 1952

Dearest Folks:

Well, we have been here [in Nazareth] one month today. It is Easter Sunday and I'm a little homesick for my sweet family, but we had a nice service this morning with Elmo [Scoggin] speaking and Paul will speak tonight. It is a beautiful day but terribly windy and cold…Dwight [Baker] is in Old Jerusalem today and he met some of the missionaries from Jordan and they had an Easter Service at the tomb site of Jesus. The traditional Easter Sunday for the Eastern World is next Sunday so they won't have any other worshippers there, probably.[1] We hope to be able to attend this next year. I know it must be a most inspirational service.

By the way, last Sunday Miss Cohn who came over on the boat with us came by to see us. She is on her way back to New York. I gave her 2 pretty pieces of Nazareth Lace to bring to you—one for Mrs. Rowden and one for you. I think they are very pretty. They are traditional pieces of work done here for centuries by Nazareth women. Let me know when you get them. Give Mrs. Rowden one of them. They cost quite a bit here and are done with one needle. We are very comfortably set up here now with a bedroom and bath and a sitting room with our furniture in it. We stored the rest of the stuff downstairs until after the meeting…

There are two cute young fellows from Pennsylvania in a farming village near here. They are Quakers and are helping the people in an agricultural way.[2] They come to our services often and were here this morning. Sit Nahil [Jeries] teaches them [Arabic lessons] too.

Yesterday, Mr. and Mrs. [James G] McDonald visited us a while. He is the former Ambassador from America to Israel.[3] He is very nice—he made me let him test Robin's bottle to see if it was warm enough just before I gave it to her…I baked a cake and cut out chickens and rabbits off of [American Easter] cards and decorated the top for an Easter cake. It is twenty minutes 'til nine at home [in Atlanta] now and everyone is dressing in their Easter outfits. I can just see them…

Much much love,

Marjorie.

The following letter dated April 14, 1952 is written to Paul and Marjorie's friends, James (Jim) Smith, and his wife Elizabeth (Betty) Smith. The Smiths had agreed to help by mimeographing letters for the Rowdens and mailing them out to people in the United States. The newsletter is written to "friends."

Letter to:
Rev. James W. Smith
Rt. 2
Conyers, Ga.

Rowden
Baptist Mission
P.O. Box 20
Nazareth, Israel
April 14, 1952

Dear Jim & Betty:

Enclosed is a double-barreled shotgun of work, as though you had nothing else to do, but, believe me, if you can find the time to mimeograph this letter and get it out, you will have helped us immensely…This is really a ministry on your part, and such a help to us.

…The Lord continues to bless us. Our freight came through without a scratch, and [it is] good to sleep in our bed once again. The children are fine and I'm thankful that they seem to have adjusted themselves to this new land very well. [It is] still mighty hard, putting it mildly, on Marjorie and me. We are homesick to beat the band, along with a hundred million other things, but "His grace is sufficient." Don't forget us in prayer.

Christian love,

Paul and Marjorie

Rowden
Baptist Mission
P.O. Box 20
Nazareth, Israel

April, 1952

Dear Friends:

So many have been interested in our trip and work that we want to take this opportunity to bring you up to date. Just before we left for New York City the Lord gave us this [biblical] promise: Deuteronomy 31:8 "And the Lord, he it is that doth go before thee; he will be with thee, he will not fail thee, neither forsake thee; fear not, neither be dismayed." To know that God would be with us and never fail us was just the thing we needed as we faced experiences that were entirely new to us in every respect.

Nazareth is a town of about 22,000 people. The population is [Arab] except for some Jewish administrators. Most of the houses and shops are very, very old and a stroll through the narrow streets with their little shops and wares, the people dressed in their colorful robes, camels and donkeys loaded with baskets, makes one think of the Nazareth of Jesus day[s]. In Nazareth we have the Truett Children's Home with nineteen children, a church, and a school. The school is a marvelous opportunity for evangelism. There are about 325 pupils from kindergarten to the tenth grade. Through daily Bible study and instruction many are being reached and are making professions of faith. Our school is badly limited by space. We trust in the days ahead we can enlarge and be able to reach more of the young people of Nazareth. They are the future and hope of our work here. Pray for them and for their teachers that God shall lay his hand upon many, and that he shall call out preachers and missionaries from them.

I wish you could be with us on a Sunday. At eleven our [church] bell rings and the morning service starts. Everything, of course, is in Arabic. One of the missionaries preaches in English and an interpreter translates into Arabic. At two P.M. we have Sunday School. This reaches many of the children of Nazareth and the church is full each Sunday School hour. At three we leave for the Cana preaching service, and at six-thirty we have the evening preaching hour. During the week there are the Believer's meetings, the R.A.s [Royal Ambassadors], the G.A.'s [Girl's Auxiliary], Bible study, and other fine opportunities of witnessing. There are many villages around Nazareth that need a witness. Our work is limited only by time and workers. Pray for the Church at Nazareth, for the school and Home, for the services at Cana, for more workers to help us in this great task. Letters from you

Shepherds bring their sheep and goats to the well in Cana c. 1952.

Passageway in Cana c. 1952

are always an encouragement to us. We may not be able to answer every letter right back but you can know that each and every one is greatly appreciated. Most of all, pray for us.

Christian love,

Paul, Marjorie, Becky and Robin Rowden

The following letters were written after the members of the Baptist Convention in Israel had their annual meeting. The three-day meeting was held in Nazareth. Assignments were made as to where each of the mission members would live and work and adjustments were made as members left for furlough in the United States or temporarily focused on language study.

Aerogramme To:
Mr. & Mrs. B. H. Cole
1546 Richland Rd. S.W.
Atlanta, Georgia U.S.A.
Mrs. Paul Rowden
Baptist Mission

Nazareth, Israel

April 17, 1952

Dearest Folks:

Well, I now know how Mrs. Dionne felt when she woke up and heard she had 5 babies.[4] Because in five minutes flat yesterday I acquired 19 [children in the Children's Home]! We sort of expected it to turn out this way, but we weren't sure until the [mission] meeting and we could all discuss it. Elmo [Scoggin] moves to Jerusalem [on] May 1st to take over Bob Lindsey's work and we move up to the Children's Home. Only the Lord could possibly know how incapable we feel for such a task...

Also it was decided that in September that Paul will take over the [Nazareth Baptist] church and the [Nazareth Baptist] school, and do the best he can for a year. That will allow Dwight [Baker] to go somewhere for language study which...as the future pastor he will need greatly to preach and witness with. At the end of that year, Paul will be free from the church and will have more time to study language along with leading the school...

The meeting lasted for seven sessions and got pretty heated at points, but I guess all conferences do. Anyway, we ended today at about 3 p.m. We have had our meals at the Galilee Hotel here in Nazareth so Emma [Baker] wouldn't be cooking all day and night. We met the Lindseys (rather Margaret Lindsey) for the first time. They are both so nice...We also met Tom and Mary Helen Francis. They are the newest missionaries besides us. They arrived last August. She will be 28 in November so she's more my age than the other 3 women... Elmo [Scoggin] was very obviously lonesome for [his wife] Hannah... [on medical leave].

We will have 5 or 6 capable native helpers. The most helpful one will be Mrs. Weippert, an Australian single old lady, who has been out in this part of the world for about 40 years and who our [Children's] Home has hired as matron. She is a fine old lady who manages the diet, kitchen...However; she is nearly 70 and can't be active too much longer.

Dr. [Theron] Rankin is coming in June for about a week.[5]...We all agreed to propose to the [FMB] in Richmond that our term of service be reduced to three years instead of five, and that we have a year free after first term and six months leave every three years thereafter. We're hoping and praying this will be passed. We're having a hot Eastern wind tonight and you should hear it howl outdoors...

Much love,

Marjorie

Aerogramme To:
P.D. Rowdens
1712 West Haven Dr. S.W.
Atlanta, Ga., U.S.A.

Paul Rowden
Baptist Mission
Nazareth, Israel

Sunday morning
April 27, 1952

Dear Mother and Dad,

This last Sunday morning in April is a beautiful day in Nazareth, and being the Sunday morning hour my thoughts turn toward Cascade [Baptist Church in Atlanta].

Later—5 p.m. Sudden interruption. Elmo [Scoggin], who was planning to preach had to go to Haifa, so Dwight [Baker] asked me if I could substitute, which I did, but which took a few minutes to plan and get ready for—so I didn't get to finish the letter. After church we used our two station wagons and carried a group to the Sea of Galilee for a baptismal service. We carried our lunches, and ate, overlooking the Sea, and then Dwight baptized a young man, one of our students in the school. In the background was a boat of fishermen casting their nets—thus a very interesting and inspiring service.

The other day I took a walk to one of the tallest of Nazareth's hills, and when I reached the top I could look out over all of Nazareth. 'Twas a beautiful sight. We are receiving your letters right along, and enjoy them very much. Tomorrow we will go to Haifa and use our Scrip certificate for the purchase of powdered milk, butter, etc. I believe the Scrip suits our needs better than [CARE packages] in that we can get just the articles we need.

Lots of love,

S

Aerogramme To:
Mr. & Mrs. B. H. Cole
1546 Richland Rd. S.W.
Atlanta, Georgia U.S.A.

Mrs. Paul Rowden
Baptist Children's Home
Nazareth, Israel

Sunday 9:30 A.M.
May 4th

Dearest Folks:

…Tom and Mary Helen [Francis] have been up here in Nazareth for about 3 days and are going back to Jerusalem this afternoon. I think we'll go back with them and stay a few days. I want to see Jerusalem. They have a little basement apartment in Bob Lindsey's house. They have just finished a six month concentrated Hebrew course and they're really tired. They went to class six hours a day and studied six hours out of class…Tom is a graduate in agriculture as well as Seminary and so the Board appointed him to do this farm job out here…

Elmo [Scoggin] has been awfully nice to us since we've been up here at the Home. He said he'd stay with us as long as we thought we needed him. We all eat with the children at breakfast and dinner everyday but at night we feed them all about 5:30 and they get bathed and go to bed. Then, Mrs. Weippert fixes a supper for us alone and it's always so nice. She fixes such pretty things as well as good things…

I don't know about other orphanages but this one is really run properly. Elmo and Hannah really have done a remarkable job. Elmo is really strict with them but his bark is worse than his bite and they all dearly love him. Mrs.Weippert is really a jewel—she takes life slow and easy but manages to turn out delicious raisin bread or nut bread…everyday. She never seems busy but she turns out a lot of work for a 70-year-old woman…Zelma [also pronounced "Selma"], the cook, can't speak a word of English but she's really fine too. She lives here too. Fida [Ateek] and Naami [Naomi Ateek], sisters, 19 and 17 years old are our attendants to the children. They are good too. Last night was Saturday bath night and you should have seen them scrubbing these…kids, heads and all. It looked like an assembly line. Well, I'll close now. Mrs. Weippert says tea is ready.

Much love,

Marjorie

Aerogramme To:
Mr. and Mrs. B.H. Cole
1546 Richland Rd. S.W.
Atlanta, Georgia U.S.A.

Mrs. Paul Rowden
Truett Home
Nazareth, Israel

May 6, 1952
Tuesday A.M.

Dearest Folks:

I stopped in the middle of getting dirty clothes ready for the [washing] machine so I could write this in time for Monseur[6] to get it to the Post Office. Monseur [Insair] is the boy who is handyman here…Sunday afternoon we took all the children for a ride in the back of the truck. They had a big time. We drove to Cana of Galilee and back, about 5 miles each way, I guess…

[Mrs. Weippert] is all provoked right now with the scrubwoman who is doing the floors "all wrong," she says. She speaks Arabic fluently…This scrubwoman is in here in the office now doing the floors. She is amazed at this typewriter and can't do her work for looking and jabbering. She is a typical Moslem woman. She wears long flowing rags with a headdress all decorated with all her money sewed on it. They all keep their wealth on their person. She is bare-footed and cleans the floor with a large rag. She keeps talking to me just like I understood every word she says. You should have seen her the other day when they brought in our washing machine and hooked it up for the first time. She almost jumped up and down…She kept looking at it and then rubbed her knuckles together as if to say, "Is that thing washing those clothes?" She is the only Moslem employee…

Naami and Fida [Ateek], the two girls who care for the children, are very nice. So is Monseur [Insair], and Selma the cook is very superior. She can't speak a word of English like the rest of them, however, and she and I have a time. She won't even try to learn English and I'm kind of glad because I have to speak to her in Arabic if I speak at all…

I had a two-hour lesson, yesterday. This is hard stuff! If you want to say, "come here," it is different if you say it to a girl than if you say it to a boy. Also it is still different if you say it to more than one person. Also there are almost one dozen Arabic words for each English word. You can say "Hello" at least 10 ways. Also the colloquial Arabic is different from the written Arabic. Hebrew is much like it, I understand.

The Lindsey family is sailing for America next week—all but Bob. He has to stay here until they get the land deal through on this farm business…Well, I must close. P.S. I shall never forget this Mother's Day 1952, when I had 21 children!

Much much love,

Marjorie

Letter to:
Mr. & Mrs. B. H. Cole
1546 Richland Rd. SW
Atlanta, Ga. USA

Near East Mission of the Southern Baptist Convention U.S.A.
Marjorie Rowden
Post Office Box 20
Nazareth, Israel

May 8, 1952

Dearest Folks:

Sunday after dinner we...went home with Tom and Mary Helen [Francis]...Early Monday morning...Tom and Mary Helen and Paul and I took off for Beersheba. Bob Lindsey also went in his car and took three of his kids and Becky with him. We drove along together and every little ways Bob would stop and tell us about the sights. He is a wonderful guide...

We saw Samson's birthplace and the plain on which he killed the lion. We saw the valley where David fought Goliath and we got out and walked down to the little creek (which is dried up now) and took a bunch of pictures. We picked up a few stones, which we thought were like the one David used in his sling. It is a lovely spot with high hills on both sides and it is easy to imagine the Israelites standing on one hill and the Philistines on the other. We stopped about noon under a big olive tree in a grove near the road and had a picnic...We then went on south to Beersheba. It is right at the beginning of the Negev desert...Beersheba is an interesting place but hot and dry and flat! We saw an ancient well which dates back to Abraham days and probably was used by him. We met a nice couple there, Mr. and Mrs. [Alvin Martin] who are missionaries under the Christian Missionary Alliance.[7] Sometimes they have no water there at all. They have a right nice mission house there, however.

On our way back we took a different route and came within sight of Gaza, which is in Egypt territory. We couldn't cross over into it but it looked about a block away from where we were...We got back about 6 P.M. mighty tired and hot. But it was most enjoyable...

Tuesday morning...Tom took Paul and me on a sightseeing excursion over Jerusalem. It is a lovely city (the newer Jerusalem that is; we can't go into old Jerusalem since it is in Jordan). Modern Jerusalem is pretty and "western looking" with wide streets and nice shops. We drove up to one point at the edge of the city, which juts out, almost to a point [in] Jordan. It is a high place, and we climbed up [to] a fortress there and could look over and down on Bethlehem. [Bethlehem, in Jordan], was about 6 miles away but we could see it as plain as day. With our field glasses we could see many churches and distinct buildings...Right there, where we were standing, we were about 10 feet from a bob-wire fence which marks the edge of Israel and then there is a space...which is "no-man's land" and then another bob-wire fence which marks the beginning of Jordan. To our left was a ridge of mountains and the Dead Sea.

Then we left and went back into the main part of town and climbed up Mount Zion (which also juts out into Arab-held territory.) … There is also a museum up there, which has relics, etc. It is a long steep climb, and I was exhausted. Here is the spot of the upper room, now a Catholic church

Standing in front of the Jerusalem Baptist Church, Jerusalem c. 1952 are (L-R) Dwight Baker, Tom Francis, Paul Rowden, Elmo Scoggin, Robert (Bob) Lindsey,

…David's tomb is there and we went in the little room where the Jews go on pilgrimages and burn candles…Over the tomb there are some huge silver jars with scrolls of the Old Testament in them. In another part of the building, down in a dark cave like place, where you have to go with candles in order to see, are some horrible things that were brought back from Germany after the purge of the Jews. There are ashes of thousands of Jews for you to see and soap made from human fat with the serial number of the Jew from which it was made and also other things made from parts of the human bodies…[8]

Tom and Mary Helen [Francis] just finished an extensive 6-hour day Hebrew course that lasted 6 months and they speak pretty good Hebrew, I guess…We ate supper at the Y.M.C.A. that night. While we were on Mount Zion we could see The Mount of Olives real good, just outside the city...

…Mary Helen and I went shopping. It was wonderful to go in some nice modern shops again. Of course there [were no shops] any bigger than Stegar's drug store,[9] but they were clean and neat and more or less modern…Right after dinner we left and drove back to Nazareth in the big red truck which we are keeping at the Home until they need it at the farm, because it is the only thing big enough to hold all the children [in the Children's Home] at one time. We want to take them on some picnics…this summer and maybe over to a beach on the Mediterranean…

You asked if there was anything that we need; I can't think of a thing. We can get lots of things with Scrip and it is better in that respect than Care. For example the Care packages sometimes contain things that we don't really need, whereas we can pick out what we need in Scrip stores. Sometimes you can pack us assorted boxes yourselves and mail them regular mail, parcel post, with heavy wrapping around the box so as to insure it getting here in one piece. It can't weigh over 22 lbs...You could include things like corn meal (which is not available at all), Swans-down cake mixes, sandwich spreads, gum, jello, pie dough, ready-mixes of all kinds, potted ham, etc. You could try a box like that sometime if you want to and we'll let you know how it gets here.

Well, I must close as I said before. Tell Bill and Pat I said I wish I could be there to see them get tied up properly.[10] That's gonna make me more homesick than anything, I'm afraid...

Much, Much love,
Marjorie

Aerogramme to:
Mr. & Mrs. B. H. Cole
1546 Richland Rd. S.W.
Atlanta, Ga. U.S.A.

Mrs. Paul Rowden
Truett Home
Nazareth, Israel

May 15, 1952
Thursday, 11 A.M.

Dear Folks:

Well, after getting all my [Children's Home] children off to school and then washing a tub of clothes and then straightening the house and then having a morning "tea," I now have a minute to write you. Mrs. Weippert and I are going to tea at 4 this afternoon up at the English [Edinburgh Medical Mission Society] Hospital. I'm real glad. I've met all of the people there, but I haven't gotten to know them well. They have about 15 missionaries there, 3 doctors, nurses, etc. Most of them are from England or Scotland. There is a new Doctor and his wife who have just arrived from London.

They have been here a little over a week. I haven't met him, but I met her last Friday at a prayer meeting that we had at the Bakers for all the Nazareth Protestant missionaries. There were about 20 of us there in all. The new doctor's wife is French and is very cute…

George Lati and his wife (both are teachers in our school here) are sailing for America tomorrow to go to college in Mississippi. The President of that college was out here last summer and gave them a scholarship. They are both fine Christian young people. They have only been married a few months. They are sailing on the *Expiditer* (the [freighter] we were originally scheduled for, remember).

One of your questions was about water supply. It is very good this year here because there was an abundance of rain during the winter. They don't think there will be a shortage at all. I understand it was dreadful last summer; the people fought over water at Mary's well. We have two nice complete bathrooms here and two kitchens with running water just as at home. The toilets are flushed like Aunt Susie's old one on the porch with a pull chain. It takes the small tank about 10 minutes or more to fill up again so we don't flush it every time, especially at rush hours like in the mornings. We boil all our drinking water 10 minutes for safety. At the end of each of our tubs is a hot water tank with a small-enclosed grate underneath for burning wood. We heat up the tanks for real good baths every Saturday night. The rest of the time we use cold water for sponge baths because both water and wood (for burning) are precious items here…

From our bedroom window you can see Nazareth with one swoop and also the valleys and mountains past Nazareth. The distances you can see in this country [are] amazing…

I just had to go chase Asa and Besillias back to bed. They are our two baby boys, ages 4. The names of these kids [in the Children's Home] sounded funny at first but now we are used to them. The other boy's names are Adnan, Edward, Ali and Damianus. The girl's names are Hideyia, Afaf, Teresa, Rima, Anne, Maladie, Katrina, Aida, Reiufi, Rhadia, Lorrice, Delal and Amira.[11]

Much love,

Marjorie

Letter to:
Mr. & Mrs. B. H. Cole
1546 Richland Rd. S.W.
Atlanta, Ga. U.S.A.

Near East Mission of the Southern Baptist Convention, U.S.A.
Marjorie Rowden
Nazareth, Israel

Sunday, 2:35 P.M.
May 18, 1952

Dearest Folks:

Well, here it is, another Sunday. We have spent 10 Sundays already in Nazareth. Time is passing quickly. Paul has gone to Haifa to take a group of teachers…from the church to say good-bye to George Lati and his wife. They sail on a freighter for New York tonight at 6. I kind of envy them. However, they probably feel like we did when we left New York for here…
Our dinner party was quite a success last night. The new doctor and his wife [Dr. John Tester and wife, Odette] and Mrs. Weippert's niece, Ruth Lenox, (all three from the English Hospital) came at 7:30 and had supper and remained until about 10. We had lots of fun…Last night I happened to think while we were eating supper of the difference in background of us six sitting there. Paul and I were born in America, Mrs. Weippert was born in Australia, Dr. [John] Tester was born in England, his wife was born in France, and Ruth (although of Australian parentage), was born here in Nazareth. Now wasn't that something? Mrs. Weippert had a nice supper with pork roast, baked potatoes, English peas, pickled beets, bread, apple pie and coffee. All of that was canned and we only open such on rare occasions. Even the apples in the pie [were from a can]. I haven't seen an apple since we left the ship…
Well, I just drug out daddy's "questionnaire" again…When we first came, Emma said she boiled all drinking water and so we do too, even for all the children here in the Home. The regular people here in Nazareth drink it straight, but they are used to it. The Arab pediatrician here said he boils all his family's water. In the larger cities like Tel Aviv, Haifa and Jerusalem, the water is treated and is safe. However, we all got our stomachs upset a little while we were in Jerusalem last week. It might not have been the water, however. When we go visiting in these homes we know the water is not boiled, of course, so

we dodge drinking it if possible. We don't mind drinking tea because usually it has been boiled in the process.

Prices are high, very high. That means everything. We have a young man living here, Manseur, who does all the buying for us so I don't know the prices, but so few things are available that you don't mind the price. You have to buy it. We eat 10-12 loaves of bread a day here [in the Children's Home]. The bread is never wrapped. You just bring it home in your hand. We buy local milk for the children. They have two glass fulls a day, but Mrs. Weippert boils it first…

…The Jews have beautiful farmlands all about, but the demand is just more than supply…We have a big out-door vegetable bin outside the kitchen door and some days Monseur [Insair] can almost fill it and other times it is empty. Mrs. Weippert is remarkable in planning nourishing meals with what is available. Today for dinner we had "*coosa mashe*" (stuffed squash). The squash here is large and green in color. But it is as good as ours, I think. Zelma, (the cook) fixed rice and meat together and stuffed the scooped out squash with it and baked it. Then she made a cream sauce for it. Also we had mashed potatoes and bread and vanilla custard. There is rarely enough meat to give each child a big serving so she stretches it good by putting it in the rice. About once a month or so we get maybe 5 chickens. You should see how Mrs. Weippert and Zelma stretch it. We have chicken soup one day, lima beans and chicken mixed the next day, stuffed cabbage or squash the next day and sliced chicken for Sunday and chicken sandwiches the next day…

We get about 3 or 4 eggs a week per person. Babies and elderly people get a little more…We can buy fresh eggs at scrip stores, however. Also, fresh meat. Also we have whole egg powder with us for cooking purposes, etc. That also is available at scrip, I think. There are two kinds of bread cooked here in Nazareth—Arab bread and "*frangi* bread" (foreign white bread). The Arab bread is brown and cooked in round flat patties. The other bread is oval shaped with baking powder in it and is more like ours. Although neither one tastes like what we were used to, we like both now.

Paul took all…of [the children] yesterday to the Sea of Galilee on a picnic. They went in the truck, but Monseur [Insair] made a tent-like covering for the back of it…They all took off their shoes and waded in the water…Paul was "pooped" when he got home. All 19 of them were running in different directions he said. It was too hot to take Robin, and Fida and Naami [Ateek] had to go and help with the kids so I stayed here and helped Mrs. Weippert get ready for our dinner last night.

We want to take them over to the Mediterranean [Sea] and play on the beach, but we're going to do it in shifts from now on…Becky has learned to respect law and order a lot more than ever here. It is good for her. Fida yells at her just like she does the other children and Becky "jumps" too. She told me that Becky obeys her orders even in Arabic, so she understands more Arabic than she can speak. Well, I'm weary of this typing. This is Sunday p.m. and I always get homesick on Sundays.

Much love,

Marjorie

Letter to:
Mr. & Mrs. P.D. Rowden Sr.
1712 Westhaven Dr. S.W.
Atlanta, Ga. U.S.A.

Near East Mission of the Southern Baptist Convention, U.S.A.
Paul Rowden
P.O. Box 34,
Nazareth, Israel

Thursday, May 29, 1952

Dear Mother and Dad:

…Becky and Robin bring us much joy as we play with them and watch them grow. Becky is quite a sight. We have a mulberry tree in our yard and we have warned the children not to eat them, because Mrs. Weippert makes jam from them, but the other day I caught 3 of the rascals under the tree eating them—mulberry stain from one ear to the other and all over them—and you can guess who one of the rascals was—Becky. So I marched them into the office and talked very severely to them, and marched three subdued culprits out. You can just bet if there's any devilment going on around here, Becky's in the middle of it! And if Robin could keep up with Becky she'd be right in the middle too! She knows just as well what "No-No" means as I do, but that just makes her want to do the wrong thing more than ever.

Children in the George W. Truett Children's Home pose with with Paul and Marjorie Rowden in back holding Becky and Robin Rowden, Nazareth, c. 1952.

...I got a $10.00 scrip [certificate] today planning to use it in Haifa but found the stores closed for the day. Last week we used the Ladies Sunday School scrip in the purchase of powdered milk, canned pears, peaches, etc. [It's] mighty good to be able to open a can of peaches when you want them and thank God for the privilege of getting it and being able to buy it. In so many, many ways we are blessed...

Had a very fine service tonight. I am leading in the study of 1st Corinthians, chapter 4 tonight. I feel so frustrated at times in trying to speak, not knowing the language and having to speak through an [Arab] interpreter. And I cannot feel free as I did at Durant and Stapleton [churches],[12] and I long for the time to speak with unction in a language other than English. Yet the Word of God and His Spirit are not bound and at the close tonight, two young men came forward on profession of faith—one, a teacher in our school and another fine young man. So God does bless in spite of us!

Lots and lots of love,

S.

The following two letters are written by Alta Lee Lovegren, Baptist missionary to Jordan, and a native of Cedartown, Georgia. She and her husband, Dr. August Lovegren were spending a year in Beirut, Lebanon studying Arabic. Following a year of Arabic language study, they would be stationed in Ajloun, Jordan at the Baptist Hospital. Finlay and Julia Graham, Baptist missionaries in Lebanon, were working in Beirut. The letters from Alta Lee Lovegren were in response to a letter she had received from Marjorie Rowden's mother, Mrs. B.H. (Alma) Cole. The Lovegrens and Rowdens could not write directly to each other, as there was no postal services between Lebanon and Israel. Alta Lee sent a letter to Alma Cole that was intended for Paul and Marjorie and asked her to resend it to them from America so there would be no indication that it had come from Lebanon. This precautionary method of communication was necessary given the political circumstances.

Letter To:
Mrs. B.H. Cole
1546 Richland Rd. S.W.
Atlanta, Ga. U.S.A.

Letter from:
Alta Lee (Mrs. L.A.) Lovegren
American Mission
Beirut, Lebanon

May 20, 1952

Dear Mrs. Cole:

August and I had your letter sometime ago and appreciated so very much hearing from you. We hope to hear from you again and will certainly add your name to our mailing lists. We would appreciate your passing such news as you can on to Paul and Marjorie. I accidentally brought the [enclosed] air mail stationery with us from the States so have written to the

Rowdens on it and will ask you to post it there in Atlanta. I am putting your return address on it and you address it to them please.

...We went to Old Jerusalem for Easter weekend and saw the Lindseys and Dwight Baker there. They said Paul and Marjorie had planned to go but didn't get their papers through in time or something like that...They also told us that the mail was rather highly censored so be sure that you do not mention our location in writing them. They are having no objection to the Baptists and the Baptist work there [Nazareth] so you need not worry about their safety.

We have been considering seriously with the other missionaries [in Beirut] your offer to send CARE packages here. This is the situation, and it is a very hard one. There are hundreds upon hundreds of people without work. There is a great need. We do have some refugees in our church but we could not give to one group without giving to all and that is a tremendous task. Also, they would not understand receiving one or two packages and not keeping on getting them month after month after month. Also, refugees usually live in large groups together—in pine groves, on the beach, anywhere they can find vacant land to put up tents. It would be almost impossible for one or two families to receive help and the others not learn of it. Then they would crowd to our church as "rice Christians" did in China to get rice—these would come for what they could get. You really couldn't blame them, but there just isn't enough to give them all. Most of these here are receiving help through the organizations to help Arab refugees. Considering all these things, the [Finlay Grahams] (the permanent missionaries in Beirut) and we, felt that it would be wise not to receive packages here. We appreciate very much your thought and offer...

Yours in Him,

Alta Lee Lovegren.

Letter to:
Mrs. B.H Cole
1546 Richland Rd. SW
Atlanta, Georgia U.S.A.

From:

Mrs. Alta Lee Lovegren
American Mission
Beirut, Lebanon

June 8, 1952

Dear Mrs. Cole,

I wrote the above letter to you on May 20 and saw Mrs. Bob Lindsey soon afterwards. Her sister and her sister's husband were traveling with her to the States. They are Presbyterian missionaries to India. They got off the boat and spent the whole day with us. We especially asked about Paul and Marjorie and she told us they're doing fine. Let me suggest to you that you write Mrs. Lindsey in care of the Foreign Mission Board and ask them to forward it to her furlough address in the states and she will write you more about the conditions, etc. than Paul and Marjorie are able to write from their station.

We happened to have a US Airmail letter, which I wish you would forward to Paul and Marjorie. Read it first. Hope you are well and are enjoying the blessings of the Lord. The more I think of the work of your Sunday School Department, the more I think they must be wonderful Christian people.

Yours sincerely,

Alta Lee [Lovegren]
Beirut, Lebanon

Hannah Scoggin had cousins who lived in Haifa. The Biebergals were four brothers and a sister. The brothers were Yaacov, Tuvia, Haim and Menachem. The sister's name was Yaffa. They graciously entertained the Rowdens in their homes. Hannah wrote that visits with them were wonderful experiences. Yaacov and Victor Biebergal owned a cinema in Haifa and, at least on one occasion, invited all the children in the Children's Home to their theater to see a movie at no cost. [13]

Letter to:
Mr. & Mrs. B. H. Cole
1546 Richland Rd. S.W.

Atlanta, Ga. U.S.A.

Marjorie Rowden
P.O. Box 20
Nazareth, Israel

June 12, 1952

Dearest Folks:

…Tuesday night we had dinner with Hannah's [Scoggin's] cousin and his wife and their two little boys. Also another brother and his wife were there. We had a lovely time. They are all just wonderful people. We had supper with still another one of the brothers week before last…They all live on Mt. Carmel, [Haifa] but in 4 separate places, 4 brothers and their wives. This couple we visited Tuesday night have a lovely apartment with a nice view of the Mediterranean…

Well, "Sherlock Holmes" Marjorie solved the "cake mystery" yesterday. I'm really getting good at this. I cooked a cake and left it in the kitchen and [the] next time I saw it, it had been picked all around the sides and top by little fingers. So we lined everyone up and began hunting for the guilty one. We let the little ones go because they were too little to reach it. We let the big ones go because they were late getting in from school and didn't have time to do so much damage. That left the middle ones. We got "not I" from all of them. We looked in their mouths for evidence and on their fingers, but no sign of cake. Finally one little girl, who had dried the dinner dishes, finally got cornered into saying she did it. "Uncle Paul"[14] had an active conference with her in the office.

We are still working on the "purple tub" mystery. One Sunday morning not long ago, someone dumped a whole bottle of purple medicine in the bathtub. We still can't find the guilty one. It is really a great life. We have so many things like this coming up that life can never be dull. They are really all, sweet children, however.

Much, much love,
Marjorie.

Letter to:
Jim & Betty Smith
Rockdale Baptist Church
Conyers, Georgia

Near East Mission of the Southern Baptist Convention, U.S.A
Rowdens
P.O. Box 34
Nazareth, Israel

June 18, 1952

Dear Jim & Betty:

…Wish we could see the Smith clan landing in Haifa and coming here to work! Believe me, fellowship is one thing that is greatly missed…Listen, lad, I have received several letters from people about the letter that you mimeographed for me saying how much they enjoyed it. Can't tell you how much I appreciate it. Saved me no end of trouble and time…

…Our work here goes on at a steady pace and always there is much more to do than we have time for. Marjorie and I are at the George W. Truett Children's Home now in addition to our other responsibilities in connection with the church and the school. We have nineteen children between the ages of 3 ½ and 9. Counting our own two we have 21. Our day starts early and ends late believe me. Keeping up with 21 children is a job. School is out tomorrow, and 325 boys and girls are happy, except those who failed; but there is much to do to get the school ready for the fall. Dwight Baker and wife are the other couple here and are doing a wonderful job. We have good attendance in church, and Bible study. This summer there is Bible school, camp, and…other items. Now we need a redheaded fella and fine girl here to help…

Finally today I finished my beginner book in Arabic and have advanced to kindergarten.[15] It is hard to get adjusted to [preaching through] a translator after a few years of preaching [in English] in the states…Jim, I find that everything I have ever learned, studied, had as a hobby, seen or worked at, has been a great help here. I used to have subjects and wonder whether or not I'd ever use them again, but now I wish that I had six or seven degrees, and 15 million talents. Well, if you can make any sense out of this letter, you are better than me…

Christian love,

Paul & Marjorie

Letter to:
Mr. & Mrs. B. H. Cole
1546 Richland Rd. S.W.
Atlanta, Ga. U.S.A.

Marjorie Rowden
Box 34
Nazareth, Israel

Wed. 9:30 A.M., June 25, 1952

Dearest Folks:

...I went to my first [Arab] funeral yesterday. It was very sad, the little 4

Fida Ateek, Nazareth, 1952

Marjorie Rowden sits on a donkey belonging to Arab man who delivered vegetables to the Children's Home.

yr. old niece of Fida and Naami [Ateek died,] after 6 months of suffering. Her mother died just two years ago this month and her father... is in the Hospital very ill with T.B...[The Ateek] home...was spic and span,[16] and everything was so orderly and quiet. They are fine Christians and are members of the Anglican Church here, although they also attend our church and the father is superintendent of our S.S. [Sunday School]. They do not have a S.S. at their [Anglican] church. There is always so much wailing and moaning over death here [in Nazareth], especially among the Moslems... It was a relief to see [the Ateeks] conduct themselves so calmly...

...Fida's father wears a red fez on his head and a long robe which most of the men here wear. Only a few, like Suhail Mu'ammar's father and Fuad [Farah's] father, wear [Western style] clothes like our men. We stayed about 30 minutes. There wasn't a word spoken, hardly. At least it was a good rest before our long hot hike back home. I had taken our [21] children down to Emma [Baker's home adjacent to the church] to stay while I went, since Fida and Naami were not here to watch them. So I came back by and picked them up and we got back home about 12:00. Hot! On the way up the hill from Emma's to here we passed the man bringing our vegetables on a donkey. He comes every day. He picked Becky up and she rode home on the donkey.

Well, we rested until 3:30 and then Emma and I had to go back to the funeral. They bury them quickly because they do not embalm here. It was even hotter this time and I had to wear high heel shoes and a hat. The Anglican church is right next door to their home so it was the same walk…It was a hot trying day, I can assure you. Trying to walk any distance on this stony ground is awful. I can easily see how "stoning" was a common form of punishment or persecution, because stones are everywhere.

On top of everything else it was Selma, the cook's, nite and afternoon off. Someone left a kettle on the kerosene stove in the kitchen and it began smoking and when we found it the whole kitchen was black as tar—you could not even see through the screens in the windows!…I nearly died right then. But lo and behold, while Mrs. Weippert and I were struggling with the kitchen and trying to get supper for the children, in walked Fida and Naami [Ateek]. I could have kissed them both…

Much love,

Marjorie

6

DR. THERON RANKIN VISITS THE MIDDLE EAST

In June 1952, the Baptist Convention in Israel prepared for the first visit of Dr. Theron Rankin, the Executive Secretary and top administrative officer of the FMB. He reported to the board members selected from Southern Baptist churches of the Southern Baptist Convention. Dr. Rankin served as a missionary to China from 1921–1935 teaching in a theological seminary and then served as the FMB Secretary for the Orient from 1935–1945.[1] Theron Rankin was the first Executive Secretary of the FMB who had served as a Baptist missionary prior to taking office. The FMB administrative offices were located in Richmond, Virginia. When Dr. Rankin opened his offices in Shanghai in 1936, Japanese militarists were planning an invasion of China and the clouds of war were gathering. His duties took him to Japan, where missionaries were being evacuated and Japanese Baptists were getting ready for the days that lay ahead.[2] When the United States entered World War II, Dr. Rankin was captured by the Japanese and imprisoned for nine months at the Stanley Internment Camp, Hong Kong. He recalled:

> During those months without sufficient clothing and hardly any food, we got down to the bare realities of life. I realized for the first time that the true realm of reality lies within our spirits and the qualities within us. The hunger and hardships reveal our character. As long as you have quality of character, you may lose everything else and still have the one thing that counts.[3]

While a prisoner of war, Dr. Rankin was vice-chairman of the American Communal Council of the internment camp and was, therefore, responsible for the welfare of fellow missionaries. He was repatriated in September

1942.[4] In 1950, as Executive Secretary of the FMB, he traveled to The Orient as missionaries were being forced out of China and efforts were being taken to move them into other areas. "We haven't lost in China," said Dr. Rankin. "We can't lose what God himself has accomplished."[5]

When he took up his duties as Executive Secretary in 1945, he found a limited number of mission volunteers. A meager overseas budget had frozen the number of missionaries at about five hundred. He began to build a foundation. In 1949, the Convention adopted a program of advance for its entire work. Remembering the World War II years in America from 1942 to 1945, he said:

> The American people just played around at the job of winning a world war until they were given a colossal task. When they realized they had to equip all the Allies in order to win, they amazed even themselves with the results. Baptists are like that; they'll piddle at the job of world evangelism until doomsday, unless they begin to see that a church of any size can be worldwide in scope if it has a world program.[6]

In his report to the FMB for 1952, Dr. Rankin stated that there were 879 missionaries serving in 32 countries. "However," he said, "the foreign missionary is not primarily concerned about building up figures, just as Jesus was not primarily concerned about the numbers. Jesus spent most of his ministry on earth preparing twelve disciples. The greatest hope for the foreign missionary is in the service he renders to help develop a strong, well-trained, indigenous Christian constituency that will be the primary evangelizing agency of the country where he serves."[7]

Dr. Rankin and his staff traveled, as time allowed, to some of the countries where Baptists had mission stations. Accompanying Dr. Rankin to the Middle East was Mrs. George R. Martin, president of the national Woman's Missionary Union, and Mrs. R. L. Mathis, President of the Texas Woman's Missionary Union.

Dr. Rankin, along with Mrs. George Martin and Mrs. M. L. Mathis, flew to Beirut, Lebanon from Europe, and visited Baptist missionaries in Lebanon and Jordan before coming to Israel.[8] Lebanon, the smallest Mediterranean country, was in the heart of the Levant, but it actually looked the most Western to Mrs. Martin. She stated, "In Beirut, the largest city, Baptist missionaries Finlay and Julia Graham[9] and Miss Mabel Summers[10]

[are] doing splendid work and have a well-organized growing church. In Tripoli, the second largest city in Lebanon, there [is] also ongoing work."[11] Finlay M. Graham, missionary in Lebanon wrote:

> Beirut provides a meeting ground and a point of contact for businessmen from near and far in the Arab East. Here may be found the chief moneychangers of the Arab world, the main regional offices of western business associations, and the American University, originally a mission school, whose influence for good cannot be denied. Despite the ardent nationalism with its concomitant aversion to the West, the opportunity to witness for Christ here in this land has never been greater.[12]

Dr. Rankin and the WMU ladies also visited Jordan. In 1937, in the Arab village of Ajloun, Jordan, British missionaries Dr. and Mrs. Charles McLean, of Church of England affiliation, began the Gilead Mission Hospital. According to a report by Dr. Loren Brown in minutes of the FMB, "[Dr. & Mrs. McLean] did excellent work, both evangelistically and medically." After thirteen years, however, they were unable to continue the work and offered to turn it over to the FMB.[13] The Southern Baptists bought the hospital and began to staff it. At the time, the FMB was seeking to initiate work in Jordan with a medical facility, and this seemed to be the Lord's leading.

Dr. & Mrs. Loren Brown, Southern Baptist missionaries, went to Ajloun in April 1952 to prepare for transfer of the hospital. Dr. and Mrs. J. T. McRae joined them during the start up. Dr. and Mrs. August Lovegren planned to work in Ajloun upon completion of a year of Arabic language study. The hospital, which faced the Jordan Valley about half way between the Sea of Galilee and the Dead Sea, accommodated forty beds and the nursing staff. In the village of Ajloun, about a hundred Christians of different persuasions met for worship but had not yet formed a church. Dr. Loren Brown stated, "The Southern Baptist entrance in 1952 into the Hashemite Kingdom of Jordan marked a great advance in the Near East mission work. Jordan was one of the few Arab states where freedom of religion prevailed; yet there were few evangelical witnesses."[14]

Mrs. George Martin wrote, "In Jordan, a reception at the Baptist Hospital (formerly the Gilead Mission Hospital) brought all the official dignitaries to meet us. The *sheik*,[15] the president of Parliament and other officials brought greetings. One of the officials told us that the Arabs like the American people, but do not like their politics. He said our politics had brought them great disaster and heartache."[16]

Dr. Rankin and the ladies crossed from East Jerusalem into the Israeli sector of West Jerusalem where members of the Baptist Convention in Israel met them. Mrs. Martin wrote, "One cannot enter Israel without realizing the paramount problem of the [immigrants]; it overshadows all other problems. Since 1948, Israel has more than doubled her population and new (Jewish) [immigrants] are still pouring in." She added, "Someone has called Israel not a melting pot but a pressure cooker. In spite of the fact that the city of Jerusalem has been divided into two cities…it remains in the eyes of the world, the Holy City, as if it were a single unit."[17]

7
LETTERS
JULY-MID-SEPTEMBER 1952

Letter to:
Rowdens Sr. & Coles
1712 Westhaven Dr. S.W.
Atlanta, Ga. U.S.A.

Marjorie Rowden
P.O. Box 34
Nazareth, Israel

July 1, 1952

Dearest Folks:

...Well, after much difficulty, Dr. [Theron] Rankin finally arrived Sunday morning in Jerusalem. He was accompanied by Mrs. George Martin, president of the whole [WMU] of the Convention and by Mrs. M.L. Mathis, president of the Texas [WMU]. The difficulty was in crossing over into Israel from Jordan where they had been visiting...They had flown to Beirut, Lebanon, from Europe, about a week ago...Bob and Tom and Elmo met them at the [Mandelbaum] Gate between Old and New Jerusalem and finally everything was O.K. and they crossed. They drove almost straight on to Nazareth.

The two women came with Elmo [Scoggin], Tom and Mary Helen [Francis] and got here about 4 pm Sunday. Bob [Lindsey] brought Dr. Rankin but they came by the farm, so they didn't get here until midnight Sunday night...We heated up the wood-burning hot water tank and the [ladies] had their first real bath in a week. We gave them our room. Dr.

Rankin stayed with the Bakers. Bob Lindsey stayed with us and the Francises stayed with the Bakers. Also Elmo stayed with us. We had people sleeping everywhere! I slept in one of the youth beds in the older girl's room and moved Robin's bed in beside me. Our room is really a comfortable one and nice and airy so they really thoroughly enjoyed it.

...Mrs. Martin is very nice and so interested in every phase of our work. Mrs. Mathis is as cute as pie! She is a gorgeous person and was dressed to perfection every minute—a real art, when you're traveling in this part of the world. Mrs. Martin looked trim and neat all the time too. Mrs. Mathis was responsible for Texas giving one million dollars to the Lottie Moon Christmas offering last year. So it was a big joke the whole time she was here. All the men called her "Miss Million Dollars." This is her first time abroad. She has been working with Dr. [W.A.] Criswell, [pastor of] First Baptist Church, Dallas, Texas for the last four years and is now Assistant Dean at Baylor University in addition to being President of the Texas WMU. She was a real sport. We made some pictures of all of them and us. While I was taking [a picture] of Dr. Rankin [and Mrs. George R. Martin and Mrs. R. L. Mathis], Mrs. Martin...said, "This ought to be good—the Brain, the Power, and the Money."

...Sunday night right after they arrived, Suhail's mother came over to see Mrs. Mathis because she had so recently been with Suhail at Baylor...Mrs. Mathis told all the news about him and made poor Mrs. Mu'amour [Mu'ammar] so lonesome for him that she sat there and wept and wept. So when she left she invited everyone to her home for tea Monday at 5...An Arab tea is something to write about. We all ate until we nearly died. She is the best Arab cook I've been privileged to eat with. Mrs. Martin didn't try to go, she rested here at home. Mrs. Mathis and Dr. Rankin went and thoroughly enjoyed it. However, Mrs. Mathis had a terrible headache...and I rubbed her neck until my fingers nearly fell off to get her in shape to go. It was more or less in her honor.

Then, Emma [Baker] had already asked everyone to her house for supper, so almost immediately we had to go there. We didn't eat until nine since we were all so full of the pastries at the tea. We finished at 10:15 and then adjourned into the living room and had a discussion with Dr. Rankin until 1:15 am. We had to take advantage of the short time that he would be with us. We discussed major issues, such as additional personnel and more money for mission work...We also brought up the subject about shorter terms of service. He said that many of the missions all around the world had sent similar requests to him and that all of them would be studied in the light of faster transportation in these days…We couldn't get much sympathy out of him, however, since he spent two 7 year terms in China. He was there 20 years in all. But his first term was 7 years without returning. Imagine!

Dr. Rankin is really a fine man and we all enjoyed being with him. We all got the giggles at the supper table and we wondered what Dr. Rankin thought about such a silly bunch. Tom [Francis] turned over the gravy bowl and we all more or less got hysterical. Dr. Rankin seemed to fit in real well. He said that next to spiritual qualifications, he put a sense of humor next. But he said he thought we all had an overdose of humor. Elmo [Scoggin] just keeps you in stitches with his remarks and Bob [Lindsey] too. They took Dr. Rankin swimming in the Sea of Galilee on their tour. He was very much impressed with all he saw. It was his first trip to the Holy Land.

Well, this morning we invited everyone up here [to the Children's Home] for breakfast since we had not had a chance to have Dr. Rankin for a meal due to their short visit. There were 12 of us in all and we had a grand breakfast at 8:30. We have been without eggs for a week, but we managed to salvage enough to give them all an egg. Mrs. Weippert cooked hot "Australian" biscuits and melted cheese on top.

…They were to go by the farm today on their way back to Jerusalem and thoroughly go over the situation. They are having a special mission meeting tonight in Jerusalem to settle the issue [about the farm]. Tom, the farm man, is rather discouraged. He feels the farm project can't be a success unless the Board gives us a larger budget to build and operate it with. So they will discuss that tonight and tomorrow they will tour Jerusalem. Then early the next morning they fly to Rome…

By the way, Mary Helen's folks sent her some coca cola syrup the other day and she brought me a small bottle. I've nearly died for a coke. I'm hoarding it like it was gold. We bought some "fiz" water to mix with it…There is lots of red tape about sending fluids in the mail, or something. Anyway, I thought it was right sweet of her to share hers with us…

Much love,

Marjorie

The following letters reference organized Baptist youth programs modeled on similar groups in America. Royal Ambassadors (R.A.) was the name of a boys and young men's group. Girl's Auxiliary (G.A.) was held for girls and

Young Women's Auxiliary (Y.W.A.) was a group for young women. The church groups met regularly for Bible study and prayer. They engaged in social activities and promoted mission projects to help the community. There were sports activities for boys and sewing activities for girls and young women. During the summer, camps were held separately for the young men and women. The camps provided opportunities for the young people to spend a concentrated amount of time together in new settings. Another church sponsored program was the yearly Vacation Bible School held for boys and girls of all ages and held at the church and school grounds for a week each summer.

Aerogramme To:
P.D. Rowdens
1712 Westhaven Dr S.W.
Atlanta, GA U.S.A.

Paul Rowden
P.O. Box 34
Nazareth, Israel

Sat. P.M.
July 12, 1952

Dear Mother & Dad:

On this beautiful Sunday afternoon in Nazareth, I guess you are [vacationing] on the beach in Daytona. Would like very much to be with you, but if I had a choice, I think it would be here, because there's so much to do, and so few to do it. There is no feeling that can quite take the place of knowing that one is in the work that God wants. Nazareth is no place like Daytona, Florida though. Ha! I would like to have supper tonight at Howard Johnsons [restaurant].

We had a very good week at [Royal Ambassador] camp. We had about 35 boys, and Dwight [Baker], Tom [Francis] and I taught, worked…in it. Thursday, Elmo [Scoggin] came up from Jerusalem [to Nazareth Baptist Church] to preach for the closing service… [while we were at camp]. I taught the book of Mark each day and really enjoyed it.

This morning I had the preaching services—spoke on Acts 9:1-20. Tomorrow morning begins the daily Vacation Bible School for a week, and I am teaching the book of Acts to the Intermediates. Dr. Rankin promised that we could have two teachers from America for our school, so perhaps in a year or so we shall have an adequate staff for the school…

Love,
S

Letter to:
Mr. & Mrs. B. H. Cole
1546 Richland Rd. S.W.
Atlanta, Ga. U.S.A.

Near East Mission of the Southern Baptist Convention U.S.A.
Marjorie Rowden
Nazareth, Israel

July 14, 1952

Dearest Folks:

…Last Thursday Mary Helen [Francis] and Emma [Baker] and I took Bill, Bron and Becky and went up and spent the afternoon and evening at the [R.A.] camp with all the boys and our husbands. It is about an hour's drive. They were really camping "out…" They slept on cots right out under the stars. The sight was a pretty one. They camped directly under two huge Lebanon cedar trees on the grounds of the Baha'i Shrine. The Baha'i religion is one, not widely known…Baha'i was one of the founders of the religion; therefore it is named for him. The Shrine is located on a large plot of ground near Acre, above Haifa, and they graciously allowed our campers to use a portion of the grounds. Bahaullah, the founder, is buried in a room there and that night we were taken on a tour of the house and Shrine by the Arab caretaker who is a devout follower of Baha'i.[1]

When we first arrived about 3 pm, we drove from the camp down to the beach about 2 miles away and let the kids play. It is a lovely beach, not quite like Daytona, but nice. Then we went into the old city of Acre and walked through the market place. It was the most picturesque thing I'd ever seen. The little narrow streets and the open shops must have been just like they are now for hundreds and hundreds of years. It was interesting, but I was

89

kind of glad to get out into the fresh air again. [In] one place a man was selling beans and had a big pot there where he would also cook them for you. Pastries were everywhere for sale with a million flies all over them. Ragged little kids were eating stuff right off the cobblestones…

We saw the thick wall that the city built as a fortress against [Napoleon] which he was never able to penetrate. We walked along the top of it. We also visited a Moslem Mosque which is the second oldest in Israel…It was very ornate with no seats. I guess everyone always stood or either sat on the marble floor. We had to go in barefooted. Five times a day the people are called to prayer…

Afterwards we walked back down to the camp and sat around the camp fire with the 40 R.A. boys and had the evening service…

Much love,

Marjorie.

⁂

Letter to:
Mr. & Mrs. B. H. Cole
1546 Richland Rd. S.W.
Atlanta, Ga. U.S.A.

Marjorie Rowden
P.O. Box 34
Nazareth, Israel

July 17; Thurs. A.M.

Dearest Folks:

…Vacation Bible School is going on this week and Paul is teaching the Intermediates and Fida and Naami [Ateek] are teaching in the smaller classes. Paul has 60 intermediates…All of us couldn't go off and leave the home, so I stayed to keep Miss Robin and the home fires going. They seem to be having a fine time. There are about 250 enrolled in all…

Tuesday afternoon we had a birthday party for 7 of our children [in the Children's Home] and for little Bill Baker. All of them have had birthdays since the last party in March. We had it down at the Bakers in the back under a big tree. I did all the planning and Mrs. Weippert did most of the food fixing. Emma made ice cream and a cold drink. We made a huge cake and cookies and sandwiches…Also I made pretty crowns for each of the 7…They wore them on their heads and thought they were big stuff…Fida said it was the nicest party the children had ever had in their life so it made me feel like it had all been worth it. We were all angry at ourselves afterwards for not remembering to invite the little Jewish boy, son of the military commander here in Nazareth, who was so kind to invite our children to his birthday party about two months ago…We will invite him up some day for a small party or something.

Selma, the cook, went to her home in a village near here Tuesday night as she always does…But Wednesday morning she didn't come back. Mrs. Weippert managed all right with breakfast, but I knew she couldn't prepare the dinner alone so she and I worked all morning peeling potatoes, "coosa" (green squash) making a salad, and so on. There are 30 here to feed so it is no small matter to cook for them. We had watermelon for desert and I cut up watermelons until I thought my hand would drop off. Mrs. Weippert was puffing and stewing so that I got right worried about her…After lunch Paul took Monseur [Insair] and they drove to Rainey [*Reineh*] (her village) to see about her. She had rheumatism in her arms and legs pretty bad, but they brought her back. I never realized how valuable she was before. I poured aspirin down her all afternoon to keep her going.

You know it is a small small world. Yesterday Paul was taking Adnan to the hospital to have the doctor look at a series of boils he is having, and on his way he drove past Mary's Well and saw a tall American man standing there taking a picture and he thought he recognized him. He was Dr. [Cannon], head of the Department of Church History in Emory Theology School.[2] When Paul was at Emory living in that private home on Springdale Road, Dr. [Cannon] had the room next to him. Well, he was delighted to see Paul. He is touring this part of the world alone and had a professional guide and hired car taking him around. He had a packed schedule and was unable to come up and see us right then, but he invited us to come to Tiberias last night and visit with him at his hotel. So we drove down and had a very delightful time last night…He told Paul that if he had known before that he was here he would have stayed with us and he and Paul could have toured Israel together and "we could sit down at each historic spot on a stone and read our Bible." I'm sure there is nothing Paul would have enjoyed more for he had great respect for this man…

It was the first time I had been to the Sea at night and it was beautiful, the stars were bright and there must have been a million. He was in the nicest hotel (only nice hotel I should say) there and we sat out on a terrace overlooking the Sea of Galilee. We drove home about 10 and enjoyed the whole evening very much…

Much love,

Marjorie.

Letter to:
Mr. & Mrs. B.H. Cole
1546 Richland Rd. S.W.
Atlanta, Ga. U.S.A.

Near East Mission of the Southern Baptist Convention U.S.A.
Marjorie Rowden
Post Office Box 20
Nazareth, Israel

Sunday, July 27, 1952

Dearest Folks:

…Wednesday Emma [Baker] started her G.A. camp for about 20 girls…We took the girls up on a mountainside outside of Nazareth every morning at 7:30 and stayed until 6 pm. Their mothers wouldn't let them go to a camp where they have to spend the night. We don't have a tent anyway. They took blankets to sit on and a lunch. The camp lasted 4 days and I think they all enjoyed it. We closed yesterday afternoon with an altar service (Paul came up to conduct it) and then they all came down to our house and Paul showed them a movie that the Education Department puts out about camping. It was a nice ending. I think they all really had a good time.

Emma taught the G.A. Manual and had the devotional with them every morning. I usually waited until 10 a.m. to go up and I taught them a study course book and used the flannel graph board…They had handwork. They painted pottery and some of the vases looked real pretty when they finished them. Also we had them put on plays each day. They had to act out some scene from the Old Testament and use the things they had with them as costumes. Yesterday the play was about Joseph being sold into slavery. It was real good. They wrapped up in blankets and made themselves look like real characters. They are all natural born actors and have no shyness at all. In the afternoon they had to lie down and rest an hour, then they had recreation and then either Paul or Dwight came up for the vesper service.

Love,

Marjorie

Letter to:
Mr. & Mrs. B.H. Cole
1546 Richland Rd. S.W.
Atlanta, Ga. U.S.A.

Girl's Auxiliary camp on hillside in Nazareth, Israel 1952.

Marjorie Rowden
Post Office Box 20
Nazareth, Israel

Sat. Aug. 2, 1952

Dear Folks:

Well, we had quite an evening last night… Emma [Baker] and I…went with Fida and Naami [Ateek] to a Moslem wedding party for the bride. It is the niece of Fatmi, our scrub-woman. Dwight drove us as far as he could, but the streets are so narrow that you can't drive far. We walked up the rest of the way to the bride's house. Up hill,

Vacation Bible School at the Nazareth Baptist Church, c. 1952.

up hill, up hill. Everything is up hill here. The stone walkways are as slick as glass…I can't imagine how one would stand up on them when it was raining.

Long before we arrived we heard the "tom toms…" and the [rhythmic] clapping of hands. We entered the small dirt floor court with the outside toilet there and the chickens and pigeons…Then we looked in the one room which is about the size of our American living room and there must have been 150 women in there, some sitting on chairs and even more on the floor. More women stood outside and looked in the window. Counting us four, there were about 10 Christians there in all. The rest were Moslem women.

The bride was sitting on a big overstuffed chair up on top of a table with satin sofa pillows, all colors, all around her. This was at one end of the room with palm leaves and flowers and colored electric light bulbs all around her and also an Oriental tapestry. She was really a pretty girl about 21 years old…There was only one man there and he was blind. (Moslem women don't like for men to see them). This man played an instrument something like our banjo. He was way over in a far corner. Many women played tom toms in the shape of vases with a tight skin stretched over one end.

There was a small clear space in the middle of the floor where the women, one at a time, stood up and danced while everyone else sang and clapped…Emma and I were given the seats of honor right up close so we saw everything. We nearly suffocated. There was every kind of a woman from a nice well dressed lady to the village Moslem women who wear 10 or 12 garments and have their faces [tattooed]. There must have been 50 small babies yelling or nursing…Every time we opened our mouth to speak to each other they all asked Fida and Naami to tell them what we said. Everyone glared at us…The wedding is this afternoon and I would like to go to it, but we have to go to a tea at the home of the organist of the Anglican church. At four this afternoon the groom will come with all the men (who also had a big party last night) and they will take the bride to the groom's house. That's all there is to it. There is no ceremony.

Well, after two hours of dancing…the bride came down and two girls danced with her around and around. Each of the two girls carried long candles in their hands. They took her out the door and she covered her face before she walked through the courtyard to another room where she changed her clothes…She kept changing clothes and coming back and dancing around with each of her "trousseau" dresses. They were really all lovely and had lots of handwork on them. She had a handkerchief and hair decoration to match each dress. She looked as if she would cry any minute. They say it would be terribly ill mannered for her to look [happy].

[A] woman got a big bottle of perfume and began slinging it all over the room. She came over to Emma [Baker] and me and literally poured the stuff on our heads. We had to try to be gracious through all of this, mind you. They watched our every facial expression. They wanted us to dance, but we told them we didn't know how. Someone asked Emma to sing a hymn. I'm afraid it would have sounded terribly out of place. She begged out of it. Then they asked one large woman to dance to Mohammed and she did…About midnight we slipped out to get some air and decided to go on home. They went on until the wee hours. We had a long walk home but we enjoyed it.

We passed three more bridal parties on the way home…Oh, yes, I got a generous pinch on the arm by a child. I think she just wanted the "feel of" an American. They crowded around us so that sometimes we could hardly breathe. I don't see how Emma stood it in her [pregnant] condition, but she said she felt fine. She had been before. That business of being stared at is true of any American. When we stop our car any place, immediately it is swarmed with people who come right up to your windows and stick their heads in and glare at you. It was annoying at first but you soon get used to it…

95

Much love,

Marjorie

Letter To:
Mr. & Mrs. B. H. Cole
1546 Richland Rd. S.W.
Atlanta, Ga. U.S.A.

From: Marjorie Rowden
Near East Mission of the Southern Baptist Convention U.S.A.
Post Office 20
Nazareth, Israel

September 8, 1952
Monday P.M.

Dearest Folks:

…This Wednesday (Sept. 10th) is our big day. The executive committee in Richmond will have a special meeting to consider our Farm Project. Bob Lindsey will go to Richmond from Louisville where he is studying now to talk with them. We are all very much concerned that the Lord's will be done in this matter since it will involve so much money. Tom [Francis] is of course particularly concerned, because it may mean whether he stays here or goes back home. We have been much in prayer about it.

Well, we have had more guests! Remember I wrote you about the Cowens who were on the boat with us. Well they were to spend a year in Israel. So Friday they arrived in Nazareth and stayed in the Galilee Hotel… [T]hey came up for tea Friday afternoon and then we drove them around Nazareth. (They were both in Israel 25 years ago studying at the Hebrew University in Jerusalem). They had supper with us Friday night and then we drove them back to the hotel. They had come on the bus that day from Safed…and it took them about 2 hours so they were very tired. They are studying the Hebrew language at a school in Safed. It is a special school for very advanced students. Both of them speak about 7 languages. He is at least 65 or 70 years old, but she is about 50. You remember that he fell on the boat coming over and he hasn't been well ever since. He really looks bad. She is very active and gads about like she was 19. She leads me in a merry chase. I like her very much...

Saturday morning Paul went for them and we took them on a walking tour of the Nazareth "sook" (market place). You have to walk...since they are much too narrow for cars. They bought some souvenirs. We visited both of the Churches of the Annunciation. Both claim to be built over the spot where the Angel told Mary that she was to become the mother of Jesus.[3] Also we took them to the "supposed" carpenter's shop of Joseph. We came back here for lunch. They were very much impressed with all our children and the Home in general...

Saturday afternoon we had a real experience. We climbed Mount Tabor (the traditional site of the transfiguration of Christ). It is a high mountain with a gruesome road. We were scared to death, but we took Dwight's jeep and so we made it. On the top is a beautiful church built by the Catholics. It is absolutely unbelievable almost that a church like that could be up there. You can see all over the world, it seems, when you get up there. On one side of it is the huge valley of [Armageddon]. Well, after we came down we went to visit a new "kibbutz" down at the foot of the mountain in the plain. A "kibbutz" is an organized group of young Jews who get together and live together and split all the profits evenly...

Pictured are (L-R) Paul Rowden, Marjorie Rowden, Charles A. Cowen, Ida Cowen on Mt. Tabor. In the background is a Catholic Church. 1952.

This "kibbutz" is called "ENDOR" [Ein Dor][4] because it is near the village of ENDOR where Saul consulted the witch, remember? It is a new kibbutz, only 4 years old. The Cowens were particularly interested in showing us this new one so we could see how much progress has been made. They personally, the Cowens, got up the money for the first children's home at this kibbutz. About half of the young Jews in this kibbutz are from America. We toured the whole thing and visited in the quarters of one young couple from Michigan and had coffee and cake. They were the finest people you ever saw. It would really do your heart good to see what those young people (120 in all) have done with absolutely nothing to start with. They have a beautifully laid out farm with their own electric generator, silos, chicken houses, large herds of cattle, farm machinery, [etc]. They lived in tents at first, then built pre-fabs, now have white stucco houses. The houses are laid out in a pretty pattern with a huge green lawn in the middle. Each couple has one large room with a private bath and porch. That's all they need because they all eat in a common dining room.

Their children are all living in houses for themselves with the others their age…In a kibbutz everyone works, so that's why the children are all taken care of together. The girl we visited was head dietician in the kitchen. We were there on Saturday, which is their Sabbath, so they were all more or less free that day. There were no trees at all when they came and now they have literally hundreds of little trees growing all over their territory. The Jews have gone in for tree planting in a big way all over the country because it was absolutely barren when they took it over. All the main roads are now lined with small trees, and all the mountainsides and everything.

…Sunday morning [the Cowens] went to church with us. They asked to go. Then after lunch we drove them back to Safed. It is about 1 ½ hour's drive. We had never been there so we were glad to see it. It is a lovely city set on a very high, high spot…

Much love,

Marjorie

Letter To:
Mr. & Mrs. P. D. Rowden Sr.
1712 Westhaven Dr. S.W.

Atlanta, Ga. U.S.A.

From: Paul Rowden
Post Office 34
Nazareth, Israel

September 8, 1952

Dear Folks:

...Today we had a meeting of the teachers for our school. It opens next Monday week. Dwight [Baker] will remain in charge until he leaves for language study and until [the new missionary couple—the Murpheys] come. Marjorie will teach a Bible course three times a week and I will teach English and Bible. We have some eleven teachers in the school now.

...We have been exposed to quite a few dishes since our arrival in Israel and enjoy most of them. We have cactus fruit, which is the fruit of the large cactus that grows everywhere here. You slice off the spiny part and underneath is the fruit, which is fairly nice. They call it [*sabra*]. Then there is pomegranate, which is cut open, and the small seeds covered with a delicious tasting capsule are scraped out and served with sugar. We often have olives for breakfast, which are very nutritious and good...

Love,

Sonny

8

FUNDING FOR THE FARM

A few months after Dr. Theron Rankin returned from his trip to the Near East, the FMB in Richmond, Virginia called a special meeting to consider the proposed Baptist farm project on land in Petah Tikva near Tel Aviv. Bob Lindsey, who was working on his doctorate at Southern Baptist Theological Seminary in Louisville, Kentucky, traveled to Richmond to provide information on the proposal. Following the meeting, a report to the FMB stated:

> The one project in Israel around which more hopes were centered than any other was the Christian Colony. It was the brainchild of Rev. R. L. Lindsey. About a year ago an agricultural missionary (Tom Francis) went as our representative to Israel. Soon after his arrival, he began to survey the situation and about two months ago he released his report.
>
> So desirous of making the right decision were we that we called a meeting of the Committee on Africa, Europe and the Near East and we asked the executive secretary and the president of the Board to sit with us. After an excellent presentation by Mr. Lindsey and a full discussion of the project, the following decision was reached.
>
> Despite the fact that Mr. Lindsey presented the matter convincingly, the members of the committee were forced to the conclusion that it was not possible to find the amount [of funds] that would be required to initiate the project.[1]

The budget report to the FMB that year was not promising. The report stated that the FMB could not make large increases in missionary staff with-

out automatically creating the necessity for large increases in appropria-
tions for fieldwork and capital purposes. In 1950, 111 new missionaries had
been appointed—a record number. In 1951, 58 were appointed. The ex-
pectation for 1952 was for 90 new missionaries to be appointed. The total
operating budget for 1953 was a little over five and a half million dollars.
This budget provided almost entirely for recurring expenses, missionary
support and field operations. It included capital needs for church buildings,
schools, seminaries, training schools, hospitals, publication plants, missionary homes and paid for 875 missionaries and their children in 32 countries. The funds also aided salaries of 3,000 native pastors, evangelistic
teachers, doctors, nurses and other denominational workers. The only fore-
seeable increase of the budget would have to be from increases in the cooperative program, whereby churches contributed a share of tithes to home
and foreign missions, and from the Lottie Moon Christmas Offering contributions by church members.[2]

In his report to the FMB, Dr. Rankin talked about the shortage of funds
for missions:

> In today's world these people, who in the past were so far
> away that they could not see what we do with what we
> have, have come now to be just across the street from us.
> They are looking into our lives, our homes, churches and
> institutions. They hear what we say and see what we do
> about what we say. And they draw their own conclusions.
> Ignore it as we may, we cannot escape the fact that the rel-
> ative smallness of what we are doing to make Christ's
> gospel known to the world is being regarded by the non-
> Christian peoples, to a distressing degree, as evidence that
> we ourselves do not believe the gospel we profess.[3]

Tom and Mary Helen Francis had been appointed for the purpose of
overseeing construction on the farm property. They had spent six months
in Israel learning Hebrew, and Tom had worked diligently putting together
a report for the FMB of the estimated costs of the proposal. The Israel mission members were disheartened by the lack of funds and the inability to
begin construction on the farm property. Tom and Mary Helen Francis were
now uncertain of their role with the Baptist Convention in Israel.

The mission was eagerly waiting for the arrival of newly appointed mission workers, Milton and Martha (Marty) Murphey. The Murpheys would

be taking over the Children's Home in Nazareth. Upon the arrival of the Murpheys, the Rowdens planned to move to another house in Nazareth rented by the mission. Paul Rowden was to assume administration of the Nazareth Baptist School and both Milton Murphey and Paul Rowden would preach at the Nazareth Baptist Church. Dwight Baker planned to travel to Jerusalem and spend some concentrated time on Arabic language study.

9

LETTERS

MID-SEPTEMBER-DECEMBER 1952

Letter to:
Mr. & Mrs. B. H. Cole
1546 Richland Rd. S.W.
Atlanta, Ga. U.S.A.

Marjorie Rowden
Baptist Mission
Nazareth, Israel

Monday, September 15, 1952

Dearest Folks:

…We have all just heard the news (a cablegram) that there can be no farm so we're together to console each other and to plan future work. Poor Tom and Mary Helen are rather lost now about what to do! They are awaiting a letter from the Board for further details…

We haven't heard any more from the Murpheys. They must be terribly busy getting ready to sail.

Much much love,

Marjorie

Letter To:
Mr. & Mrs. P. D. Rowden Sr.
1712 Westhaven Dr. S.W.
Atlanta, Ga. U.S.A.

From: Paul Rowden
Post Office 34
Nazareth, Israel

September 20, 1952

Dear Mother & Dad:

...We have been working on [renting] a house...trying to get some agreement about it. The house is very nice and Lord willing we shall get it, but it does not have electricity yet, and that is a serious problem as we have so many electrical appliances...Seems that because the newness of the country that they are about six months behind in doing all the wiring...

...Wednesday and Thursday night there was a Youth for Christ rally in the YMCA here in Nazareth that we sponsored...

Robin is a cool-aide fiend now.[1] She will see you drinking it and she will turn around and back up to you which means "pick me up" and then she will point to the glass and grunt which means, "say chum, how about sharing that stuff with a friend."

Tomorrow night I am preaching on "Questions." There are four questions that we must honestly answer. Is the new birth necessary for me? Our natural condition is described in Romans 7:15-21. How do I get the new birth? [It's] God's work and our work. God calls us to salvation and provides salvation and we, for our work, must simply put our faith in His finished work. [Galatians] 3:26, John 1:12. Can I know if I have the new birth? There are many ways of knowing. [Galatians] 5:22 tells us many ways. John says that we know that we have passed from death to life because we love. Do I have the new birth? This is the most important question. We may have worldly fortunes but do we have eternal life? We may have titles but do we have a new name in the Lamb's book of life? We may see Kingdoms, but do we know the King of Kings? We may see lands but are we bound for the land that is fairer than day? We may have a nice house but are we going to have a place in the house of many mansions? We may see many flocks but have we seen the Lamb of God that taketh away the sins of the world?

Each day is filled with its many duties such as having devotional period with the children every morning, painting sores, seeing officials about trying to get cement to fix some cracks in the walls of the house, paying the help, problems of the school, dealing about a new house, getting the screens painted, going to services, and preparing messages, trying to get stove pipe for a new stove for the Home, trips to Jerusalem for Mission meetings, trips to Haifa for purchases, etc.

We are very happy to get a teacher [Frank Currie] for our tenth [grade] class from Bob Jones University. He graduated from there last June and came to Israel for a visit and decided to stay. He needed a job and plans to study Hebrew on the side. His fiancée is coming out in November and they are going to be married here. He seems to be a very fine and spiritual fellow and I think that we will be helped by his coming. That relieved Dwight and [me from] having to teach the tenth [grade] class…

…The Lord continues to be real to us and supply our every need. Morning by morning there is new joy in Him. We are seeking day by day what Ezra sought in Ezra 8:21: "To seek of Him a right way for us, and for our little ones, and for all our substances." Will close now. Hope this finds all of you well and happy.

Much love,

S

Letter to:
Mr. & Mrs. B. H. Cole
1546 Richland Rd. S.W.
Atlanta, Ga. U.S.A.

Near East Mission of the Southern Baptist Convention U.S.A.
Marjorie Rowden
Post Office 20
Nazareth, Israel

Tuesday
September 23, 1952
Dearest Folks:

Well, school started yesterday and there is a little quietness around here now, at least in the mornings. They all leave at 7:45 and come in at 12:15 for their dinner. The younger ones take a nap and the older ones go back for afternoon classes. Paul is trying to learn all about the principal's job so he stays down there all day. He isn't teaching any classes now that Frank [Currie] has been employed. [Paul] will take over as principal as soon as he feels he knows enough about it so Dwight can leave for language study—probably in 6 weeks.

I am teaching high school Bible three days a week for only one period, so that isn't too bad. It gives me a chance to leave the Home for a while and also makes me get down and dig in my Bible to keep ahead of the class. It is a difficult course to teach to this group of people at this time. It is Old Testament history and deals entirely with the Jews, of course. I have to be very careful to remember their recent history here in Palestine and to be very tactful…It's hard for these Arabs, who have recently lost their dignity (not to mention their homes, many of them) to think of this as the "Promised Land." I trust that I can help their attitude a little bit as well as teach them the plain facts of the Old Testament. It won't be easy. They are a fine bunch of young people.

It has been some job getting all these 20 children ready for school. Their clothes all had to be repaired and their shoes sent for repairs. Mrs. Weippert is busy now making school bags for them. They require a clean outfit each day…Becky marches off with them each morning. She thinks she's big stuff…

The other afternoon while the Francises were here, it was terribly hot and still so we drove down to the Sea of Galilee. It is 600 feet below sea level there and we nearly suffocated until we got in the water, but then we had a wonderful time. It was as calm as a fish pool. We took four large inner tubes and we each one sat in one and floated half way across it seemed. We made a long train out of us four and our tubes and paddles together like a rowing team. We really made good speed. We laughed about going on to Lebanon or Syria or Jordan, but changed our minds. Anyway we got cooled off. You can see these three countries from the Sea of Galilee…

Much love,

Marjorie

Aerogramme To:
Mr. & Mrs. B. H. Cole
1546 Richland Rd. S.W.
Atlanta, Georgia, USA

From:
Marjorie Rowden
Box 34
Nazareth, Israel

October 3, 1952

Dearest Mother:

…Well 'tis Saturday morning and this place is all a buzz. We have so much to do on Saturday mornings. A pipe is stopped up in the kitchen. Monsour [Insair] is trying to fix it. He is mad with Selma, the cook and they won't speak to each other…I have 4 children sick in bed today with colds. Rima has an upset stomach and vomited 5 times last night. Fatmi, the Moslem washwoman is cleaning all our floors today and she just cut her bare foot on the corner of a bed and is lamenting in loud cries of anguish. She is *[majnooni]* (a little crazy). 'Tis a great life on days like this!

Paul is yelling at me to get the 6 youngest ready for him to take to the hospital for their regular check-up. Fida [Ateek] has a terrible sore throat and wants to go along to see the doctor. Robin is as good as gold and is sound asleep. Becky is trying to take a cold so I made her stay in bed and she is sitting up coloring. She has no fever. After dinner we have to start our Saturday scrubbing of children and their shampoos. Then at 5 we have their supper ready and show them a movie and dump them in their clean beds. As Fida says: "*Nushcor Allah*," (Praise the Lord!).[2]

I am enjoying my Bible class so much, although I wish I didn't have quite so many students. I have 51 who are 14, 15, and 16 years old. Last week I got two more who are Moslem boys from a nearby village. They know very little English and they have never laid eyes on a Bible before. I really don't know what to do. We are so thrilled to have them that we have to be patient, but I guess I'll have to coach them outside of class the whole year in order for them to come anywhere near passing. It was really a thrilling experience to hand them two Bibles and show them the inside for the first time in their lives. Our first assignment was to read Genesis 1:1-35…[They] had no idea where to start…

Much much love,

Marjorie

Aerogramme To:
Mr. & Mrs. B.H. Cole
1546 Richland Rd. S.W.
Atlanta, Georgia

Marjorie Rowden
Box 34
Nazareth, Israel

Friday, October 17, 1952
Dearest Mother and Daddy:

…Hope you all have had your trip to the mountains by now. There are no trees here to turn yellow and red. But the government is planting them like flies all over the place. In another ten years it will look like a different country.

…I am really enjoying teaching in the school…I have 50 in my Bible class and we are having a wonderful study. All the kids are so interested and good. They all stand when I walk in the class and stand to recite. An American teacher would drop dead to have such respect.

Also I organized the YWA girls last week with 11 to begin with. We received our manuals and little emblem pins this week. They have to work hard to earn the pins. We are making green scarves for our white blouses and embroidering the YWA emblem on the back of the scarf…

Much much love,

Marjorie

Letter to:
Mr. & Mrs. B. H. Cole
1546 Richland Rd. S.W.
Atlanta, Ga. U.S.A.

Near East Mission of the Southern Baptist Convention U.S.A.
Marjorie Rowden
Post Office Box 20
Nazareth, Israel

October 20, 1952
Monday Morn.

Dearest Folks

Did I tell you all about the experience I had the other day in a Moslem village? Well, I have a real nice little Moslem boy in my Bible class who lives in a Moslem village about 10 miles from Nazareth... I was real anxious for him to get started off well in the Bible class because it was completely new to him and I knew he'd never like it if he got behind. I kept asking him when he could stay after school and let me help him privately a little. He always said he had so far to walk that he couldn't stay. So finally I told him one day that if he'd stay an hour or so and let me help him I'd drive him home. So after we finished I put him in the front seat with me and off we went. I knew his village was near the little city of Afula, but off the highway about 5 miles, so I decided I'd just drive him to Afula and let him out.

Well on the way home we passed this very distinguished Arab man dressed in strict Arab garb. Kahled asked me to stop the car. This man was the [mukhtar] of Kahled's village and also his uncle. [Mukhtar] means he was the head of the village. [Kahled] introduced me and the man asked me (in Arabic – I'm getting sharp) to have coffee at his home. I said thank you I'd like to sometime. I didn't know he meant that particular afternoon. So he followed our car in his truck. I tried to explain to Kahled that I couldn't possibly that afternoon and besides that when I did come I'd like to have my husband with me, because I know he'd like to come too. Well, he was insulted no end. He insisted that I go at least to have a look at the village. I drove through this narrow winding little path for miles and miles. Finally we got there. If it had rained the road would be impassable. But it hadn't rained in months so I nearly got stuck in the dusty sand instead. When we neared the village all the women were dressed in their colorful Moslem clothes and were carrying water pots on their heads. When they saw an American car with an American woman in it they almost stampeded me. They were all over the car in no time at all. Kahled felt real important and kept talking out the window to all of them in Arabic. I never did completely stop until I got in the center of the village and found a place big enough to turn around in. Children, chickens, dogs and everything scattered when I started turning around. Some of them looked actually like they had never seen a car before. The dust was so think I could hardly see.

Kahled kept insisting that the *mukhtar* would be very sad if I didn't have coffee. He said, "It is not good to turn back when the visit is half made." They always tell you "It is not good…" I told him that I was very sorry but "good or no good" I was not going without my husband. I wasn't actually afraid because they have utmost respect for a foreign woman, although they haven't much for their own women. But I didn't think it would look so good and besides it was about 5 P.M. and I wanted to get out of there before it started getting dark. So he finally got out and said good-by. I came back and told Paul. He said now we really must make an effort to go out there for coffee because they will be really hurt with us…My, it was really an interesting place. I wish you could see it… My, oh, my, if we could just lead that boy to know Christ it might be an entrance into that whole Moslem village, because he is the nephew of the *mukhtar* and rather important. He told me later that he liked to read the Bible we issued him and that he did not realize how interesting it was. He is making good grades in my Bible class now.

Well, Saturday we went to tea in a wealthy Jewish family's home. We go from one extreme to another. This man is the father of the girl who married the youngest son in the [Biebergal] family (Hannah's relatives). She is expecting her first baby before long so she and [Manachem], her husband, were visiting her folks for a few days. They called and gave us an invitation to come to tea and meet them. We really thoroughly enjoyed it. They spoke only Hebrew and no English at all. [Manachem] and Marsha spent the whole afternoon interpreting for us. The oldest [Biebergal] son and his wife, Sarah, have a new baby about 6 weeks old, which we never have found time to go visit. So we plan to do that Tuesday night. We feel that all these people are really genuinely interested in us, although they admit they are not interested in our theology. They are at least very tolerant. We like all of them very much and have appreciated all the nice things they have done for us. They have really gone out of their way to entertain us.

Much love,

Marjorie

Aerogramme To:
Mr. and Mrs. B. H. Cole
1546 Richland Rd. S.W.
Atlanta, Georgia USA

Marjorie Rowden
Baptist Mission
Nazareth, Israel

Monday, October 27, 1952

Dearest Mother and Daddy:

Saturday afternoon we had a beautiful baptismal service at the Sea of Galilee. It was the first one I had been able to attend and I'm sure it was the most impressive one I have ever seen before. We went to a spot where there were lots of smooth rocks on the shore and small ones all along the edge of the water. It is near the end of the dry season and the Sea was very low. There were about 30 of us sitting on the edge on the big rocks as Dwight took the two candidates, an Arab man and his wife, out into the water. It is the bluest, clearest water in the world. In the background are the mountains of Moab, which are in Jordan now. And to the north is Mt. [Hermon], the tallest one of all, with snow on its top. We had Scripture reading and sang a hymn or two. It was so quiet and impressive. As each of the candidates came up out of the water and walked to the shore, the congregation sang "Oh Happy Day, when Jesus took my sins away." It was in Arabic, but the tune was the same and I'll never forget that sight. I took our three oldest children and Becky along.

Last night after church we had the Lord's Supper. There are only a handful of baptized believers but last night there were the two new ones and it was a blessing just to have communion with them…On the back row their four little children sat as still as little mice. We feel encouraged because this is actually the first real family we have had to join the church with us. Although we have large congregations we have only about 15 who have made open professions of faith and have been baptized. Many have made professions, but due to family and other reasons they will not be baptized. Here it indicates a complete break with the old traditional Christian or Moslem religions, which are continued simply in name only. The Nazareth young people are hungry for our type of Christianity and flock to the church in droves, but when it comes to being baptized into our church, their parents usually give them lots of trouble. One of the 16-year-old boys in my Bible class made a profession of faith about three weeks ago. He is the happiest Christian you have ever seen, but his family has given him much unrest ever since…

Last week I had my 2nd YWA meeting with 13 girls. Since then I have enrolled two more girls—making a total of 15…Yesterday after church a most distinguished Arab man met me outside the gate, under that big Baptist Church sign; you know? (From pictures) He had his two daughters with him. He wanted me to take them into the YWA and he handed me all kind of money to get them books, manuals, YWA scarves, [etc.] with. He said he knew it would be a fine thing for them and begged me to take them. They are both students in our school. I thought to myself that a father in America would never be that interested in his daughter becoming a YWA…

Much love,

Marjorie

Letter to:
Mr. & Mrs. B. H. Cole
1546 Richland Rd. S.W.
Atlanta, Ga. U.S.A.

Near East Mission of the Southern Baptist Convention U.S.A.
Marjorie Rowden
Post Office Box 20
Nazareth, Israel

November 3, 1952
Monday Night, 7:15 P.M.

Dearest Folks:

…We have really had a full week behind us. Last Sunday Selma, the cook, got mad for the hundredth time in about a month…So Selma just walked out…Mrs. Weippert was sick in bed with bronchitis at the time and there I was—no cook and no Mrs. Weippert. For three days Monsour [Insair] and Fida and I, and Mrs. Weippert when she felt like it, cooked and cleaned the kitchen…Finally we got a widow woman near here to come in and help out a short while each day. Tomorrow we are getting Monsour's sister, Zahara, to come and take the job…

I had already planned a Halloween party for the children this past Saturday night so I had to do all the work myself. But I didn't mind so much. We really had a wonderful party, with pumpkins, balloons and even a real life ghost (Monsour) [Insair]. We ate apples off strings and played a game with peanuts. I think everyone enjoyed it. We also celebrated 7 of the children's birthdays. All day Friday I cooked cakes and put orange colored icing on them. Also I cooked 100 cookies and made 38 dishes of orange jello.

…Well, after the party Saturday night, all the children went to bed and we sat around the [dining] room table and had an informal mission meeting. Tom and Mary Helen [Francis] announced their resignation and said they plan to fly home in January. We all more or less have been expecting them to do it…It will just break my heart to see them go, but I don't blame them in the least. They came out for a specific job and since the farm didn't materialize, their job is done…

We received a big box of good used shoes today from Oneilda and her circle girls. We were thrilled to death to get them. We were about shoeless!—the children I mean. We also got a small box of nuts and food items from a church in St. Louis. We used most of this at the Halloween party. There are a couple of Christmas boxes on the way, I think now. I just hope they get here before Christmas…

Much love,

Marjorie

In the U.S. presidential election of 1952, incumbent President Harry S. Truman decided not to run. There had been two years of stalemate in the Korean War. General Dwight D. Eisenhower, Republican, won the Presidency in a landslide vote ending twenty years of Democratic control of the White House. A few days after the U.S. presidential election, Chaim Weizmann, the first President of the State of Israel, died at his home in Rehovot. Weizmann, born in Russia, had been active in the Zionist movement. England's Premier, Winston Churchill, sent a telegram to Israeli Prime Minister David Ben Gurion that read: "I am deeply grieved to hear of the death of my old friend Dr. Chaim Weizmann. The world has lost a distinguished citizen and Israel a faithful son."[3] In the following letter, the Rowdens talked about listening to news on Voice of America.

Aerogramme To:
Coles
1546 Richland Rd. S.W.
Atlanta, Georgia USA

Marjorie Rowden
Box 34
Nazareth, Israel

Wednesday, November 5, 1952

Dearest Mother and Daddy:

Well, Paul and I have been listening to the *Voice of America* broadcast of the election returns...It is just a little after midnight there now. We just laughed as we pictured all of you glued to the T.V. or Radio right now...

...I'm [surely] enjoying my Bible class. We have finally gotten the Children of Israel out of Egypt and now we are studying the Ten Commandments...Last week we studied the Passover and I asked Rachel and Elliott—our two Jewish students—to tell us about the way the Jews observe it now. They were real interesting and we all enjoyed hearing them. They said that most Jews only have the Passover feast one night, but their family always had it two nights because they were still in Egypt. After all these years their family has just now...come out of Egypt into the Promised Land.

They have been living in a tent ever since they arrived here and they were about to decide—like the people of old—that it was better in Egypt. But...now they have finally gotten a little one room prefab house and they are thrilled to death. In Egypt their father was an office worker, white-collar man. Here he has done everything from digging ditches on up. But at least they are in Israel now where they won't be persecuted because they are Jews. They are typical of the thousands and thousands of Jews who have immigrated here in the past few years. Every Jew in this country, almost, has a story to tell that would fill up a book, from the ones who spent years in Hitler's concentration camps to the ones who have fled from one country to another all their life seeking freedom. Will close.

Much love,

Marjorie

Aerogramme To:
Mr. & Mrs. B. H. Cole
1546 Richland Rd. S.W.
Atlanta, Ga. USA

Marjorie Rowden
P.O. Box 34
Nazareth, Israel

Sunday, November 9, 1952

Dearest Folks:

...Tomorrow all four men, Paul, Dwight [Baker], Elmo [Scoggin] and Tom [Francis], are going on a 4-day trip to [Eilat]. It is way down at the bottom of Israel on the Red Sea and on the desert. It is the southern most inhabited place in Israel. They are taking the jeep and the big red truck with all their water and food and gas and everything for 4 days—bedding...There is no actual road so they will just drive through the desert-like country. Because this territory still is endangered with Arab snipers they have to take an army representative with them and guns. They say it really isn't very dangerous but I'd feel better if they were all back again…Paul is as excited as a child before Christmas…

Much, much love,

Marjorie

Letter to:
Coles
1546 Richland Rd. S.W.
Atlanta, Ga. U.S.A.

Near East Mission of the Southern Baptist Convention U.S.A
Marjorie Rowden
Post Office Box 20
Nazareth, Israel

November 15, 1952

Dearest Folks:

Paul came in from his trip [to Eilat] last night about 8 P.M.. They had a real nice trip they said. The four men went and they took an [Israeli] Army Major with them for protection and a Jewish guide. So they were really escorted in style. They spent one night in [Eilat] and said the Red Sea just looks like all the other seas. They slept out on the beach. From [Eilat] they could look over into Arabia, Jordan and Egypt. The road down there is terrible and they said they were shaken to bits. Paul said the land was not sandy at all but was rocky and barren and mountainous. He was really surprised. This is part of the wilderness that the children of Israel wandered through. I always thought a wilderness was a wooded place, but this wilderness is nothing but barren wastelands. They went swimming in the Red Sea and cooked their own food…They camped out the whole time.

Frank [Currie] [the new teacher at the Nazareth Baptist School] is about to crack up waiting for his bride [to arrive from America]. We tease him all the time about how he is going to live here in Nazareth with a new wife.

You never see Arab men showing any affection whatsoever to their wives. They don't even sit with them in church. It seems to be a great sin to even be seen with them. You never see a man and woman or boy and girl holding hands, but the men hold hands with each other all the time. Boy, this is a man's world if I ever saw it. When I drive the car they all stare at me like I was a freak—especially the poor women who hide behind heavy garments and veils and water-pots and everything else to keep from being seen by men or anyone. At times I get rather indignant about the matter. Mary Helen and I together really get upset and I feel like I'd like to be a Susan B. Anthony[4] and free womanhood in this Arab culture. Christ and Christianity have been the main power behind the raising of the standard of womanhood in Western civilization...

Much love,

Marjorie and all

Toward the end of 1952, Milton (Murph) and Martha (Marty) Murphey arrived in Nazareth. Murph was born in Cleveland, Ohio, the son of a teacher. Marty, born in Swazzee, Indiana, grew up in a rural area. Her father traveled through five neighboring states selling a feed supplement for farm animals and assisted farmers in treating poultry diseases. During World War II Murph served in the military and was shipped to England and then across the English Channel to France. After the war, both Murph and Marty graduated from Taylor University in Upland, Indiana and then married. Murph graduated from the Southern Baptist Theological Seminary in Louisville, Kentucky and Marty worked as a social worker for dependant families in the Louisville, area. The couple moved to California and both taught at Linda Vista Baptist Bible College and Seminary in San Diego. They applied to the FMB to be appointed as missionaries and accepted an appointment to Israel although they were unclear about what their specific job would be. The Baptist Mission asked the Murpheys to take over the Children's Home and help with the Nazareth Baptist Church.[5]

Aerogramme To:
Mr. & Mrs. B. H. Cole
1546 Richland Rd. S.W.

Atlanta, Georgia U.S.A.
Marjorie Rowden
P.O. Box 34
Nazareth, Israel

Friday, December 5, 1952

Dearest Folks:

Just a quick note (which I probably won't have time to finish) to say we are all fine but mighty busy. Last Sunday we all spent the whole day in Tel Aviv waiting on the boat [the Murpheys and Frank Currie's fiancée were on], which never came. We drove back to Nazareth and spent Monday, [and] then early Tuesday we went back to Tel Aviv. It is amazing how confused and badly informed these business concerns are here. We called several times to find out from the American Export office the arrival time. We got as many different answers as the different number of people we talked to.

When we all met in Tel Aviv Tuesday again...Mary Helen and I were determined to be there after all our efforts so we all spent Tuesday night in a hotel in Tel Aviv...Poor Frank was so upset and nervous, as all grooms are, that he didn't enjoy the wait very much. We stayed in an ocean front hotel that was real nice for a foreign country. We all met in the dining room for breakfast and it faced the sea. While we were eating we saw the old ship sitting out in the water. It had come in during the night. Frank got indigestion from his breakfast, which, by the way, was fish, tossed salad and sliced tomatoes. We had taken a bottle of [Nescafé] so we managed a cup of coffee. Afterwards we drove to the port and met Elmo. The 6 of us stood for two hours waiting for the custom officials to let the passengers off. They had to come in on a little boat like we did, but the water was calm as glass. The day we arrived, the waves were so high that the boat would go completely out of sight from land. Anyway they climbed on shore about 10A.M. and we had all our "*howdy do's*" and welcomes.

Paul and I felt so much like old experienced missionaries the minute they landed since they will be the "greenies" now. The Lord has really blessed us here and the time has flown. It hardly seemed possible that it was 9 months ago that we landed...We just fell in love with the Murpheys and Carol right from the first. Murph (Mr. Murphey) is about Paul's size and seems more like Paul in make up too. Marty (Mrs. Murphey)... is the jolliest soul I ever saw. Everything is funny to her. It's a good thing…The Murpheys went to Jerusalem with Tom and Mary Helen but we brought Carol straight on to Nazareth. We got here about noon yesterday and Mrs. Weippert had a lovely meal waiting for us. All in Nazareth were lining the streets to see the American bride. Frank wanted to keep her hidden until after the wedding but a steady stream of visitors has appeared ever since we hit the town…

Much love,

Marjorie

Letter to:
Mr. & Mrs. B. H. Cole
1546 Richland Rd
Atlanta, Ga. U.S.A.

Marjorie Rowden
P.O. Box 34
Nazareth, Israel

Wednesday, December 10, 1952

Dearest Folks:

…Well Carol and Frank [Currie] finally got hitched. Boy, it was hard work but we really had a lovely wedding and reception…After the wedding, we came here for the reception. Carol had bought a gorgeous [Madeira cutwork tablecloth] in the Azore Islands on her way so we put that on the table. The three-tiered cake looked beautiful. We opened one of our precious cans of nuts and American candy and served it along with the cake. We had about 60 guests. Afterwards, I gave each guest about one grain of rice apiece and we all threw it at them when they left in Dwight's jeep for Jerusalem. We laughed about scooping up the rice and putting it in the next day's soup. I got Monsour [Insair] to tie old shoes and tin cans to the back of the car. He couldn't understand why but he did it anyway. When they left and rode down the hill to the outskirts of the city, it was the most Americanized sight

I had seen yet with those tin cans bouncing on these ancient cobblestones streets. The people of Nazareth stood and lined the streets and looked with their mouths standing open. We thoroughly enjoyed it all.

It seems like there is so much to do in the next two weeks. My YWA girls are so enthusiastic about their work and I have two regular programs to plan for them this month, plus our Day of Prayer for Foreign Missions, which we will have on the Sunday afternoon before Christmas. This will be the first time they have ever had anything like this in their lives. Since we can't send our offering out of the country I thought we'd give it to Dwight and Paul to be used in the…service at Cana of Galilee on Sunday afternoons…Wish you could see my 15 YWA girls in their green skirts, white blouses and green scarves with the gold YWA emblem embroidered on the back. They really look snazzy. I have an outfit too. We wear them to every meeting.

As soon as I finish with them I will have to start all the million things I have to do here. I thought we'd decorate our tree on Monday before Christmas and then we'll have to wrap all the presents and sort everything equally…

We missionaries got a rather pitiful letter from Dr. Rankin last week telling us that we will all have to cut expenses and that they will have to cut the number of appointees to new work. The money seems to be running out. It is a terrible situation when a nation such as America can't give any more for mission work around the world than they do. Southern Baptists ought to be ashamed of their small number of missionaries compared to the number they could have if they'd give to support them. We have been begging for more helpers here for a long time but they don't think they can send us any more. Our whole budget, every item, for next year was cut. This is one of the most expensive missions to keep going all because of the inflation here…

Much love,

Marjorie

Letter To:
Rowdens

1712 Westhaven Dr. S.W.
Atlanta, Ga. U.S.A.

Paul Rowden
P.O. Box 34
Nazareth, Israel

Sunday night
December 14, 1952

Dear Mother & Dad:

Dwight says that they had a good service at Cana today. About 95 there. I had a good S.S. class last night. This coming Saturday night I am giving my boys a party, here at the home. We are planning a nice Christmas. We have been playing records of Christmas carols everyday and really are getting in the mood. I can [visualize] Rich's store [in Atlanta] and Davidson's all decorated and the windows filled and the crowd of shoppers everywhere. I think that next Monday we shall get a tree and put it up here at the home and decorate it.

Young Women's Auxiliary (YWA) members, Nazareth Baptist Church, are pictured with Marjorie Rowden in center back row, 1952.

All the packages that you have sent have arrived in good shape. The Scrip stores are better stocked now than they have been in a long time and we can get more of the ordinary items that we want. I can buy Scrip whenever I want at the bank. The Murpheys seem to be mighty nice folks and I think a good addition to our work...

Love,

S.

Letter to:
Mr. & Mrs. B. H. Cole
1546 Richland Rd
Atlanta, Ga. U.S.A.

Marjorie Rowden
P.O. Box 34
Nazareth, Israel

December 20, 1952

Dearest Folks:

This is the week before Christmas and we have been in a real dither. In the first place Dwight and Emma had some guests from Tel Aviv for 3 days and they had to use Frank and Carol's room. So Frank and Carol [Currie] moved up here in our room. In the second place it was the last few days of school and I had lots of loose ends to tie up in my Bible class, such as notebooks and book reports to collect. In the third place we had two days of Christmas plays at school, put on by all the classes and each one of our 21 children had to have costumes. You should have seen us trying to get up white dresses for angels...

The high school put on a 5-act play, which lasted about 1 ½ hours and was really wonderful. In the fourth place the weather is beginning to get rainy and cold and Fida [Ateek] and I are still in the process of unpacking coats, wool skirts, sweaters... And I'm here to tell you it's a big job when you have 21 children! I'm still covered in D.D.T. powder from head to toe, that these things have been packed away in. None of them fit this year and they all have to be altered. But I was real proud of all of them this week in the school plays. They all looked so good. In the fifth place, Paul's Sunday School class of young men had their Christmas party here tonight…In the sixth place I had a YWA meeting Thursday and have our Lottie Moon Day of Prayer tomorrow afternoon. I have planned a real good program for them. Afterwards we are going in a group to take gifts of food and clothes and toys to a needy family near by.

In the 7th place I have been trying to get this huge house decorated for Christmas. I have put up all kinds of red candles, pine branches, red bows…We plan to put up our tree Monday. Monsour [Insair] and I will go up to the Hospital in the truck and cut one [from the mountainside on the hospital property]. In the 8th place we have been trying to sort out the toys for Santa Claus to give on Christmas Eve night. We have to be sure that each child gets an even amount as the next. In the 9th place, we spent 2 days this week taking all our kids [in the Children's Home] to Haifa to see "Cinderella." The film was showing at the [Biebergal's] cinema and they invited our Home kids free. We had a rare time with this mob, but they enjoyed it. Two of the little boys got carsick and we had to clean up the mess but 'twas all part of the job.

…You remember the Jewish couple we met on the boat? They spent 2 days with us this summer. Well, they wrote the other day and they are coming to spend Christmas with us. They are due here on December 22 and will stay through the 25th. They are really lovely people and so very highly educated. We enjoy having them…They are the kind who are very interested in everything and that's why they want to spend Christmas in Nazareth even though they are [not] Christians. They plan to return to New York in the early spring. She teaches school there and he is a retired attorney. He is also a writer of some renown…You remember the picture we sent you of them and us taken together on top of Mount Tabor? The guard up there asked old Mr. Cowen if Paul was his son and he said, "No, but I wish he were."

One of my Bible students is learning the carpenter's trade and so he made 4 little doll beds for us for our 4 older girls for Christmas…A Sunday School class in St. Louis sent 20 new pairs of pajamas out the other day so they will each have a new pair under the tree. Also candy and gum…

Christmas noon we will kill the old big turkey gobbler and give all the children here a real sharp dinner. I have already decorated the [dining] room with red streamers and a small Christmas tree in the middle of each table. Christmas night, after all the children are in bed, the Bakers are having the whole mission group for a turkey dinner.

This is Saturday night and as the day gets closer, I get a little more homesick, but I'm thankful I have so much to keep me busy. I was thinking today that if I were home I'd decorate the tree today probably since it is the Saturday before Christmas. Well, only 4 more Christmases after this before we come home. If time passes as quickly as it has then it won't seem like anytime at all.

Well, I must go to bed. Tomorrow is another busy day. By the time you get this Christmas will be over and you all will probably be real glad of it. Will be praying that this new year will bring many blessings to our wonderful parents who mean so much to us.

All our love,

Marjorie and all.

Rowdens
1712 Westhaven Dr. S.W.
Atlanta, Ga. U.S.A.

Paul Rowden
P.O. Box 34
Nazareth, Israel

December 20, 1952

Dear Mother & Dad:

...I had a very good Bible study this morning in the book of Matthew, chapter 5, and verse 3: Blessed are the poor in spirit. I had long wondered at the exact meaning of this verse and being unable to get much help from Commentaries, I took my Greek New Testament and a Greek concordance and studied up on it and I really received a blessing in study. How marvelous is the word of God, fit for our every need. The word, "blessed" becomes very meaningful when studied in all of its uses, and the word "poor" in the sense used here means: conscious of one's spiritual need, thus the verse could read, "Happy indeed is the person who realizes how destitute of spiritual knowledge and power he is, compared to what is available to the child of God, and thus hungers for more spirituality, for his is the Kingdom of Heaven." The Bible, however, with its rich wording can say all of this in a few words.

Lots of love,

S.

Letter to:
Mr. & Mrs. P.D. Rowden Sr.
1712 Westhaven Dr. S.W.
Atlanta, Ga. U.S.A

Paul Rowden
P.O. Box 34
Nazareth, Israel

Sunday, December 28, 1952

Dear Mother & Dad:

…We had a very fine Christmas. All the children went to bed Christmas eve night with visions of sugarplums dancing in their heads. We finished decorating and laying the gifts out after they went to sleep…Christmas morning we got the children up and dressed them and then had breakfast. While they were eating breakfast, Frank [Currie] came up and dressed in a Santa suit the English Hospital had, and when they finished we all marched into the living room where Santa was.

All the children were [as] excited as [could] be. The Cowen's were here—the couple that came over on the boat with us—and Frank and Carol [Currie], [the Murpheys] and Dr. & Mrs. [John] Tester…There was bedlam until about noon with all the children playing with their toys and shooting their cap pistols and running all over everything. The Cowens enjoyed it immensely. At 9:30 we went to the church and had a brief Christmas service in which everyone brought some produce, can goods or money. After this we had communion. Then Frank [Currie], Monsour [Insair], Yusef Qupti—the translator—and [I] went to seven very poor people with the food and money…That night all of us ate down at the Bakers for supper. At both places we had turkey and dressing. Here we had English pudding and sauce for dessert and at Emma's we had apple pie and ice cream.

…The Murpheys are planning to come here to live and learn about the home on December 30 and live in Mrs. Weippert's room as she is going to Cyprus on that day for a month. Every year she has the month of January off and she spends it in Cyprus… Dwight is planning to leave at the end of January for Jerusalem to study language for a while. Murphey will be in charge of the Home and I will work with the school, and Frank, Murph and I will have the services of the church…

…I am speaking tonight on "What Will Happen in 1953?" It is a message based around the sudden coming of the Lord. I had a very good Sunday School class last night with ten boys there…The people at the English Hospital came here singing carols, which we enjoyed very much and we enjoyed the Christmas records that we had…There was a big crowd [of Catholics] in Nazareth from all over Israel [who came] to the midnight Mass at the Catholic church. I gave Marjorie a tea set, which consisted of a tray, six glass holders, and six glasses to fit in them. People drink hot tea here out of such things. She was very pleased with it. She gave me a tie rack and six bow ties. Can you imagine? I am wearing bow ties now! All the other members of the mission wear them so I had to take up the habit. We took a big box of food up to John and Odette Tester at the Hospital for their Christmas and they certainly appreciated it…

Much love,
S.

10
Letters
MID-JANUARY to FEBRUARY 1953

In January 1953, the Rowdens crossed from Israel to Jordan. The follow-
ing is the wording of a 1955 certificate of registration of Paul Rowden, required
as proof of American citizenship. The certificate was typical of the forms sub-
mitted by Americans when they applied to travel to Jordan. It illustrates the
requirement to declare one's religion along with other identifying data.

American Consulate
Jerusalem
CERTIFICATE
No. 326

> I, Paul Dennis Rowden, Jr. do hereby swear or affirm that
> I am an American citizen of the Protestant Christian faith,
> born at Atlanta, Georgia on December 27, 1924, that I am
> the bearer of United States ordinary passport number 28,
> issued to me by the American Consulate, Haifa, on No-
> vember 15, 1955, and that the following is an accurate de-
> scription of myself:

Height: 5 feet 10 inches
Hair: Brown
Eyes: Blue
Distinguishing Marks: Scar on Left Ring Finger
Occupation: Administrator.

Signature – Paul Dennis Rowden, Jr.

Palestine, City of Jerusalem,
Consulate General of the United States of America.

Subscribed and Sworn before me this 23rd day of November, 1955.

Signed: Sara M. MacDonell
Vice Consul of the United States of America.
Fee: $2.00. Service No. 326.

Letter to:
Mr. & Mrs. B. H. Cole
1546 Richland Rd. S.W.
Atlanta, Ga. U.S.A.

Rowdens
The Jerusalem Y.M.C.A. (Old City)
P.O. Box 23
Jerusalem
(Hashemite Kingdom of Jordan)
Jerusalem, Jordan

January 5, 1953

Dearest Folks:

Today has been one I shall never forget so I must write now while it's all-fresh even though I'm dog tired. The day started at 5:30 A.M. when Paul and I left Nazareth…We arrived in Jerusalem at 9:30…and stayed there until 11 A.M., when Paul, Dwight and I drove over to the Mandelbaum Gate and met our tour. We went through Israeli officials and customs, walked about 100 yards through "no man's land," and then went through Arab (Jordan) officials and customs…Mandelbaum Gate actually isn't a gate at all. It is only a place in the road with a railroad gate over it. All the houses around this area are shell pierced and half demolished from the Arab-Jewish war. Only one wall still stands in many houses.[1]

We were met on the Jordan side by an Anglican minister who directed us to St. George's Hospice where we have a room for four days. It is also an Anglican School and the Hospice and School are built around an open courtyard. The buildings are all of stone. Our room is like a refrigerated morgue. Dwight has the room next door. I've never been so cold in all my born days—no heat at all!

…We had wonderful new [Desoto] touring cars. We went the new road, which leaves Jerusalem out by the Garden of Gethsemane and the Mount of Olives and goes winding up and down barren brown hills for about 15 miles to Bethlehem. The shorter route, which we took coming home, was only 6 miles. But going we got a real good look at the "wilderness of Judea." I've never seen such complete desolation in all my life. No life at all anywhere…

We drove on to Bethlehem, which is on a hill overlooking a large field where logically the shepherds were watching their flocks by night when Christ was born. We drove up into the city and went in the Church of the Nativity, which is supposed to be built over the manger scene. This church was built in 320 A.D. and is the oldest one in this part of the world. The entrance is so small that you have to kneel in order to get in. Inside 3 religious groups have a sanctuary and altar, the Greek Orthodox, the Roman Catholic and the Armenians. Down underneath in a cave is the supposed sight of the birth. Nuns and visitors were pushing each other as they knelt and kissed the spot marked…The shepherd's field was much more impressive to me because it is still natural and probably just as it was.

Mandelbaum Gate in West Jerusalem, Israel, 1953

Afterwards, we were given an hour to shop in the little Jerusalem stores…It was nearly dark but Dwight, Paul and I started walking and ended up at the Damascus Gate leading into the actual Old City, which is walled in completely. I want to get a picture of it tomorrow. We walked inside and straight down the lines of literally hundreds of little shops along a narrow stinking street. But my, how picturesque! Food is plentiful here and it did us so much good to see it all on display, even crudely displayed. We can eat up a breeze here but we can't take any back across [to Israel].

Marjorie

In the following letter Paul Rowden talks about an upcoming visit to the mission from Dr. George Sadler, Foreign Mission Board Secretary for the Orient, Europe and the Near East. In 1920, Dr. Sadler and his wife traveled to Nigeria where Dr. Sadler served as principal of the Baptist College and Seminary at Ogbomosho from 1921–1931. He resigned as a missionary in 1931 for medical reasons and became a pastor. In 1939, the Foreign Mission Board asked him to take up his foreign commission once again as an area secretary. He crisscrossed the globe for many years and also served as Acting President of the European Baptist Theological Seminary in Zurich, Switzerland during its opening year of work in 1949–1950 while continuing his area duties.[2]

Aerogramme To:
Mr. & Mrs. P. D. Rowden
1712 Westhaven Drive S.W.
Atlanta, Ga. USA

Paul Rowden
PO Box 34
Nazareth, Israel

Sunday, January 18, 1953

Dear Mother & Dad:

…The electric wires are strung in front of our [rental] house and I hope by the end of the month that we will be able to move into the house. The arrangement that we have here is working out nicely with the Murpheys living down stairs in Mrs. Weippert's room while she is away in Cyprus on vacation. She is due back however, at the end of the month and we would like to be gone by then so the Murpheys can move into our apartment. The weather here is quite cool and you would get a big laugh at my wearing apparel if you could see me. I put on my long woolen underwear, a wool shirt that I thought I could never stand, a sleeveless sweater, a long sleeved sweater, and then a coat when I go out. The people here are not used to heat much in the winter so that this is about the only way to keep warm.

School is going along nicely. I have the chapel services three times a week and in it I am teaching the book of Romans, which I am enjoying studying as I find time. I am also over a period of time trying to make a detailed study on the sermon on the mount going back to the original Greek for some words, and have found this to be very rich. Looks like I'll be all year on it however, since there are so many interruptions and demands on our time. Last night I had thirteen boys between the ages of 18 and 20 for my S.S. class.[3] We seem to have a fine spirit and it is certainly a fine opportunity…

…Dwight may soon go to Jerusalem for language study. I am more or less in charge of the school now, and have turned many of the responsibilities of the Home over to the Murpheys. We usually divide the church services up among Frank [Currie], Dwight [Baker], Murph [Murphey] and myself. However when Dwight comes back from language study he will be in charge of the church completely. Today I am taking the service at Cana.

Dr. Sadler, the secretary for this part of the world for our Board may come in a month or so to visit us, and to help us make plans for the future. We have been having considerable rain, and everything has turned very green and beautiful. Well it will soon be church time so I guess I had better stop and get ready…

Lots of love,

S

Letter to:
Mr. & Mrs. B. H. Cole
1546 Richland Rd. S.W.
Atlanta, Ga. U.S.A.
Marjorie Rowden

P.O. Box 34
Nazareth, Israel

Sunday, January 18, 1953

Dearest Folks:

Well, this week has passed by quickly like all the others. Sunday night we accidentally picked up a week-old newspaper and read the death announcement of Mr. [Charles] Cowen, the old man on the boat with us who spent three days with his wife with us Christmas. He died less than a week after he was here [in Nazareth]. We wired Mrs. Cowen in Tel Aviv immediately to see if we could help her in anyway. They were to sail for the States this coming Thursday. Now she will go back alone. He was buried at the kibbutz (community settlement) where they had planned to settle in on their return to Israel in about a year. I don't know whether she still plans to immigrate here now or not. She wrote us a lovely letter when she got our wire. We plan to go to Haifa to see her embark next Thursday. They have no children. He was about 20 years older than she.

Wednesday was a beautiful day and so we took the Murpheys and [their son] David, and Becky and packed a picnic lunch and went to the Sea of Galilee. They had never been. Mount [Hermon], in Syria, was covered in snow and was in plain sight. It was beautiful. We ate by the water. We started driving to Capernaum, a horrible road, and it was too wet and boggy so we parked the car and walked. It was a long hike and the two men carried their kids piggyback. But we enjoyed the trip very much…

Much love,

Marjorie

Aerogramme To:
Mr. & Mrs. P. D. Rowden
1712 Westhaven Dr. SW
Atlanta, Ga. U.S.A.

Paul Rowden
Box 34

Nazareth, Israel

February 1, 1953

Dear Mother & Dad:

In thirteen days we will have been in Israel eleven months. Time does get by so rapidly out here. Our school is half over, as the children have had their first semester examinations and start to-morrow on the second term. All of us are well and happy.

Paul Rowden sits in his rocking chair holding his daughters (L) Robin and (R) Becky, Nazareth 1953.

Next Saturday afternoon Monsour [Insair], the boy that has worked for the Home so long will get engaged. This is a big occasion here. Since Dwight will be away I will be the "big shot," the kawaga, [*khawajah*] in Arabic, and have charge of the ceremony. A big group from Nazareth will go to this village where the girl lives. We will go to her home and then I will ask the father of the girl for the hand of his daughter for Monsour. Then he will say yes (all of this has been prearranged) and then I will have some scripture and a prayer and then place rings on both of their hands and then say "*Mabruk*" (congratulations) and then there will be sweets served and everybody shouting. Two weeks ago we went to the village and visited the home of the girl and made arrangements and Monsour gave the girl some material to make a dress out of [for the occasion]. He has only seen the girl about three times in his life. Out here the parents do the [marital] arranging etc.

Becky went to a bridal party yesterday afternoon with [Marty] Murphey and Naomi [Ateek]. They said that she really had a good time and sat by the bride and clapped her hands with the rest. Quite a gal eh? Robin is a very independent soul these days. She doesn't want anyone to tell her what to do. This morning she woke up at 5:15 and wanted her warm milk. It was still very dark and she heard me getting up and became very quiet, but when she found it was I and not her mother, she became very angry and started to yell again.

After some milk to warm her tummy she was more satisfied and agreed to sit in my lap, along with Becky who had awakened by this time, so at 5:45 this morning I was sitting by the heater rocking two gals.

This morning I will preach at church. Last night we had a very good Sunday school service with my boys. Had thirteen there. Dwight and Emma [Baker] leave on Tuesday morning or noon for Greece [on vacation]. We will go to Haifa to see them off. They are going by boat and later from Athens may go to Istanbul. We are hoping that the house will be ready by Thursday with electricity finished, meter installed, water running and other things finished up.

Love,

S

11

WE GO WAY BACK

Mid-February 1953, the Rowdens moved about a mile from the Children's Home to a newly constructed house of cut stone in Nazareth on a road leading east out of town toward Haifa and the Mediterranean Sea. Paul and Marjorie relied on Rev. James W. (Jim) Smith and his wife Elizabeth (Betty) Flanders Smith to format and mimeograph form letters and to mail them out to people who were interested in the Baptist work in Israel. The Rowdens and the Smiths had long been friends. Jim Smith and Paul Rowden both attended Boys High School in Atlanta and were in the Bible Club together.

Jim recalled that Paul would share books about missionaries with him at the club meetings. Marjorie and Betty went to Girls High School and Agnes Scott College in Atlanta although in separate years. Jim served in the U.S. Air Force from 1943–1946. During his service in the Pacific Theater of Operations during World War II, he was stationed in New Guinea, the Philippines, Okinawa and Japan. In each of these areas he had the opportunity of observing the spiritual and physical needs of the people. During this period of time, Paul was serving with the U.S. Navy as a Hospital Corpsman.

Paul and Jim stayed in contact through correspondence. After being discharged from the military, they both attended Emory University in Atlanta where they renewed their friendship. During college days the two couples double-dated. Paul and Jim were each the best man in the other's wedding. After Jim and Betty married, Betty could not return to Agnes Scott College because the college did not accept married women. The couple attended Baylor University in Waco, Texas where they both graduated with B.A. degrees. Jim Smith was licensed to preach at the Kirkwood Baptist Church in Atlanta but was ordained by the Prairie Hill Baptist Church in Prairie Hill, Texas. In September 1953, Jim was serving as the pastor of a Baptist church in Pine Lake, Georgia and working on his Bachelor of Divinity at Columbia Theological Seminary in Decatur, Georgia. Betty was teaching school. In a not-so-subtle manner Paul and Marjorie began encouraging their long-time friends to consider mission work as they shared the need for help.

12

LETTERS

MID-FEBRUARY–APRIL 1953

Letter to:
Jim & Betty Smith
Box 115
Pine Lake, Ga. U.S.A.

Rowdens
P.O. Box 34
Nazareth, Israel
February 24, 1953

Dear Jim and Betty:

We have tried to get around to getting another form letter written for months but can't seem to slow down long enough. In fact we still haven't written one. If possible I will try to include one in this envelope, if not I'll just mail this alone.

…In January [Milton and Marty Murphey] arrived at the George W. Truett Home to take it over. We all lived there together for 6 weeks packing our stuff and unpacking theirs, waiting for our house to be finished. Last week we moved in and we are still in that state, where everything is in the middle of the floor. But we are enjoying being to ourselves after so long a time, although we surely do miss all the children and co-workers at the Home. It is only about a mile away so we go back and forth real often. Sunday we brought one of the little girls from the Home here to our house to spend the day. We want to do that each week. It will be nice for them and for our two [children].

…Dr. Rankin was out here last June and we talked the teacher matter over with him and he promised us help. We suggested that the Board appoint us a couple of teachers for a three-year contract term to do educational work. After the three years the teachers would be free to return or to renew the contract. Contract missionaries are not rare with our Board. We had a fine agricultural couple [Tom & Mary Helen Francis], out here for our farm project that have just left. They were on a three-year basis.

I hope all of this doesn't sound too "pointed," BUT we know a certain young couple who would be just what we need! With your Seminary training ending in June, with pastoral experience and with Betty's teaching experience, I can't think of a finer couple.

Marjorie
Continued on my letter…Paul.

Paul Rowden
P.O. Box 34
Nazareth, Israel

February 28, 1953

Dear Jim & Betty:
…Today, Saturday, we are …worming. You have heard of worming a dog, well, lad, now you are hearing of worming four good Southern Baptists. For some time we have suspected the sad truth but hated to face it…It's a marvel with the filth one finds in these Arab towns that one survives on first arrival from the sterility of the States. There is a Scottish Mission hospital here and we have two good doctor friends who are trying to kill both the worms and us now. Pleasant subject isn't it? Bread is never wrapped, tossed around, falls on the streets…[T]he water supply is not safe, and vegetables rawly eaten without real cleaning and soaking in salty water are liable to send one running in the night! Ah, but there are better sides to the Mission life.

We have been here almost a year (the 13th of March) and God has been very real and good to us. The work here seems to be looking up in a special way but not without apprehension for the future. Last Sunday we had in the Church, some seven professions from among our students…It is not easy to make a break however with customs here and persecution in one form or another comes. There are the disappointments when some fall away and are unfaithful...

...I think Marjorie has largely told you about the need of a school couple...they would do everything from preaching to teaching and 101 other things. The Mission is largely interested in a couple that would feel a desire for full time appointment but if these are not forthcoming then a temporary appointment would do...I would not paint the work as desirable however. There are times that the strain is so great that even a best friend would not seem as a friend at all. I don't want you to come! The only way we would rejoice to hear of your coming would be that God will just not let you alone, and that your life is so miserable that you can't be happy without coming...

The Lord has been especially good to us in helping us to make the adjustment and in the coming year I am looking for a richer experience in the work. There have been some of the deepest meetings with God that I have ever had, while I must say that there have been times when it was just slow plodding by faith and saying with Job, "Oh that I wish I might find *Him*."[1]

Christian love,

Paul

In 1952, after his visit to Israel, Dr. Theron Rankin asked Dr. George Sadler, the FMB Secretary for the Orient, Europe and the Near East, to meet with the mission in Israel and see if the farm could begin development with a small amount of funds. In March of 1953, Dr. George Sadler traveled to Israel and met with the mission. He agreed that construction on the farm property could begin on a small scale and at less cost than originally projected. The mission decided to move the Children's Home to Petah Tikva—on the farm property, with the goal of also using the property for summer camps and retreats.

Letter to:
Mr. & Mrs. B. H. Cole
1546 Richland Rd.
Atlanta, Ga. U.S.A.

Marjorie Rowden
P.O. Box 34
Nazareth, Israel

Thursday, March 19, 1953

Dearest Folks:

...It is pouring rain outside and it is our main mission meeting today. Paul has gone on ahead to start the school day so he can be free the rest of the day. Our meeting will be at the Baker's. We are waiting for Elmo and Hannah [Scoggin] and Miss Fenderson and Dr. [George] Sadler to come in from Jerusalem any minute. Dr. Sadler arrived in Jerusalem last Monday morning. Monday night Elmo took him to speak at his group in Tel Aviv and after the meeting drove him on here. Dr. Sadler spent Monday and Tuesday nights here with us. Elmo [Scoggin] stayed at the Home. Last night they returned to Jerusalem so he could attend the Rotary Club and also speak at Elmo's prayer service.

Today we have the main mission meeting all day long and tonight...Sunday morning Dr. Sadler will preach for us here in Nazareth. Sunday night we take him to Lyyda Airport Hotel where he will spend the night and fly out early Monday morning. It will have been a very busy week. I don't see how he stands this traveling, speaking and strain. He is 65 years old, he said, and has "an international stomach" that will stand all kinds of food, etc. He is flying all the time so that saves time. This is the 10th country and mission station he has visited since he left home 3 weeks ago.

...He is very much impressed with our new home and says he didn't expect to find anything so nice. Two years ago he was here for the mission meeting and also the year before that. So far the spirit seems wonderful and Dwight and Elmo and Dr. Sadler too are encouraged. He is a tough old bird and says just what he thinks whether you like it or not...There have been times in the past when he has been ready to close down this field. Now he is much encouraged and has more or less promised us three more couples real soon. He is very much impressed with Frank and Carol [Currie] for which we are thankful, since we hired them before we consulted the [FMB]. However, they are leaving us in July. We are so sad about it. Frank feels he must go back and get his Seminary training now while he is still young and we have to agree with him.

139

We need teachers so badly, good, trained, Christian ones…Paul had to fire one of our High School teachers last night. Until the end of this school year Carol [Currie] will take her classes. We hope by next fall to have some from home or find some better ones here. Murph will probably teach some next year, and I can take more classes next year than I have this year…

Much love,

Marjorie

In April 1953 the Rowdens traveled across the border to Jordan for Easter services. Milton and Marty Murphey and Frank and Carol Currie traveled with them. They received permission to travel in their car and visited biblical sites in Jordan. The following two letters were written from Jordan.

Letter to:
Mr. & Mrs. P. D. Rowden Sr.
1712 Westhaven Dr.
Atlanta, Ga.

Paul Rowden
Jericho, Jordan

Friday night
April 3, 1953

Dear Mother and Dad:

Well, here we are with Zachaeus, in Jericho. In this Easter period Israel permitted Milton and Marty [Murphey], Frank and Carol [Currie], Marjorie and [me] to come over. We came across [the border to Jordan] about noon, and spent some time in old Jerusalem and then came on here to Jericho to spend the night…we are spending the night here in a very nice hotel—"Winter Palace."

In Jerusalem it was chilly but here below sea level, it is like summer. We were able to bring the car across after much trouble of trying to get passes for it. The Israel passes have a lot of red tape, but the Jordan side is easy going. Tomorrow we plan to go back to Jerusalem and tour around and early Sunday be at the Garden Tomb for the sunrise service…We also use this opportunity to buy Arabic books for the school, since they are not published and cannot be bought in Israel…

Love,

Sonny

Letter to:
Mr. & Mrs. P. D. Rowden Sr.
1712 Westhaven Dr. S.W.
Atlanta, Ga. U.S.A.

Paul Rowden
Jerusalem, Jordan

Monday night
April 6, 1953

Dear Mother and Dad:

Since I only wrote you a short note from Jericho [Jordan] I'll try to supplement it. We had a very enjoyable trip, and one that covered all of the spots that we had so much wanted to see and have read about…Because there were so many visitors at the Easter season we knew that it would be very difficult to find a place to stay [in Jerusalem, Jordan], and thus it was. We went several places hunting and then ate at the American Colony Hotel.[2]

We decided that we would drive to Jericho and spend the night and see the sights there…Then we packed up and drove to the Dead Sea. I wanted to go in swimming but there was no bathhouse. The water is extremely salty. It is a mammoth piece of water. On the way back to Jerusalem we [drove] the old Jericho road, which goes up, up, up toward the city. We stopped by the place where perhaps the Good Samaritan Inn was and took some pictures[3]… After dinner we walked about and then took off for Nablus, old Shechem which is first mentioned in Genesis 12:6…Here was the early capital of the Northern Kingdom. Very near to it is Jacob's Well where the 4th ch. of John has its background. It was quite an experience to sit there and read that chapter.

...Early the next morning (Easter) we left for Jerusalem. We arrived at the Garden tomb about 6:30 A.M...The Garden tomb is one of the most interesting spots in the world. It is an excavated tomb dating back to the time of Christ. It is in the place very near where Jesus was crucified, thus fitting John's description. There is a very beautiful garden all about the place...What a thrill it was in the early Easter morn to sit there, facing the empty tomb...

After we left this service we went to the Garden of Gethsemane, and to the Mountain of Ascension. Here we could look across all of the city that Jesus had looked at so much...We saw the wailing wall, and then went to the [C]hurch of the Holy Sepulcher, which is also a place believed by the Catholics to be the place of burial...but nowhere [as] impressive as the Gordon's tomb and the place of the skull where we went to the sunrise service. After some shopping we crossed back to the new Jerusalem [in Israel] and by 8:30 P.M. we were home...

Lots of love,

S.

⬿

Aerogramme To:
Cascade Baptist Church W.M.S.
Mrs. B. H. Cole
1546 Richland Rd. SW
Atlanta, Georgia USA

Marjorie Rowden
Box 20
Nazareth Israel

April 22, 1953

Dear Friends of the W.M.S: [Women's Missionary Society]

...It is spring in Nazareth now and the green hills all around us are covered in a profusion of wild flowers. "The lilies of the field," that Christ spoke of are growing like weeds in every spot. But yet in the hearts of most of these people there is very little beauty and very little sunshine.

Right now I'm sitting in the only private room of the Anglican Mission hospital here in Nazareth. Becky is sitting over here cutting out paper dolls and recovering wonderfully from an emergency appendectomy. The hospital is very old and the equipment is poor and inadequate, but the love of Christ and the presence of the Great Physician are more than abundant here.

A real pitiful drama of life goes on here everyday. Last Sunday night, the 2nd night after Becky's operation, Paul arrived here at the hospital after preaching the evening service in our Baptist Church. He and I were about to "change shifts" and I was going home to spend the night while he stayed here. In the ward next to us there was a middle aged Arab man very close to death. The nurse on duty asked Paul to come in and have prayer with him. Although the man spoke only Arabic and Paul prayed in English, his eyes showed that he appreciated that little touch of personal interest. Just one minute after Paul turned and walked away the man passed into eternity.

Oh, how miserable we felt in those next few minutes when we stood and tried to give what comfort we could with the big barrier of language between us. Thirty minutes after the death, Paul drove the three sons home in our mission truck with the body wrapped crudely and placed in the back of the truck. The wife and two daughters walked sorrowfully home. It would have been improper for them to ride. We feel the need more everyday for time for definite language study. So far we don't have enough personnel to do the work much less give up some for language study. There is much witnessing that we can effectively do in English or through an interpreter, but instances like the one I just related proves to us once again how badly we need time to study. We covet your prayers that God will speak to the hearts of many young people and call them into this field.

This year Paul has taken over the job of heading our 350-student Baptist School. Tending to the hundreds of little problems and supervising 15 native Arab teachers is a real job. The week before Easter holidays began we had an extended chapel period for three mornings. The last morning we had a wonderful service with 29 young people and one teacher making professions of faith. And at least that many more gave forth a desire to walk closer to Christ…

…It would be hard for me to explain to you just how it makes one feel to be sitting on a stone right in front of the open tomb of Christ on Easter morning. Only a few of us were [there]…As we sat there in silence before the spot where Mary Magdalene heard the risen Savior speak to her, we were all too moved to even talk. Finally the Bible was opened and the story of the death and resurrection of Christ was read again. Never had it sounded like that before! When we sang "Up From the Grave He Arose," it was as if it were a brand new song to our ears…

The doctor just came in and said we can take Becky home tomorrow. Before then I have a Bible class at school to teach, a YWA meeting to plan for, and a house to clean up (which has sadly been neglected this week.) So I'd better say good-bye for now. We wish each one of you could come and visit us and see for yourselves this wonderful land where our Savior lived on earth but where, today, He is little thought of. We know that you have been praying for us or how else could we have been blessed so much.

Very Sincerely,

Marjorie Rowden

13

MEDICAL MISSIONS

The Edinburgh Medical Mission Society (EMMS) Hospital sat on top of a hill in Nazareth. Dr. William Bathgate, Dr. Doris Wilson, Dr. John Tester, nurses and staff at the hospital were pivotal as medical care providers. In letters home, Paul and Marjorie referred to the hospital as the "English," "Anglican," "Scottish," or the Edinburgh Medical Mission Society (EMMS) Hospital. Often it was just called the "hospital."

In 1841, when the EMMS began training students for medical service, medicine had only just begun to be thought of as a part of the missionary endeavor and many were skeptical of such moves. The EMMS represented the first major breakthrough in the use of medical missionaries.[1] In 1906, the British Church Missionary Society seized the opportunity to buy hillside property in Nazareth. It was on this hill that the EMMS hospital was later built.[2] Dr. William Bathgate, a New Zealander of Scottish origins and an EMMS student, traveled to Nazareth in 1921 to become the director.[3] Dr. Bathgate's niece, Dr. Doris Wilson of Scotland, later joined him and greatly contributed toward health care of women in the area. A school of nursing was begun. In 1952, Dr. John Tester joined them. He eventually became the director when Dr. Bathgate retired in 1956.[4]

William Bathgate had thought about going into the ministry when he was growing up in New Zealand. One day he read a London Missionary Society magazine about four missionaries working in the Belgian Congo who died through lack of medical help in sickness. Appalled at this needless waste of Christian life and service, Bathgate dedicated his life to the mission field as a doctor.[5] When he arrived in Nazareth, Dr. Bathgate's predecessor told him to go out into the Arab homes and get to know the people. Dr. Bathgate traveled on horseback to surrounding villages and Bedouin camps. He carried along his bagpipes to play, adding greatly to his welcome among the Arabs.[6]

During the Palestinian Arab revolts 1936–1939, Dr. Bathgate's car was stolen and found on a road—stripped of tires. The local population became incensed and took matters into their own hands. They discovered the thieves and retrieved the tires for him. Word spread that no one was to steal from him again.[7] Nazareth was later captured by Jewish troops fighting with the British military forces. During this time the hospital was cut off from help until an anonymous donor sent a Red Cross lorry with supplies.[8] In 1948, during the Arab-Jewish war, the normal population of Nazareth increased with thousands of Arabs from the surrounding villages. The EMMS Hospital helped to administer a soup kitchen and distributed food and clothing on behalf of the United Nations and the International Red Cross.[9] In 1948, in honor of his years of service, His Majesty King George VI appointed Dr. Bathgate, *Officer of the Order of the British Empire* (OBE). Yet the residents simply called him the beloved *hakeem* (doctor) of Nazareth.[10]

From time to time, Dr. Bathgate would attend the Nazareth Baptist Church as a visitor. Dr. Bathgate praised Rev. Dwight Baker, "for extending a warm welcome to visitors as guests into the house of the Lord. That kind of welcome," he said, "suited those attending from other churches and showed an Eastern courtesy," and the sermons were "given in simple language in a spirit of devotion and earnestness." Dr. Bathgate recalled that the subject of one service was "Sin, Forgiveness, Judgment, The Cross, and The Holy Spirit." He noted that the Arab interpreter "gave a perfect rendering of both the teaching and the spirit of the message, in Arabic." But he was pleased that the service was kept to an hour "so that even the youngest did not weary and the nurses were able to get back to duty."[11]

Dr. Bathgate loved children and personally knew all the children in the Children's Home. Dr. Herbert W. Torrance, a doctor and medical director at the Scots Hospital in Tiberias recalled, "…When walking down a narrow street one day, with its guttered centre, I recollect a child running out of a doorway with him, chattering away as if to its own father."[12] Dr. Bathgate brought a few babies to the Children's Home when they were left on the doorstep of the hospital. For many years Dr. Bathgate came to the Children's Home at Christmas dressed as *Father Christmas* and handed out presents. In 1948, a baby girl was left at the EMMS Hospital the week before Christmas. At the same time, one of the little girls at the Children's Home asked Father Christmas for a baby sister. When Father Christmas came to the Children's Home that year, the little girl was astonished as an infant baby girl was laid in her arms.[13]

In 1953, Dr. Bathgate was an elderly man with brilliant white hair. He and his staff provided constant medical services to the Baptist mission members including the delivery of quite a few babies. When I was five years of age and living in Nazareth, I had appendicitis. My mother thought it was a stomachache, but as time went by and I doubled up in pain, she decided to seek medical help. My father was out of town and by the time she was able to find transportation to the hospital, I was seriously ill. Dr. Bathgate sedated me with ether. When the appendix was removed, he found gangrene. If my appendix had erupted, my condition could have become life threatening. The letters of my parents are filled with references to medical services provided by the EMMS Hospital and the friendships made with the staff.

The EMMS Hospital was expected to be a self-supporting institution; it operated with limited funds and had no vehicular transportation. Staff walked the mile-long road that twisted and turned as it ran up the hill from the Nazareth market. In 1953, in appreciation of the services which the EMMS Hospital rendered to the Baptist Convention in Israel and to the children of the Children's Home, the FMB appropriated two thousand dollars for purchase of an automobile for use by the EMMS Hospital.[14] As the British Mandate and rule in the Middle East came to an end in 1948, some of the British mission hospitals in the Middle East closed as funds dried up. Fortunately the EMMS Hospital in Nazareth continued to operate.

In 1953, Dr. August Lovegren was beginning his service as a doctor in the Baptist mission hospital in Ajloun, Jordan, the governmental seat for the area. Dr. & Mrs. Lovegren, who had been appointed at the same time as the Rowdens, spent the first year in Arabic language training in Beirut, Lebanon. In 1952, Baptists had concluded purchase of the hospital in Ajloun from an independent British doctor and had begun staffing it with doctors and nurses. Baptists also continued the educational and evangelistic ministry that the British had initiated by working with Christian Arab nationals in the area. Alta Lee Lovegren wrote, "From more than seventy-five villages of north Jordan, patients walked, or rode donkeys or camels to arrive at the hospital."[15]

Alta Lee Lovegren performed numerous administrative tasks for the hospital as accountant and bursar, paying salaries to national hospital staff. "Everyone," she said, "had multiple jobs."[16] She often accompanied her husband to visit the sick. One afternoon Dr. Lovegren was called to Rajib, a village 35 miles from Ajloun. He and Alta Lee and the pharmacist set out in a car that had to be left nine miles from the patient's house. It was after dark when they started on the final leg of the trip, across a steep mountain. The three of them took turns riding the one horse that was provided. When they reached the house, the patient was only partly conscious. He was suffering from an infection of the brain. After giving him emergency treatment, they made an attempt to transport him to the hospital for an operation, but it was impossible to do so in the dark. As people heard there was a doctor in the village, they brought their sick to the house for treatment by Dr. Lovegren. At first light they tied the patient on the back of a horse for the nine-mile ride. He bore the marks of the ropes around his wrists and ankles for days afterward. When they reached the hospital they provided intensive treatment and the man eventually made a complete recovery. He would not have survived without the treatment and praised God for the help he received at the hands of the Christian doctors.[17]

Dr. William Bathgate, Director of the EMMS Hospital, greets children in Nazareth, c. 1953.

14

LETTERS

JULY–DECEMBER 1953

Aerogramme To:
Rev. & Mrs. James W. Smith
Box 115
Pine Lake, Ga. USA

Paul Rowden
P.O. Box 20
Nazareth, Israel

July 10, 1953

Dear Jim & Betty:

We were delighted to have your recent letter...Marjorie is at the church at a Y.W.A. meeting and so I am at home for a change. I guess that this week has been the busiest yet and I trust that the next shall provide breathing space. Our school had its graduating service two weeks ago. School officially was closed, but not for us. We have been trying to get the registration, fees, parents meetings, new teachers, taxes, book work, scholarship considerations lined up for the fall so that we can do the backlog of simple items we have had to overlook during the rush. I believe that we are about to get into shape.

We also have had the four preaching services of Nazareth, the S.S., and the Cana work. Milton Murphey and I have been dividing this up. He and his wife are at the Children's Home. Dwight Baker, the other worker here in Nazareth is away in Jerusalem doing language work. Next March when he finishes, the plans are for us to do our language work in Hebrew. This summer there is a R.A. camp at Acre, a VBS at Nazareth, and GA & YWA camps.

Our hearts were made to beat faster when we read that you were open-minded to the Will of God and the Mission Field. We certainly hope that you receive a blessing from your trip to Ridgecrest.[1] On one side I wish that we had never mentioned to you about Missions. This is because we now know an aspect of the Mission field that only experience can teach. One never hears about the problems of adjustment of a new worker to language, people, new diseases, living conditions…There is that wearing care of work that tries to rob a worker of his spirituality. There are those differences of opinion among fellow workers, and sometime conflicts of personalities. There are the disappointments of months and even years of work that seem so fruitless. On the other hand we cannot help but cherish your presence on some Mission field, and if it is the Lord's Will, do all we can to attract you. If this is what the Lord wants for you in spite of all the above things, there is a joy and satisfaction that is most rewarding. There seems to be an unusual opportunity in the Middle East at this time. I believe that among the Arabs there is more response than ever before.

Some great preachers and thinkers feel that the Middle East: Jew and Arab being the most difficult group to work with, the Gospel ought to be taken to the receptive places like Brazil and Japan. This is a decision you will have to make for yourself…I also think that God calls others to go to the hard places. If there is not a time of sowing in a hard place there is never a time of reaping…

…It seems that education and hospitals are one of the few ways of reaching Moslems. However I am becoming more and more convinced that education as such is not sufficient. One must have the aim of as much evangelism as possible among the students; otherwise the school in the end is a failure and a waste of God's money. It may be the approach to better things as hearts are sowed with the seed. Well, perhaps this will throw more light on your thinking. Let us be hearing from you soon. Congratulations for both of you on finishing schools!

Christian love,

Paul

To Members of Cascade Baptist Church
Atlanta, Georgia

Rowdens
P.O. Box 20
Nazareth, Israel

August 1953

Dear Friends:

It has been several months since we last wrote about our activities in Israel. We are ever grateful and aware of our tremendous debt to you at Cascade because of your financial support, prayers, letters, interest and concern for us. We never cease to be thankful also for what the Church meant to us as children and young people.

...We realize that some may ask why it is necessary to send workers to the land of the Bible. One trip here would answer that question for good. Here in Nazareth there are twenty thousand people. Most of them have never heard that they must be born again. True it is a city of churches, bells and feast-days, but it is still a city of extreme darkness. When a person is born here, he is born into a religious community; Greek Orthodox, Roman Catholic, Moslem and that settles the matter. His salvation is left up to his religious leaders along with his religion. Consequently they know nothing of the Bible or evangelical Christianity. There is a great void of ideals and goals in life and many "isms" have made a great headway. By our Christian homes, the orphanage, the school, and the church, we are holding the light of Jesus the Messiah up.

Furthermore we are in a brand new Jewish state of several million people. Most of them know Christianity only through a State Church, which either persecuted them or stood silent in their tragedy of six million deaths. What a vast opportunity to show them what real Christianity is. Then, we are on the edge of the hardest, most heart-breaking and fruitless mission field in the world, the Moslem field. Our Nazareth school has many fine young people who under the leadership of God, because of their Arabic language and customs could mean much toward the evangelization of these people. Nothing is too hard for God. Who knows but what in our day God shall pour out a mighty revival in the Middle East?

We have just closed a week of Vacation Bible School with about 200 children. Last week we had a very fine Royal Ambassador Camp near Acre (old port of [Ptolemais]) with 32 boys. During the week the boys learned much, had a good time, and there were five professions of faith. In two weeks the G.A. and Y.W.A. day camp starts. We have a very fine group of girls. In a few more weeks after that, school will start again with its busy days of teaching, administration, and Christian guidance of about 325 young people. We wish you could attend with us a service at Cana and hear all the children sing in the Sunday School service. In all of those activities we value your prayers very much. We have come to grips with forces of darkness that can only be conquered by the prayers of God's people. Will you pray for us?

Christian love,

Paul and Marjorie Rowden

Paul Rowden stands before a group of boys at the Royal Ambassador (RA) Camp near Acre 1953.

Newsletter
Jim and Betty Smith
Pine Lake, Georgia

Rowdens
Nazareth, Israel

September 1953

In our Nazareth Baptist School we are proud to say that we have the very best group of young people that Nazareth has to offer. Some 300 Arab students file into our school grounds daily and are exposed to the Gospel of Christ as we know it, love it and teach it. Though education is a fine thing, we are not here merely to educate these young people. Education alone can never save a soul, nor produce an active, fruitful Christian. Each student attends daily chapel services and is required to take a course in some phase of the Bible. Education plus Christ is what we have to offer.

Both the Baptist School and the Children's Home seek to undergird and strengthen our Baptist Church. Attendance at our two Sunday services and the mid-week service is almost 75 percent from our student body in the school. Most of the 300 students are very responsive to a type of Christianity they have never known before; one in which they learn to read the Bible for themselves, one in which salvation is a free gift to a responsive soul, one in which there is real joy and peace…

Almost the entire membership in our very active R.A., G.A., and Y.W.A. groups is made up of our Baptist School students. Actually these meetings take the place of our extra curricular activities. So closely is our school and church linked that school activities are constantly bringing not only the students, but often their parents, into the program of the church. Although the parents, for the most part, are too bound by their traditional church to dare to stray far away, they are eager for their children to take advantage of the new way of life, which we teach. A strict system of discipline and honesty, so drastically new to these people, makes our character building advantages stand out in an attractive light.

The YWA was only organized last year and after ten months of work they have met every requirement for their standard of excellence. All but one or two of the 17 girls enrolled are believers and are eager to learn how they might help in the spread of the Gospel around the world.

Although only a part of our 15 fine Arab teachers are genuinely Christian (in the sense that they have made an open profession of their faith in Christ), there is a definite evidence of their increasing interest. Two teachers made professions of faith during this past year; one has shown remarkable growth in spiritual matters and will be a great value to us in the school this coming year, as well as in the church. Nearly all of them prefer our church services to their own.

With the addition of the 11th grade this year, and the coming of two new missionary teachers, the Herman Pettys, we expect our school to be an even greater lighthouse for the truth of our Lord…

Paul & Marjorie Rowden

Aerogramme To:
Rev. James W. Smith
Box 115
Pine Lake, Georgia U.S.A.

Paul Rowden
P.O. B. 20
Nazareth, Israel

Sunday, Nov. 8, 1953

Dear Jim:

Something that has been long neglected, in fact neglected since you got home from the Pacific area some eight or so years ago, I'll finally do—and that is—write another personal letter just to you. As I look back over the period of time that our good Father first brought us together, I can certainly see multitudes of blessings. I remember our fellowship at Emory [University], our concern in the things of God, and then the separation due to the war and our correspondence…

During these days also came the tremendous event with Marjorie and Betty, in which you held me up as I walked out to the marriage alter, and vice versa, as you soon did. Then have been these days of spasmodic fellowship with you and your fine wife…There is no doubt at all in my own mind as to your future Jim, Lord sparing your life—that I'll be able to proudly say, "I knew Jim Smith when…." With all its hardships & heartaches, there's nothing like a burden to preach the gospel and do the will of God...I'm glad that in spite of us, God still works. I've preached messages sometimes so badly that if the pulpit stand had been larger, I'd have crawled inside. Yet, somehow, God still works—doesn't He, and even gives fruit for our stumbling tongues. My, [it's] good to serve God, give our best, and let God do the rest.

In three months we will have been here two years. I'm sure that three more will be necessary before we really reach a place of halfway usefulness. The frustration of having a heart full of Jesus to preach, but inadequate grasp of language to preach it in is great. Beloved, let this letter make up for neglected years of not stating our appreciation of you. "I thank God upon every remembrance of you," and that is often.

Sincerely,

Paul

⚜

Letter to:
Mr. & Mrs. B. H. Cole
1546 Richland Rd. S.W.
Atlanta, Ga. U.S.A.

Marjorie Rowden
Box 34
Nazareth, Israel

Saturday
August 29, 1953

Dearest Folks:

Well, I will make a noble attempt to start a letter. It is nearly 6 P.M. and Paul should be here with our supper guests any minute. We are having an Arab Brethren Pastor and his wife and two children, from an Arab village near here...

At 2 P.M. this afternoon I had a small party with the Y.W.A. girls here at my house for Rachel. Rachel (the girl who has lived with Emma for two years and gone to [the Nazareth Baptist] School) is getting married. She brought her boy friend up to meet us all. He seems real nice and I'm very happy for her. So this afternoon we had our YWA "Bible Presentation" program and a handkerchief shower for her. It was lots of fun and it was real impressive when we gave her the Bible. She is already the second of my YWA girls to get married.

Well, three days this week Emma [Baker] and I had camp for about 40 girls...We met each morning at 7:30 and stayed until 5 P.M. We had breakfast and lunch at camp. We really had a full schedule, with two study courses each day, Bible lesson once a day, devotional each day, singspiration (Marty [Murphey] leading that), handwork, and recreation. Each afternoon one of the men came and gave the inspirational address. It was real successful, we feel.

... Each day the girls put on an extemporaneous play from a Bible story. The last day they [put on the play of] Moses and the [bulrushes]. They used Becky as a baby all wrapped up in a blanket and she played her part real well, didn't giggle at all like the rest of them did. The first day we put on "The Good Samaritan." None of the girls wanted to be the donkey on which the wounded man was carried to the inn, so I had to be it. I'm sure my knees will never recover from the experience...

Monday afternoon, August 30, 1953

Seems I got detoured somewhere, but here I am again to try to finish this epistle. Sunday morning (yesterday) I took over Emma's Intermediate Girls S.S. Class. She started an adult women's class. I haven't even had a chance to ask her how she came out. We are very anxious to start a good class with the women. As soon as June Petty arrives she will take over the Intermediate Girls (only she doesn't know it) and I want to go to help Emma in the women's work. The reason we haven't had a women's work before now is that all the women only speak Arabic and we couldn't teach them in English like we can the girls and boys. Up until now we haven't had what we believed was a real good "believer" among our educated women who could translate for us. We felt that the person who translated should have experienced what they are saying. But now since Mouneera [Munira] (my YWA helper and one of our school teachers) has become such a fine believer we are going to use her for a translator.

Wish you all could have seen Robin getting her hair washed Saturday. She was a sight to behold. She always starts out real brave but ends up crying because she won't hold her head down and the soap runs in her eyes. So this Saturday I washed Becky's first and told Robin to watch. I told Becky to act real happy so Robin would be inspired. So Becky did a bang up job of acting happy. She sang and sang all the time I was washing her hair. So when time came for Miss Robin she proudly stood up on the stool by the sink and said, "I not cry: I sing!" So as soon as I got the water on she started singing. In a few minutes she raised her head and got her eyes full. She stopped a minute and thought and started singing at the top of her voice, "Will you be ready when Jesus comes?" She couldn't see out of either eye for the soap, but she was determined to be brave. I laughed so hard at her selection of a song for the occasion that I had to stop and sit down. Khuzni and Becky were standing there laughing their sides off. Robin opened one eye, and screamed, "Mama, wash the hair—Oh will you be ready when Jesus comes...*tra la tra la tra la.*" She is the funniest soul I ever saw.

Much love,

Marjorie.

Herman and June Petty, newly appointed Baptist workers, arrived in the port of Jaffa in September 1953 with their two children, David and Ann. They were met by the Baptist missionaries in Israel who welcomed them to the mission. Herman Petty received his B.A. from Hardin-Simmons University in Abilene, Texas in 1947 and received a Bachelor of Divinity from Southwestern Baptist Theological Seminary in 1951. He served in the U.S. Army from 1943-1945. June received a B.A. from Hardin-Simons University. She received a Masters of Religious Education from Southwestern Baptist Theological Seminary in 1952. Both Herman and June Petty had experience teaching and began work shortly after arrival teaching in the Nazareth Baptist School.

Letter To:
Mr. & Mrs. B. H. Cole
1546 Richland Rd. S.W.
Atlanta, Ga. U.S.A.

Marjorie Rowden
Box 20
Nazareth, Israel

Saturday, September 12, 1953
Dearest Folks:

...I haven't had a chance to do much all week since the Pettys have arrived and we have all been busy. We all went to the boat Tuesday morning and met them. They are very nice and just as "Texas" as they can be...I believe they will fit into the mission and the work real well. They would appreciate your prayers, I'm sure, in these hard first few months. They are both from the country and are just good old plain people. They have been so appreciative of all we have done for them...

Yesterday we moved them into their house. Their furniture won't arrive until October but we all pitched in a few pieces and I believe they will manage until they can get their freight or until they can go to Scrip stores and buy something...Of course they don't realize how fortunate they are as new arrivals, but they certainly have things better than any of the rest of us had it. They are the first couple to have a place to live just sitting there waiting on them. But we are happy for them. School starts in two weeks and they both will have a full teaching load...

Lots of love,

Marjorie and all.

Aerogramme To:
Mr. and Mrs. B. H. Cole
1546 Richland Rd. SW
Atlanta, Georgia USA

Marjorie Rowden
P.O. Box 20
Nazareth, Israel

Sunday, November 22, 1953

Dearest Mother and Daddy and Bill and Pat:

Well sir, the rains have arrived! We will now pause while I swim to the next high spot...

…Tuesday we got a cable from George and Antoinette Laty [Lati], the young couple from our church who have been in Clark College, Mississippi for 18 months. They said, "Meet us at airport tomorrow." The weather held up the planes all over Europe, so they didn't get here until yesterday. We haven't seen them yet. They are still in Jaffa visiting relatives. They may get here this afternoon to Nazareth. My, are we thankful to see them. The Lord has certainly provided for us. One of our teachers quit about three weeks ago and Paul and Murph [Murphey] have been trying to teach biology, chemistry, and history…So now George [Lati] can take over those classes, plus preach as often as possible. And the main thing we want him to do is to take over the Cana of Galilee work with the hope of building a church later. Oh, how wonderful to have a trained capable Arab young man to work with us now, who can do preaching and teaching in the language of the people. In May, Fuad [Sakhnini], our other young man in the States, will be coming back. Both of these young men are solid Baptists in addition to being on-fire-for-the-Lord Christians…

Must close,

Love, M.

Letter To:
Mr. and Mrs. B. H. Cole
1546 Richland Rd. SW
Atlanta, Georgia USA

Marjorie Rowden
P.O. Box 20
Nazareth, Israel

Sunday, December 13, 1953

Dearest Folks:

…We have had more water troubles this week. There is no particular shortage but our landlord upstairs proceeded to cut our pipeline off last week because the tank on the roof was overflowing. He forgot to turn it on again and yesterday we gave out of water. This is the second time this has happened. But there is no use in getting angry about it; they could make life miserable if we did. We sure have to strain to keep relations good. Elliot, [a student who is living with the Bakers] was here all day yesterday working [in] our little garden out front, so he and Paul went up on the roof and took several big buckets full of water from the landlord's tank and put it into ours, but it won't last long. We are using it by the thimble-full. We hope city water will come in tomorrow or Tuesday.

Last Monday afternoon we all drove to Natanya (about 50 miles) to see Rachel, [Elliot's sister], get married. She and Marc were very happy…They were married on the flat roof of the Rabbi's office. Four boys held a canopy over the couple while the ceremony was going on. They drank wine from a glass and then the Rabbi threw the glass on the floor and broke it, to symbolize that no one but these two would ever drink from that glass. The whole service was in Hebrew and was conducted with the same amount of disorder and confusion that marks all religious events in this part of the world. Everyone kept right on moving and talking and laughing. It is really funny to us who have been used to order and reverence.

In the Jewish faith it is necessary for the men to always wear hats in religious services. Only a few had on hats, but the others made four cornered hats out of their handkerchiefs. The women do not have to wear hats. Rachel was so thrilled to see us all there. Even Hannah and Elmo [Scoggin] drove down from Jerusalem. [Marc and Rachel] didn't have but a little money since they had spent everything Marc had earned in the bank trying to rent a two-room apartment. So they came to Nazareth to spend their honeymoon…I enjoyed having them. Marc is a sweet boy and very much in love with Rachel. He allowed Dwight [Baker] to have a short…service for them Thursday night after prayer meeting. All of Rachel's friends came and it was very sweet and impressive. Marty sang and afterwards Marc asked her to write the words of the hymn for him to keep. Dwight just spoke briefly and asked the Lord's blessings on their marriage…

I am having all the mission adults for a Christmas dinner the night after Christmas. And then on the 27th Paul and I are having dinner with the Pettys so we can celebrate Paul and Herman's birthdays. Herman [Petty] will be 32. Paul will be 29. Paul is still the youngest man on the field. And Elmo [Scoggin] is the oldest at only 37. We are all between the ages of 27 and 37, which is good in many ways. (Except Miss Fenderson, of course, but she will retire in about two years.)

Paul preached this morning and it was very good. Did we tell you that last Sunday, Dalal made a profession of faith? She is the eldest of the little girls at the Children's Home. She is 10. We were all so happy. It was like one of our very own [children]. Well, this morning Damianus [made a profession of faith]. He is the oldest boy…

Thursday night we had George and Antoinette [Lati] for supper. They are so cute and love the Lord's work so much. Going to America really gave them a new outlook on the fields here…We are turning over the Cana work to George. He also will teach full time in the school. At present they are living in the Petty's spare room, but are looking for a place to live alone…we will be thinking about our sweet folks back home and praying that you will have a very happy Christmas.

Much love,

Marjorie and all.

15

NAZARETH NATIONAL BAPTISTS

Each summer the Royal Ambassador (R.A.) young men and boys and their leaders left Nazareth for a weeklong camp. Paul and Marjorie wrote of a R.A. camp held in 1952 on the grounds of the Baha'i Gardens in Haifa, near Acre. Dwight Baker also wrote of this R.A. camp as being especially memorable and significant:

> Even at five o'clock in the morning there was little respite in the Galilee from the August heat, but that was no sweat for the 35 well-packed campers—each carrying his own bedding and food for a week. The boys showed up to board an old truck, perching themselves atop a mountain of bedding and boxes. Singing accompanied with cadence clapping shortened the two-hour trip to the Baha'i gardens on the Mediterranean.
>
> Following their daily activities the boys gathered around a campfire each evening to share an evangelistic hour. After each service the opportunity was extended to receive new life in Jesus of Nazareth, they're near-kinsman. Although the young Arab men were from Christian homes, they had never been discipled to follow Nazareth's humble, yet most exalted citizen. The boys knew the historical Jesus but that was the extent of their knowledge of Him.
>
> After six fun and study-filled days and nights, the final Sunday night service ended, but there were no Christian commitments from the young men. I rose to share my own Christian experience with them. The struggle going on in their minds and emotions became apparent, but at each

moment of truth, courage seemed to fail them. As one last appeal went out, even as the words were spoken, one, two, then three, and finally eleven campers were recruited for Jesus before the campfire. Counseling and prayer continued well into the night. Eleven young men shook free of their fear and uncertainty and followed Jesus into new life. Many of the young men became active in the Nazareth Baptist Church and the church not only experienced a deepening of its spiritual life, it increased in numbers. A spiritual renewal broke out in the church, spread to the school and homes, and moved out into the surrounding villages.[1]

In 1953, the Nazareth Baptist Church increased in membership. "Young men and women dedicated their life to Christian service through the church and became active in the Sunday school program, the Nazareth Baptist School, Royal Ambassadors (R.A.), Girl's Auxiliary (G.A.), Young Women's Auxiliary (Y.W.A.) and the Women's Business Circle. Munira Assel, Antionette Lati, Subhiya Toubassi and Fida Ateek assumed important roles of leadership among the women."[2]

"With so many young people needing a spiritual home in which to grow and share their faith," wrote Dwight Baker, "the church was challenged to give the very best of its efforts. Under such stimulation, along with a heightened confidence in the future, the Nazareth Baptist Church underwent reorganization."[3] Since 1950, the goal of Arab Baptists and the American mission workers had been the reorganization of the church. It was once a strong organization, but war and lack of leaders brought it to low ebb, and it functioned only as a mission or chapel. Each year, a few converts were baptized. From the new members, God raised young men who became aggressive leaders among the youth. A revival began. This awakening had a revitalizing effect. Following a week of study into the meaning of church membership and Baptist beliefs, Baptists of Nazareth paused during the last week of October, 1953, to formally reconstitute themselves after the pattern of a New Testament church, independent and self-supporting, except for the pastor's salary. Elmo Scoggin from the Jerusalem Baptist congregation was elected moderator of the organizational council, which consisted of pastors and laymen from Nazareth and Jerusalem. Twenty-nine members signed the Church Articles of Faith. Visitors and members then joined in observing a simple but impressive communion.[4]

George Lati was already a lay preacher and leader of young men in the church when Paul and Marjorie Rowden arrived in Nazareth in 1952. He had been a teacher in the Nazareth Baptist School and was active with the R.A. young men. He encouraged Emma Baker to begin a program for girls that was similar to the Royal Ambassadors. She held a day camp for girls and soon thereafter organized the group into a Girl's Auxiliary.[5] After higher education in the United States, George Lati returned to Nazareth and was particularly helpful in the church outreach work in villages around Nazareth. George had been a nominal communist in his youth. His parents lived in Acre and were members of the Greek Orthodox Church. George became a believer under the Baptist ministry and the influence of his friend, Fuad Sakhnini. He began attending the Baptist Church and was baptized by Pastor Dwight Baker. "George became one of the most active and effective lay evangelists I have ever known on any continent," said Dwight Baker. For many years George conducted preaching services in the home of his parents in Acre. "We used to go all day and preach and minister in the Arab villages from morning to night. One day we came in late and George's elderly mother scolded him and said, 'George, you and Brother Baker must rest.' 'No mother,' he said, 'we will work for Jesus here and rest in heaven.'"[6] George Lati's nephew, Issa Saba, said he grew up following his uncle around to preaching stations, giving out the hymnbooks and helping in any way he could.[7] "[George] helped dozens of students while he was teaching," said Dwight Baker. "He bought them food, clothing, paid their doctor bills and provided every other kindness you can imagine. He was a big booster of the Lottie Moon Christmas Offering, handing out Christmas Offering envelopes and encouraging people to give sacrificially."[8] George Lati died in 1993. Today some Baptists in Nazareth have renamed the Christmas Offering for missions, the 'George Lati Christmas Offering' (or the 'Lati Moon" Christmas Offering), instead of "Lottie Moon," and the donations are given to the poor and underprivileged.

Fuad Sakhnini, a teacher in the Nazareth Baptist School, had been studying in the States, at Gardner Webb College in Boiling Springs, North Carolina. He returned to Nazareth in 1953 with an A.A. degree in Bible. Fuad Sakhnini and his brother Fayiz were Baptist converts from the Greek Orthodox faith under the ministry of the Brethren led by an Arab lay preacher, Jameel Hissan. Upon the death of his father in 1945, Fuad assumed responsibility for his widowed mother, two brothers and two sisters. During the Arab-Jewish war in 1948, Fayiz moved to Lebanon and became a Baptist pastor and evangelist under the leadership of Baptist missionary Finlay Graham.[9] Fuad Sakhnini remained in Nazareth and began teaching Bible at the Nazareth Baptist School. Sometimes he preached at the Sunday services at the Nazareth Baptist Church. He progressed rapidly in his knowledge of the Bible and public speaking. When Rev. Dwight Baker arrived in 1950, Rev. Baker assumed the pastorate and Fuad would translate.[10] In 1959, the Nazareth Baptist Congregation selected Fuad Sakhnini to be the pastor and he was ordained. The congregation then sponsored Sakhnini as he attended the International Baptist Theological Seminary in Ruschlikon-Zurich, Switzerland.[11] He returned and took over the responsibilities of being pastor to the congregation[12]

Yousef Qupti also accepted preaching responsibilities in the villages in addition to his regular work as a teacher in the Nazareth Baptist secondary school. During the early days of the school, as WWII disrupted its operation, the American Baptist missionaries were recalled and Qupti was given the keys in the hope that the school could soon be reopened.[13] Yusef Qupti often provided translation from English to Arabic at the church services.[14] He later studied at the International Baptist Theological Seminary in Ruschlikon-Zurich, Switzerland. He became an active lay preacher and schoolteacher.

Emile Nusair was born in Nazareth in 1926. He attended primary and secondary schools in Nazareth. In 1944, he completed his secondary studies in Jerusalem. In 1957, he obtained a Bachelor's Degree in Education and Sociology from the Hebrew University in Jerusalem. In 1958, Nusair became the Principal of the Nazareth Baptist School. He was the first national to succeed an American principal. He retired in 1991. When Emile Nusair passed away in May 2006, after many years of service to the Nazareth Baptist School, the administration building was named for him in gratitude for his service and to keep his memory alive.[15]

Fuad Haddad began working as a teacher at the Nazareth Baptist School in 1953. He had formerly taught at another school in Nazareth and was active in the Royal Ambassadors. He completed his Masters Degree in English Literature at the Hebrew University in Jerusalem. When Mr. Emile Nusair retired as principal, Fuad Haddad succeeded him and remained in that position until 1998, when Dr. Ousama Moalem succeeded him. "*Ustaz Fuad*," as students and staff respectfully called him, was involved with the Nazareth Baptist School as the General Director until 2004, and his influence was significant. He encouraged church and student groups in America to travel to Nazareth to participate in one of the many programs at the school, such as spiritual emphasis week. Fuad Haddad continues to be involved with the school as the Chairman of the Board. Haddad's wife, Abla, a graduate of the first twelfth grade class to graduate from the Nazareth Baptist School, served at the school as primary teacher for 35 years.[16]

Monsour Insair was the young man who worked at the Children's Home. Dwight Baker married Monsour and his fiancée in 1954. In the early sixties, Monsour became the lay pastor of the Cana Baptist Church. Dr. R. G. Lee, pastor of the Bellevue Baptist Church in Memphis, Tennessee, came to Israel in 1961 and preached to more than two hundred villagers crowded in the little Cana Chapel. Upon Dr. Lee's return home, he requested and received financial contributions for the work in Cana. The donations were used to fund construction of a Baptist Church in Cana with a pastor's apartment on the second floor.[17] Monsour and his wife were the first occupants of the new center.[18]

The Baptist-sponsored George W. Truett Children's Home in Nazareth, unfortunately, underwent numerous turnovers of administration over its first ten years—beginning with Julia Hagood Graham who moved to Lebanon after marriage to Finlay Graham, followed by Kate Ellen Gruver and Elizabeth Lee, who left the Israel mission field in 1950, followed by Elmo and Hannah Scoggin, who administered the Home for a year, followed by Paul and Marjorie Rowden, and then Milton and Marty Murphey and later, Bob and Margaret Lindsey. On a positive note, so many of the mission members interacted with the Home children through the years, that the children became part of the extended mission family. The mission children and Home children built close relationships. They celebrated holidays together, sat in classrooms together and, by and large, acted like brothers and sisters. Both missionary children and Home children called the Baptist missionary adults by their first name following the word "Uncle" or "Aunt." Therefore there was "Uncle Paul" and "Aunt Marjorie," "Uncle Murph" and "Aunt Marty," and so on. Fortunately for the Home children, two young Arab women provided consistency during those years—Fida and Naomi Ateek. In addition to caring for the children, the Ateek sisters were active in the programs of the Nazareth Baptist Church and the Nazareth Baptist School.

The arrival of the Ateek family in Nazareth was not by choice. Fida and Naomi were two of ten children of Stifan and Nevart Ateek. The Ateek family was from Beisan, an Arab town of approximately six thousand about 20 miles south of the Sea of Galilee. In May 1948 during the Jewish-Arab war, Jewish soldiers evacuated the town. The Arab Christian residents were put on buses and taken to Nazareth. The Ateek family found refuge with some friends who gave them two rooms until the family could rent a small house.

Fida and Naomi found jobs working in the Baptist Children's Home. They taught nursery and kindergarten at the Nazareth Baptist School and participated in the church programs. Their father, Stifan Ateek, a silver and goldsmith, was brought up as an Eastern Orthodox Christian, and later became active in the Anglican Church. Mr. Ateek was instrumental in building a small Episcopal (Anglican) church in Beisan, where he was a lay reader.[19] Occasionally Stifan Ateek led the services at the Nazareth Baptist Church and served for a while as Superintendent of the Sunday school program even though the family continued to be active in the Anglican Church. In addition to her many other duties, Fida began a G.A. group for young girls. Naomi Ateek later worked for a Children's Evangelical Fellowship.

Fida Ateek married Suhail Tawfiq Ramadan. Suhail was raised as a Greek Orthodox. He attended secondary school at the Nazareth Baptist School. He and his father ran a local business making windows and mirrors. Suhail made a profession of faith in Jesus while attending the Baptist sponsored Royal Ambassador Camp but it was many years later that he decided to be baptized in the Baptist tradition because his father had forbidden him to do so. Adopting the Baptist doctrine and practice was viewed as a betrayal to the Greek Orthodox faith and the family. After he was baptized in the Baptist Church he continued working with his father and attended Bible classes and Brotherhood meetings but avoided attendance on Sundays due to his father's wishes.[20] In time, however, he became a deacon in the Nazareth Baptist Church. In 1968, with his father's blessing, he traveled with his family to receive theological training at the International Baptist Theological Seminary in Zurich, Switzerland. Upon his return, he and Fida served for thirty-five years ministering and developing the Baptist Church in Tur'an, an Arab village not far from Nazareth. In 1980, Suhail Ramadan began a prison ministry and was the first Christian Arab to be made a chaplain for prisoners in the Galilee area prisons. He was one of the first believers in the unity of the body of Christ in the land and participated in the United Christian Council in Israel. "The UCCI helps foster unity, strengthen relationships, and build community within the evangelical body in Israel and beyond."[21]

Many of the young men and women who became leaders and educators first participated in the youth groups. During the early fifties there was a spiritual awakening that chartered the direction of the church and its ministry for years to come. In time, the Nazareth Baptist Church and school were turned over to Arab national Baptists. Dwight Baker began teaching theological courses for Baptist workers who wanted to further their biblical education and who went out to the surrounding villages to preach and teach.[22] The church outreach programs in villages around Nazareth resulted in the establishment of new Baptist congregations in the Galilee area.[23]

Pictured from (L-R) are Fuad Sakhnini, Yousef Qupti and George Lati, Nazareth c. 1953.

16

LETTERS

JANUARY 1954

Letter To:
Mr. and Mrs. B. H. Cole
1546 Richland Rd. SW
Atlanta, Georgia USA

Marjorie Rowden
P.O. Box 20
Nazareth, Israel

Tuesday night, January 19, 1954

Dearest Folks:

...Sunday we had a fine day. Paul preached Sunday morning and George Laty [Lati] Sunday night. Aida, one of the little girls from the Home spent the day with Becky and Robin. After church everyone came over here and we kept vigil until 11 P.M. waiting for Elmo [Scoggin] to arrive from Jerusalem with Miss Juliette Mather and Miss Harriett Mather, her sister, who is head of the Mather School of Nursing at New Orleans Baptist Hospital, and Miss Josephine Jones, Executive Secretary for Florida WMU. Miss Juliette Mather is editor of all the mission magazines: *Royal Service, Window, Sunbeam*, etc...[1] ... They crossed over into Israel Sunday morning from Jordan.

They left the States in September and this is their 4th month of traveling, but they looked in fine shape...Yesterday Elmo and Dwight took them on an all day tour of Galilee. They are real travelers. They never got tired. They started out yesterday morning at 7:30 and got back last night at 6:30

just in time for a special meeting we had planned for them with our G.A. and Y.W.A. girls. They were thrilled with all our girls. (I was real proud of them too.) They all wore their uniforms and looked so pretty. They sang for them in Arabic and in English and quoted their G.A. and Y.W.A. mottos for them. We had about 50 girls to come. All three of the women spoke, but Miss Juliette [Mather] brought a wonderful message about all the fine girls that she had met with all around the world. The girls just loved her to death and almost wouldn't let her leave last night…This morning we had to get up at 5 A.M. to get them off to the plane. They are already in Rome [Italy] now and probably have already seen the whole city!

…Dwight's mother is arriving by plane here in the morning at 7 A.M. All the Baker clan have gone to Tel Aviv tonight to spend the night so as to be johnnie-on-the-spot in the morning. She will stay 3 months. If I were Dwight I think I'd be so excited I wouldn't sleep a wink. It has been almost 4 years since they left. She has never seen the two youngest children [Carol and Steve]. We keep hoping *our* folks will break down and see how easy it would be to come.

Paul and I are both sitting here with a stack of Bible test papers to grade and dreading to start. He is making headway with his stack. Final exams are next week and we have got to start preparing them and then grading them and figuring semester averages…

Must close. Good night.

Much love,
Marjorie and all.

Letter To:
Mr. and Mrs. B. H. Cole
1546 Richland Rd. SW
Atlanta, Georgia USA

Marjorie Rowden
P.O. Box 20
Nazareth, Israel
Sunday, January 24, 1954

Dearest Folks:

Well, here it is Sunday again…Katrina, from the Home, spent the day with us. She and Becky are now in the middle of the living room rug playing the Candyland Game. They are all excited. Robin is supposed to be asleep, but I hear…noises coming from her room. Dwight preached this morning and Yusef Qupti will preach tonight. He is our official translator and a dedicated young man. We are sending him to our seminary in Zurich, Switzerland next year for a year's study.

Dwight's mother arrived all safe and sound last Wednesday A.M. at 7. She had spent two nights and one day on the plane and was pretty tired…She will be here three months. Becky was "right pitiful" when she saw Bron and Bill [Baker] so excited. She came home and said, "Mother, why doesn't my grandmother come to see me?" I told her [their] Grandmother would…be grandmother to all the kids while she was here.

Much love,

Marjorie and all

17

RACIAL SEGREGATION, QUAKERS AND ARTIST

As the year 1954 began, the *Atlanta Constitution* reported that William Hartsfield, the Mayor of Atlanta, returned from a tour of the Holy Land. Hartsfield reported, "Walking from the Arab section of Jerusalem to the Israeli side was like moving from an ancient, backward city of 2,000 years ago into a modern metropolis." He said that he was nearly shot while trying to get a vial of water from the Jordan River because "no person is allowed to approach the river," due to the trouble between the Arabs and Israelis. An armed sentry ordered him back.[1]

Oral arguments ended before the U.S. Supreme Court on the issue of the constitutionality of racial segregation in the public schools.[2] Governor Herman Eugene Talmadge[3] addressed the Georgia General Assembly and promised, "As long as I am your governor there will be no mixed schools in Georgia."[4] The Israeli media covered the racial controversy in America. In the Middle East, ethnic groups with skins ranging from white to every shade of brown and black mingled together in the markets. It was puzzling to many Israelis as to why the color of one's skin was such a divisive element in American society.

Two young American men serving with the American Service Friends Committee (Quakers) in the Galilee area could not have been more different— Don Rosedale was white, blonde and over six feet tall, while William (Bill) Miner was 5'8" and black. They made a striking pair.[5] The young men were living in the Arab farming village of Tur'an helping farmers to update their farming methods—replacing Harold Campbell and Herbert Pollack, the young Quakers who had worked in Tur'an previously. Bill Miner and Don Rosedale occasionally attended the Nazareth Baptist Church services and became friends with the mission workers. Don Rosedale was a conscientious objector and elected to serve his country through the service arm of the Quaker organization rather than in the military.[6] Bill Miner was rejected for military service and classified as 4-F due to poor eyesight. He majored in Public Health and Social Work and his college professor suggested that he contact the American Friends Service Committee to determine if they needed qualified men to volunteer for service abroad. He was young, unmarried and he volunteered even though he was not a Quaker because it offered a good experience to serve his country. Bill had also studied music.[7]

Both Bill Miner and Marty Murphey had wonderful singing voices. One evening they gave a vocal recital at the Nazareth Baptist Church. Marty Murphey laughingly recalled that she and Bill met prior to going to the church for the recital, and, when Bill saw that Marty was dressed up, he got some material and made a bowtie to go around his shirt collar so he would look dressed up as well.[8] The concert was well received by the attendees who packed the church and heard—what to a Nazareth crowd—might have been a rather eclectic program of music—both sacred and secular, including Oscar Hammerstein's *Indian Love Call!*[9]

Along with the musical concert, the members of the church welcomed a new artist into their midst. Marjorie wrote an article published in *Royal Service* about the visit of Dwight Baker's mother, who came to Nazareth for a visit in early 1954. "Grandmother's visit was not merely a pleasure call," wrote Marjorie. "She also came to work! Besides being the busy wife of an active rural evangelist, she was an accomplished artist. She wanted to make a lasting contribution to the Baptist church in Nazareth, so in her luggage was the equipment for a baptistery painting."[10] Dwight took her to view the Jordan River and she took several pictures, which she used for her painting. Her goal was to finish the drawing during her three-month stay. "Almost from the first day 'Mom' was the 'talk of the town.' Each group in the church gave a special party in honor of *Im Mr. Baker* (mother of Mr. Baker). The [Young Women's Association], the [Girl's Auxiliary] and the [Royal Ambassadors] all wanted to entertain her. She showed her appreciation at each party by giving an inspiring artistic chalk talk. The young people were thrilled beyond expression and sat motionless as her hands drew a message from the Bible right before their eyes!"[11]

"The highlight of Mom's visit was the unveiling of the baptistery painting. Her last Sunday night in Nazareth, the church was packed, every seat was taken and many were standing around the edges. After a brief message the lights were dimmed and the curtains pulled back [to view the drawing]…The hundreds of hushed sighs told in their own way the deep-felt appreciation of the audience. The Jordan River, which in reality is very near Nazareth, seemed to be flowing into the church baptistery."[12]

18

LETTERS

FEBRUARY to EARLY APRIL 1954

Aerogramme To:
Coles
1546 Richland Rd. S.W.
Atlanta, Georgia U.S.A.

Marjorie Rowden
Box 20
Nazareth, Israel

Sunday, February 7, 1954

Dearest Folks:

…Wednesday night we had two American fellows for supper. They are Quakers and are here on an Arab farm project not far from Nazareth. They are real nice. One is a colored fellow. He has a beautiful singing voice. The other boy is 6 feet 5 inches tall and very handsome. Their mission here is helping the people to learn to farm better.[1] We enjoyed having them so much. They are both from Ohio. Paul and I remarked after they left that seeing this colored fellow willing to spend two years out here helping the Arabs, made us even more ashamed than ever at what we read in the magazines about Georgia's attitude toward race problems.

Did I tell you about the graduation ceremony we had last week? Well, Becky finished the first half of her first grade course that we are studying at home.[2] So we had graduation. Robin and Paul were the audience. Becky marched in and recited all the poems she had learned, told the 12 months of the year, the four seasons [in America] and their characteristics, stories about how each day got its name...Then she read them a story from her book, and then she spelled lots of words. After that she identified about 12 famous pieces of art. Then I gave her a certificate, having successfully finished the first half of first grade. Robin and Paul clapped and clapped. Becky thought she had done something magnificent. After it was all over, Miss Robin decided that she wanted to graduate too. So Becky and Paul had to be the audience while she recited parts of all of Becky's poems (real good too) and she sang a song in Arabic and counted to 10 in English. She thought she was very clever, too.

...You have never witnessed anything so horrible as the way people carry on after a death here...When I arrived [at the home of the family of the deceased] this morning, the men were all sitting around outside. Inside the women had prepared the body in the wooden coffin right in the middle of the room. And everyone sat in rows of circles around it and shouted and screamed and chanted... The whole idea is to wring [out] the utmost of grief from the family of the dead. The more weeping and screaming there is, the more beloved the dead person was. No one tries to comfort the family at all. They just bend over the coffin and scream and yell...I asked Georgette [Jeries] who was sitting by me, about it. She said that it isn't good to offer sympathy to the family until about three days later.[3] That first three days are dedicated to the person who died...I was talking with June [Petty] about it later. And we decided that it is just a form of great entertainment for those women. It really is. They have nothing in their lives to make them interesting. They are ignorant and have to work so hard. They just wait eagerly for a wedding or a funeral because it is their rare chance to get out and let off a little steam. The funeral is this afternoon. Paul is getting ready to go. The women are not allowed to go. They must all stay behind at home.

...We are already thinking about our annual mission meeting; it will be our third one since we arrived. But we don't want to have it until Bob [Lindsey] gets back [from furlough]. Elmo and Hannah [Scoggin] are getting anxious to leave, but can't go until Bob returns. Elmo has been offered two different departments in which to teach at the Louisville [Southern Baptist Theological] Seminary during his year at home, during which he will also work on his doctorate. I think I wrote you before that we hear he had been offered a teaching position at our International Seminary in Zurich. We are just holding our breath. I'm really afraid he won't come back to Israel after his furlough...

Much love,

Marjorie and all

With the arrival of Herman and June Petty to work in the Nazareth Baptist School, Paul and Marjorie Rowden planned to move in the spring of 1954, at the end of the school year, to Jerusalem for a year of Hebrew language study.

Paul & Marjorie Rowden
Nazareth, Israel
March 5, 1954

Dear Friends at Cascade:

It is Spring in Israel! Surely no other place in all the world is quite as beautiful. The four, cold, rainy months that we have just passed through make this season even more wonderful. We wish that you could take a walk with us over the hills of Nazareth and see the colorful array of "the lilies of the field" that Christ spoke of. There are millions of them, peeping out from behind every rock. It is interesting to watch the people as they come out from their stone houses all over the hills and stretch in the warm sunshine, almost like bears who have been sleeping all winter. Everywhere you see long lines of raw sheep wool hanging out in the sun. This is what their mattresses are stuffed with, and the stuffing is pulled out and washed each Spring. The little children's shoes, which are always about 6 sizes too large anyway, are thrown away and they wiggle their bare toes in the soft sand. They won't put them on again until, perhaps, December.

We in the Baptist Mission have other reasons for being happy also. This week we are having our annual "student revival" week. Of course the whole year our primary aim is to lead the students to know Christ, but each Spring we look forward to this emphasis week. Last year, on the last day of the meeting, we had 27 professions of faith and that many dedicated lives. Much prayer and preparation has gone into the planning of this week and we are expecting great things from the Lord. With 360 students enrolled this year we have kept busy from morning until night. It is marvelous to watch how the Lord has worked in the lives of our young people. It is easy to tell which ones have been longest in the

Rev. Dwight Baker is at the pulpit in the Nazareth Baptist Church, c. 1954.

school, and which ones are new and are still amazed at the things they hear and learn.

Since our last letter to you, our Baptist Church has been reconstituted and many have been added to the membership. This past Sunday morning we had 320 in Sunday School. The Sunday School is literally bursting at the seams. We have 3 classes meeting in the tiny balcony of the church.

We have been in Nazareth two years this month. Seems almost impossible! During this period we have had no time for language study. We have "picked up" enough Arabic to get along, but still feel very handicapped when we have to deal with people who know no English. But even our Arabic is no help to us when we leave the city of Nazareth, because the official language of the country is Hebrew. So now, at long last we are getting our turn for concentrated language study. We are leaving Nazareth next month and will move to our main Jerusalem mission house, for one to two years studying Hebrew. It will not be easy to settle down to studying after spending these past two years in active service. But we realize that no really effective and lasting work can be accomplished on any mission field until the missionaries learn the language of the people. We will need your prayers greatly that the Lord will give us patience as we struggle with Hebrew conjugations and vocabulary.

Becky and Robin are excited over the prospects of moving to Jerusalem where there are actually "sidewalks" and "parks with swings in them." That is where they will learn their Hebrew—painlessly! They seem to have just "absorbed" Arabic while we were here in Nazareth. Oh, for the mind of a child! Becky has been attending first grade in our Baptist School, conducted entirely in Arabic, all this year…

We had an exceptionally nice Christmas this year—thanks to many of you. We were so grateful for the many lovely Christmas cards, and especially those, which had little personal notes, attached. The children were so pleased with the cards that had balloons tucked inside – and there were many of them, too. Thank you from the bottom of our hearts…

Very sincerely,

Paul and Marjorie Rowden

Aerogramme To:
Coles
1546 Richland Rd. S.W.
Atlanta, Ga. U.S.A.

Marjorie Rowden
Nazareth, Israel

Sunday, March 28, 1954
Dearest Folks:

…This has been a busy week. I have been practicing an Easter play with my Y.W.A. girls all week, plus giving tests to my Bible class, plus chasing Marty [Murphey] all over the place to get her to direct the choir portion of my play. Marty is going to give a vocal recital some evening in our church and she has been practicing up a breeze. She has a gorgeous voice. She and I drove down to [Afula], a little Jewish wide place in the road near Nazareth this week to see if we could find a beauty parlor. Well sir, we found a piece of one. The operator couldn't speak English or Arabic—only Hebrew, French and German. We had a rare time. She didn't know how to even roll up hair. Marty got hers fixed first, and after I saw how she looked, I gave up and told the woman to just wash it…Marty is an automatic tickle box anyway, and it was all we could do to keep from rolling in the floor during this painful experience. All week we have been calling Tel Aviv to see when Bob and Margaret [Lindsey's] boat was arriving. Finally we got the signal and flew off to meet them Friday morning at 5 A.M. We all had lots of fun waiting for the boat to get unloaded. They had to get off the main boat about ½ mile out to sea and come in on a little tugboat just like we had to do. We were all there; Hannah and Elmo [Scoggin] came down to Tel Aviv from Jerusalem. The Lindseys all looked wonderful after two years in the States. Their 5 children looked so good. The baby boy [Robert], who was born in the States while they were home, is a little doll. Bob is now "Dr." Lindsey. Their two little girls are both 8 years old right now. Barbara was 8 on the boat and Margaret [later called Lenore] will be 9 next week. Donnie is two months older than Robin. David is 11.

After we greeted the Lindseys we Nazareth guys, 8 of us, had to head for an Arab village way up in North Israel. There is a devout Arab pastor there (Brethren Mission Church) who has invited us to his home many, many times for dinner and we have never been able to go… His home is very humble but he is such a wonderful little man. They had a good dinner for us. We were all really ready for the bed Friday night after so much activity. But, bright and early yesterday, Saturday, we had to get up and start out again. Hannah had prepared a feast in Jerusalem to honor the arrival of the Lindseys. It was a wonderful day. We were all together, thirteen of us [missionaries], for the first time. It is the largest crowd ever to be on the field at one time in the history of the [Israel] mission. We will all be together again on the 12th and 13th of April for the meeting, and then Elmo and Hannah [Scoggin] will be leaving. We have taken up lots of our stuff to Jerusalem already and we will move up the day after Easter. At least those are our plans now.

…Our mission house in Jerusalem is in a nice neighborhood and you'd almost think you were in America… It is a very nice building with the church next door. It is a corner lot and we have a 4-foot wall with fence on top of it that goes all the way around our property…

Margaret [Lindsey] would like to study some more Hebrew too. Paul and I will attend an *ULPAN*. That is the name of special Hebrew language schools set up all over the country to teach people Hebrew. See, so many Jews are here who have never known Hebrew, either. There are all kinds of *ULPANS*, some of which last all day, some which meet at night for working people, some which are only two hours a day with no homework, for house wives…

…Wish you could see Bob's thesis. It is 368 pages long…Did you all get a copy of the [July 1954] *Commentary* magazine at a newsstand? It has his 4th chapter as an article in it. Well, I must close.

Much love,

Marjorie

Aerogramme To:
Rev. & Mrs. James W. Smith
Baptist Church
Pinelake, Ga., U.S.A.

Paul Rowden
Box 154
Jerusalem, Israel

Saturday, April 9, 1954

Dear Jim:

...March 13 marked our second anniversary... of arrival in Israel. We can look back and really see the hand of God with us. Very soon the first person we saw walk the aisle in response to the preaching of the Gospel here, will be baptized. As you see, there is a period of testing and examination before the believer is baptized, usually not as long as this particular one (2 years) but enough to know if they mean business and are ready to pay the price...

Christian love,

Paul

19

BAPTISTS FROM THE
UNITED STATES EMBASSY IN ISRAEL

The Americans with the Baptist Convention in Israel interacted on occasion with the U.S. Embassy and consular staff. On American holidays, like July 4th and Thanksgiving, the U.S. Embassy would host events for Americans in Israel. Occasionally, staff from the U.S. Embassy would make a courtesy visit to the Nazareth Baptist Church for services or drop by for a home visit with the Baptist Mission members. In 1954, Lynn Davis was a U.S. Army Attaché in the Office of Military Attaché at the U.S. Embassy in Tel Aviv. He and his wife, Helen, had been members of a Baptist church in the States. One Sunday they drove from the modern embassy community of Herzalia, near Tel Aviv on the Mediterranean Sea, to the narrow streets of ancient Nazareth. Along the sides of the main street in Nazareth, Arab men sat on small stools and sipped strong, black, Turkish coffee. Lynn asked for directions to the Nazareth Baptist Church and someone pointed to a spot just around the bend in the road.

In an article for *Commission,* a Baptist Magazine, Marjorie wrote, "Lynn and Helen Davis had a deep desire to serve their country in a noble and fitting manner as its representatives in a foreign country. But life for Lynn and Helen Davis was not complete in just fulfilling these duties and obligations. They were anxious to find fellow Baptists."[1]

At the church service, "Lynn and Helen smiled as they tried to decide which side was 'up' in the Arabic hymnal," wrote Marjorie. "But the first tune was familiar and they sang in English from memory as their neighbors sang in Arabic. The spirit of the Lord was so real as they sat there. The young couple went forward and united with the church [as members], so different in many ways from their church back home, but so similar in its love for Christ."[2]

Most of the time Lynn Davis's assignment with the U.S. Embassy in Tel Aviv kept both him and Helen busy meeting with important officials, at-

(R-L) Lynn Davis, Helen Davis, Becky Rowden, Erice (?) stand in front of "No-Man's-Land," between Israel and Jordan. A sign informs people that there is "Danger" if you go beyond the barbed wire (near Jerusalem, c. 1954).

tending receptions for foreign ministers and participating in endless affairs for diplomatic dignitaries. At the age of 23, Lynn Davis had been a Master Sergeant in the 82nd Airborne. He was stationed at Fort Bragg in North Carolina where he was in training to go to Korea. Looking at his options, Lynn considered application for G-2, Army Intelligence. However, he did not qualify because he was under the age requirement of 25. A U.S. Army General wrote a letter to Army Personnel on Lynn's behalf, asking for a waiver of the age requirement. Three days later Lynn was accepted in G-2 and soon thereafter received orders to go to Israel.[3]

Lynn was assigned to work as a U.S. Army Attaché in the Office of Military Attaché at the U.S. Embassy in Tel Aviv. His responsibilities also sometimes covered collection of information for the U.S. Navy. The U.S. Air Force officer had a two-engine propeller-driven C-47 and occasionally took Lynn when he went on flights up and down the coast of Israel. Lynn had a counterpart in the Israeli military and, as authorized, they would brief each other. Lynn was kept appraised of hostile events and border skirmishes between Israel and neighboring Arab countries and filed reports through his office.[4] Lynn and Helen were able to travel to neighboring countries and visited with Baptists in each country they visited.

Many Sundays, Lynn and Helen not only attended Nazareth Baptist

Church services, but also helped with the programs. Helen became involved with the Young Women's Auxiliary, Girl's Auxiliary and with a choral group. Lynn began teaching a teenage boy's Sunday school class. Over the next two years Lynn and Helen Davis became faithful members of the church. Sometimes they invited the mission members to their lovely home in Herzalia on the Mediterranean Sea. Lynn and Helen Davis made a notable contribution as lay workers in the Nazareth Baptist Church. In later years Lynn Davis worked at the Southern Baptist Sunday School Board (now LifeWay) in Nashville, Tennessee.

20

LETTERS

APRIL 1954

Aerogramme To:
Coles
1546 Richland Rd. S.W.
Atlanta, Ga. U.S.A.

Marjorie Rowden
Nazareth, Israel

Thursday, April 15, 1954
Dearest Folks:

...Saturday noon this young consulate couple from Tel Aviv came to spend the weekend with us...They are Helen and Lynn Davis...working with the American consulate here. They are Baptists and fine young people. They are so thrilled to find a church connection here and have been at all services for 4 Sundays in a row. They drive all the way here and back each Sunday or spend the weekend with one of us. She taught June [Petty]'s Sunday School class Sunday and did a marvelous job. Anyway, all of us went to the Sea of Galilee for a picnic Saturday afternoon. Then Saturday night Paul and I had to drive to Haifa to have dinner with the Chaikins (our dentist and her husband.) They gave us a small farewell party since we are moving and gave me a lovely Yemenite pin for a gift. They have really been sweet to us. Sunday we spent most of the day receiving guests in Nazareth who came to tell us good-bye...

Then Monday A.M. bright and early our annual mission meeting started and lasted until yesterday, Wednesday afternoon. Bob and Margaret Lindsey and [their] two baby boys stayed here. These past three days have been like a mad house. But Soriya [Shurrush] [who helps with housework] has been wonderful and somehow gotten order out of chaos. We had the actual meeting at the Bakers house and all [the] children stayed up at the Children's home. We met all morning, all afternoon and three hours each night. But I think we had a good meeting and accomplished quite a bit. The Scoggins are leaving by plane the 26th of this month. We are moving to Jerusalem next Wednesday. Half of our furniture has already gone and the place looks real bare.

...Guess you have read about our municipal election last Monday. The Communist Party in Nazareth won by a great majority... [E]lection day was wild here. It was interesting to watch these people, most of them voting in a democratic way for the first time in their lives. Our school was a voting station and even heavily veiled Moslem women came to vote. Police patrolled the streets continually all day. But people were excited...Our green dodge got a rock slung at it and [it] busted the front windshield. We were not in it. I don't think the boy meant to really hit it. But Dwight [Baker] had a big argument with him and his father. His father said he couldn't pay for it, so [the boy] is going to [provide labor and] work...in Dwight's garden...

Paul has gone to Afula this morning with Dwight to see about getting their new visas. We have to renew them each year. We enjoyed having Bob and Margaret [Lindsey] with us these past three days. Their three older children are

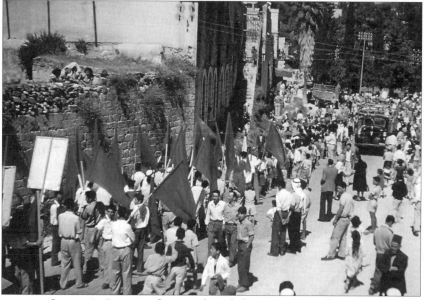

Communist Party parade moves through downtown Nazareth, c. 1954.

185

real sweet and the two little boys are cute, but real boys...Margaret is a quiet person and has her hands constantly full. Bob [Lindsey] is a real character and a half. He is very different from Elmo [Scoggin] who is very precise. Bob is brilliant but gives you the impression that he hasn't got a brain in his head. He is an easy going, slaphappy, dreamer sort of person, while Elmo is a bundle of energy and an efficient sort of person. Bob is the type of person who is the brain of the mission but who would never, never be able to be the treasurer. He'd get us in such a mess that we'd never get out. So Paul has inherited the treasurer's job from Elmo. I really dread it because it is the biggest job of all. With inflation and currency changes all the time it is a mess. Well I must close.

Much love,

Marjorie

The Baptist mission in Israel finally received funding for construction on the farm property in Petah Tikva, near Tel Aviv. The first buildings would house the Children's Home and staff. Milton Murphey was tasked with the responsibility of reviewing bids and overseeing the construction of buildings. The letter of April 18, 1954 references the go-ahead to begin the Baptist settlement.

Aerogramme To:
Coles
1546 Richland Rd. S.W.
Atlanta, Ga. U.S.A.

Easter Sunday Night
April 18, 1954

Dearest Folks:

...Our Petah Tikva farm [land] is about a half mile off the main highway, half way between Nazareth and Jerusalem. That makes it all very handy. We will be able to have all our meetings and so forth there from now on. We now have secured permission to start building the children's home there.

This week various contractors are putting in their bids. By another month we hope to get really started. Our plans are to put the children's home up as the first building on our farm and work from there, rather than try large scale building as we had thought last year. Later on we want to put up a school maybe…

…Hope we can get reasonably settled in our apartment [in Jerusalem] tomorrow. We are taking Monsour [Insair] along to help get us settled. The truck is coming at 6 in the morning. We are hiring one. Hope it doesn't fall apart on the road. We will follow in the car. Also Bob and Elmo are arranging for some men to be there to help unload when we arrive. I am <u>so</u> tired of moving. We have moved 16 times in 8 years! This will be the fourth place in Israel. Hope we will stay in Jerusalem at least 2 years. All this moving makes you feel like you wish you didn't own a single piece of furniture. June [Petty] is going to keep our dining room suite. Marty [Murphey] has one of our beds. Dr. and Mrs. [John] Tester took our kitchen cabinet. Emma [Baker] has our big wardrobe (which we had built here.) June will take a small dresser. We won't be able to get much in three rooms…I surely have enjoyed my nice new big house these past 14 months. It has been a real pleasure. But, on the whole, we will enjoy Jerusalem's climate and modernism more than Nazareth, I guess.

Well, I must close and start packing up stuff again.

Much love,

Marjorie

Aerogramme To:
Coles
1546 Richland Rd. S.W.
Atlanta, Georgia

Marjorie Rowden
Box 154
Jerusalem, Israel

Tuesday April 27, 1954

Dearest Folks:

Well, here we are in Jerusalem. We moved up last Wednesday and have had a time trying to get settled. So far we seem to be getting more used to these small rooms each day...Hannah and Elmo [Scoggin] and [daughter] Scarlett are flying out day after tomorrow. They are disposing...of their furniture and things. If they are planning to come back they will surely have to start from scratch. We have gotten loads of nice stuff given to us by them, canned goods, etc. Margaret Lindsey and I are going to have a supper for them tomorrow night upstairs at their house. All the Nazareth folks are coming up. They will have to spend the night at the Y.M.C.A...

Paul starts his Hebrew studies in an *Ulpan* this afternoon from 4 to 8 P.M. He just left for his first lesson. The class has been going two weeks, but he shouldn't have any trouble catching up. We are planning to sail for Cyprus on the *S. S. Messopia* on June 1st and return on same boat on June 21st. So I will not start an Ulpan class until after we come back. The Murpheys are all going too. Murph [Murphey] and Paul still want to spend a week of that time in Turkey, so hope they get to go. Marty and I and the 4 children will stay at the Dome Hotel in Kyrenia while they are gone...

...We are only one block from a whole line of grocery stores and other shops. The shelves are full of good things to buy. It is impossible to imagine how this country has changed in these past two years. Here we can get everything we want—there wasn't a variety like this in Nazareth...We get fresh milk delivered to the door each day, but I boil it before we drink it. But we get pure pasteurized cream at a shop near by. Paul sits and eats it like peanuts. He is getting fatter by the minute. We also get little half-pint bottles of *lebania*, which is a thick buttermilk-like stuff, which is delicious. This is also pasteurized. Israel is fast becoming more and more like a little America. Paul and Elmo [Scoggin] got stones thrown at them yesterday when they went a little too close to the wall dividing the Israel Jerusalem and the Jordan Jerusalem. Our house is way on the other side of town, so we don't have to be in that part unless we just wander over there. We are also on the side of town from which the road leads north towards Nazareth, so we can leave pronto, if ever necessary.

Wish you all could see the Orthodox Jews here in Jerusalem. Last Friday evening at sundown, one young orthodox fellow marched down the sidewalk out front blowing a horn to announce the Sabbath had started. They cut their hair like other men, except they let their sideburns grow and they form one long curl down each side of the face. Even little orthodox boys have the same hair dress. They all wear black coats and long stockings. Some wear big coonskin looking hats…It is very interesting. Our mission house is just one block from the Israel Kenneset [Parliament]. It is like living one block from the national capital in Washington. Also we live one block from the chief synagogue in the world. There is a national museum around the corner. Hannah [Scoggin] bought us a year's membership to the museum…

Orthodox Jewish boy, West Jerusalem, Israel, c. 1954

Much love,

Marjorie and all

21

CORONATION

OF QUEEN ELIZABETH II

During the summers of 1953 and 1954, the Rowden family traveled to Cyprus for a few weeks of vacation and stayed in the Dome Hotel in Kyrenia. Cyprus was a short hour and-a-half flight from Israel. Kyrenia was a beautiful and quaint little spot on the northern side of the island, about 50 miles from Turkey.

On June 2, 1953 Queen Elizabeth II was crowned sovereign of Great Britain and symbolic head of a commonwealth of nations embracing one-fourth of the world's population.[1] Cyprus was then a Crown Colony. In Nicosia, the British troops stationed in Cyprus along with the local militia conducted a ceremony with marching bands. A reviewing stand was set up for dignitaries. The governor of Cyprus announced the coronation from a platform that was constructed especially for that purpose. There were celebrations all day and a huge fireworks display that evening. The Rowdens were among the spectators and watched the coronation celebrations from a balcony overlooking the square.

Americans were much taken by the young new Queen of the United Kingdom. The American networks used jet aircrafts to carry the film from England to the States. The *Atlanta Constitution* reported that transatlantic planes would be converted into flying photographic and sound labs manned by technicians who would prepare the film in flight, so it would be ready for instantaneous telecast once the planes reach the United States. Weather conditions permitting, all three of the American television stations would put the coronation on the air. The largest audience in Atlanta television history watched the historic coronation of Queen Elizabeth.[2] "The coronation pageantry brought misty eyes, warm hearts and a long day of excitement for thousands of Atlantans," reported the *Atlanta Constitution*. "In every part of the city, they lingered by radio and television sets from 4:15 A.M.

until 11 P.M. to catch the unfolding of a great day in Britain's royal history."[3]

In Israel, in Ramat Gan, north of Tel Aviv on the Mediterranean Sea, the coronation was celebrated at a garden party given by the British Ambassador, Sir Francis Evans. Israeli President Ben-Zvi and Prime Minister Ben Gurion and their wives attended. President Ben-Zvi sent a message to Queen Elizabeth: "It is my privilege to extend to Your Majesty on behalf of the people of Israel and myself best wishes on the occasion of your coronation and to stress the hope that your reign may be blessed by the Almighty with lasting peace and length of days and be marked by prosperity and happiness for all the peoples of the Commonwealth."[4]

Marjorie Rowden stands on balcony overlooking the square where ceremonies took place celebrating the coronation of Queen Elizabeth II, Nicosia, Cyprus, 1953.

22

LETTERS

JUNE 1954

Kyrenia, Cyprus
June 12, 1954

Dear Friends,

...Right now we are enjoying a restful change for a few days on the lovely little island of Cyprus.[1] We are actually only 150 miles away from Israel, but it seems like a thousand. The food here is wonderful and we are about to eat ourselves to death. The food situation in Israel is much improved over the last year, but some things are still rather scarce and very expensive.

As you know, we have been working in Nazareth among the Arab minority of Israel ever since we arrived. It has been a thrilling experience and a most fruitful work. But last month we finally packed our belongings and moved to Jerusalem. At long last we are getting our period of language study...

Work among the Jews is hard, unfruitful, and very discouraging. The people themselves are very fine and very friendly, but they want nothing to do with our Christian faith. Israel's Declaration of Independence says that there is religious freedom, but in reality there is no religious freedom for the Jew at all. There is an open campaign in the daily newspaper against Christian missionaries. At least two Jerusalem missionaries have been refused visas this past month and have had to leave in despair. For example, all our mail is censored and the least little thing mentioned in our letters about money sends a policeman hurrying over to have us explain the transaction to him.

At our annual mission meeting in April, Paul inherited the job of Mission Treasurer, which is a trying job in any mission, but in Israel it is really a complicated task. Part of the extreme caution on the part of Israel is understandable since their country is new and very economically unsettled. And, sad though it be, the Jews' relationship throughout the centuries with so-called "Christians" is enough to cause them to distrust us all forever! They have done a magnificent job of building a nation in these past six years—it is almost impossible to believe that a group of people could be as devoted to a task as the Jews are to rebuilding Israel! Somehow you can't help but catch the enthusiasm of the masses as they labor willingly night and day.

...Jerusalem is a lovely place, very modern and very clean. It is still a divided city—half of it being in Israel and half in Jordan. Armed guards from both sides are on 24-hour duty and shooting is spasmodic but continual. It is an odd and uncomfortable feeling to stand on our side of Jerusalem and look over into the Old City where the Moslems still have possession of much of the area sacred also to the Jews. After these past six years of so-called peace, the hatred between the Jew and the Arab seems more intensified than ever...

Next door to our mission house stands the attractive little Jerusalem Baptist Church. We have one service a week there and two services a week in the Lindsey's living room. We find that the few Jews who are brave enough to come to our services are much more at ease in the home than in the church. All of the services are conducted in Hebrew...

...Please pray for the work in Israel...The country is open to Baptists now, but we do not know for how long. Our completely democratic approach—our belief that every man should have the right to choose his own faith and represent himself alone before God—appeals to the great mass of young Israelis...Pray that they will soon turn to Christ who can give them the freedom that they seek so greatly.

Very sincerely,

Marjorie and Paul Rowden
Box 154
Jerusalem, Israel

23

BAPTISTS IN JERUSALEM
1923–1954

Baptists arrived in Jerusalem in 1923, when the FMB of the Southern Baptist Convention appointed Rev. and Mrs. J. Washington (Wash) Watts to Palestine and Syria.[1] The Watts settled in Jerusalem and began language study.[2] Rev. Watts began regularly scheduled meetings for Bible study and prayer. With the help of a Jewish convert, a few hymns were translated into Hebrew. Four believers were baptized one year but economic and social persecution forced some to move away from Jerusalem.[3] One Jewish believer began preaching the gospel to a small group in secret. Sometimes Dr. Watts prepared sermons for him to translate. The evangelist spoke in Hebrew and sometimes in Yiddish, German or Russian. Dr. Watts said, "Oh, how I did rejoice in hearing him preach the first time! He had said he could not. But the message, that had been grasped in his own struggle for faith, and with which his heart had been filled and become familiar through personal work, was ready. He has the natural talents for preaching."[4] Messages came to the group in Jerusalem of other small gatherings in Jaffa, one at Petah Tikva, one at Haifa and one or two in the Valley of Jezreel. These groups were meeting quietly—studying the gospel.[5]

In a mission book entitled, *Palestinian Tapestries,* Mrs. Wash Watts stated, "The Jewish believers were torn between two desires. They wanted to confess their belief in Jesus as Messiah. At the same time they wanted to remain a part of their people, loyal to their nation, especially in its great effort to establish a national home in Palestine. If they openly became believers, then they would be branded as traitors and become outcasts."[6]

About 1925, due to generous donations, Baptists in Jerusalem were able to acquire some land. Mrs. Pattie Witherspoon of Winchester, Kentucky and two sisters from Macon, Georgia—Mrs. Tero Amos and Miss Annie Callaway—contributed funds for property acquisition in Palestine. The sisters became interested in Palestine after their pastor, Dr. Martin Wood, pastor of the Vineville Church, Macon, Georgia, traveled to Palestine and became deeply impressed with the needs and opportunities in Jerusalem. Mr. J. F. Easley of Plainwell, Michigan, a Northern Baptist, who had given the bell for the Nazareth Baptist Church, contributed funds for construction of the mission house. A small comfortable house was built with foundations that would allow for a second floor to be added later.[7] A Jewish Christian evangelist lived in the home and used it for worship gatherings and meetings. The Watts saw the construction of the home before returning to America in early 1928, but were not able to return to Jerusalem due to illness and retired October 2, 1929. Just before the Watts left Palestine, another missionary was appointed.

Miss Elsie Clor was an American Jewess who converted to Christianity in Chicago and wanted to serve among her people in Jerusalem. During World War I, Elsie, a trained nurse, sailed for France with one of the first Red Cross units that followed the soldiers into the trenches.[8] Arriving in Palestine in 1921, she worked for the Christian and Missionary Alliance in Jerusalem. However, in 1926, the Alliance notified her of its inability to continue support. In 1927, she was appointed by the FMB to work in Jerusalem. The Baptist church in Jerusalem was built in 1932-33 with funds from the Lottie Moon Christmas offerings donated in Southern Baptist churches over a period of four years. It was constructed next to the Baptist Mission house. Miss Clor spoke at the dedication service.[9] The church was made of stone and stucco and located on the Henrietta Szold Road—later renamed Narkis Street.[10]

Miss Clor began the Jerusalem Good Will Center located on the Baptist property—modeled on the early twentieth century settlement houses in America. The Jerusalem Good Will Center provided social and religious services primarily for women and children including a mothers' meeting, a children's story hour, girl's and boy's clubs, a weekly prayer meeting, a Sabbath school on Saturday morning conducted in Hebrew for Jewish children, a young people's Bible class in Hebrew on Saturday afternoon, a Sunday school on Sunday morning for Jews, Arabs, British and Americans and night classes in English with the New Testament being used as a textbook. In the summer, Vacation Bible Schools were held.[11] Miss Clor left Palestine before the outbreak of WWII and did not return.

Eunice M. Fenderson, of Minnesota, was born in 1893, and received her education at the University of Minnesota and Moody Bible Institute, Chicago, Illinois. She felt a call to missionary service and went to Jerusalem right after college where she studied Arabic for two years. After four years of mission work in Syria and seven years of mission work in Jerusalem with Miss Elsie Clor at the Jerusalem Goodwill Center, Miss Fenderson was invited to work with the Baptists and was appointed by the FMB in 1936. She worked a few years and then returned to the States for seven years. She returned to Jerusalem in 1947 and continued her work with women and children.[12] When she retired in the late fifties, her term of service in Palestine-Israel totaled thirty years. Dwight Baker wrote, "She kept very little of this world's possessions for her own use, preferring to give them to the needy of the Holy City among whom she worked."[13]

Dr. Leo Eddleman was appointed to Palestine in 1936. For about eighteen months, while studying Hebrew, he was the pastor of the little Baptist church in Jerusalem.[14] Dr. Eddleman stated that Jewish immigration was at such an augmented rate that in 1937 Jerusalem became a predominately Jewish city for the first time in sixteen centuries.[15] The church was rapidly becoming a small beacon light in the center of a large cultured Jewish section. Services were held in Hebrew attended by 10-30 people. On Sunday afternoons, a service was held in English and translated into Arabic. It was attended by English tourists, Arabs and Arab speaking Jews.[16] During World War II, the mission workers in Palestine were recalled. During their absence, a retired Presbyterian missionary, Rev. William McClenahan, who lived in Jerusalem, helped with the small congregation, giving them counsel and encouragement.[17]

In 1939, as a college student, Robert (Bob) Lindsey traveled to Palestine, lodged with a Jewish Hebrew speaking family in Jerusalem and studied Hebrew for a year before returning to the States to complete his college and theological seminary education. Bob and Margaret Lindsey arrived in Jerusalem at the end of 1945.[18] Bob Lindsey became the pastor of the Jerusalem Baptist Church. The congregation had scattered during World War II and he began the task of rebuilding. The congregation was a cosmopolitan mix of Arabs, Jews, and expatriates—of Russian, Polish, Austrian, German, Dutch, American and other nationalities.[19] Miss Violet Long was appointed to work in Palestine and arrived in 1946. However, her time of service in Jerusalem ended at the outbreak of hostilities between Arabs and Jews.

On Saturday November 29, 1947, the United Nations voted on the Jewish and Arab partition of Palestine. Word of the vote was received in Palestine in the early morning hours of November 30th. Bob Lindsey wrote:

This has been a historic day. …We live in a Jewish section of Jerusalem with thousands of inhabitants…by one-thirty this morning (people) had thrown coats around their pajamas and dashed out to the street to join other pajama-clothed…people and to run together to the Jewish Agency building some two blocks from us. …Shouts rang out in the street in front of our window: "There is partition!"

It was an amazing sight. Only a few days ago (British) policeman and soldiers had been in disfavor with the Jewish population. Now they were singing and dancing the national "Hora" with the people.

When we got to the Jewish Agency building, big circles of people had formed in the streets and were dancing and singing…Two or three impromptu speeches were made from a balcony. There were old men and women. There were whole families.[20]

The violence that followed the UN vote for the partition of Palestine signaled the beginning of the Arab-Jewish war. There were explosions that shattered glass and plaster of buildings including the Lindsey's residence at the Baptist mission house. People were invited into the house if they had nowhere else to stay. The increasing civil unrest ultimately made it necessary for those serving in Palestine to leave.[21] Margaret Lindsey and the children returned to America. Bob Lindsey was in Tel Aviv when Israel declared independence. He was unable to return to Jerusalem due to the fighting and joined his family in America. The family returned to Jerusalem in the spring of 1949.[22]

The Baptist property was located in the Jewish section of Jerusalem and that section of the city was frequently under severe barrage during the summer of 1948. About 700 people were killed. With the exception of one member, the local congregation evacuated.[23] With the return of the Lindseys, the work was begun again. Repairs were made on damaged buildings and Wednesday evening prayer meetings were started. A Saturday morning Bible study class was organized for adults and a preaching service in Hebrew was begun on Saturday evening. Miss Eunice Fenderson returned and began a ministry with women.[24]

One of the early problems to which the State of Israel immediately addressed itself was the absorption of the thousands of exiles that were flocking to Israel from the detention camps of Cyprus, from the displaced persons camps of Europe and from dozens of other lands. Baptists wondered about the destiny of the new nation and their role as Christians in a Jewish state.[25] The Arabic-speaking members of the Jerusalem Baptist church had fled and did not return. A few of the Jews immigrating to Israel were Baptist. A number of these found their way to the Jerusalem Baptist church.[26]

Young Israelis who engaged in discussions with Bob Lindsey asked questions like: "How can there be a good God if six million Jews can be slaughtered in Europe?" "Do you believe that Yeshua (Jesus) was born by a virgin?" "How can you believe in science and God too?" "Why do Christians persecute the Jews?" "Why do people in America discriminate against Negroes?" "Who are the Baptists and what do they believe?"[27] Bob Lindsey wrote, "The young Israeli, if Jewish in background, tends to judge all religious movements by the fanatic Jewish orthodoxy that he dislikes, or by a distorted Catholicism, which he has heard, exists in other countries. This is one reason why Baptists in Israel avoid the use of the word '*Christian*' when endeavoring to explain their faith. Instead they used the word '*believer.*'"[28]

Some believers who were Jewish (most of whom insisted that they were still Jews and preferred the term "Messianic Jews") experienced persecution from time to time at the hands of Jewish extremists.[29] Messianic Jews often chose to form their own fellowships. They continued to practice their faith within Judaism as Jews. Christian religious rituals were foreign to many of them and had little or no meaning. In 1948, a pastor began a ministry called, "The Messianic Assembly of Israel." Worship services in Hebrew were held on the Sabbath in a room at the Y.M.C.A. There were other Messianic Fellowships scattered throughout the land, living mainly in agricultural settlements.[30]

Bob Lindsey believed that the greatest single need of work was suitable literature. He came to the conclusion that a new Hebrew translation of the New Testament was badly needed, especially by the young Hebrew-speaking Christian congregations or Messianic assemblies in the State of Israel. In 1951, with the aid of a couple of Israeli translators who worked from English and French texts, Lindsey completed a preliminary trial translation. Lindsey later began his translation of the Synoptic Gospels into Modern Hebrew from the Greek text. In the course of his research, he concluded that these Greek texts were dependent upon an earlier Hebrew written account of the life of Jesus.[31]

In 1950, Baptists in Israel were invited, along with four other evangelical groups, to conduct services that would be broadcast by the national radio. Bob Lindsey wrote, "Although Baptists broadcast only once in five months, the influence of this medium is wide. Early in November 1950, Baptists were the first evangelical group in the history of the country to broadcast the Gospel in Hebrew."[32]

In January 1950, Elmo and Hannah Scoggin arrived and began their language study in Jerusalem. Elmo was born in the mountains of Rutherford County, N.C., the first of 10 children, and was raised during the depression. He attended Furman University in Greenville, S.C. and was working delivering shoes when he met Hannah Pearlman behind the counter in a store in Charleston. He was Baptist. She was Jewish. They fell in love and were married. After Elmo finished his studies at Southern Baptist Theological Seminary in Louisville, Kentucky, they were appointed to Israel. In 1951, they moved to Nazareth to assume responsibility for the Children's Home. The Home was turned over to Paul and Marjorie Rowden in the spring of 1952.

When the Lindseys went on furlough in 1952 for two years, Elmo and Hannah Scoggin lived in Jerusalem, studied Hebrew and Elmo became the pastor of the Baptist church. Elmo Scoggin's sermons in Hebrew indicated his skill as a linguist and underscored the necessity for new workers to master the language as soon as possible. In a country of immigrants, where nearly half the people were engaged in learning the language, Elmo Scoggin's fine use of Hebrew was well received.[33] In 1954, as the Lindseys returned to Israel and to Jerusalem, the Scoggins left for America.

Bob Lindsey was now Dr. Robert L. Lindsey, having completed work for the Th.D degree from the Southern Baptist Theological Seminary in Louisville, Kentucky. However, most people continued to call him "Bob" or "Pastor Lindsey." Dr. Lindsey's doctoral dissertation was entitled, "The Philosophy of a Christian Approach to Jews."[34] It was later formatted as a book entitled, *Israel in Christendom: The Problem of Jewish Identity.*[35] A portion of the dissertation was published in *Commentary* by the American Jewish Committee and entitled, "Israel's Coming Crisis Over 'Jewishness.'"[36] There was much interest in the article and it became a useful study for students of Jewish-Christian relations.

In *Israel in Christendom*, Dr. Lindsey states that "never since the days of Bar Cochba[37] (thought by some Jews to have been the Messiah) have there been so many Jewish ideologies competing with one another for general Jewish "acceptance."[38] He wrote,

> The mistake of modern Jews and Christians is to suppose
> that the New Testament reflects a conflict between people

we today call Jews and Christians. Nothing is farther from the truth. The New Testament conflict is a Jewish family quarrel complicated by large numbers of Gentiles flocking to become Jews who find in Jesus the simplest and most meaningful gate to that reality. Only when Pharisaism succeeded in divorcing the Christians from their Jewish identity many years after the last books of the New Testament were written did the Christians abandon their claim to be Jews.[39]

In light of the recent historical establishment of the State of Israel, Dr. Lindsey discussed the dynamics of Zionism, ultra Orthodox Judaism and the nationalism of the Israeli-born Jew known as a *sabra*.

The *sabra* (Jew born in Israel) understands perfectly the greatness of the Law, but he also knows that he must be redeemed from it. He finds his redemption in Israeli nationalism and he finds it kind of grand that Jews nearly two thousand years ago should have felt the same need for deliverance from the Law...The significance of Zionism lies in the re-creation of the term 'Jew,' even if the dimensions of its use seem cramped with the...State of Israel. As such it may give Christendom the key to its existence. Just as importantly it has opened the road of nominal Jews to world fellowship, for the Israeli revolt against Orthodoxy means not only that Pharisaism is an empty shell out of which the new-born chick has just burst but that a nominal Jew may now accept any Jewish form of faith available to him. The New Testament faith is one of these forms. Jews have made a semantic return to the first century. Sooner or later so called Christians will make their own semantic surrender.[40]

Rabbi Herbert Weiner of Temple Israel in South Orange, New Jersey, traveled to Israel several times in the fifties to interview Christians, Moslems and Jews. He asked them how life in modern Israel affected them religiously. Rabbi Weiner interviewed Dwight Baker and Bob Lindsey in the course of his research. In *The Wild Goats of Ein Gedi, A Journal of Religious Encounters in the Holy Land,* published in 1961, Rabbi Weiner stated that he was intrigued about the "leap backward in time" which Judaism and Christianity both take in modern Israel. "In a sense it brings them back to a period in history before they were divided..."[41] A written report sent to the FMB by the Baptist Convention in Israel said:

> The new Jew in his own land is uninhibited; he is open-minded; he is seeking truth. As a Jewish writer puts it: 'One thing ...is certain. Nobody in Israel pays lip service to religion. You may be an Orthodox Jew, or a free-lance seeker of God, or have a romantic attitude toward Judaism as the most precious treasures of the national past, or be altogether opposed to religion. Whatever the case may be, you profess what you believe and act accordingly.' Baptists here [in Israel] feel that this open and frank approach to religion—the willingness of the people to hear all sides of the question and then act in accordance with their beliefs—is an open door [that] heretofore had been closed. To the stimulus of this challenge, Baptists of Israel have set to their tasks.[42]

Bob Lindsey, now in charge of the work in Jerusalem and pastor of the Jerusalem Baptist congregation, spent time counseling with visitors and answering the questions of inquirers and church members. He prepared translations of books and articles. He wrote sermons and served as Executive Secretary of the Baptist Convention in Israel. His office was also a clearinghouse for literature and preparation of manuscripts.[43]

In the summer of 1954, Paul and Marjorie Rowden moved from Nazareth to Jerusalem for a year of language study, lived at the Baptist house with the Lindseys and assisted with the ministry at the Jerusalem Baptist Church. However, they also frequently traveled to Nazareth to assist with special school and church programs.

Letters
JULY–AUGUST 1954

Aerogramme To:
Coles
1546 Richland Rd. S.W.
Atlanta, Ga. U.S.A.

Marjorie Rowden
Box 154
Jerusalem, Israel

July 3, 1954

Dearest Folks:

...One week ago we drove to Nazareth...Sunday A.M. Paul preached the baccalaureate sermon and it was real good. Monday night we went to the graduation service [for the Nazareth Baptist School] at the YMCA building in Nazareth.

...The Communists won the majority votes in the last municipal election. But although two months have passed the city council has been unable to elect a mayor due to the division among all the council members...Every time the council meets to elect a mayor, it ends up in a huge free-for-all brawl; everyone gets beaten up and they get put in jail...Anyway, we were a little afraid there might be a demonstration at our graduation exercises, so Dwight asked for a police guard outside. Last time we had an American consul for a speaker, [the consul's] car was painted red during the service.[1] So this time we took precautions. But it was really funny to see how many they sent. All we asked for was one policeman. We got two carloads—about 10-12 men guarding the whole place. The communists got in a big balcony across the street from the [YMCA] and sang at the top of their lungs trying to disturb our service.

Then we came back to Jerusalem to spend our first night listening to shots across the Jordan-Israel border all night…They opened fire on each other about a mile from here and it lasted all night long and started again the next day. But the Mixed Armistice Commission intervened and it got quiet after a while. Yesterday I had to go visit my dentist down in that territory and I was really a little scared, but it all seemed to be over. They have these flare-ups about every two or three months…They say here that it was the biggest assault since the Armistice was signed in 1948…Tomorrow is the 4th of July and we are invited to a reception at the American Consulate at noon…

Much love,

Marjorie and all

Aerogramme To:
Coles
1546 Richland Rd. S.W.
Atlanta, Georgia USA

Marjorie Rowden
Box 154
Jerusalem, Israel

Friday, August 13, 1954

Dearest Folks:

…Paul is downstairs studying with Dr. [Rosen], professor at the Hebrew University from whom he takes one lesson a week. Becky is outside with Barbara and Margaret [the Lindsey girls] taking their Hebrew lesson. Georgette [Jeries][2] teaches them together one hour each afternoon. I just finished a two-hour session with her. We stopped long enough to drive over to the Railroad Station to get Aida Tobassi [Toubassi], a friend of Georgette's from Nazareth, who was coming up for the weekend. But she wasn't on the train. Guess she decided to come by bus.

In 45 minutes we have our Friday evening service over next door in the church. Tomorrow morning at 9 A.M. I have S.S. [Sunday school] with the kids. At 10 Bob [Lindsey] has S.S. in his living room with all the adults. Tomorrow afternoon, Paul, Bob and Margaret and I are invited to Herzalia (near Tel Aviv on the beach) to have a steak fry at the home of the Lynn Davis's. I think I wrote you about them. He is with the American Consulate there. They are Baptists and wonderful young Christians. They have put their church membership in our church in Nazareth, and Helen Davis is teaching a young adult women's S.S. class. All the ones from Nazareth are coming tomorrow night too. We are looking forward to it. They can get all kinds of American products all the time and we expect to drink ourselves full of Coca-Colas...

I was glad to hear that the W. O. DuValls are coming this way next spring. I hope that they will investigate all the angles. Tell them to be sure to check and double check about the difficulty with Israeli visa in the Arab countries. All the time very rich and very intelligent persons get here only to find that because they came to Israel first that the Arab countries would not accept them. Last month one of Paul's professors from New Orleans Seminary made the mistake of coming to Israel first. After saving his money all these years to make the trip, he had to go home without seeing Lebanon, Egypt, Jordan and Syria...The process is best to visit all the Arab countries first, and then come to Israel last. Also there is a method by which the Israeli visa is issued on a piece of paper rather than stamped in the passport...[For] the same reason...we aren't allowed to visit any of these [Arab] countries. Because we have Israeli visas in our passport...

We are going to write Dr. [George] Sadler to publish a statement about this situation in the State [Baptist] Papers before all those people come this way after the Baptist World Alliance next year.[3]

Much love,

Marjorie

cℐɔ

Letter to:
Mr. & Mrs. B. H. Cole
1546 Richland Rd. S.W.
Atlanta, Ga. U.S.A.

Baptist Convention in Israel
Marjorie Rowden
Baptist House, P.O.B. 154
Jerusalem, Israel

Monday Morning August 30, 1954

Dearest Folks:

I keep talking to Robin trying to get her in the mood for *gan,* the private kindergarten next door,[4] and she seems interested. The other night in her prayer she asked the Lord to help Donnie [Lindsey] go to *gan* without crying. She didn't pray for herself [to attend *gan*]. As for Becky, she is about to burst for school to open. The school is at least a half mile away so I will have to drive them over...The school is in the same building with Hadassah Hospital. It use to belong to the Anglican Mission and when the State of Israel came into being, they took over the hospital but the Mission still operates this small private school on the same grounds.[5] There are only about 15-20 children who ever attend. They are mostly missionary children or consulate

West Jerusalem, c. 1954

children because it is all in English. A very elderly single missionary—Miss Clark—is principal and major teacher…

…Saturday morning we had a wonderful service. There was a larger crowd than I have ever seen. There were also some interesting Jewish Christians from the States who were tourists and visited the service. Bob [Lindsey] is really enthusiastic about the work. We still haven't started the building at the farm yet—seems that there is always something to hold us up…

Much love,

Marjorie and all

25

ULPAN

Of the thousands of Jews immigrating from all over the world to Israel in the years after the 1948 war, most could not speak Hebrew. Classes for intensive teaching of Hebrew, called "ulpanim" were offered everywhere. My father once described his ulpan experience to an American church congregation:

> The teacher would draw a dog—a "*kelev*" and he'd say, "*kelev*"—in Hebrew. If he took the time to say it in every language, people would never learn Hebrew. We were forbidden to speak in any language but Hebrew, and so we learned a few basic words, and then new words were explained. One day, a young lady turned around and broke the rule, because she spoke to me in English and she was not suppose to speak anything but Hebrew. And she said, 'I *bet* I can tell you where you came from.' And I said, 'All right, you tell me.' And she said, 'You came from somewhere down in the south of the United States, probably from—no you came from *Georgia*.' And I said, "Well now how in the world did you know that?' She said, 'You're the first person I've ever heard who could speak Hebrew with a *southern* accent!"[1]

My father focused on learning Hebrew as he rocked in one of his rocking chairs, like Jews who rock back and forth while praying or reading the Torah. Bob Lindsey was amused by his rocking habit. He said, "Paul loved rocking chairs. He had two—one downstairs and one upstairs. He made up a piece of 3/8 plywood and would sit down in the rocker and put the plywood on the arms and study with any number of books."[2] According to Bob Lindsey, Paul was probably the only Baptist missionary in history that rocked the entire time he studied languages."[3] Many Arabs and Jews living in Israel spoke both Hebrew and Arabic and used the two languages interchangeably. It is notable that Georgette Jeries, who initially taught the Rowdens to speak Hebrew, was a Palestinian Arab from Nazareth. In the larger cities, English was also spoken. The Israeli government encouraged everyone to learn Hebrew in order to have a common language. In letters home, Paul wrote that one of his Hebrew teachers was Professor Haiim B. Rośen, Hebrew and Semitic Linguistics Scholar and Professor of Hebrew at the Hebrew University in Jerusalem. Dr. Rośen wrote a textbook on Israeli Hebrew that was widely used and is still in use today.

26

Letters

SEPTEMBER 1954

Aerogramme To:
Coles
1546 Richland Rd. S.W.
Atlanta, Georgia USA

Marjorie Rowden
Box 154
Jerusalem, Israel

September 18, 1954

Dearest Folks:

Here it is—another *Shabbat*.[1] We had Sunday School and Bible Study this morning. Murph [Murphey] is here working on last minute details for the Home [in Petah Tikva] and he had lunch with us…Paul went to Nazareth with Bob [Lindsey] Thursday A.M. and stayed until last night. They met with Dwight [Baker] and Murph [Murphey] and Herman [Petty] over some important matters concerning our projected work in Tel Aviv [Petah Tikva]…The contractors are supposed to settle the whole thing this week…

Well, Paul and I spent this week at the *ulpan*. So far we are getting along fine, but they are carrying us awfully fast. If I had not had private lessons with Georgette [Jeries] all summer, I would not have the slightest idea what was going on. And I am in the bottom class…An *ulpan* is just about the most interesting place I've ever been. My class has about 20 students. They are mostly working girls that have emigrated here from every country in the world. They don't know Hebrew so they come after work and study in this *ulpan* for 2 to 4 hours. The teacher speaks only Hebrew. From the first day she talked only Hebrew. You just have to try to figure out what she is saying. She says a new Hebrew word, then someone who thinks they understand it tells it to their neighbor in German. She tells her neighbor in French. She tells it in Yiddish. She tells it in Spanish. She tells it is Arabic. Finally, I get it in English. Then we all settle down to learning it in Hebrew. You'd be surprised how much we have learned in one week like that. We all have to talk to each other in Hebrew because it is the only language we have in common. I go from 4-6 o'clock. Margaret Lindsey goes with me. She is in number 2 class. Then we come home at 6 and Paul goes until 8. Paul is also still taking private lessons for two hours each morning with a woman down the street. Then once a week he has a lesson with Dr. [Rośen], a professor at the Hebrew University, who is the author of our Hebrew book. Well, I must close.

Much love,

Marjorie

Aerogramme To:
Coles
1546 Richland Rd. SW
Atlanta, Georgia USA

Marjorie Rowden
Box 154
Jerusalem, Israel

Sunday, September 26, 1954
3 P.M.

Dearest Folks:

Well, yesterday was a big day in the life of the Israeli [Baptist] Mission…[A]t noon we left and drove down to the farm in [Petah Tikva]. The

Pettys, Bakers and Murpheys met us there from Nazareth. They brought three of the kids from the home plus all their own. Lynn and Helen Davis (Embassy, Tel Aviv) also came over. We got out in the middle of the big field and had our groundbreaking ceremony. It was such an inspiring time. After all these years we all felt like weeping to think we were really going to see something put up on the farm. Murph...gave the message. Bob led in prayer. It was a great day for us all but I was especially happy for the Murpheys and also for Bob because he has had visions for that area all these many years. The three children from the home, Dalal, Ali and Reufi dug up the first spade of dirt. We made a whole roll of color slides of the occasion. The work is to start this week. They promise to have it finished by June, but we will be happy if they finish by the end of next summer...

After the service we all walked down to the Yarkon River's edge (on our property) to a lovely spot that the men on the farm have cleared out for us. They have built picnic tables and benches and everything. We all brought a big lunch so we ate until we nearly popped. One of the old men on the farm brought his white donkey over and took all the children for a ride around the farm, one by one...

This past week has been *Rosh Hashana* for the Jews (New Year). Wednesday started year 5715. It was a big time for most of them. All the schools were out for three days. One of the girls who comes to our services all the time took Margaret [Lindsey] and me on a tour of the synagogues on the eve of the New Year when they have their main service. It was absolutely wonderful getting to see the way they celebrate the New Year in the various groups.

We visited a very Orthodox synagogue where the men all wear these big fur hats and long white coats. They chant Psalms and then pray loud and long for forgiveness. Then we went to a Spanish Jewish synagogue where this girl's father used to be Rabbi before he died. It is more modern and the men wear just plain hats. (In all the synagogues the men are the only ones who participate; the women can go in a back room and look through a small window or through a curtain or something). Next we went to a synagogue where the Yemenite Jews worship. It was fascinating. The men, all with long white beards, sat around bare-footed on the floor and chanted their Psalms and prayers. Also we went to one where Jews from Persia attend. It had beautiful Persian rugs and tapestries all over the place. It was a very interesting time. After the service the people all went home and had a big New Years meal. It was interesting to walk through the narrow streets and look in all the windows and see the tables all set for the special meal with candles, wine, special fruits, etc. and flowers. This Thursday is *Yom Kippur*, Day of Atonement. It comes ten days after the New Year. On that day the Jews will stay in the synagogue all day and pray for forgiveness.[2] Then five days after that will be a very happy feast of the Torah, the giving of the law.[3] Well, I must close for now and go to *ulpan*.

Much love,

Marjorie

Groundbreaking Service at the farm in Petah Tikva, September 1954

27

PENINA

The young woman who took Marjorie Rowden and Margaret Lindsey on a tour of the synagogues referenced in the letter of September 26, 1954, was Penina Nehama. She was instrumental in helping Baptist Americans to understand and appreciate Jewish religious expression and tradition. Penina openly studied the New Testament and the teachings of Yeshua (Jesus). In articles written for Baptist mission magazines, the real names of Jews attending services with Baptists were often changed or omitted, to protect them from those who vigorously opposed any Jews associating with believers. When Paul Rowden wrote an article published in *Commission* about Penina, he used the name "Rebekah" rather than her real name.[1] However, Penina spoke freely and openly about herself and her beliefs; therefore, those who later wrote articles about her used her real name.[2]

Penina was born in Jerusalem, Palestine around 1930. Although her father was a rabbi, he allowed Penina and her sister to receive an English education at the Anglican Mission School in Jerusalem, but cautioned them not to believe any of its religious teachings. He died when Penina was eight, but Penina, her sister and her invalid mother continued to live in a synagogue-owned house in the *Mahane Yehuda* quarter near the Baptist House. There were threats from some Orthodox Jewish neighbors against the family because the girls continued to attend the Anglican Christian School.[3]

One summer Penina attended a Vacation Bible School sponsored by the Baptist Mission where she met Miss Elsie Clor and Miss Eunice Fenderson—who early on, recognized her leadership qualities. They were impressed by her ability to speak in several languages—Spanish, Ladino, Arabic, Hebrew and English. During the siege of Jerusalem in 1948, Penina served as a messenger in the Israeli Defense Forces.[4] Large numbers of people were displaced because of the war. After the 1948 war, Penina helped Miss Fenderson in working with women who came to the Baptist House. Most of them spoke a form of Spanish, Ladino or Arabic. Few could speak

213

Hebrew. The women studied the Bible and sewed quilts and clothing, which they helped to distribute to those more unfortunate than themselves. Penina accompanied Miss Fenderson to the area near Jerusalem's "no-man's land," the border between Israel and Jordan, where families lived in crude rooms built of rough wood in an impoverished crowded section of the city. They sought to bring what comfort they could with food, clothing and medicine. Wherever possible, they would leave a Bible in the language of the household and built friendships with the people.[5]

An unrelenting delegation of Orthodox Jews visited Penina's invalid mother using insults and threats hoping to prevent Penina from associating with Christians—all to no avail. Her mother said, "She is old enough to decide these things for herself."[6] Penina worked as a secretary in the office of the Baptist House in Jerusalem. She was unable to do strenuous work due to rheumatic fever—a heart condition that limited her strength.[7] In 1955, a Jewish heart specialist from America came to Jerusalem and offered to operate on Penina's heart but did not promise success. It was a risk that only Penina could decide to take. She prayed about it. "We all prayed about it," said Paul Rowden. "She decided to have the operation."[8] In an article for *Commission*, Paul wrote, "In the days before the operation, [Penina] lay in bed armed with [gospel] tracts which she fearlessly distributed to any who would take them. The doctors and nurses said they had never seen anyone go into so serious an operation with the cheerfulness and faith that she showed.[9] On the evenings before and after the operation the entire Baptist congregation prayed together for her."[10] Penina slowly recovered. She continued her spiritual growth and believed in the love and power of Jesus.[11] In 1956, Bob Lindsey baptized Penina in the Sea of Galilee.

Penina had many friends. Among her special friends were the boys and girls of the Children's Home. To them she brought her special warmth and was *"doda tova"*—good aunt.[12] When people, especially students from the Hebrew University, engaged Penina in a debate about her belief she said, "I am a Jew, the daughter of a rabbi, but I am also a believer in Jesus."[13] She embraced her Jewish heritage. Penina's heart finally gave out and she died in 1961. Prior to her death she represented Baptists of Israel at the Baptist World Alliance in Rio de Janeiro, Brazil in 1960 and had begun theological training at the Southeastern Baptist Theological Seminary in the United States.[14]

Orthodox Jewish extremist political groups in Israel were, and still are, very opposed to any missionary activity among the Jewish population. Some Jewish groups sought to reduce the influence of Christian relief and educational ministries in Israel.[15] One evening as Paul and Marjorie Rowden ate at one of their favorite cafes in Jerusalem, a young woman came in with a basket asking for contributions. She had a card pinned to her dress, showing the cause that the money would go for. It was in Hebrew and Paul and Marjorie could not translate it. Wanting to contribute to the many worthy causes in Israel, they put money in the basket and were given buttons to wear. When they arrived home, Bob Lindsey took one look at their buttons and burst out laughing.[16] They had contributed to *Keren Yaldenu*.[17] *The Jerusalem Post* noted that the purpose of *Keren Yaldenu* (Our Children's Fund), is "to keep children from the influence of Missions," and is "composed of 13 women's organizations…During its [first] five months of existence, the fund took more than 300 children out of foreign education institutions and placed them in Jewish schools."[18] There was concern that religious teachings in Christian schools would undermine the Jewish identity of the children. The organization was especially concerned about Jewish children of immigrants whose parents were not particularly religious. Along with social and educational programs, the *Keren Yaldenu* felt it important to establish programs that taught Jewish values and tradition so the children would identify with their Jewish heritage.

The fear that two particular Jewish children would be "lost" to Roman Catholic influence and beliefs came to the forefront in Israel in 1953 through a series of articles in the media. The *Jerusalem Post* described the effort by the Office of the Chief Rabbi of Paris to obtain release of two Jewish brothers, taken in and protected by a French Catholic family in the early forties. The desperate Jewish parents requested that the Catholic couple take their sons to prevent their deportation to concentration camps. The Jewish parents did not survive the Holocaust. The Catholic couple, who raised the boys from a very young age, resisted a French court order requiring transfer of custody of the boys to their biological aunt in Israel. The boys then disappeared from their home in France. The press reported that the boys were thought to have been "smuggled" into a convent in Spain. The Chief Rabbi in Paris accused the French Catholic hierarchy of supporting the disappearance of the boys. The Archbishop of Lyons protested the allegation by the Rabbi's office.[19] Through the Archbishop's efforts, the boys were found in a private home in a small Basque village and returned to France. "After a considerable international furor over Catholic refusal to comply with the Court order," said the *Jerusalem Post,* "an agreement was reached between the [parties] to place the children in a 'neutral' educational and religious atmosphere…[at the home of a] French Jewish leader…[while the aunt traveled from Israel to France to look after the boys].[20] In July 1953, the boys arrived in Israel under great scrutiny of the media.[21] The story was, at heart, one of anguish—for the Jewish parents trying to protect their sons from the Holocaust, for the French Catholic surrogate parents losing custody of two 'sons' they had raised, for the Jewish aunt, determined to reclaim her nephews and bring them to her home in Israel, and for the boys, torn from one family and placed in another. The press, however, primarily portrayed the story as a battle between Catholic Church hierarchy and Jewish rabbis in France. This type of media fueled religious sentiments.

After 1948, when Judaism became the official religion in Israel, numerous political parties were formed representing various interests of the population. Jewish Orthodox political parties opposed separation of religion and state on the grounds that the *Torah* was the law of the Jewish people. They regarded the Jewish Reform movement as nothing but a transitory state between diluted Judaism and Christianity.[22] The Jewish Orthodox political parties, though few in number, wielded power through coalitions in parliament and their rigid religious stance often clashed with the vast majority of secular Israeli Jews.

Staff within the Israeli Ministry for Religious Affairs debated the status of Christian groups. In *Cross on the Star of David, The Christian World in Israel's Foreign Policy, 1948–1967,* Uri Bialer offers an "interpretation of the complicated [foreign policy] issues relating to Israel's relations with the Christian world in general and the Catholic Church in particular in those early years."[23] Bialer states:

> One of the most important points of contact between Israel and the Christian world, which was inextricably connected to the question of Israel's foreign relations, was missionary activity. Knowledge of the basic facts on this activity in the first years of statehood is vital to understanding the perspectives of both sides and the dialogue between them. A Christian missionary is one who carries out a mission. The duty to disseminate the religion is one of the fundamental tenets of Christianity and is fulfilled through intensive activity and the establishment of relevant institutions and organizations. Long before Israel came into being, it was considered imperative to spread the message of Christianity in the Holy Land, the cradle of that religion.[24]

Christians of evangelical persuasion maintain the New Testament teaches that every believer should "go into all the world and preach the gospel..."[25] When Christians share their faith, it is to carry out this teaching. However, nearly two thousand years of persecution and forced or coerced conversion to Christianity at the hands of Christendom had resulted in a stereotypic Jewish view of the term "mission" or "missionary". "A missionary [is] typically viewed, not as one who serves, but as one who attempts to manipulate others through fear or deceit to change one's religion against one's will..."[26] "Baptists in Israel [therefore], do not use the word 'missionary,' because it is used by Orthodox Jewish extremists to describe 'one who seduces or steals children and forces them to become Christians.'"[27] Ray Register, author of the book, *Back to Jerusalem, Church Planting Movements in the Holy Land,* states, "It is ironic that Messianic Jews who believe in Jesus as Messiah are...called 'missionaries' by the Orthodox Jewish extremists, as a method of slander or derision. [How-

A poster on a wall in West Jerusalem with the picture of a young girl. Under the picture in Hebrew it says, "Donate to Keren Yaldenu" (Our Children's Fund). Next to the poster is an advertisement for the Walt Disney movie, "Peter Pan." Jerusalem 1954

ever], the secular public recognizes that a greater threat to Israeli society is extreme Orthodox Judaism, which tries to squeeze the country into its mold and restrict religious freedom."[28]

The Israeli parliament, press and public opinion were increasingly occupied with complex relations between the state and Orthodox Jewry. The issue came up on many occasions, such as the debates on unified state education and the keeping of the Sabbath on the municipal level. There were occasional clashes between the police and Orthodox Jewish demonstrators, who attempted to bring traffic in Jerusalem to a standstill on the Sabbath by force. There were also a number of attacks on non-kosher butchers and missionary offices.[29]

Letters
OCTOBER–NOVEMBER 1954

The letter of October 7, 1954 by Paul Rowden was in response to a request by Dr. Ben R. Lawton for information about the Baptist Convention in Israel. Dr. Lawton was the Visiting Professor of Missions at the New Orleans Baptist Theological Seminary at the time.

Letter from:
Rev. Paul D. Rowden, Jr. Treasurer
P.O. Box 154
Jerusalem, Israel

Letter to:
New Orleans Baptist Theological Seminary
Ben R. Lawton
3939 Gentilly Boulevard
New Orleans 22, Louisiana

October 7, 1954

Dear Brother Lawton:

Since today is *Yom Kippur* of the Day of Atonement, things are at a standstill here in Jerusalem and perhaps it will give me a little time to try to answer your letter…

…Israel is a young field even though Southern Baptists have been here about thirty years, off and on. Dr. [Washington] Watts[1] can give you past history should you desire it. However there have never been more than a few missionaries at the most here at any one time, and only a few of these [were] men, until recently. The field is young in the sense that in 1948 the country became a nation, Israel, largely Jewish. At this time vast changes took place in Mission work, since quite a bit of it had been with Arabs. In many respects the work had made great progress among the Arabs, with large church congregations and also quite a few Jews (I am speaking of general mission work by all evangelical groups).

The war between the Arab states and the Jewish people changed all this. Most of the Arab members of churches fled; as did a large number of Jewish members (many to England, as they were members of various English sponsored work, largely Church of England)...The Jewish believers [in the gospel] felt that in an entirely Jewish governed state, they would be persecuted. Consequently the work has begun as though Baptists had entered a new field. Under the British mandate, missions had been more or less favored or helped; now Missions and missionaries are quite despised here and are considered a blot on the country, and thus are treated so.

...We are a Mission of mostly young people, six couples with children, and a single lady worker. One couple is now on furlough. The set up at present is that there are two couples in Jerusalem, one handling meetings in the Jerusalem and Tel Aviv area (Tel Aviv being the largest city in Israel), while the other couple is in language study. The single lady worker handles various women's meeting and children work and some relief work. One couple is in charge of the George W. Truett Orphanage, at present the buildings of which are being erected in the center of Israel, also near the population center of Israel. Israel has about a million and a half Jews plus about 175,000 minorities as Arabs, Druze, etc. In Nazareth we have two couples, one acting as pastor of the church and the various mission points out from Nazareth. The other couple is in charge of the school (primary and secondary). Nazareth is the only all-Arab town left in Israel of any size.

Concerning our organization: I will not repeat statistics, as the ones in the annual report of the Board are correct. Even though we are small in personnel we have tried to organize on a basis of a democratic organization and also look to the day when we trust that our personnel shall increase. Besides the annual meeting of the Mission we have quarterly meetings of the executive committee.

The executive committee [of the Baptist Convention in Israel] is composed of the chairman, secretary, treasurer, plus the respective heads of the two institutions of school and Children's Home. This is an entirely Foreign Mission organization, as there is yet no local or national organization. The work is extremely difficult among the Jewish people but there is a nucleus of a church in Jerusalem...

In Nazareth there is an organized church of active Arab believers. Two young men have received education at two…colleges in the states, while a third is engaged in studies at the seminary in Zurich…The other two young men are very active in village mission work, in the school as teachers, etc. Thus we have not been faced with the need of working out a relationship with a national organization. I personally believe that our organizational setup is very effective for the present. Request for funds are made at the Mission meeting for the following year. These budgets are discussed and approved, changed or rejected in the meeting. I am sorry that I can't give you any information about relations with a national convention. We are looking to the day when we can.

We do consider it part of our work to establish a self-sufficient national organization. To this end we are planning for the immediate future a greater participation of the members in the Nazareth church in sharing responsibilities of local mission and evangelistic work. They have been doing this in an increasing way for the past year. They contribute to the expense of the school and we look and plan for the day when they will completely run the school. We are continuing our work of preaching, Bible study, youth camps, adult camps, translation of worthy Christian books, tracts, school work, radio…For the distant future we have in mind a type of Junior College to prepare Christian workers beyond our High School, plus a greatly enlarged literature and translation work as this seems to be one of the most effective ways of reaching the very literate Jewish people.

In answer to your question about past general methods and their need of modification, all I can say is that up until recently the Mission never had enough workers to actually say that they had a plan or method. It was simply a matter of trying to hold on, in the absence of help of fellow-workers, and do the best one could in the matter of preaching and working. I might add that during the [British] Mandate, Community Center, relief, and children's work was more effective than now. The Jewish state handles relief work fairly effective[ly] and opposes such Christian activity. The orphanage work will not be expanded for the same reason…

We do not have any particular anti-American attitudes, but we do not have any overwhelming pro-American feeling. There are several other major missions in Israel: the Anglicans, Presbyterians, Christian and Missionary Alliance, the Brethren, Church of God Assembly. Many "Faith" workers come and go all the time. The press is very hostile, and critical of missionaries. They have stirred up quite a bit of bitterness toward us. We are having great difficulties renewing our visas due to the religious element in the government.

In Israel among the Arab minorities are Greek Orthodox, Greek Catholic, Roman Catholic, and Anglican communities. All but the Roman Catholic seem to be losing ground. There is a Moslem group also among the [minority groups]. The major population is of course Jewish. I would say that roughly only 20 percent of these are really orthodox while the rest are non-religious or only observe a few of the more serious Holy days, such as the Day of Atonement. Thus I might say that Israel is in a spiritual void at present among both the Jewish and Arab element. We are seeing results of this among our Arab work by real interest in the Baptist message. Among the Jewish people there is an interest in Christianity I believe, but there is also centuries of resentment of persecution by so-called Christians...

...Perhaps the greatest strains have been in the matter of getting the language of the people. Because we are a small Mission there have been many other things to keep us busy besides the matter of study and yet we realize that we must have uninterrupted study to properly prepare ourselves. This problem is not yet solved but we believe that in a matter of two more years we can permit each new worker to have uninterrupted study for at least a year or more. I have found one of the greatest personal helps to me here was the experience of being a pastor of a church in America...

Sincerely,

Paul Rowden

Aerogramme To:
Coles
1546 Richland Rd. SW
Atlanta, Georgia USA

Marjorie Rowden
PO Box 154
Jerusalem, Israel
Sunday, October 10, 1954

Dearest Folks:

…We are having so many holidays these days that we don't go to the *ulpan* half as much as we stay home…

The bulletins [about the Baptist Convention in Israel] seem to never be going to get printed if we don't stop having so many holidays. We have everything ready to print now but they won't do it until after next week. Hope they get there [to America] by Christmas.

The weather here in Jerusalem is so nice. Paul and I get out and walk around the block almost every night before we go to bed. It is nice to be living where there are sidewalks. Also there is a nice Oriental restaurant not far down the street. We go down there for supper about once a week. They serve Arab food and we love Arab food.

Jerusalem has the same dry summer and wet winter like Nazareth and the rest of Israel but it is just higher up here and the air is really invigorating. There are lots of advantages and also some disadvantages about living here. All in all, it is nice. I miss my nice big house in Nazareth and also I miss the friends there. But otherwise we are very happy here…The services are getting better all the time, in attendance, and in spirit. Also we are beginning to understand more of it so naturally it seems better to us…

Much love,

Marjorie

Aerogramme To:
Rev. & Mrs. James W. Smith
Box 115
Pine Lake, Georgia USA

Paul Rowden
P.O. Box 154
Jerusalem, Israel
October 12, 1954

Dear Jim & Betty:

…Trust that all of you are well and that things are making progress the way you want. Sounds like you are awfully busy these days in the church. [It's] wonderful to be able to stand back sometime and see the way that God blesses our feeble efforts in the church. How important are these lives we come in contact with and what a responsibility to shepherd them.

We are somewhere in the halfway mark, I suppose, in our language study… I have had along with the language study the matter of being treasurer, which has caused a bit of work. There is a matter of months in language study when everything looks dark. It seems that you are making no progress, you don't understand a thing that is being said and you forget half that you've learned, but just about the half year mark things begin to take on a more encouraging outlook. In some of the conversations that you hear you catch words and phrases, and you are able to talk a little bit. After this the steepest part of the ascent is over but for the rest of your life you are still pushing upward learning more words, idiom[s]…After Christmas I plan to spend quite a bit of time on the New Testament with my teacher learning the phraseology [in Hebrew] that means so much to us in English. I am also hoping that it will be a means of light entering into the mind and heart of my teacher who is so sincere and seeking, in trying to follow the Old Testament and related teachings.

Tomorrow we are going to a camp in the middle of Israel (geographically). [T]his is on a piece of land that we are building the children's home on. [It is] good to report that work has started. We have tents…and really plan to rough it. (Real pioneers!) All the members of the mission, children and members of the Nazareth church and Jerusalem church plus others are coming and we plan to have something like Ridgecrest with study course by Arabs and Jews and us and ought to be the first of its kind in Israel… Be assured of our many thoughts of you. As Paul said, "We thank God upon every remembrance of you."

Christian love,

Paul

Aerogramme To:
Coles
1546 Richland Rd. SW
Atlanta, Ga. USA

Marjorie Rowden

Box 154
Jerusalem, Israel

Saturday, October 16, 1954

Dearest Folks:

…We are all so elated over our camp [in Petah Tikva] this week…Sometimes our faith is certainly small. We were all worried half to death about whether the camp would turn out to be anything at all, especially with the mixing of the Jews and Arabs. But the Lord was certainly present with us. The whole three days and two nights were filled with spiritual blessings. All of us benefited.

Camp opened Tuesday night, but Paul waited until Wednesday morning to go so he could take Margaret [Lindsey] and me and all 7 of our children. We looked like migrant farmers or something by the time we all got in the car with all our mattresses and bedding and suitcases and water jugs. There were about 13 people in it in all. Miss Fenderson had sort of planned on going, but she took one look at us all and changed her mind. We left here about 6:30 A.M. and got there by 8. Dwight [Baker] taught a fine study course on Baptist Doctrines. Bob [Lindsey] translated it into Hebrew. All the ones from Nazareth understood English, so the camp was conducted in just the two languages. Arabic wasn't used very much.

At 11 A.M. each morning we had messages by Paul and Murph [Murphey]. Then we went on hikes or swam in the Yarkon River in the afternoons. Then both nights we had wonderful evening services. We had an average attendance of about 45 or 50. At least 30 of these stayed the whole time. About 15 came each night after work from Tel Aviv. We had a huge brush arbor built right out in the middle of our big field. The women all slept in the three little pre-fab houses that the farm workers use. The men had tents. It was really "roughing it" but we all had a marvelous time. Becky and Robin had lots of fun. Becky had never camped out like that so she thought she was doing something real big. Each morning before breakfast we had morning watch [devotional] down on the bank of the river. We ate all our meals on a big flat trailer attached to the tractor, which we pulled from one shady spot to another. [There were about] two long blocks of rough ground between the tents and the river so when we went down there we all climbed on the trailer and the tractor bumped us all over there. It was just like an old fashion hayride. The children thought they were in heaven.

The U.N. [United Nations] would have dropped dead if they could have seen Arabs and Jews having so much fun and fellowship together. But the highlight of the whole time was the last night when we had testimony time…[O]ne by one they stood up to tell what the Lord had done for them. It was absolutely wonderful. A fine Jewish boy gave the best testimony of all. He was just overcome completely when he tried to tell how much it meant to him to find that there were other Jewish young people in Israel who had followed Jesus.

At the end, Bob asked four people to come up and sing "What A Friend We Have In Jesus" in their mother tongue. A boy from Nazareth sang it in Arabic. Marty [Murphey] sang it in English. A Jewish girl sang it in Hebrew, and one of the farm workers, a Russian Baptist, sang it in Russian— all at the same time! It would have thrilled you to hear it. Then each one in turn prayed in their own language. At the close we made a big circle and prayed for the strengthening of the bond between us all and for the individual growth of each one. I'm sure there has never been a moment like that in the history of this nation. It was worth all the mosquito bites and lumpy mattresses and rough living at camp. Next summer, Lord willing, the Home [buildings] will be there and it won't be so rough.

It was so good to be with June [Petty] and Emma [Baker] and Marty [Murphey] at camp. I surely do miss being with them. June is doing a grand job of being principal of the grammar school. And Herman [Petty] seems to have the High School well in hand too. Dwight [Baker] worked hard on this camp. He really shines when it comes to organizing. Bob [Lindsey] shines in just about every other way, but without Dwight's help at this thing it would have been a mess. That Bob Lindsey is a character like unto which you have never seen. He never worries too much about anything. They turned off our phone last month for three days because Bob forgot to pay the bill. And yesterday the electric company came to cut off the electricity but Margaret begged them to wait one more day until Bob got back from camp. He is just about the most likeable guy you ever met but he is really a nut at times. The other day at camp he jumped in the river up stream and put his shoes on a small board and floated them down the river so they'd be there when he arrived himself. I've never seen anything so funny as those shoes floating down the river all alone. [Also,] I'll show [you] the picture of the car he built when he was out here for his first term about 1940. It was made out of old parts and he had a motorboat body to it. Drove the thing all over Israel.[2] Once he drove Dr. [George] Sadler from Jerusalem to Tel Aviv on a motorcycle.

This Baptist camp held on the farm property in Petah Tikva features a service held under a brush arbor. Standing (L-R) is Dwight Baker and Bob Lindsey, 1954.

Must close,

Marjorie

Aerogramme To:
Coles
1546 Richland Rd. SW
Atlanta, Ga. USA

Marjorie Rowden
P.O. Box 154
Jerusalem, Israel

Wednesday, Nov. 17, 1954

Dearest Folks:

…Last Wednesday night the Lindseys and Paul and I had an invitation to the American Marine Corp's annual birthday ball… [O]n the invitation it said they would have the birthday cake cutting and the ceremony at 11

P.M. So we decided to drive over just for that part of it. We had a time waiting until 11 P.M. without going to sleep, but we managed…

The party was held at Government House, which is in "no man's land" between Israel and Jordan. It was a real experience to drive through several blockades with guards to get to the Government House. Now it is the U.N. Headquarters. We felt like real "big wigs." When we got there we found that nearly all the Americans helping to celebrate the Marine's birthday were from the Jordan side. We saw people we hadn't seen in years. It was a funny feeling to know that we couldn't go a step further in their direction and they couldn't come a step further in the Israel direction, but for an hour we all met "in the middle." And had such a good time. The Marines stationed on both sides of Jerusalem were there in uniform and they marched and we all sang the Marine hymn. I haven't felt so patriotic in years…

Much love,

Marjorie

Aerogramme To:
Mr. & Mrs. B. H. Cole
1546 Richland Rd. S.W.
Atlanta, Georgia U.S.A.

Marjorie Rowden
P.O. Box 154
Jerusalem, Israel

Wednesday November 24, 1954

Dearest Folks:

Boy, winter has arrived in full force. Up until three days ago it was summer. Then it rained two days and nights—now it is cloudy and cold as ice. Our little "under-the-ground" apartment is wonderful. The minute we come in the door we feel like we're in a steam-heated house, and so far we haven't started the stove. We hate to start it because it will have to be kept going and it will make us all take colds I'm afraid at first. And besides, Miss Clark doesn't have heat at her school so it will be a great change for Becky to go from a heated house to an unheated [classroom]. However, even though Jerusalem gets colder than Nazareth we don't feel it as much since here it is a dryer cold. In Nazareth the dampness penetrates through and through and no amount of heat helps. Most of the people in Israel go all winter without any heat at all—it is amazing but they stay very healthy. We have one Coleman heater for this downstairs apt. and we have another one in our large bedroom upstairs…

Paul and I took our daughters to see the techni-color movie *A Queen's World Tour* the other night. It is just the movie of Queen Elizabeth's trip around the world last year, showing all the places she visited and the natives on all the Islands. She looked lovely in it. Becky was simply thrilled to death. Ever since our first trip to Cyprus at the time of the coronation last year Becky has talked about Queen Elizabeth just like she was a little British child. If you all have the chance to see the film, don't miss it.

…I have forgotten whether I wrote you about this young Jewish woman whom we know here who has become a Christian… [L]ast week she was fired from her job as a government school teacher because of her becoming a Christian. It has become a real issue and it will be interesting to see how it comes out. All the papers have written it up pro and con. Some agree that she is a traitor to the Jewish faith and nothing is too bad to do to her, while others think it has put "religious freedom" to a real test here. They may not agree with her belief but they think she should have the right to believe as she wants. Much has been said about what would happen if all the Jewish public school teachers in the States were fired all of a sudden. She is going to press the case into the higher courts. Bob [Lindsey] is so excited over it all he can't sleep or eat. The outcome of this thing will determine quite a number of things. Well, I must close…

Much love,

Marjorie

29
THANKSGIVING IN JERUSALEM 1954

In 1954, the Rowdens attended a Thanksgiving meal and program at the Jerusalem YMCA. Bill Miner, who worked with the American Friends Service Committee (Quakers), was the Master of Ceremonies. He recalled that in attendance were American businessmen, tourists, missionaries, military, government officials, consuls and embassy staff—Americans from all walks of life. The gathering was very informal. There was no speaker, but there was prayer and reading of the Scripture. Songs that were likely to have been sung were, "We Gather Together," "Come Ye Thankful People Come," "Now Thank We All Our God," and he remembers that everyone sang, "Home on the Range." He believes that the group probably sang "America." Bill didn't recall how he ended up being the MC but he learned about the gathering from the American Friends administrative office in Acre, and he believes someone from the administrative office may have suggested him for the honor. He said that most Americans that were traveling in Jerusalem stayed at the YMCA or at the King David Hotel across the street. Bill estimated an attendance of approximately 120-140. A banquet room was used for the gathering and everyone sat around and visited.[1] Little paper turkeys and other Thanksgiving decorations were set out on the tables.

At that event Paul and Marjorie met a well-known writer, Sholem Asch—a Jewish novelist and playwright. He first came to the United States in 1909, was naturalized in 1920, and lived in various parts of Europe and the United States. He settled in Israel in 1956.[2] One of the most widely known Yiddish writers, he won his first success with the play, *The God of Vengeance*. He made long visits to Palestine and in his last, most controversial period of writing, "he attempted to unite Judaism and Christianity through emphasis upon their historical and theologico-ethical connections: (1943; *The Nazarene)*, a reconstruction of Christ's life as expressive of essential Judaism; *The Apostle* (1943), a study of St. Paul; *Mary* (1949), the mother of Jesus seen as the Jewish 'handmaid of the Lord.'"[3] However he was widely criticized by many Jews as a self-appointed Apostle to the Jews. One writer stated, "Jews have become used, and inured, to the missionaries who century after century have laid siege to the Jewish people, but who beleaguer them from without. Sholem Asch however, worked from within, as a Jew among Jews."[4]

30
LETTER OF NOVEMBER 28, 1954

Aerogramme To:
Coles
1546 Richland Rd. SW
Atlanta, Georgia USA

Marjorie Rowden
Box 154
Jerusalem, Israel

Sunday, Nov. 28, 1954

Dearest Folks:

...Last Thursday we had a wonderful time over at the YMCA Thanksgiving dinner...We sat at the middle [of a] long table. [Sholem] Asch, the very famous author of such books as *The Apostle, The Nazarene, Mary*, etc. was there and sat at the head of our table. It was a real thrill. He made a short speech at the end. I told you before that he was in the country and had received a very cold reception due to his books on Christian themes. He is going back to the States this week. He is an old man about 78 years old. Looks like [Albert] Einstein.

The food was delicious, turkey, dressing, potatoes, boiled onions, beans, salad, soup, pumpkin pie and coffee. The master of ceremonies for the occasion was our friend Bill Minor [William R. Miner] who is out here with the Quaker group—he is a Negro from Ohio—and he is a wonderful person. He had supper with us one night in Nazareth last winter. He has a wonderful voice. Paul and I sat there at the dinner and thought how really wonderful the whole thing was—[Sholem] Asch is a Jew, Bill Miner is a Negro, and [we] were all kinds of religions—but we were all Americans. Thanksgiving day was really nice for us this year in Jerusalem...

Yesterday a bunch of [Jewish] religious fanatics got out in the street here in Jerusalem and made a human blockade so that cars could not pass down the street on the Sabbath. The police came and there was a huge free for all. One Hebrew University student was beaten unconscious for smoking. He is in the hospital. Two newspaper men were beaten because they were taking pictures...It reminds you of how zealous the Apostle Paul was before his conversion.

Well, I must close. We are getting excited about the telephone call. Surely trust the line will be clear.

Much love,

Marjorie

31

THE SPIRIT OF THE SEASON

In a letter to her mother Marjorie wrote, "I'd rather hear your voice this Christmas than anything else in the world." Alma Cole, Marjorie's mother, shared the letter with her friend Mrs. John E. (Mary) McGarity, a member of Cascade Baptist Church in Atlanta. Mary McGarity decided that as a gift to the family, she would set up a long distance call between Paul and Marjorie and their parents, who had only been able to communicate by mail. Setting up the call was no easy task. With only one cable line to Jerusalem, a long distance telephone reservation had to be made weeks in advance. It was a daring venture because so many things could go wrong and so much hope was riding on its success. Mary had telephone conduits set up at her house at 1619 Beecher St. SW, Atlanta, and borrowed additional extensions so every one of the four grandparents could have an individual phone.[1]

Mary reached out to the Cascade Baptist Church members for a special offering to pay for the call. They reached into their pockets and contributed forty-six dollars, a large sum in 1954. The minister and the congregation prayed that the call would come through clear and fine. The morning of the hookup, the Jerusalem operator telephoned Mary at 8 o'clock in the morning to be sure she and the family would be standing by at noon in Atlanta. It would then be about 7 P.M. in Jerusalem. The actual time that the call would go through could not be precise. The parties had to remain on standby. The chief operator in Atlanta became so interested in this effort that she made a special point to personally help handle the connections.[2]

In Jerusalem Marjorie rushed home from her afternoon *ulpan* class and prepared supper. Several hours ahead of time, they went up to Bob Lindsey's office where a phone was located and waited. Finally the phone rang. In an article in the *Atlanta Journal Constitution* entitled, "Telephone Call to Jerusalem Carries the Spirit of Christmas," Hugh Park wrote, "Everything went excellently. There was a little crying at first and then

Becky and Robin spoke to their grandparents from Jerusalem. This capped it, of course. The conversation lasted 11 minutes. By the time it was over, the Jerusalem operator had apparently caught the spirit of the season for she said, 'I'm charging you for only 10 minutes.' The 10 minutes cost exactly $46."[3]

32

Letters

DECEMBER 1954

Aerogramme To:
Coles
1546 Richland Rd. SW
Atlanta, Ga. USA

Marjorie Rowden
Box 154
Jerusalem, Israel

Monday, December 13, 1954

Dearest Folks:

Well, it seems so funny to be writing you again after talking to you last night. It seems kind of like a dream now. All of you sounded just wonderful and we could hear you so clearly. After hearing your voices we could hardly realize that it had been nearly three years. Made us want to jump through the wire and hug you around the neck. Well it is only two more years now. This time two years from now I'll already be packing my suitcases.

Well, last night I rushed home from *Ulpan* and fixed supper. Paul didn't want to go to the *Ulpan*. At 10 minutes to 7 we went up to Bob's office where the phone is and parked ourselves. Becky and Robin were like birds out of a cage. They giggled and jumped and twisted and turned and acted silly in general. Paul and I tried to act very calm. But we waited and we waited. (I chased Margaret [Lindsey's] kids out about 16 times). They were about as excited as we were. Finally I took the girls downstairs and bathed and dressed them for bed. Paul stayed by the phone. Then when we finished dressing we went up and stayed by the phone while Paul went down to dress. Then the phone rang. I ran to the door and yelled for him and he came up half dressed and half undressed. Becky was really funny—when the phone rang she sobered up in a hurry. She got out her little list of all the things she had written on it to talk to you about. The time went so fast that we didn't get to say anything that we had planned. Becky was heart broken because she didn't get past item one on her list. Robin was a real dude. She stood there and kept jumping up and down and saying "Me, daddy, me!"

After we all said goodbye we went back downstairs and Becky and I had a good little cry. Paul merely rocked and looked rather sober—Robin promptly went to sleep. Becky was real touched by it all. I think it brought back lots of little memories that were just about to fade away in her mind…

This Wednesday week (22ⁿᵈ) Becky's school is having their Christmas play. Becky is a shepherd. They will have a tea afterwards for the parents. Then on Thursday (23ʳᵈ) the YMCA is having a big Christmas party for all the Christian children. I am on the committee to help wrap gifts and candy and have to go over Wednesday morning and work. They are having a Santa Claus and everything. Also that same Thursday we are beginning our three-day conference here at the church. It will go through Christmas Day. At first I felt real bad about having so many people and so much activity going on around here on Christmas Eve and Christmas Day. It seemed unfair to all our children, but I realize that was a very selfish thought. It is a time of year that such a meeting as this will have more effect than any other time. Also it coincides exactly with *Hanukah*, a Jewish holiday season, and the people will have some holidays from their work…

Much love,

Marjorie and all

P.S. Dearest Mother and Daddy: Well, sir, I could weep bucketfuls if it would help any. It was just marvelous to hear your voices. You both sounded like you were in the next room. And I got real thrilled hearing your good ole Southern Accents!

Aerogramme To:
Coles

1546 Richland Rd. SW
Atlanta, Ga. USA

Marjorie Rowden
P.O. Box 154
Jerusalem, Israel

Saturday, December 4th 1954

Dearest Folks:

We just finished our Shabbat dinner. Dwight [Baker] ate with us. He is
here for a few days trying to get permission to take his older two boys, Bill
and Bron, over to Jordan with him and Emma [during] Christmas. Margaret [Lindsey] and I are planning to go across too. We all have to go to the
Consulate office Monday and fill out some forms or other.

Well, we really stepped out in high society last night. Sergeant and Mrs.
Frank Gross left for the States today, so last night Consul-General and Mrs.
Cole had a dinner party for them. They were asked to invite 6 friends, so
[the Lindseys and Rowdens] were selected. We felt real honored. It was really nice. Frank and Mildred Gross (he is in the Marines and connected
with the Consulate) have been our close friends for quite some time so we
hated to see them go.

The American Consul-General here in Jerusalem is Mr. William Cole.
He is a real big shot. It was a real experience to have dinner at the Consulate
on gold-rimmed State Department china. Mrs. Sarah McDonald, Vice-Con-
sul, was also there…Also the other guest was Father Pat, the Roman
Catholic priest here in Jerusalem. He is from the States too. It was some
mixture, wasn't it?

We started out by sitting in the long consulate drawing room having
cocktails (we got coca-cola and were thrilled to get one), after half an hour
we went down to dinner in the huge dinning room. We had servants waiting on us hand and foot. And had a wonderful dinner… After the dessert we
had fruit, which was served beautifully. They had some gorgeous apples,
which we never see here. Bob [Lindsey] sat next to me and was so excited
over peeling that big apple that the thing got away from him and slid across
that slick polished table half a mile away. He had to stretch out to get it and
I nearly bursted trying to keep from laughing. Nothing bothers Bob, however.

237

After the fruit, the 5 women retired to a private salon for our after-dinner coffee. The men drank theirs in the dinning room. Then half an hour later we all met in the drawing room around a big open fire for more talk and cocktails (more cokes). We all "put on the dog"[1] real good, but when we got back out in the car we cut loose and laughed ourselves sick. I think I'll see that freshly peeled apple flying across that shiny State Department table for the rest of my life. The Gross's had…Paul and me over at the YMCA for dinner with them last Tuesday night. We enjoyed it lots. They have two cute little boys. I hate to see them leave; they are going home on a U.S. Naval vessel and won't get there until the middle of January. I feel for them.

We have been getting all kind of crazy publicity in the local press here lately. This week some screw-ball reporter interviewed Murph [Murphey] about our new building at the farm and about the Baptist work. He must not have understood English at all and in addition he made up lots of stuff and printed it. It is the craziest thing I ever read. Well, I must close. I hope you can read this. This typewriter did a bad job of writing today. Paul is working at the desk and I am trying to write this on the coffee table and it is a little low. Oh well.

Much love,

Marjorie and all

The following letter was written by Paul Rowden to Dr. O.M. Seigler, pastor of the Cascade Baptist Church in Atlanta.

Letter To:
Dr. O.M. Seigler
1631 Alvarado Terrace, S.W.
Atlanta, Ga. USA

Paul Rowden
P.O. Box 154
Jerusalem, Israel

December 19, 1954

Dear Dr. Seigler:

Here finally, is a long overdue letter. As you know, we are in language study here which is a full time job in itself, but I am also the treasurer of the Mission which involves a lot of time consuming reports, trips to the Bank, Post Office, auditor, etc. so that I have neglected a lot of important things. I planned several months ago to set aside a few days before Christmas to try to be a better father, correspondent, husband…and get away from the verbs, nouns, and grammar that is all the time getting in my way…

Marjorie and the children are well. Becky and Robin are looking forward to the visit of ole Mr. Santa. We have our tree up and decorated, and are enjoying it along with a record of favorite carols on the phonograph. Becky is doing well in school even though it is quite different from an American school. The Anglicans have a small English speaking school here that she attends and she is becoming quite British. Robin is three and a half and is really enjoying the tree for the first time and thoughts of old Santa.

Marjorie is making quite a bit of progress in study but of course does not have the time that I do, having the responsibility of cooking, children, etc. The Lindseys are in charge of the work here, while we live in an apartment under them. They have five children, so, plus ours we have quite a family. Marjorie has a S.S. for them each week. Of course the day of rest here is on Saturday so we have our worship services then and on Friday night when Sabbath begins. On Wednesday night we have Bible study and prayer service. In addition to the services here Bob Lindsey goes to Tel Aviv weekly for a meeting. Tel Aviv is the largest city in Israel besides being very modern and a relatively new city…

We are encouraged with the way that work in general is going here. Naturally we have quite a bit of opposition. In fact there is a league organized to attempt to combat Missionary activities: "Society for Defense Against Apostasy," and an organization called "[Keren Yaldenu]" which seeks "to protect" the children from missionaries. I think that the anti-Christian attitude is very understandable in the European Jews who have come to Israel in the past ten or more years. In fact I wonder that we should be treated by most people as nicely as we have.

Europe is cursed by infant baptism, thus producing people calling themselves Christians who know nothing of what it means to be a Christian, of regeneration, of kindness, love, of "loving our neighbor as ourselves." Thus a "Christian" nation caused the death of 6 million Jews. It is incomprehensible—6 million people, some by torture, some by experimentation, etc. Yet how quickly the world has forgotten; [it] is now bringing Germany back into the "Society" of nations. We know that in no sense is Germany Christian [any] more than America is Christian. There are people in each country that have been motivated by a personal faith in the Lord Jesus Christ and seek to live circumspectly; clean, righteous lives, but the rest know nothing of the golden rule. But the curse of state church and the Roman [Catholic] Church over the years have placed a great hatred or at least contempt in the European Jewish heart for "Christianity." Shalom [Sholem] Asch the great writer (*The Apostle, Mary, The Nazarene*) said recently, it was only when he came to America that he realized what real Christianity was as he saw it in the lives of people who personally, rationally, freely accepted the "Way" of Christ.

This is a big job we have here (Baptists have the message in this hour, of the competency of the free individual soul before God) to help people realize that the message of the Bible is something that each person must take or reject for himself. That we as Baptists want only those who understand and who voluntarily of their own free will want to become [Christian] and Baptist.

A problem, which 99 percent of the people don't realize in America that are interested in the work here, is that of religious community. Both among the Arabs as well as the Jews is this blot on human freedom to accept or reject. It is impossible for anyone theoretically to be an atheist or unbeliever in religion. Every person born here in the Middle East is born with a religion. Here a baby is Jew, Christian, or Moslem. He has no choice in the matter. Thus Nazareth is filled with people (I suppose 60 percent of the population is "Christian") who are incensed when asked if they are Christian: "Of course, I have been one all my life." There is no such thing as civil marriage or divorce. Inheritance, etc., lies in the hands of priests or rabbis, thus they wield a power all out of proportion to their real influence. The rabbinate recently would not marry an American Marine in Tel Aviv to a Jewish girl. They said that either the boy would have to become a Jew or that the girl would have to become a Christian. Consequently they went to Cyprus near by and had a civil marriage in 15 minutes.

As I said, we have been treated fairly by everyone, government offices, stores, etc. I believe that the responsible people in the government are fair in their dealings with Christians. The courts deliver sound judgments. Most of the Jewish people except the more religious of the European background, or who have been persecuted I think, do not much care that there are people called "Missionaries" in Israel.

What the future shall be no one knows. It is difficult to renew visas.

There may come a time that the religious [political] block shall cause all of us to be expelled, but whether we remain or not, there are cracks in the wall that are widening day by day. The people have the land. No longer can the British be blamed for everything as they were in the mandate. Now Judaism, and all that it involves, has free sway. Yet it is not offering people and especially the young people anything really vital. As an English Rabbi recently said of Billy Graham, "He has something to offer the people, sincerely, with no doubt on his part, matters of life, of sin, of salvation, of life after death, of the requirements of God."

The religious Jews here seem to be unable to grip the loyalty of the youth, and many older people. In a profound editorial, the editor of the English language paper here recently said (Regarding whether the film, *The Robe*[2] should be shown in Israel [or not,] for fear of the effect that it might have on people… the Censorship committee was considering banning it.): "This is indeed a sad commentary upon the positive presentation of Judaism in Israel….Unless some modern approach to the spiritual famine is found there will be a drift away from Judaism into untried and dangerous paths which all the censorship and controls in the world may not stop."

The handwriting is on the wall. I don't believe that there is a possibility within Judaism to stop the trend that we are seeing now. What this signifies for the future I don't know. What this has to do with prophecy I am not sure. One thing I know: God is busy guiding these remnants from every land, but now [guiding them] in THE LAND [Israel], to the Messiah that they have rejected so long. The middle wall of partition is being broken down and the day is coming when there shall be no male or female, Jew or Greek, bond or free, but we shall all be one in the Lord Jesus Christ.[3]

…I feel in the light of the investment that Cascade is placing in this country that you will be interested in these things.[4] We here feel that this is the day for Baptists in this country; that the past thirty years of labor is beginning to bear fruit; that a momentous day is approaching for Israel. Pray with us that we might be and do all within our power for the lasting good of this nation.

Israel is beset within and without with enemies. The Communists seek to cause trouble. The surrounding nations are continually provoking Israel with bloodshed, and economic boycott, the people are new in many respects and not a welded, one-purpose group, there are ever the threats of the Arabs and pending wars; yet through it all a strong nation is being produced, a nation that is trying to move towards complete democracy. Thus what we stand for and what we are attempting we believe to be well worth all the costs.

We appreciate the weekly bulletins, and follow the work of Cascade with great interest. Dad reports continual progress. Again, the best of wishes.

Sincerely,

Paul Rowden, Jr.

Letter To:
Rev. & Mrs. James Smith
Box 115
Pine Lake, Ga., USA

Rowden
P.O. Box 154
Jerusalem, Israel

December 19, 1954

Dear Jim & Betty:

…Almost had a revival reading about…what you said about [being open to a call to] the Mission field if the Lord wills and wants. I don't know what to say. I am thrilled beyond words, and at the same time I am praying that the will of God will be plain to you two. I say this because I know how discouraging mission fields can be…

Yet on the other hand, these things bother one very little if God has called him because God provides, as he promised. Then there is the joy that comes as one sees the Kingdom of God being established in a country, as one sows the Word knowing it shall not return void, in being faithful in well doing, knowing that in due season we shall reap if we faint not, knowing that every effort in trying to carry out the will of God will not go unblessed or unnoticed.[5] It has been good in learning the lesson that—more important than anything else— is the doing of God's plan for our lives. More important than soul-winning, and I think much when I say this, more important than building a big and influential church, and on and on, for if we are in the will of God we shall be doing the thing that—back in eternity—God planned for our lives.

…What I am trying to say is that life faithfully lived on a field, a life that has patiently tried to do the will of God in season and out of season is a mighty influence on a field. In the states this is true also. My question is, when half the world is entirely without Christ and another quarter is nominal Christian, has the young minister in the states really honestly sought the will of God? Naturally I would not be human if I did not want you to come to this field. On the other hand it makes me all the more fearful that I may influence you over against the real will of God so that your life here would not be happy. You may be sure that we shall be much in prayer in the coming days…

Love,

Paul

The following letter was written by Paul Rowden to the Honorable Senator Walter F. George, U.S. Congressional Senator from Georgia. Walter F. George (1878–1957) was one of Georgia's longest-serving members of the U.S. Senate (1922–1957). He distinguished himself in terms of his diplomatic influence during World War II (1941–1945) and the early years of the cold war. He graduated from Mercer University and Mercer's School of Law in Macon, Georgia in 1901. The Mercer School of Law is named after him.[6]

Letter To:
The Honorable Senator Walter F. George
Senator from Georgia
Washington, D.C.
U.S.A.

Paul Rowden
P.O. Box 154
Jerusalem, Israel

December 20, 1954

Dear Sir:

I am writing to you because the permanent residence of my wife and I, as well as that of all our relatives, is in Georgia.

Yesterday was observed by the United Nations as "Human Rights" day. We know that behind the "Iron Curtain" there is no such thing as respect for individual human freedom. However, it is disconcerting to find nations of the "free" world, which receive much American aid, violating basic human rights.

The November COMMISSION, official organ of the Southern Baptist Foreign Mission Board, reports in the November issue that the Second Baptist Church, Madrid, Spain had been closed and sealed by the Spanish policy. Today, even though the American Embassy protested, the church is still closed. The Southern Baptist Foreign Mission Board owns this property. This is only one more incident against the Protestant community of Spain.

...In Western Germany, at a meeting addressed by a member of Dr. [Konrad] Adenauer's[7] Cabinet, there was a demonstration with shouts of: "Jewish swine," and calls for new gas chambers and concentration camps. People were insulted who did not stand when DEUTCHSLAND UBER ALLES was sung. (TIME, December 6, 1954, THE JERUSALEM POST, December 10, 1954.)

Living abroad for three years has helped me to see America as others see it. I have found that we advance far more in the eyes of foreign people whenever we take a stand on a moral issue concerning basic human rights of mankind, than we do simply by pouring out money and other aids. Let us not soon forget that Western Germany only a few years ago was responsible in a large measure for the death of six million innocent Jews. While we seek this Germany as an ally may we also take the leadership of the free world that rightly belongs to us, by frequently and loudly proclaiming the things we believe to be the inalienable rights of every man.

Very sincerely,

Paul Rowden

Aerogramme To:
Coles
1546 Richland Rd. SW
Atlanta, Ga. USA

Marjorie Rowden
Box 154
Jerusalem, Israel

Christmas Eve
10 'til 10 P.M.
December 1954

Dearest Mother & Daddy:

Well, I'm sitting here waiting so I might as well occupy my time. The gals are both asleep—all excited to death about Santa coming tonight. Paul has driven over to Mandelbaum Gate to [get] a young woman from Texas who was in Jordan and by some manner got permission to cross over here for our service tonight. Paul got word from the American Consulate today that she was coming across at 5 P.M. and [to] please meet her.

What a day we have had! For the past 2 weeks Bob [Lindsey] has been rushing against time to get a lounge room ready for our big Christmas conference. We finally finished it this afternoon at 4 and had a big tea in it at 5. It was packed full of young people from Tel Aviv and here—perhaps 50-60 (which is no less than a miracle.) After the tea this P.M. we had a service in the church at 6 'til 7. Then at 7:30 they all went to the Y.M.C.A. for a big carol singing. After that our crowd was going to sing carols in the streets. (I hope they don't get stoned). Right now we are waiting for them to get back to our new lounge room for coffee and doughnuts...Margaret and I stayed here instead of going to the Y.M.C.A. to sing carols since we had to be with the children some and get them to bed. Robin & Becky have their stockings hung up on our cement block fireplace. Looks real cozy down here with our Christmas tree and our fireplace.

We had lots of beautiful flowers (gladiolas and roses) sent to us by various people in Jerusalem, so the house is all pretty-fied. The florists here do a booming business all year long because these people use flowers so much. No good Jewish home would be without special flowers on Shabbat (Saturday) or any feast day.

Your check for $25 came today! On Christmas Eve. Thank you so much! You should have sent $5 and stopped. Anyway we will try to use it wisely...Must close. Merry Christmas! Won't be long until we will spend Christmas at home again.

Much love and kisses,

Marjorie and all

33

THE BROCHURE

Marjorie Rowden served as the publicity chairman for the Baptist Convention in Israel. In addition to writing articles for Baptist mission magazines, she designed, wrote and edited the "1954 Christmas Greetings Pictorial Report of the Baptist Convention in Israel." On the front, was a map of Israel with the geographic location of Baptist stations. Close to 6,000 copies were printed in Jerusalem and mailed to America for distribution to Baptist churches and seminaries. On the very back of the bulletin was a square box with no picture. Beside the empty box was the statement:

> Here is an empty space. It should have been a picture of a missionary couple, but we had no picture to put here. Whose picture will fill this empty space? Could it—should it—be yours?[1]

Rev. Jim Smith, pastor at a church in Pine Lake, Georgia, was busy getting ready for the Christmas season. His wife, Betty, spoke at numerous WMU meetings in the Atlanta area. She shared stories of the Baptist work in Israel from letters written by the Rowdens. Betty said, "Soon I began to see [us] in that picture frame. The Lord used that 'empty space' on the back page of the bulletin in His call to Jim and me![2] Jim said, "It took our attendance at the annual meeting of the Georgia Baptist Convention in 1954 to truly hear the Lord's direct call to the mission field. Dr. Baker James Cauthen, Executive Secretary of the Foreign Mission Board, was the featured speaker at one evening session. Dr. Cauthen said, "I feel that in this auditorium, there is a young couple who has already been called by the Lord to serve Him overseas! Without hesitation, Betty and I went forward during the hymn of Invitation."[3] By Christmas 1955, Jim and Betty Smith would be newly appointed members of the Baptist Convention in Israel.

CHRISTMAS GREETINGS

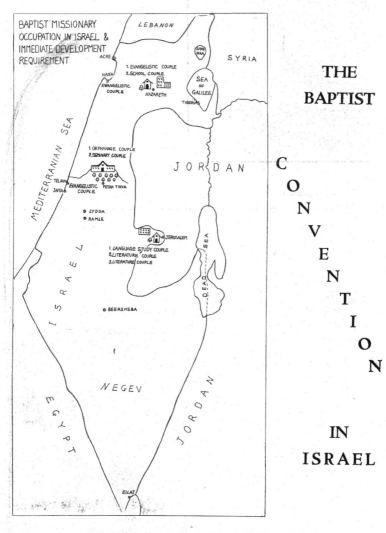

BAPTIST MISSIONARY
OCCUPATION IN ISRAEL &
IMMEDIATE DEVELOPMENT
REQUIREMENT

THE

BAPTIST

C
O
N
V
E
N
T
I
O
N

IN

ISRAEL

PICTORIAL REPORT, 1954

JERUSALEM STATION

Southern Baptists have had work in the "City of David" since 1923. Dr. Robt. L. Lindsay, pictured at right with his family, is Pastor of the Jerusalem Baptist Church and has served on the Israeli field for many years. Mrs. Lindsey is of missionary heritage. Her father and mother are still actively serving in Korea under the Presbyterian Church.

Translation and literature work form a large portion of this busy Jewish center. The three weekly services and Bible Study are conducted entirely in Hebrew. Private consultations and Scripture study with earnest Jewish men and women occupy much time each week.

The Jerusalem Station also sponsors a weekly Bible Study Class each Suday evening in the Tel Av.v area. Plans for a permanent Baptist work there are well underway.

The B. Elmo Scoggins, shown below as they left Israel for their first furlough, are now in the States. Mr. Scoggin served as head of the Jerusalem Station for two years, was mission treasurer, and spent time in language study.

For one year Mr. and Mrs Scoggins served as directors of our George W. Truett Children's Home in Nazareth. Their daughter, Scarlett, is shown with them.

248

Miss Eunice Fenderson, at left, is a veteran of thirty years in this part of the world. In addition to the three regular Baptist services in Jerusalem each week, conducted by the pastor, Miss Fenderson carries on work with several groups of women and young people.

A major part of Miss Fenderson's consecrated ministry has been among the hundreds of immigrants in Israel.

At right she is pictured with her weekly women's sewing class. Bible study follows and many of her women have professed faith in Christ. Her work, also, is done entirely in Hebrew.

The Jerusalem Baptist Church is small but attractive. It is located in one of the finest residential areas in new Jerusalem. Situated on a busy corner, it stands with open invitation to all. The main service of the week is held here each Friday evening at 6 o'clock.

249

NAZARETH STATION

Located on seven hills, Nazareth is a city of 20,000 Arabs. Evangelical Christianity is almost unknown, although "nominal Christianity" is professed by two-thirds of the population. One-third is Moslem. In this town where Jesus lived as a youth the Baptist Church stands as a real witness to Him.

Church activities are wide. Each year the three R.A. chapters go to camp on the Mediterranean coast. Vacation Bible School attracts hundreds of young people each summer.

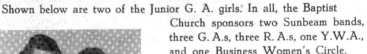

Shown below are two of the Junior G. A. girls. In all, the Baptist Church sponsors two Sunbeam bands, three G. A.s, three R. A.s, one Y.W.A., and one Business Women's Circle.

The Nazareth Baptist Church is at present experiencing a real revival. During the past two years over two hundred young people have made public professeions of faith. Baptism is their next step — and it is a difficult step in this part of the world.

250

With 360 students the Nazareth Baptist Grammar and High Schools offer scholarship plus Christ to the youth who attend each day.

The school maintains a high standard of discipline at all times. Chapel attendance is expected of each pupil. Bible classes are required subjects. Because of the many students who have found Christ as their Savior, the campus is unique as it radiates a Christ-like atmosphere.

The most important contribution that the school has made is that of a "feeder" into the Church. There we are training those who will perhaps be the leaders of our church tomorrow.

The Nazareth Station sponsors a Sunday service at the ancient village of Cana-of-Galilee.

Shown at right is a portion of the large group which is always in attendance.

The Dwight Baker family has been in Nazareth for over four years. Pastor Baker is shown here with his wife and four children. Mrs. Baker is active in all church organizations. Under their leadership the Nazareth Church has seen great vitality and great progress. Mr. Baker has also served as principal of the Nazareth Baptist School.

The Paul Rowdens, at right, have served in Nazareth for two years; first as directors of the Truett Orphanage, and until recently Mr. Rowden was principal of the Baptist School. Mrs. Rowden was active in all school and church activities.

At present they are in Hebrew language study in Jerusalem. Their two daughters are shown with them.

The Herman Pettys, on the field a little over a year, have been actively associated with both the evangelistic and educational work in Nazareth. In September Mr. Petty assumed the principalship of the Nazareth High School. Mrs. Petty serves in the same capacity in the Grammar School. They have two children.

PETAH TIKVA Station

As this bulletin goes to press the early stage of building a new home for the George W. Truett Orphanage is going on at Petah Tikva. Mr. and Mrs. Milton Murphey, shown at right with their two sons, are in charge of the Home and its nineteen little Arab orphans.

The Truett Home is over eight years old and has never had a permanent, nor adequate, home. Excitement is running high as both children and workers anticipate a new place to live and work and play on our Baptist Farm grounds.

The Truett Home children, shown below, are now housed in Nazareth and have been attending the Nazareth Baptist School and Church. Three of the older children recently made professions of faith. The new Home, located in the middle of the State, will mean that Baptists will have set up another mission point in Israel.

34

LETTERS

JANUARY–FEBRUARY 1955

The following letter was written when Marjorie Rowden was visiting in Jordan during the Christmas season.

By Air Mail
The Hashemite Kingdom of Jordan
Letter To:
Rev. & Mrs. James Smith
Baptist Church
Pine Lake, Georgia U.S.A.

Marjorie Rowden
American Colony Hotel
Jerusalem, Jordan

January 7, 1955

Dear Jim and Betty,

...Yesterday Margaret Lindsey, Dwight Baker and I crossed over into Jordan. We are allowed to stay here 3 days. It is a peculiar experience to pass through bob-wire fences, armed guards, and 2 government investigators, and a half block of "no-man's land" to get over here. We are only allowed to do this at Christmas and Easter...Margaret and I left Paul and Bob with our 7 kids—there is no telling what condition we will find them in when we go back.

We had a wonderful experience last night. We caught a taxi to Bethlehem about 9 P.M. and went to the Church of the Nativity for the Christmas

Eve Mass of the Greek Orthodox. Their Christmas is 13 days after ours. It was a real [pageant] with all the robed priests marching up from the shepherd's field to the church, with lots of little choir boys and candle bearers. Bethlehem is only 30 minutes ride from here. We went back again today and spent the day with some fine Presbyterian missionaries there that Margaret knew from childhood days in Korea.

There is an awful lot of prejudice against Israel over here—we have to be so careful to act like plain American tourists. Margaret and I have to be on our toes to keep from speaking Hebrew (and [it's] hard when you've been doing it everyday at home). I'm so thankful that in Israel I have had the privilege of working with both Jews and Arabs because we can see both sides and have learned to love each group. Even the missionaries over here are so prejudiced against Israel that it pops out in all their conversations.

We are all excited over the news from Dr. Sadler that you are definitely under consideration. But Paul and I will not let ourselves think about it too much—the disappointment would be more than we could take. But since this is my only chance to write an uncensored letter, I want to tell you that if you are appointed to be sure to have *teacher* or *housewife* put on your passport and all official papers. Don't dare let them write *missionary* on it. The Jews are just allergic to that word. There will be many other things you will need to know but Paul's daddy can explain money matters, etc. to you. Until then we'll just pray that the Lord's will—will be done in it all.

With love,

Marjorie Rowden.

Aerogramme To:
Coles
1546 Richland Rd. SW
Atlanta, Georgia USA

Marjorie Rowden
Box 154
Jerusalem, Israel

January 22, 1955

Dearest Folks:

...We had a good Sunday school and Bible study period this A.M. It was such a gorgeous day that we took all the kids and a picnic lunch and went out to [Ein Kerem] (about 5 miles from here) for lunch...The climate up here in these Judean hills is just wonderful...The kids had a big time romping up and down the hills this afternoon. We built a little fire and roasted wieners (canned ones) and made some coffee. Margaret and I spread big blankets out on the grass under some ancient olive trees and played with the three little kids while Bob [Lindsey] took Becky and their 3 older ones on a hike over the mountain...

I am knitting a sweater for Robin. I finished one for Becky and it looks real cute. It is white and she wears it to school real often with her green or red or navy corduroy pants. I don't know why I waste time knitting. The sweaters they make here in the country for sale in the stores are just beautiful now—much prettier than the ones at home. But in winter everyone knits and you sort of get the "bug" and want to be making something too. I should be studying Hebrew instead...the work on the Home at Petah Tikva is really going to town with all this nice weather. They are under contract to finish the entire building by June 30. Don't see how they will, but surely hope so...then they are scheduled to move the Home and all the kids in June. They have busy days ahead. We want so much to get the Home all moved and sort of set-up before the 4000 Baptist [tourists] start arriving out here this summer.

Paul is still plugging away at this Hebrew everyday. He is really making wonderful progress. We have both been advanced to "[*Kita Bet*]" (second class) in our *Ulpan* classes...

Of course Bob [Lindsey] has long since graduated. He could probably teach the *Ulpan* teachers a thing or two. He is, without exception, the world's oddest guy. Right now he is playing his piano so loud that everyone in Jerusalem is no doubt hearing him. On top of that he is singing in Italian at the top of his voice...the other night he came down here all excited over a new invention he is working on. It is a gadget that cuts the tops off of soft-boiled eggs so you can eat them in the shell with a small spoon (British style.) Now he is working on an idea of how to push a button in your car and send a tract out the side to a pedestrian on the road...Last week he and Margaret planned to have a small party with a few friends. Margaret wasn't feeling well so they decided not to have it. But Bob forgot to tell the people he had invited. His office looks like a junk pile. Nobody can ever find anything, but Bob. He knows exactly where to find everything. Yesterday he had a very important business appointment with two men but he forgot about it so they sat in his office and waited half the day while he was down the street in the printing press [office] trying to get out a new hymnal in Hebrew. Margaret was frantically pouring coffee down the men trying to keep them happy until Bob "woke up" and came home.

Well, I guess that is enough of that. Seems strange to think we have been in Jerusalem for 10 months already. We will have our annual mission meeting in April and it will be decided what we will do. There are so many possibilities. Please help us pray about it…

Much love,

Marjorie.

Aerogramme To:
Coles
1546 Richland Rd. SW
Atlanta, Georgia USA

Marjorie Rowden
Box 154
Jerusalem, Israel

Sunday, February 13, 1955

Dearest Folks:

The Murpheys and Pettys and Bakers gave a big Valentine Party for all the Nazareth people – [EMMS] hospital staff and other British and American workers there. They had about 30 people in all. We had a hilarious time. The British never had been to a Valentine party before. They had a turkey dinner and the whole party was banquet-style. At the close we put on a "mock wedding." I have never laughed so hard in all my life. We, who were in it, dressed up so funny that we looked like—I don't know what. I was the vocalist and sang, "I Love You Truly." You can imagine how lovely it was. One of the Quaker workers from Pennsylvania –a 6 foot 4 inches guy, [Don

Rosedale]—was the bride. Murph [Murphey] was the groom. Emma [Baker] was the bride's father and was a scream. The whole affair was so nice. Marty had the place decorated so nicely. June and Herman [Petty] sang and acted out "School Days."

We are having terrible troubles in Tel Aviv with our meetings there. I think I wrote you that we were building a small meeting hall on the roof of a 5-story building. Well, the rabbis and the orthodox people got worried and went to the municipality and they stopped the works. We have lots of money invested in it. The whole problem that has Bob [Lindsey] all in the air is whether we ought to fight it or try something else. He is all for fighting. He is even ready to take a pup tent up there and "squat" for months if necessary. He thinks if the papers back home got a hold of this religious intolerance, Israel would be in a real bad mess. They are the ones who are always yelling "Anti-Semitism" every time Jews are refused anything. He is ready to warn the government that there are 10 million Baptists in the States who won't like this at all since an awful lot of their tax money is coming to help this country.

The rest of us are trying to temper Bob down a little and sensibly decide what would be the best course of action. Frankly we don't know right now. If we fight it could mean we make a wonderful contribution to religious freedom in this country forever. Or it could mean we would all get kicked out of the country. We had a long prayer meeting over it this morning and we are trusting the Lord to lead—if Bob will just wait for Him to lead. Please help us pray about it. The press is full of wild tales about us every day in several newspapers…

Much love,

Marjorie.

Aerogramme To:
Coles
1546 Richland Rd SW
Atlanta, Ga. USA

Marjorie Rowden
Box 154

Jerusalem, Israel

Saturday, February 19, 1955

Dearest Folks:

Paul left us last Thursday and hasn't come back yet. Early Thursday A.M. he and Bob [Lindsey] left to go to the Farm to meet all the other men for their executive meeting. Neither of them came back that night like they were supposed to have. Bob stayed on business in Tel Aviv and Paul went home with Herman [Petty] to Nazareth. It seems that they discussed the possibility of Paul and [me] moving to Haifa after our language study period and so Paul struck right out to hunt for a place to live. We have thought for a long time that we would like living in Haifa for several reasons—one, it is only 45 minutes from Nazareth and we could always help out there whenever we were needed; secondly, we have no work in Haifa at present, thirdly, we could get a teacher and continue our language study while we made friends in Haifa and helped out in Nazareth. Another reason, it is the most beautiful spot in the country. It is built at the foot of and on the side and top of Mt. Carmel overlooking the Mediterranean…

Bob came back home yesterday for about an hour, just long enough to grab some more clothes and food and go back to Tel Aviv. He is fighting this building-stoppage business with tooth and nail. He had trouble down there last night and flew back up here to Jerusalem this morning to get our lawyer and flew right back again. Margaret is so worried about him. He doesn't even stay here long enough to explain what is going on. He is just fed up with being pushed around by these Orthodox people (who are behind the building being stopped). Don't confuse this with the Children's Home at Petah Tikva. So far it is doing fine. Work is progressing real fast. But this other business was our meeting place in Tel Aviv. We will keep you posted on the outcome…

Last night and this morning were our regular times for services. But both Bob and Paul were gone. Mr. [Roy] Creider,[1] [Kreider] a fine Mennonite fellow, working now with the Christian Missionary Alliance here, came over and held the services for us. I enjoyed [the services] being in English for a change, although we had them translated into Hebrew also. Usually our services are strictly Hebrew…

Well, I surely would like to know what the future holds for us in the next year or so. There are many possibilities…I just hope that wherever we go that we can stay put until furlough time—this moving is not much fun…

Much love,

Marjorie

Aerogramme To:
The B. H. Coles
1546 Richland Rd SW
Atlanta, Georgia USA

Marjorie Rowden
Box 154
Jerusalem, Israel

Friday P.M., February 25, 1955

Dearest Folks:

…We wrote you all about our trouble in Tel Aviv over the building we were putting up. Well, it still isn't settled. I was real interested in a little article that came out on the front page of the *Jerusalem Post* of last week. It said that President Eisenhower had made a speech before some large Jewish group and had said that he thought it was a good idea to have *MORE* synagogues in the United States. The reason was that people who worship are usually better neighbors and citizens. It was a very democratic thing to say. That same day the Baptist group in Tel Aviv got kicked illegally out of the few square feet of space they had managed to lease for meetings. This is a real democratic country, isn't it? I wish there was some way we could effectively let the…Baptists in the States, whose money goes in taxes to help support Israel, know about this.

Oh, last Sunday we had a fine day. Paul brought back one of the Nazareth cars so for a change we have two here in Jerusalem. After our Sunday morning prayer meeting Paul and I packed a lunch and put Becky and Robin in and drove off. We drove down to the farm and had the best time. We ate lunch by the river[2] and Paul went swimming—it was so warm. The new building is going up so fast. None of the Murpheys were there since they have responsibilities in Nazareth on Sunday. Becky and Robin made long fishing poles out of bamboo and played in the water. We have a beautiful picnic spot made there, with a rustic log fence rail around the banks of the river. The trees are thick and the shade is wonderful. We have picnic tables and chairs. It is about 100 yards back of the new building. Must close. Enjoy your letters.

Much love,

Marjorie

(L-R) Bob Lindsey and Paul Rowden review the destruction of a meeting room that had been under construction, but was torn down under the direction of the municipality. Tel Aviv, c. 1955.

35

BAPTISTS IN TEL AVIV

Tel Aviv merged with Jaffa in the fifties as the city grew down the Mediterranean Sea coast. Tel Aviv is an economic hub, known for its coastline high-rise apartments, hotel beach resorts, cafes, shops and secular lifestyle. Numerous embassies and consulate offices are located in the city including the U.S. Embassy.

Baptists first worked in Tel Aviv for a brief time in 1927. Rev. and Mrs. Washington (Washington) Watts were stationed primarily in Jerusalem, but spent a few months in Tel Aviv determining if a small group of Christians could begin meetings to study the Bible. Watts wrote:

> Early in the year came a request from a group of friends in Tel Aviv, the new Jewish city of 30,000 or more beside old Jaffa. Friends wanted us to help them build up a meeting. It was decided that Mrs. Watts and I should move to Tel Aviv. We thought that it would be impractical to do mission work openly in the city itself. Tel Aviv has been claimed as the only 100 percent Jewish city of the world. Nevertheless, we decided to try to at least live within the city limits. How glad we are that we did! Friends have been gained and neighbors are quite friendly despite the fact that we are now known to be missionaries. However within a few months the prospect of real work seemed to vanish. Some of the "friends" who had asked for help got mad because Gentiles came to do the helping. The others appeared too afraid of the situation to do anything worthwhile.[1]

The Watts were scheduled for furlough and returned to the United States in 1929. In the early 1930s, Rev. Roswell Owens traveled periodically to Tel Aviv for meetings but was working primarily in Haifa. According to Rev.

Owens, there were about eighteen to twenty Baptists, most of them having emigrated from Russia, living close to Tel Aviv. However, there was no Baptist worker who was appointed to work full time in this all-Jewish city.[2]

During the later part of 1937, Rev. and Mrs. H. Leo Eddleman moved to Tel Aviv to try to begin work. Rev. Eddleman said, "The people here are antagonistic to foreign influence, especially the preaching of the gospel. [However,] services for small groups have begun on Friday and Saturday evenings."[3] The Eddlemans were not able to stay and support the groups for long, for in 1938, Rev. Eddleman was asked to move to Nazareth to take over as pastor for the Nazareth Baptist Church allowing Rev. Louis Hanna and his wife to have a furlough.

Southern Baptists aided a small group of Baptists of Slavic origin in securing land close to Petah Tikva near Tel Aviv in 1949. This group, organized as an agricultural cooperative, had regular services on Saturday (the Sabbath) inviting friends and Messianic Jews to join them.[4]

After his return to Israel in 1954, Bob Lindsey began holding services in Tel Aviv every Sunday night. In early 1955, he decided to undertake a project for a Baptist Center in Tel Aviv. Space was purchased in the cultural and entertainment center of the city, just off Dizengoff Circle. The goal was to construct an enclosed apartment that could be used to house Bible classes and discussion groups already underway. Plans were drawn and an application was submitted to the municipality for a permit. An employee of the municipality gave verbal approval that an official permit would be forthcoming and that construction could commence. However, rather than wait for the issuance of the official permit, construction was begun. In a matter of weeks, Jewish religious extremists heard that a Christian center was being erected in the heart of Tel Aviv. The Orthodox Jewish extremist leaders were successful in having the permit and construction of the center blocked by the municipal authority. When the construction was three-fourths completed, a municipal stop-work order was nailed to the entrance, forbidding further work until a permit was secured. Bob Lindsey attempted to occupy the apartment but was prevented from his attempt to establish "squatter rights." A demolition crew, sent by the municipality, finally razed the construction to rubble.[5] One appeal after another went unheeded. It was decided to take the matter to court. After much delay, the Baptists lost the case. However support and assurance of solidarity came from many quarters. The secular press was indignant that religious fanaticism was allowed to express itself in such an undemocratic manner. Baptists were recognized as pioneers in the struggle for religious liberty in the fledgling democracy.[6]

Bob Lindsey wrote a report on the Israel Baptist Convention, looking back at 1955 and early 1956. "Despite the loss of the Tel Aviv property," he wrote, "other places of worship have been purchased and earlier plans for a Hebrew-literature production center are making progress. The difficulties in Tel Aviv point up a central problem for the young State of Israel. While neither the government nor the majority of citizens approve of such discrimination, the years of persecution known by many Israeli citizens and the present insecurity of the state hinder the advance of such ideals as separation of church and state and the complete integration of minority and majority groups. As in other lands, Baptists in Israel continue to labor and suffer for these ideals."[7]

36
LETTERS
MARCH–MAY 1955

The following letter references the celebration of "Purim." Purim cele-brates and commemorates the foiling of a plot to kill the Jews of ancient Persia. According to the book of Esther in the Bible, Haman, an advisor to King Ahasuerus, convinced the King that all the Jews should be killed because they did not keep the King's laws. Queen Esther, who was Jewish, interceded with the King and pleaded for mercy on behalf of the Jews. The King rescinded the order and hanged the wicked Haman. Purim is celebrated as a happy festival with a carnival atmosphere. Children at school or synagogue put on special parties and plays. Little girls usually like to dress up as Queen Esther.

Aerogramme To:
Coles
1546 Richland Rd. SW
Atlanta, Georgia USA

Marjorie Rowden
Box 154
Jerusalem, Israel

March 6, 1955 Sunday night

Dearest Folks:

…Nothing new on the Tel Aviv business except that the municipality sent a crew up last week and proceeded to tear down all that had been created. There was about $5500.00 invested in the materials. Don't know exactly what we will be able to do about it all. Very troubling situation.

It is Purim (Feast of Queen Esther) here in Israel now. The official day will be next Tuesday. There will be a large parade and city-wide carnival in Tel Aviv…All the children in Jerusalem are out of school for most of this coming week and already they are marching around the streets in all kinds of costumes and masks. Robin and Becky have masks and are pulling out all kinds of things to use as funny pretty costumes. Erice, the little girl next door, was just over here a few minutes ago. She has made herself an outfit from one of her mother's old evening dresses and had lipstick from ear to ear.

The Truett [Children's] Home is going up real nice and fast in [Petah Tikva]. It will be a large rambling ranch style building, all on the ground floor, except the Murphey's apartment, which will be on the second floor up over the boy's dormitories. There are 5 separate units to the floor plan, each connected to the other with long open but covered corridors, patio-like. It will be lovely when it is finished, even a swimming pool is being built (which some of us feel is superfluous, especially since the river is only 100 feet away), but it will all be nice for our various camp groups, R.A. retreats etc. We have made some pictures of the building in process and will send them to you when it is finished…

Must close,

Marjorie and all

Aerogramme To:
Coles
1546 Richland Rd. SW
Atlanta, Ga. USA

Marjorie Rowden
Box 154
Jerusalem, Israel
March 19, 1955

Dear Folks:

'Tis another Saturday evening. I just got the girls off to bed. Paul is upstairs doing something with Bob [Lindsey] in the office. Everyone is frantically trying to get their various reports ready for the annual mission meeting. We leave here tomorrow and will drive to Nazareth by way of Haifa and hope to get there in time for services in Nazareth tomorrow night. The mission meeting starts Monday A.M. I hope we can finish in two days, but I doubt it. We [had] lots of important issues to come up. Paul has been working on the treasurer's report all afternoon.[1] Bob is General Secretary so he has an enormous report to give. I am publicity chairman and I have been trying to get together all the articles and bulletins etc. that we have managed to get out this year. I think it helps the people back home to know more about our needs and thus they can pray and give and study about the work more intelligently.

There is a real interesting thing happening in Israel right now. You know, there is no such thing as civil marriage here. Everyone is married, divorced, buried, etc. by his or her religious community, either Jewish, Christian or Moslem. Well, that means that there can be no intermarrying because no group will marry outside its own people.[2]

The children celebrate Purim: (R-L) Barbara Lindsey, Becky Rowden, Margaret Lenore Lindsey, and friend, Erice (?), Jerusalem, 1955.

There is a boy here in Haifa, Jewish boy, who wants to marry a Christian girl. She does not want to become a Jew just to get married and he doesn't want to become a Christian. Therefore it is impossible for them to get married. They have begged for a civil marriage but [have] been refused. It is such a feudalistic kind of law. Well, anyway, the boy is staging a hunger strike now to bring notice to the situation. He said he is even willing to fast until death if it will bring about reformation of such an unjust law. It has really attracted attention too. The government is begging him to give in and break the fast, but he is determined. It is the 4th day or 5th day today. Yesterday Bob drove over and spent 2 hours with him. We are of course very interested in this. It is the core of the whole problem here—a hand full of Orthodox Jewish people are putting an unbalanced amount of pressure on the whole country, when 85 percent of the people are not religious at all. It will be interesting to see how it comes out.[3]

Also Eleanor Roosevelt is in the country right now. Last night she was at the King David Hotel, a few blocks from here. Bob went over to see her but wasn't very successful. She has always been very interested in Jewish problems and has been a real friend to Israel.[4] Well, I am tired and I have a heavy day ahead tomorrow. So I'll close.

Much love,

Marjorie and all

Aerogramme To:
Coles
1546 Richland Rd. SW
Atlanta, Georgia USA

Marjorie Rowden
Box 154
Jerusalem, Israel

March 24, 1955, Thursday

Dearest Folks:

Another annual mission meeting is over. We got home last night about 7:30, had mid-week service at 8. We were dead when we finally got to bed. We left here last Sunday noon and drove to the farm—building going up fast—drove on to Haifa where we looked real good [for a place to live], then drove on to Nazareth. Early Monday morning we started our meeting and it lasted all day, evening session, all day Tuesday, evening session (with wiener roast sandwiched in) and all of Wednesday A.M…

The Truett [Children's] Home report was very good for this year. Marty [Murphey] has done a fine job all this year, almost alone. Murph [Murphey] has been down on the farm most of the time trying to untangle all the problems there and supervise the building. We have about 5 employees on the farm who run tractors, plant [crops], etc. They have to be kept in line. The farm has just about been self-supporting this year, however, and shows great improvement. In a few years the Truett Home should be earning its own way there. Also the 6 little boys will get a good farmer's education. We also discussed starting a very small Bible college level there, letting students work half a day on the farm to pay tuition. It would be a very small project at first. This year we graduate our first high school class in Nazareth and some of those students might be interested in such a plan, also our 20-man faculty in Nazareth needs lots of extra teaching in such a school as this. The Rowdens will take over the Baker's work [when they go on furlough] until the Smiths, or someone, arrive and will live in Haifa probably. It will be nice to get back into all the activities of the church and school…

We are expecting some 3 or 4 thousand Baptists through here in June, July and August [traveling before or after the Baptist World Alliance in London]. As it is developing we are going to have a terribly busy time with them. Bob and Margaret will receive them here in Jerusalem, and then they will go on to the farm—[where the children and staff] will be just moving in and in a grand mess. Then they will come to Nazareth… I will be more fortunate in Nazareth than Margaret [Lindsey] will be [in Jerusalem] because I will have all the G.A. and YWA girls to help out…

…I have kept one decision that was made to tell you at the last, since you should keep the best for last. We discussed furloughs considerably, and decided that it is always best if we can go home one couple at a time, so that no two couples are gone home at once. We are due to go home in March of '57, but the Murpheys are due to go 6 months later. So the mission voted that the Rowdens should go home early rather than the Murpheys go home late. So—the Rowdens will leave Israel in July 1956, which is a year from this July. It was such a shock that we still haven't gotten used to the idea…This

Posing for the camera are (L-R back standing): Herman Petty, Martha (Marty) Murphey, Emma Baker, Eunice Fenderson, Dwight Baker; (L-R kneeling): Bob Lindsey, Marjorie Rowden, Margaret Lindsey, June Petty, Milton (Murph) Murphey. This picture was taken by Paul Rowden in Nazareth, 1955.

is subject to approval by the Board in Richmond, but we do not foresee any difficulties. Dr. [George] Sadler and Mrs. Sadler are to be out here in September and we will have another lengthy meeting with them, probably.

Much love,

Marjorie.

Aerogramme To:
Rev. & Mrs. James W. Smith
Box 115
Pine Lake, Georgia U.S.A.

Rowdens
Box 154

Jerusalem, Israel

April 1, 1955

Dear Betty & Jim:

…We decided to keep the lower half of the house that the Truett [Children's] Home is now in, for you…The Murpheys hope to have the children out and moved to the new place at Petah Tikva by June. Murph's mother arrived this past Tuesday to spend a few months with them…

The Bakers are running around like chickens with their heads cut off trying to tie up all the loose ends and get ready to fly home next month [for furlough]. I wish it could be possible for you all to see them when they get there. He is going to school at Princeton [University] next year.

We had a very fine meeting last week in Nazareth. There was a fine spirit and we settled lots of major problems. We are so grateful to the Lord for the harmony we have with one another and for the way we are able to work out our problems together. It is not true of all missions and it is not easy to do when you think that we all have different backgrounds and different ideas, working under strained and difficult situations. But we have all been so grateful to the Lord for the way we have been able to work together. The Lord has been so good. We could never thank Him enough.

Love,

Marjorie

Aerogramme To:
Coles
1546 Richland Rd SW
Atlanta, Georgia USA

Marjorie Rowden
Box 154
Jerusalem, Israel

April 3, 1955, Sunday Evening

Dearest Folks:

Thursday Paul and I went to Haifa and stayed all day…We had lots of decisions to make on the new apartment. I wish you all could see it—my, is it going to be nice. It is one of 4 apartments in one building (two apartments downstairs and two upstairs). We have one of the downstairs apartments. They have not been completely finished so we had to decide on wall colors, have pipes put in for our heating stoves (they thought we were crazy!—they just don't use [heating stoves] here), have proper pipes put in for the boiler and washing machine, etc., have electric plugs put in the right places. We have two large porches; one extends the length of the living room and one bedroom and is on the mountain sloping side, overlooking the Mediterranean Sea. We are right on top of the mountain overlooking the [sea]. You just can't imagine how lovely a spot it is.

We are two blocks from the new shopping district on Mt. Carmel. You'd never know you were outside of the States if it wasn't for the Hebrew signs and the language you hear all around you. The house is located at the end of a dead-end street and there is almost no traffic problem with the children. All the homes around us are new and the people are very nice looking; we don't know any of them yet, of course. There is a lovely little pine forest park half a block up the street with benches and picnic tables. There is a nice private kindergarten for 4 and 5 year olds nearby. There is also a very good Hebrew public school there we are thinking of sending Becky to next year. Since we will be coming home in July of next year she will be able to go to 3rd grade in the States. She has already finished 2nd grade work with me in the Calvert Course and also at Miss Clark's school. So it won't hurt her to go to Hebrew school next year even if she doesn't learn anything much because of the language problem. I believe, however, that after we spend the summer months in Haifa with just Hebrew-speaking children around that she will know it well enough to get along in school next year. She can speak it right well and understands real well, but most of this year she has been with English speaking children.

…This week "*Pessach*" (Passover Feast) starts. We are real thrilled over being invited into a real Jewish home [in Jerusalem] to eat Passover supper this coming Wednesday night. Margarlit (Bob [Lindsey's] secretary) is from a very well-to-do family here. They have invited the Lindseys and us for Passover…The people across the street from us invited us all to their house and when they found out we were already going out they asked if our 4 older children could come. I think Becky will be old enough to appreciate it. She knows the [Biblical] story [in Exodus] of the Flight from Egypt and the Passover Angel very well.

Much love,

Marjorie

Aerogramme To:
Coles
1546 Richland Rd SW
Atlanta, Ga. USA

Marjorie Rowden
Box 154
Jerusalem, Israel

April 8, 1955

Dearest Folks:

…We had the thrilling experience of attending our first Passover Seder (the Passover ceremony and meal). The family that invited us has a lovely home and everything was really lovely. We sat down to the table at 7:45 and did not get up until about 11:30. The father conducted the ceremony with all of us reading with him in unison from the Passover books (all in Hebrew; most of it was scripture passages or sayings of Rabbis down through the ages…The father had a large plate in front of him with various foods on it representing various things. He had a big bone representing the Passover Lamb, bitter herbs to represent the bitterness of slavery, etc. We all partook of bites of these things. Then we had the actual Passover meal that was very elaborate and delicious. The dishes and silver were beautiful and only used this one time each year. We had about 5 courses and each one was wonderful. Then the last part of the ceremony was carried out after the meal and consisted of more Scripture passages, questions and answers about the journey out of Egypt and singing. Some of the Passover songs are real cute and especially liked by the children in the family.

Becky and [the Lindsey girls], Barbara and Margaret, went across the street and had Passover with a very nice family. The father even explained much of the ceremony to them in English. They have a precious little girl about 10 years old and a baby boy about 2. The Jews are very kind and very careful to see that no one is left out of having Passover supper even if they are Gentiles…

This Sunday will be Easter. We are all uniting for a sunrise service over at the Scotch Church, right next to the Old City walls. Bob [Lindsey] is to lead the singing. I hope it will be a nice morning. We will watch the sun rise over the Mount of Olives from this side. Dwight [Baker] and Murph [Murphey] and his mother will be having sunrise service only a few yards away at the Garden Tomb, but they will be in Jordan. Sunday afternoon we plan to take all our kids (plus the little girl across the street and the little boy in the family where we ate Seder) to a nice grassy place near here and have a big Easter egg hunt. They are getting excited…

Much love,

Marjorie and all

Letter from:
Paul & Marjorie Rowden
Baptist Convention in Israel
Jerusalem, Israel

April 15, 1955

Dear Friends:

One year ago this month we left Nazareth and moved to Jerusalem for our year of Hebrew language study. I wish I could say that now "we know it all," but that wouldn't be true in the least. But we have put in many, many hours, days, weeks and months of study this past year and we feel that we have a good Hebrew foundation upon which to build. Paul has been spending the mornings with a private Hebrew tutor and the afternoons in an *Ulpan*, which is a special class for Hebrew language students. He has conducted the Bible study three times lately in Hebrew, in the absence of the regular speaker, and managed real well. He was rather comical throwing in an English word here and there when he didn't have a Hebrew one at that particular point in his thinking. Once we were all amused when he mustered up courage in the middle of a public prayer to switch from English into Hebrew. It was a half and half prayer, but I'm sure the Lord understood!

This is Passover Week in Israel. There has been no bread on the market for 6 days and everyone is getting a little tired of eating "*matza*," plain unleavened, unsalted crackers (See Exodus 12:14). We were fortunate to get a few loaves of Arab bread brought up to us from Nazareth, but we didn't keep it long when our Jewish neighbors found out we had some. One Jewish friend walked three blocks in very bad weather to get a loaf from us. The result now is that we are sitting here eating "*matza*" and all our Jewish neighbors are eating the [Arab] bread. But day after tomorrow everything will be back to normal again…

Very sincerely,

Marjorie and Paul Rowden

Aerogramme To:
Coles
1546 Richland Rd SW
Atlanta, Georgia USA

Marjorie Rowden
Box 154
Jerusalem, Israel

April 16, 1955

Dearest Folks:

[We]…took two cars and drove down to Sodom on the Dead Sea. It is a long hot tiring trip but I'm glad we went. We left here at 6:30 A.M and got to the [Dead] Sea at 11:30. We stayed about an hour and waded in that bitter, salty water, then drove back to Beersheba and ate lunch at 3:15. Then we drove on back to Jerusalem just in time to get changed for our regular 6 P.M. Friday night service. We all looked like wrecks. The dust was 3 feet thick on us from traveling down in the Negev all day. My hair was so dusty and sticky I couldn't comb it. Margaret Lindsey looked so funny because her hair is very black and it turned completely gray on the trip. We are actually only one hour's drive from the Dead Sea at Jericho, but Jericho is in Jordan. So the nearest we can get to the Dead Sea and still be in Israel is at Sodom. There is now a big salt factory and mineral industry going on there. It is very very hot—I don't see how the men work down there. I wish you could see the scenery around that area—not a living thing for miles and miles and the mountain formation is the most unique I've ever seen. In an odd sort of way it is absolutely beautiful…

…Sunday night Dwight [Baker] is having a big baptism service in the church and we want to be there for that…Dwight has done a grand job in these 5 years. He and Emma have both worked hard and faithfully…We are planning to have a farewell supper party at Lynn and Helen's home in [Herzliya] (half way between Nazareth and Jerusalem) for them before they go. Lynn and Helen [Davis] have practically become part of us since they have been working in the country…

The Jerusalem water supply…busted, or something, yesterday. The Lindseys had no water when we came home from Sodom last evening. We still have some, but all the neighbors have none and have been over borrowing. I think a pipe might be broken in the main line leading up to Jerusalem.

Picured above is the road to Sodom in the Negev Desert with the Dead Sea in background, 1955.

Anyway they will get it fixed before too long, I hope. The water situation is not going to be good all summer due to the drought. This has been practically a waterless winter...

Much love,

Marjorie and all

Rev. & Mrs. James Smith
Box 115
Pine Lake, Georgia USA

Rowdens
Box 154
Jerusalem, Israel

April 23, 1955

Dearest Betty and Jim:

Paul Rowden replaces a flat tire in Negev Desert. From (L-R) Margaret Lenore Lindsey, Becky Rowden and Barbara Lindsey look on from the side of the road.

...One day we took two cars and drove down to Sodom to the Dead Sea. It took us 6 hours each way and we were half dead at the end of the day, but it was worth it...Bob Lindsey drove the leading car and got us all on the wrong road and we drove for hours in a dust storm. He is the funniest character you will ever have the privilege of knowing, also the best natured. We saw hundreds of wild camels, that is, when we wiped the sand out of our eyes...Then to top it all, Paul had a flat tire and we spent an hour in the boiling sun and dust changing it. We took along a lunch but we couldn't eat because it was full of sand too. We took 5 of the older children along and they went wading in the Dead Sea. We were thankful we hadn't taken the little ones.

With love,

Marjorie

In a letter of April 13, 1955, Marjorie Rowden wrote of a tourist company in Israel that paid for Bob Lindsey to fly to the United States. The purpose of the trip was to allow Dr. Lindsey the opportunity to select Baptist ministerial students to travel back to Israel with him, to visit the Biblical sites in Israel and to learn where Baptists had ongoing programs. The ministerial students were to coordinate with Israeli tour guides in order to prepare for thousands of Baptist tourists expected to travel through Israel in the summer of 1955 before or after the Baptist World Alliance in London.

Aerogramme To:
Coles
1546 Richland Rd SW
Atlanta, Georgia USA

Marjorie Rowden
Box 154
Jerusalem, Israel

May 7, 1955
Saturday

Dearest Folks:

…Paul had the service last night in the church with someone translating for him. It was nice to hear a sermon in English for a change, but I'm sure he could have done it in Hebrew if he had tried real hard. Then this A.M we had the Shabbat A.M. Bible study class and [Paul] did the whole thing in Hebrew. I was real proud of him. We sure do miss Bob [Lindsey] around here, but this is powerful good experience for Paul's Hebrew.

Murph [Murphey] is down in the dumps about the building [at the farm]. They promised to finish by June first, but it will be at least two more months he thinks before it will be sufficiently done to move in. He is getting tired of living in a hut 5 days a week away from his work in Nazareth and his family, and watching all building procedure like a hawk to be sure it gets done properly. Also he is having trouble with some of the hired help on the farm.

Paul and I have some friends, two couples, whom we met in the *Ulpan*. They come over and visit and we go and visit real often. They are lots of fun. Both of the women are Americans who have come here and married. One is from Seattle married here to a man from Baghdad, and the other is from Brooklyn and married to an Israeli-born man. All of them are Jewish. We have the best time. The woman from Brooklyn is a big talker and a scream. She thinks she is a great artist and Paul has the most fun making fun of her art…

We are graduating our first [secondary] school [twelfth grade] class this June. We are so thrilled over it… [It] is a real milestone in Baptist History out here…

Did we tell you that Roy Sewell is sending Paul a nice new…suit by his Pastor who will come here after the Baptist World Alliance? He wrote and asked him what size and color he liked.[5]

Much love,

Marjorie and all

37

THE FIRST NAZARETH BAPTIST
SECONDARY SCHOOL GRADUATION

In June of 1955 the first twelfth grade class graduated from the Nazareth Baptist School. It was a historic event in the history of the school. Marjorie wrote, "In a sea of pastel, nylon and black bow ties…young people in Nazareth marched down the isle of the Baptist Church to become the very first graduating class for the Nazareth Baptist [Secondary] School. Smiling under their white cardboard mortarboards they represented not only an achievement in their own lives, but also a landmark in Baptist history in the Near East."[1]

> The …graduates, having come to the school in the days of its infancy, had literally grown up with the institution. Each year as they grew older a new class was added to take care of their needs. Along with their knowledge of history, algebra and science, these young people left school with a thorough understanding of the simple truths found in God's Word… In Nazareth the Baptist Church and the school are closely related. Almost any afternoon in the week you will probably find a church group meeting in one of the classrooms. A map or a poster will be on the wall and a mission program, taken straight from *Tell* or *Ambassador Life* will be in progress. Many times these programs must be painstakingly translated into Arabic by the leader or by an older student, but the message goes forth fresh and stirring to their hearts. Each school day begins with a thirty-minute chapel service. All 360 students attend whether they are Christian, Moslem or Jew. In addition, every student must take a Bible course. When Sunday

comes the students are free to attend any church they wish. But it is a real thrill to see them come to the same campus where they have been all week, to hear more about Christ and His love for them."[2]

As Herman Petty presented certificates to the…graduates, he expressed the feelings for all Baptists as he wished each graduate a full and happy life—a life in which the principles of Christ might be the guiding light of their future.[3]

Picured above is the twelfth grade class of the Nazareth Baptist School, Nazareth c. 1955.

38

Letters

JUNE 1955

Aerogramme To:
Coles
1546 Richland Rd SW
Atlanta, GA USA

Marjorie Rowden
Box 6096
Haifa, Israel

Saturday, June 11, 1955

Dearest Folks:

Well, what do 'ya know? Here we are in Haifa at last. Wednesday morning at 7:30 the truck came and about 11 A.M. we left Jerusalem…We are the only ones in the building right now, but tomorrow the couple upstairs over us move in…This morning another neighbor in a house next door talked to me a long time over our balconies. Both of us were very apparently struggling with our Hebrew. After half an hour of struggling we laughed to find out she was from England and I, from America, and English was sure used from then on.

This morning we had breakfast out on our porch overlooking the Mediterranean [Sea]. Boy, is this the life! It is the Sabbath so everything was quiet and lazy-like up and down the street. In Jerusalem the Orthodox Jews kept Sabbath in the same manner as the Pharisees of old—watching everyone else to see if they were observing all the rules and regulations. Here in Haifa our neighbors sleep late, do odd things around the house and seem to be really making it a day of rest…

Last night, we drove over to Nazareth to the Senior Class banquet. It was our first Senior class and they all looked so nice around the table—21 in all. Marty and June worked hard on the banquet and also Mrs. Murphey Senior, who is also here. She wrote the class poem and the class song for them. We all like her very much… We will all go back in the morning for Sunday School and church. Paul preaches tomorrow. It is so good to be back in this neck of the woods where we can go to a real service on Sundays. The people in Nazareth all miss the Bakers awful much. They worked mighty hard and faithfully for these past 5 years.[1]

…Lynn and Helen [Davis] are in Beirut (they can go anywhere since they are [U.S.] Consulate people) to meet the pastor of their church back home. They will travel around through Lebanon and Jordan and come back into Israel the last of the week. Their pastor will bring our baccalaureate sermon in Nazareth next Sunday…Was thrilled to hear that Dwight and Emma [Baker] will be in Atlanta…Hope you get to have a nice long chat with them…

Well, I must close. Somewhere in the middle of this letter I stopped to cook dinner. After dinner we drove down to the beach and all went swimming. We came back, ate supper, put the kids to bed. It is now 10 P.M. and we are sleepy. Must get up at 5 or 5:30 in order to get everything done here before driving to Nazareth for S.S. at 9:30.

Much love,

Marjorie

The following letter is Paul Rowden's response to the news that the Southern Baptist Foreign Mission Board had appointed friends Jim and Betty Smith to the Baptist Convention in Israel.

Aerogramme To:
Rev. & Mrs. James W. Smith
Box 115
Pine Lake, Georgia U.S.A.

Paul Rowden
Box 6096

Mt. Carmel
Haifa, Israel

June 20, 1955

Dear Jim & Betty:

Still have to pinch myself and still can't believe our good fortune in your coming [to Israel]. We have been in Nazareth since Thursday as there is much work to do. In fact so much that we could use five couples and not take advantage of all the opportunities.

All this summer we shall be largely there for the Bible schools in Nazareth and Cana, camps, church services, etc. Friday night the eighth class received their diploma and tonight the 12th theirs...

I am answering your letter, which I found in the P.O. when I returned, the first thing before I do anything else so please excuse the mistakes. I have been trying to get the budget report ready for Dr. Sadler. A book practically has to be written for that. It was good to have some time to study for a year but it is also good to get back into the work—and there is plenty. The first year you'll be doing Dwight [Baker's] work as pastor and teaching some in the school and then we'll see as to the way the Lord leads.

Let me stop here in the middle to say again that you have no idea how much it means to know of your coming...I would bring enough wearing apparel for several years...winter suits, summer things, overcoat, raincoat, sweaters, flannel pajamas, cotton pajamas, etc. Clothing is good, but all of us are buying here as we wear out our stuff. Don't worry about customs. We'll settle that here until such a time that you can pay.

...I am glad I brought such things as a few bottles of iodine, band aids, sal hepatica (if you like this), bring some good vitamins, and vitamin drops for the baby. The public health department in Atlanta will give you typhoid shots and the vaccination. They will furnish you with the international certificate for vaccination and inoculation...You might want your baby doctor to do it for [your daughter] Jackie. Bring a bottle, better [bring] three or four large size of aspirin (you'll probably take all of them before you leave!) Bring a typewriter, clock, books, lamps, desk, living room equipment, bedroom, kitchen—no cabinets, however.

...Well, I am sure the minute I put this in the box, I'll think of something. Be assured of our concern and know how you feel—only more so.

We didn't know a soul out here. You'll really like the Herman Pettys in charge of the school. Fire your letters away.

Christian love,

Paul.
P.S. Bring a camera and plenty of film.

39

BAPTIST TOURISTS VISIT
THE MIDDLE EAST 1955

The Baptist World Alliance, a worldwide Congress of Baptist churches and organizations, met in London the summer of 1955. The Southern Baptist Convention was a member of the alliance at that time.[1] Some attendees planned to travel in large groups to the Middle East before or after the conference. Many a tourist had been denied entry to Arab countries because they had made the mistake of traveling to Israel first. If Israel stamped the passport of a visiting tourist, that tourist would not be allowed entry into any of the surrounding Arab countries. Fearing that most Americans were not aware of this, the mission had asked Dr. George Sadler of the FMB to publish information in the Baptist newspapers of each state so tourists would know to visit the Arab countries first, and then cross over into Israel.

Most of the Israeli tour guides were not familiar with the New Testament biblical sites that interested Baptists or, for that matter, where Baptists had churches and programs. The *Christian Century* reported that the government tourist office in Israel arranged a meeting of nearly half of their registered guides so that Bob Lindsey could address the special needs and interests of the Baptist visitors—"thus rendering a valuable service to all Christian tourists."[2]

Bob cautioned the Israeli tour guides that Baptist tourists would not be interested in seeing too many Roman Catholic churches, even though the churches protected many biblical sites. He told them that Baptists would more likely want to see the places where Jesus preached, healed and ministered to the needy.[3] Marjorie Rowden prepared a bulletin about Baptist work as handouts for the tourists. The handout said:

> Express your faith while in Israel just as you do at home.
> Your very presence can help change a great many false con-

ceptions about the Gospel. Encourage your group to pray and worship. Join in singing anywhere you wish. The people of Israel are friendly and will feel complimented by your interest in their land and your expressions of spiritual devotion. Do not hesitate to answer any questions put to you about Baptists. People in this land are often curious about evangelistic denominations. They read of Billy Graham and his mass meetings and they find it hard to understand such religious movements. This is your mission field as well as ours. We need your help and your advice. May God bless you as you travel homeward to your own place of personal service for our Lord.

The tour for Baptists in Israel included West Jerusalem and the Jerusalem Baptist Church, the new Baptist Center in Petah Tikva, the Nazareth Baptist Church and school, the Sea of Galilee and biblical sites around the Galilee area. Also tourists were informed that a hall had been purchased in Tel Aviv, where a literature center was to be opened and that work was being established in Haifa.[4]

Alta Lee Lovegren, Baptist mission worker in Ajloun, Jordan, also wrote an article providing pointers for the Baptist travelers and described what tourists could expect to see in Lebanon and Jordan. She suggested that tourists should bring sunglasses for sensitive eyes and good walking shoes. They should notify missionaries of the date of arrival and make all reservations for lodging and travel beforehand. The first stop, she recommended, was Lebanon. "The oldest Southern Baptist work in Lebanon is located in the cosmopolitan city of Beirut where there is a Baptist church," she wrote. "There is also work in smaller communities that are a little more difficult to reach."[5] She pointed out that Baptists did not have any work in Syria and the Baptist work in Jordan was only three years old. It centered on the village of Ajloun where there was a Baptist Hospital, a girl's school and a small church. Alta Lee warned tourists that there were no hotels in Ajloun, but a number of guests could be accommodated at the Baptist Mission if advance notice was given.[6] Ajloun served as the governmental seat for the area. Alta Lee Lovegren wrote:

> The mission hospital is known favorably all over north Jordan. The Arab people are gracious and very appreciative of anything that one tries to do for them. As you stand atop

> the hill in the town of Ajloun you see the minaret of the
> Moslem mosque and the cross-topped spire of the Catholic
> Church. But to find the Baptist-meeting place you have to
> enter town, go down the main street, turn off on a side
> street and walk down to a small room that is rented by the
> Baptist Mission. The room is made of mud, straw and
> dung. It contains a very old organ, a small pulpit stand and
> a few unpainted benches. But there is standing room only
> [for services].[7]

Alta Lee cautioned tourists: "Many will want to visit Israel also. You will re-member that the Arabs and the Jews do not consider that a permanent settle-ment has been made to end their last war, though a truce was signed. There are no communications between Israel and the Arab world so you will have to se-cure information concerning Israel elsewhere. As you travel here and there, you will not want to forget that you represent America and Christ to the people of these lands. Most non-Moslems expect that Americans are Christians. You will have the opportunity as a tourist to represent your Lord and you do not want to fail in that. Welcome to the Middle East."[8]

As Baptist tourists began arriving in Israel, so did the press. Baptists were viewed as "one of the most rigorous missions in Israel."[9] An article in *The Chris-tian Century* reported that 1,300 Baptist tourists, most of whom were predom-inantly Southern Baptist, had passed through Jerusalem and more were expected.[10] One group of tourists filled the little Baptist church in Jerusalem and spontaneously burst into singing the Doxology: "Praise God from whom all Blessings flow…" "Never before have the rafters of the church shaken with such enthusiastic Baptist singing," they said.[11] "There is so much Catholic, Moslem and Jewish influence in the Holy Land that it is 'like an oasis in a desert' to find a simply-constructed little Baptist church where one can lift up his voice to God in prayer and song."[12]

More than one tour group learned about Jewish kosher dietary laws. On one occasion meat was on the luncheon menu but when some of the tourists asked for coffee, they were served—but without cream. It was explained by the Jewish staff that no dairy product could be served in the same room where meat had been served until one hour had elapsed. However, powdered milk solved the problem without offense to anyone. Breakfast at a hotel in Tiberias on the Sea of Galilee caught some Southern Baptists by surprise. It consisted of hard-boiled eggs, kippered herring, cucumbers, tomatoes, olives, block cheese, cream cheese, marmalade, half a grapefruit, butter, bread and a hot drink.[13]

40

LETTERS

JULY 1955

Aerogramme To:
Coles
1546 Richland Rd SW
Atlanta, Ga. USA

Marjorie Rowden
Box 6096
Haifa, Israel

Monday, July 11, 1955

Dearest Folks:

Well, at long last we are spending a few days in our apartment in Haifa. Last week we had Vacation Bible School [in Nazareth] all week and it was a wonderful success! We had 298 children on average each day, with 350 the last day. We held it each day from 3 to 6 in the afternoon and it was much better than rushing around to get there in the mornings. Almost everyday without fail we had one, two, three busloads of [Baptist] tourists drop in during Bible school. They made pictures and got some wonderful firsthand mission information. Usually Paul took them into the church and talked to them for about 10 minutes about our work in general, then they walked around taking pictures and talking with us all.

Thursday Roland Q. Leavell's[1] tour arrived with two huge buses loaded— about 64 people on that tour. It was just wonderful to be with them: Dr. and Mrs. J. D. Grey (First Baptist Church of New Orleans), Dr. and Mrs. Jimmy

Middleton, etc. and also the new president of the Southern Baptist Convention, Dr. C. C. Warren and his wife. They took pictures and talked to us all. Mrs. Leavell was so sweet to me when I was at New Orleans [at the seminary] and always seemed so interested in us...

Dr. Leavell talked to Paul a long time about the possibility of Billy Graham coming out here next year. He said Billy Graham talked to him a long time...and asked him to feel out the situation. If he comes, Dr. Leavell will come with him.[2] They stayed with us for about an hour and then the buses took them to Haifa to their hotel for the night. They invited us to have dinner with them, but we had our regular service Thursday night in Nazareth and couldn't leave until it was over. So about 9:30...June and Herman [Petty] and Paul and I drove over here to Haifa. We had a long chat with all the tour [members] again and then we piled Dr. and Mrs. Leavell and Dr. and Mrs. Middleton into our car (we four were already in, so you can imagine how crowded we were) and drove them up here to the top of Mt. Carmel to our apartment for coffee and cake. We stopped just at the top and got out to look at the city from the top. It is one of the most beautiful sights you ever saw. The city looks like a great crescent of lights all around Haifa harbor and all up the mountainside. They were so thrilled with the view. As we all stood there looking down over the city everyone commented on the huge task before us as we think we two are the only Baptists in this whole city, with...very few believers of any kind. Then we drove on to our apartment and they visited with us about an hour. Dr. Leavell prayed the sweetest prayer of dedication of our new home and of us to the service here. It was worth a million dollars to us. Then we drove them back to their hotel and then we four drove all the way back to Nazareth and to our children.

It was about one [a.m.] when we got home and then a policeman stopped us in the middle of Nazareth and asked us to take a poor old Arab woman up to the hospital who had taken poison and was very ill. Well, sir, we really had a night. We got to sleep around 2...

Then the next day was Friday and the last day of Bible School. We all felt it was the best one we had ever had. About 36 local workers helped. Also about 9 [people] went out to Cana each morning and held a school for them, with an average of 100 children each morning. Just as we finished Bible school...Dick Hall's[3] busload drove up. Mrs. [W. O.] DuVall[4] came jumping off the bus along with the Monroe Swillys,[5] the Courts Redfords,[6] and the Searcy Garrisons,[7] etc. We had a gay old time saying all the same things over and over again and showing them all around the church and school.

...Paul drove over to the hotel [in Haifa] and picked up Dr. and Mrs.

[Dick] Hall…, Dr. and Mrs. Courts Redford, and Dr. Searcy Garrison. They came over for about 2 hours and ate grapes and cookies and we had a wonderful evening together. Dr. Hall led us in prayer before they left. Mrs. Hall left her shawl here; I don't know what to do with it. Guess I'll keep it until I come [to Atlanta] next year.

Much love,

Marjorie

Letter from: Rowdens
Haifa, Israel

To: Friends at Cascade (Baptist Church)
Atlanta, Georgia

July 13, 1955

Dear Friends at Cascade:

…Six weeks ago we left Jerusalem and our year of Hebrew language study behind us and moved to Haifa, Israel's chief port city. Haifa is the most beautiful city in Israel – built right on the edge of the blue Mediterranean Sea and all up the sides and top of Mt. Carmel. You will remember that it was on Mt. Carmel that Elijah called down fire from Heaven to defeat the priests of Baal many, many years ago. We have bought an apartment right on top of the mountain. Stretched out below us are thousands and thousands of new apartment buildings, each occupied by Jewish people from all over the world. Practically none of them know, or even want to know, our Savior. You can well imagine the helplessness of our situation as we realize how incapable we are of our task. But we continually rely on the Scripture verse, "nothing is impossible with God," and trust Him to lead the way. There are 200,000 people in Haifa. We are the only two Baptists! There are a few other Christian groups here, but the surface has only been scratched.

This is an extra busy summer in an extra special way. Touring Israel in huge modern buses these days are thousands of Baptists. Almost every day we have the pleasure of showing our work to 50 or 60 Baptists who are on their way to the Baptist World Alliance in London. What a thrill it has been to see so many of our friends and former associates…Dr. Leavell's tour [group], consisting of over 60 persons, was personally introduced to Israel's Prime Minister, Moshe Sharett. I believe both were impressed with each other.

We have one more year in Israel before our furlough time arrives. We are praying that this year might be more blessed of the Lord than any previous year. This, our first year in Haifa, struggling to use the Hebrew language that we studied all last year, will not be an easy year. Our main task will be to establish ourselves and our children and to try to become a part of our community. We shall be making new friends and will be seeking to build a Christian atmosphere about us and our home that will stand out as something different and something desirable to the Jewish people around us. We hope to start a small Bible study class in the near future. We hope you will be praying for us…

Very Sincerely,

Marjorie and Paul Rowden

41

BAPTISTS IN HAIFA

In the summer of 1955, the Rowdens moved to Haifa, a city built on the slopes of the Carmel Mountains overlooking the curved bay and Haifa port on the Mediterranean Sea. About twenty miles east-southeast is Nazareth; Acre is 13 miles to the north and Tel Aviv, 60 miles to the south. Baptists had a small presence in Haifa in the 1930s. In the book, *Palestine Tapestries*, published in 1936, Mrs. J. Wash Watts wrote, "The first [Baptist] missionaries who established the Near East Mission recognized Haifa as having importance in Galilee as the center of work, but they could not know in the 1920s how rapidly it would grow. The laying of the oil pipeline from Iraq, and the building of a great beautiful harbor under Mt. Carmel drew thousands of Jews and Arabs to the city. Suddenly Haifa became a fast growing and flourishing port city."[1]

In 1929, Roswell Owens and his wife, Doreen Hosford Owens, were appointed for service in Palestine and spent their first two years in Jerusalem. In 1931, they moved to Nazareth.[2] They found that some members of the Nazareth Baptist Church were leaving Nazareth and moving to Haifa, due to persecution by those opposed to the new Protestant group. Owens wrote, "When it was heard that we were planning to hold services [in Haifa], several homes were opened to us where we were invited to preach the gospel. The need is tremendous and the opportunity is ripe to begin a new station. This, however, has become impossible because of the awful curtailment in our mission budget and now [I only go] twice a month for services."[3]

Roswell Owens was a graduate of Howard College (now Samford University) in Birmingham, Alabama and received a divinity degree from Southern Baptist Theological Seminary in Louisville, Kentucky. In Louisville, he met Doreen Hosford. They were married in 1927. Doreen Hosford was born November 10, 1905, in Rosario de Santa Fe, Argentina. She was the second daughter of Irish parents.[4]

In 1933, the Owens set out for Haifa as a new mission station. Mrs. Watts wrote, "They were without any budget save their salary and house rent; without any equipment save a dozen hymnbooks."[5] Following a visit from Dr. Charles E. Maddrey, Executive Secretary of the FMB in 1934, an allowance for a small mission hall was provided and furnished. They bought five benches. The congregation was Arab."[6] In the 1934 annual report to the FMB, Rev. Roswell said that he had the privilege to preach to members of the English and German communities [in addition to the Arab community]. He wished he "might transport Southern Baptists to Palestine and give them a vision of the need for the gospel of our Lord."[7]

One day, a young man named Augustine Shirish, whom the Owens knew from Nazareth, came to their home asking if there were some work that he could be given. Augustine Shirish and his wife had become members of the Nazareth Baptist Church due to the ministry of Shukri Musa, in the late twenties. Augustine was a shoemaker. However, he was finding it hard to make a living in Nazareth. Friends and family boycotted his business when he left the Greek Orthodox Church to join the Nazareth Baptist Church. The Owens employed Augustine to do their shopping in the market and Augustine also continued to work as a shoemaker. When he wasn't working, he became a student of the Bible. Owens increasingly put him in charge of the services that had been started. In 1934, the FMB provided a salary for Augustine for one-half his time. This enabled him to begin a systematic course of Bible study under the guidance of Rev. Owens. "[Augustine] became a fine worker in the struggling Haifa mission,"[8] said Rev. Owens. Augustine became particularly significant when the Owens family was stricken with scarlet fever and quarantined. He did the preaching, as well as the marketing.[9]

In 1936, Elias Saleebi[10] came to Haifa to help with the work. Elias was born in 1906 to Lebanese parents. He was also "born into" the Greek Orthodox Church, but the family did not attend services regularly. Elias worked at the American University as an assistant gatekeeper and later in the post office on campus. He studied on his own and read the Bible along with many other religious books. Through friends, he became interested in the little Baptist church near the campus. Here he came to know Rev. Sa'eed Jureidini, a Lebanese Baptist pastor, and learned about the teachings of Jesus. He was baptized in 1926. Elias Saleebi organized a religious society on the American University campus for the purpose of Bible study and witness among the university students. Rev. Roswell Owens, on a visit with Baptists in Beirut, was so impressed with Elias Saleebi, that he requested that he come to Haifa to help him in the ministry. Rev. Jureidini told Owens that Elias was "a young Timothy" of unusual promise. The reference was to Timothy of the New Testament, a faithful assistant to Saint Paul, the Apostle as he began his missionary journeys. In 1936, Elias moved to Haifa when the FMB made an appropriation for his salary and he began more intensive training with Rev. Owens. Elias Saleebi was recognized as a good orator and a talented preacher.[11]

Mrs. J. Wash Watts wrote of the organization of the Haifa Baptist Church:

"In the spring of 1936 the First Baptist Church of Haifa was organized. To this newly organized church there came four applicants for baptism and church membership. A bus was chartered and the members went to the River Kishon for a baptism service. The Kishon's headwaters unite in the Jezreel Valley and flow diagonally emptying into Haifa Bay just north of Mount Carmel. At the church organization meeting, Elias Saleebi …effectively explained the duties of church members and …Augustine…explained the meaning of the lovely baptismal scene."[12] Owens referred to Augustine and Elias as the "two Timothies."[13]

In October 1940, Rev. Jureidini traveled from Lebanon to Palestine to participate with missionaries in the ordination of Elias Saleebi at the Haifa Baptist Church.[14] Rev. Owens began teaching the equivalent of seminary training to a small number of Arab ministerial students.[15] However World War II disrupted the ministry. In 1941, after Italy entered the war, Haifa was bombed, with the aim of putting the refineries and port out of action. The Owens went to Jerusalem but then left Palestine and returned to the States.[16] Following World War II, the Owens family was not able to return. Rev. Saleebi took the leadership of the work in Haifa and on Sunday evenings he preached at the Nazareth Baptist Church. During the week he taught, witnessed and visited in the homes of families. He contracted tuberculosis and in 1942, he had to enter a sanatorium in Lebanon. Thereafter, he remained in Lebanon and became pastor of the Beirut Baptist Church.[17]

Paul and Marjorie Rowden planned to connect with other Christians in the city and to begin Bible study for those interested in learning about the gospel. The city was now primarily Jewish, with most Arabs having fled or having been ordered to evacuate during the 1948 war. Since Dwight and Emma Baker were on furlough, the Rowdens took a leadership role with many of the programs at the Nazareth Baptist Church. Many of the Arab national Baptists were assuming leadership positions as well and the programs were growing. The Rowdens drove back and forth from Haifa to Nazareth on most weekends. Jim and Betty Smith would soon be arriving and the mission had asked Jim to be the pastor of the Nazareth Baptist Church until the Bakers returned.

Paul Rowden looks over the city of Haifa and the Mediterranean Sea in 1955.

42

Letters

AUGUST to MID-SEPTEMBER 1955

The following letter of August 2, 1955 was written by Searcy S. Garrison, Executive Secretary-Treasurer of the Baptist Convention of the State of Georgia regarding his visit in Israel.

The Executive Committee of the
Baptist Convention of the State of Georgia
Searcy S. Garrison, Executive Secretary-Treasurer
Baptist Building
291 Peachtree Street
Atlanta 3, Georgia

August 2, 1955

Rev. & Mrs. Paul Rowden
Box 6096
Haifa, Israel

Dear Friends:

I wish to thank you again for the privilege, which was mine in visiting your home upon our recent visit to Haifa. The fellowship with you and the visit to the mission station in Israel are among our happy memories of the journeys incidental to attending the Baptist World Alliance.

Because of our visit with you we shall be even more interested in the work, which you are undertaking for our Lord. As you begin the work in Haifa we shall be in especial prayer for you. I sincerely hope that you will be able to develop a strong growing church in Haifa to witness to the people of Israel concerning our Lord.

We were impressed with the new Children's Home, Camp and Educational Center which is being built in [Petah Tikva] Israel. I believe that this will be a fine facility, which will be useful in promoting the work there.

I am sure that your Atlanta and Georgia Baptist friends would wish to join me in sincerest greetings. Only today I was speaking with one of the ladies from the Cascade Church, and she was very much interested to know that we had recently visited in your home. These Cascade friends are proud of you and are supporting your ministry with their daily prayers.

We shall all be happy to see you upon your return home for your furlough period. I hope to have the privilege of fellowship with you during your furlough and also I hope to have the privilege of presenting you to some of our Georgia Baptist groups while you are here.

Thank you again for your gracious hospitality, and with sincerest good wishes, I remain,

Fraternally yours,

Searcy S. Garrison

Aerogramme To:
Coles
1546 Richland Rd S.W.
Atlanta, Ga. USA

Marjorie Rowden
Box 6096
Haifa, Israel

August 29, 1955

Dearest Folks:
…This past week has been "camp week" for both of us. Paul took 35 RA boys and 3 workers and he and Herman left for the farm [in Petah Tikva] last Monday A.M. at 5:30…I had to see about registering Becky in school.

Everything is so complicated here. I had to see a dozen different people and go to 50 offices, it seemed.

Camp opened [in Nazareth for G.A. and Y.W.A. girls] at 8:00 A.M. Wednesday and we stayed until 6 P.M. in the evening.[1] We had three gloriously wonderful days. I've never had a better camp…Helen Davis…was wonderful help. She is so talented and a wonderful speaker for girls. We had 55 girls and they were all so cooperative…and the 5 Arab women helpers really put their hearts into the camp. For the first time I had someone ready and prepared for every job and I just sat back and watched everything. I had the morning devotionals each A.M. and the rest of the day I let the others work. I had the two American nurses from the English [EMMS] Hospital helping too. One came down to direct an hour's recreation each day and one came down for the closing inspirational message each afternoon. We had study course books, Bible study, enacted plays about famous women missionaries' lives. In all we had a fine time. Each girl brought her own food and water for each day. We even had a morning "tea time" and an afternoon "tea time."

Friday afternoon after our camp closed Helen and I and Becky and Robin left Nazareth and drove to the farm for the closing night of the R.A. camp…They had a fine week. The closing service was fine…We spent Friday night at the farm…The place is beginning to take shape although Marty and Murph [Murphey] have a long way to go before they will be anywhere settled. Marty is about to walk herself to death all over that huge place trying to get everything fixed. Their furniture from the States has arrived but it is still in port pending a lot of red tape, which is the usual procedure. The children [in the Children's Home] all seem happy as can be in their new home. The swimming pool is finished and is the main attraction. Murph's mother is still here and will be here until February, which means she will have stayed a whole year. She has worked very hard in all this moving…

Yesterday, Sunday, we started a week's revival meeting in Nazareth. Paul is preaching and is doing a wonderful job…

…I had to take Becky to the school [in Haifa] for a test this A.M. and she starts next Thursday…The [Hebrew *Reali*] school is about 5 blocks from here and is a private one. It is reported to be the very best school in Israel. Fees will be about 15 dollars a month. Robin will go to a private kindergarten (I hope she will go!) and that will be about the same price each month. The Board pays these schools for us which is nice.

…After the Smiths come we hope to settle down here in Haifa and have a good long rest. Of course, Paul will still have to go over [to Nazareth] real often for a while and help Jim [Smith] out. And also Herman [Petty] will be there to help. I will keep my Sunday School class and my YWAs. But the burden of the pastorate will be lifted. It has been so hard this summer to live in two houses and travel [between Haifa and Nazareth]...

Love,

Marjorie

Aerogramme To:
Coles
1546 Richland Rd. S.W.
Atlanta, Ga. USA

Marjorie Rowden
Box 6096
Haifa, Israel

Tuesday September 6, 1955

Dearest Folks:

Becky and [Paul] got up before daylight this morning and drove to Jerusalem for the day. Paul had lots of business to attend to and Becky wanted to go and see Barbara and Margaret [Lindsey girls]. Dr. and Mrs. [George] Sadler are in Jerusalem with the Lindseys now...

Guess you all have been reading the papers about our border trouble with Egypt. Some Egyptians penetrated deep into Israel territory last week and made an attack almost to Tel Aviv. Things looked bad for a couple of days, but all seems under control now...

Well, we are counting the days now until the Smiths arrive. We eat our breakfast and supper out on the porch facing the Sea and each day we think how much closer they are to our shores...They will probably stay here with us from Thursday through Sunday or Monday and then move on to Nazareth so they can begin getting used to things. The Baker's house is there furnished, but I imagine June [Petty] will put them in her guest room. The first Sunday afternoon that they are here my YWA girls are having a big tea for them at the church in order to meet everyone...

I really feel for new missionaries those first few weeks, but when I think how much better off they will be than we were I think they will be in Heaven. They already have met the Bakers, the Scoggins, Bob [Lindsey] and they know us. We had never laid eyes on anyone! We all get a big bang out of sitting around and seeing who can tell the biggest tale of woe about how horrible it was when they first came…

Well, we had a wonderful week of revival meetings this past week in Nazareth. Paul preached twice on Sunday and Monday through Thursday nights. The church was packed all the time and it is really the first real revival meeting we have had since we got here. Nearly the whole membership of the church went forward for rededication and there were 10 professions of faith. We really felt the presence of the Holy Spirit…Fuad Sakhnini translated and he is wonderful at it. He and Paul were both preaching so strong and fast that they couldn't wait for one to stop the sentence before the other started. Up until this week Paul's preaching has been a little altered to suit the Arab congregation, but this week I could shut my eyes and almost imagine I was back at [church] at Crossroads [Alabama] again. It was good to hear that kind of preaching. The church is making lots of progress and Jim [Smith] will find it a joy to work with the people I'm sure. Sunday A.M. we had baptism and Paul baptized two candidates…

Much love,

Marjorie.

Aerogramme To:
Coles
1546 Richland Rd. SW
Atlanta, Georgia USA

Marjorie Rowden
Box 6069
Haifa, Israel

September 12, 1955 Mon.

Dearest Folks:

'Tis a mighty fine day here in Haifa. The sea is so clear and blue and the breeze is wonderful. Becky is in school and Robin is playing paper dolls. I haven't had time to see about her kindergarten, although she assures me she isn't going…

Becky started [school] last Thursday and has been 4 days so far. She just loves it and walks home by herself each day with the other little children…It seems to be a very good school and her teacher is very understanding when something comes up that Becky doesn't quite understand in Hebrew. Becky's name in Hebrew is "Reef-ka" so that is what all the children and the teacher call her. I'm glad she has a Hebrew name. Poor Robin will have a time explaining her name.

We had to buy half of Haifa for Becky to start school with. She brought home a list a mile long of [required school] supplies and it took Paul and me half a day to translate the list [from Hebrew] before we could start buying! What experiences we do have.

Becky has to wear a certain kind of dress so we spend half the time keeping it washed and ironed and the school emblem sewed on and off…The first day of school all the older students put on the cutest play welcoming the newcomers. They had costumes and a child's orchestra and special seats for all the new mamas. It was so nice. This country spends more energy and time and money on their children than any place I have ever seen. Each child looks like a fashion plate out of Vogue Magazine.

Well, Dr. [George] Sadler and Mrs. Sadler have come and gone. Dr. Sadler got here from Jordan last Monday with a good case of stomach trouble from eating unclean food and was in bed in Jerusalem two days and

Becky Rowden with flower garland around head holds a textbook following a school program celebrating the giving out of the first grade books at Reali School in Haifa, 1955. The book cover written in Hebrew says, "Reading Israel."

had to have a doctor. But he recovered nicely. Bob and Margaret [Lindsey] had lots of interesting things planned for them. Thursday we all went to the farm [at Petah Tikva] for our dedication ceremony. It was very sweet and Dr. Sadler brought just the right message. We had a buffet supper afterwards. We all stayed there overnight and slept all over the place. Then Friday A.M. we had an all-morning meeting with Dr. Sadler and brought him reports from all the stations. Mrs. Sadler is very charming and we all enjoyed having her.

Well, just three more days and the Smiths will be here. We got a letter from them mailed from New York. The boat will probably arrive here sometime Wednesday (day after tomorrow) in the nighttime. Everyone is coming here early Thursday A.M. and we will go down to the port. It is always a thrilling time…

Much love,

Marjorie and all

The Baptist farm, later called Baptist Village, in Petah Tikva.

43

THE BEGINNING OF BAPTIST VILLAGE IN PETAH TIKVA

The Baptist Convention in Israel finally saw the construction of a new home for the children of the George W. Truett Children's Home located in Petah Tikva inland from Tel Aviv. To the south on a small hill sat the ruins of the once Roman city of Antipatris. To the west, just out of sight was the Mediterranean Sea. To the north were large groves of orange trees. And on the east, running directly on the line of the property, was the Yarkon River. Development of buildings on the farm or Baptist Village (*Kfar Ha-Baptistim*), as it was later called, had long been a goal of Bob Lindsey. He worked tirelessly promoting the project and soliciting funds from the FMB. The farm property lay on the Plain of Sharon, centrally located between the Galilee area and Jerusalem. For over a year Milton [Murph] Murphey had tackled the overwhelming job of overseeing construction. He was finally able to see the fruition of his labor as the first buildings on the farm were completed.

The main building was in the form of an "H". A large multipurpose room was located in the middle while the two wings included offices, classrooms, and bedrooms, dining room, kitchen, utility rooms and quarters for the workers. One of the wings had a second story that contained an apartment where the Murpheys would live.[1]

Marty Murphey labored to get the furnishings in shape before moving time. The mission ordered new furniture for the farm buildings. It arrived at the port in Haifa but due to the usual red tape, was left on the docks and some of the furniture was soaked by rain before it could be retrieved. Marty and Helen Davis walked up and down streets of Tel Aviv looking into shops for anything they could find in the way of material for curtains, bedspreads, pillows and rugs, but, said Marty, "There was little of anything for sale."[2]

Marty Murphey recalled moving day. Murph drove Marty and their three small children to the farm, dropped them off and returned to Nazareth in order to bring a truckload of Home children and staff the next day. Marty settled her children in for the night, but at dusk the mosquitoes swarmed and bit them all relentlessly. Marty fled to the construction crew for help and was given insect repellent. Murph returned from Nazareth the next day with a caravan of children, staff and meager furnishings. The children arrived—excited to be in their new home. Gone was the crowded Nazareth house with the small dirt yard; now they had five buildings and acres of open farmland to call home. Everyone walked through mud where the walkways ended. Some of the children exuberantly knocked each other in the mud for sheer fun.[3] The children's bedrooms opened onto outdoor corridors. Walking around at night required dodging of frogs and flying insects. Soon a group of young men from Nazareth arrived for their week-long R.A. camp. Although some products were grown on the farm, most of the food had to be purchased daily from the markets in Tel Aviv. Three cooks prepared meals for the children, staff, construction crew, agricultural farm workers and campers. Marty Murphey relied heavily on Fida Ateek and other staff to help the rambunctious children adjust to a new schedule.[4] In an article for *Commission,* Marjorie Rowden wrote:

> The rooms [at the farm] were painted with bright colors with wide outdoor corridors in which the children can run and stretch their growing limbs. There is a playroom with a large stone fireplace at one end for long rainy days and a dining room. There are classrooms where the children can study their lessons each day—lessons in three languages, Arabic, Hebrew and English. The children will have farm duties and household jobs… It was fitting that our regional secretary, Dr. George W. Sadler, Foreign Mission Board Secretary for Africa, Europe and the Near East, along with his wife, could be here to inspire us to greater heights. We assembled on the veranda to dedicate the new buildings to the Lord. Mr. M. G. Griebenow, missionary for the Christian and Missionary Alliance, led in prayer and Paul [Rowden] read a Scripture passage. Milton Murphey introduced Dr. Sadler, who, with dignified simplicity, commended the land, the building, the people, the activities and the future into the hands of the Lord. He recalled the many that had a great or small part in making the center possible."[5]

The Baptist Village was modeled somewhat like the Israeli *kibbutz*. It provided an agricultural and communal form of living. The members of the Baptist mission felt it was a good location for rearing and educating the Home children so that they could better take their place within Israeli society and the larger world. In this new location, the children would no longer be singled out as "orphans." In many Israeli *kibbutzim* children were housed together, and in that respect, the Baptist farm was no different. The mission members frequently met at the farm for business meetings since it was centrally located. Camps were held yearly. Everyone enjoyed the swimming pool, the open fields and the picnic area by the Yarkon River.

When asked about the contribution the Baptist Village would make to the Baptists in Israel, Milton Murphey said:

> The Baptist center symbolizes the determination of this Christian community to play a constructive role in the development of the new state. The farm, more than any other Christian institution, speaks eloquently of Baptist determination to take root in the soil of Israel and to make a home there. To their credit, Baptists are making a genuine effort to hasten the process of peaceful integration between Israeli Jew and Israeli Arab…This solution is based on the Scriptures, which teach us that Jesus…is able to make all people brothers.[6]

The Baptist Village became a central meeting place for believers of all races, ethnic backgrounds and nationalities. They met and studied the Bible together. A Baptist congregation was established and services began. Milton Murphey served as pastor of the church and invited other Christian speakers to preach and teach.[7] Israeli youth were avid hikers and when they dropped by Baptist Village for a visit, tours were given.

The Murpheys spent the majority of their 27 years on the mission field at the Baptist Village and oversaw its successful development into a thriving center of activity. Marty Murphey, who had taken voice lessons during college, trained under excellent Israeli voice teachers. Over the span of her career, she established choirs at Baptist Village that performed throughout Israel. She planned special events, such as musical concerts featuring nationally known musicians and concert soloists for the widening circle of Israeli friends. Marty invited singers from all over the land to join the *Singers of Praise* choir in presenting the oratorio, *Messiah*, by Handel and *Elijah* by

Mendelssohn. The choir was invited to perform in churches and concert halls in various towns and cities of Israel.[8]

Pictured above are the children in the Children's Home at the farm in Petah Tikva (L-R front row): Hadiya, Bacilla, Adnan, Asa, Damianus, Ali, David Murphey, Edward; (L-R second row): Raufe, Lorice, Katrina, Milady, Rema, Afaf; (L-R third row): Rhadia, Dalal, Amira, Aida, Therese, Ann; (L-R back row): Helen Davis, Fida Ateek, Mrs. Murphey Sr. (?), (?) (?) Marty Murphey, Fuad Haddad, 1955

44
LETTERS
LATE-SEPTEMBER–DECEMBER 1955

In September 1955 Jim and Betty Smith arrived in Haifa with their young daughter, Jackie. The Smiths spent the first few days living with the Rowdens, catching up on news and renewing their friendship. Jim became pastor of the Nazareth Baptist Church while Dwight Baker was on furlough. The following letters were written after the arrival of the Smiths.

Aerogramme To:
Coles
1546 Richland Rd SW
Atlanta, Georgia USA

Marjorie Rowden
Box 6096
Haifa, Israel

Sunday, September 25, 1955

Dearest Folks:

Here it is another week gone by. Jim [Smith] and Paul made lots of progress in the port. All the things have been opened and inspected by customs officials, but no amount [of customs tax] has been set yet. As soon as bookwork is over the things can be shipped to Nazareth…

…Jim was going to preach his first sermon in Nazareth today… [Paul and Jim] should be about ready to start back home to Haifa about now. It is almost 8 p.m. Tomorrow is *Yom Kippur,* the Day of Atonement, so it is a high holy day here in Israel.

Herman [Petty's Nazareth Baptist] school opened last Monday, short two teachers. I don't know how he is making out. Also Jim is supposed to be over there teaching, but he can't go until the freight is settled. Then it will take them a few days, at least, to get the house arranged comfortably…

Much love,

Marjorie and all

Aerogramme To:
Cole
1546 Richland Rd. SW
Atlanta, Ga. USA

Marjorie Rowden
Box 6096
Haifa, Israel

.

Thursday, October 6, 1955

Dearest Mother:

Monday we went down to the farm to our annual Baptist conference. We had our first one last fall, you remember, and met under a brush arbor and slept in shacks. Well, this year we had our nice new building. We had about 65 people to attend for the 3 days, both Jews and Arabs. It was a thrilling experience. Jim [Smith] said it was better than Ridgecrest…We had an early morning service at 6 a.m. down on the river bank each morning, then breakfast, then from 9-11, Paul taught the book of John. It had to be translated into two languages. That meant every sentence was said three times.

Then at 11 we had the message of the morning. We had lunch and then the afternoons free. One day Margaret [Lindsey] and I took all our kids and drove into Tel Aviv to the zoo. They saw all the animals and also rode on lots of children's fair rides. It was a thrill to them. It really is the nicest zoo I ever have been in…

Then after supper each evening we had the main service of the day with lots of singing (in three languages, also some Russian and French thrown in)

Jim and Betty Smith (R) are greeted in the Nazareth Baptist Church, 1955.

and the message of the evening. The testimonials each evening were thrilling. Right in the middle of all the others, Jim [Smith] got up and gave the sweetest testimony, which meant much to everyone. All the people, both Jews and Arabs, like him very much and he has really adjusted himself to everyone wonderfully.

He and Paul got out and went off two nights and had fun together after the meeting. One night they drove into Tel Aviv and ate ice cream at the Brooklyn Ice Cream Bar until they nearly popped. The next night they took a long hike around that part of the country. The moon was real full. They stayed with all the men in one part of the building and I stayed with all the girls and women in another part. We were crowded, but it was lots of fun…

Much love to all,

Marjorie

Aerogramme To:
Coles
1546 Richland Rd. SW
Atlanta, Ga. USA

Marjorie Rowden
Box 6096
Haifa, Israel

Tuesday P.M.
October 25, 1955

Dearest Folks:

Paul and I are both dying in these *Ulpans!* Boy, what work these teachers do give. I am in a small group of 12 women who study two hours, three mornings a week. Our teacher is a man from Germany who has been teaching Hebrew here for 22 years. Most of the women in my class are from England or Europe somewhere. There are about 3 Americans. All of them are Jewish, of course. There is one very sweet woman who was formerly from Mississippi. She has invited me to her home for morning coffee next time before our class. It is quite a different group from the one I studied with last year in Jerusalem. There the students were from all walks of life and all different parts of the world. These women this time are in the "upper crust" and most of them are married to professional men who know the language perfectly and who are insisting that their wives learn the stuff. Most of them admit that they could very easily do without Hebrew lessons and just use their English, but their husbands make them come. Most of them are real cute and lots of fun. I feel real sorry for the poor man who is trying to teach us. But he makes the work very difficult and I'm sure we are learning something.

Becky is still enjoying her school. I was worried a little at first because she had to go in first grade again because she didn't know how to read and write Hebrew well enough to keep up with the second grade work. But she seems very happy...They are going very fast and making much progress. Of course it is all very simple to Becky except the Hebrew language itself...Miss Robin is...going to kindergarten. Most of the time she is very happy and comes home bubbling with real and imaginative things that happened. But once in a while she has a bad day...and so she screams bloody murder the whole time. Everyday [when] I go [to get them], I usually buy them a popsicle on the way home.

Robin doesn't get one on the days that she cries at school, so she tries to control herself. Some days, however, she has a victorious look on her face, as if it was worth it to lose the popsicle! She is a real sight. Her teacher is real fond of her and does everything to make her happy. The kindergarten is a wonderful place, with 3 huge rooms full of toys and educational objects, climbing things, etc. and a large play yard full of all kinds of [interesting] outdoor things...

Much love,

Marjorie

The following letter is a correspondence from Paul Rowden as Treasurer of the Baptist Convention in Israel, to the Israeli Censorship Authorities for Letters, who monitored monetary transactions of incoming and outgoing mail. Paul furnished Dr. Saul Colbi in the Ministry of Religious Affairs Office, at the Christian Desk, with a copy of his correspondence and sent him an article that had been published about Baptists in Israel.

Paul Rowden
The Foreign Mission Board of the Southern Baptist Convention
2037 Monument Avenue
Richmond 20, Virginia

Censorship Authorities for Letters
Post Office
Haifa

November 1, 1955

Dear Sir:

I thought that it would be of interest to you to know that over the past few months I have received on behalf of the Baptist Convention in Israel, the following U.S. dollar cheques which came in letters that were uncensored:
August 17, 1955 - $508.70—cheque no 7906—Drawn on Chase, New York, October 17, 1955-$6,559.57-cheque no 8029—-Drawn on Chase, New

York, and October 17, 1955-$6,000.00-Cheque no 8028—Drawn on Chase, New York

These cheques have all been turned over to Barclays Bank, Western Branch, Jerusalem, which Bank handles all our accounts. Here we receive IL1.500 for each dollar. We would like for you to know that we are always glad to cooperate with the existing laws and agencies in Israel. This is only one example of money turned over to the Bank. This has happened on many occasions in the past.

Very Sincerely,

Paul Rowden

Treasurer, Baptist Convention in Israel

cc: Dr. Colbi

Dr. Saul Colbi responded to Paul Rowden in the following letter. Dr. Colbi was born in Italy and was a graduate of the Law Faculty of the University of Rome. He became an expert in Canon Law. In 1939, he settled in Mandatory Palestine, and until the establishment of the State of Israel, pioneered in an agricultural settlement. In 1948, he joined the Israeli Ministry of Religious Affairs and was entrusted with the Christian Desk.[1]

State of Israel
Ministry of Religious Affairs
Department for Christian Communities
Jerusalem, Heshvan 22nd 5716
Israel

Mr. Paul Rowden, Treasurer
Baptist Convention in Israel
Hator Street 6
Mt. Carmel
POB 6096, Haifa
Israel

November 7, 1955

Dear Sir:

I read with much interest the clipping from the *Christian Century*, which was enclosed in your letter of November 1, 1955. I never doubted the attitude of goodwill of the Baptists toward the State of Israel.[2]

Furthermore, I acknowledge receipt of the copy of your letter addressed to the Censorship Authorities for Letters. Your behavior is to be highly appreciated, and should be taken as an example by other church representatives and institutions.

Yours sincerely,

Dr. P. Colbi, Director of the Department.

Four graduates of the Nazareth Baptist School [NBS] lived at the farm in Petah Tikva one year in order to teach educational subjects to the Home children. The NBS secondary school graduates taught the Home children part of the day and then various members of the Baptist Mission taught classes to the NBS graduates as a way for them to begin their higher education.

Aerogramme To:
Coles
1546 Richland Rd. SW
Atlanta, Georgia USA

Marjorie Rowden
Box 6096
Haifa, Israel

November 4, 1955,

Dearest Folks:

...Becky went to the farm with [Paul] after lunch today to visit all the kids while he teaches his three-hour church history course…[Paul] always comes home with a car full of green vegetables, which last us from one week to the next…

…Margaret Lindsey is coming here by taxi Tuesday from Jerusalem and then she and I will drive over to Nazareth for a mission study course with our two [women's church] circles. Margaret will teach them all about Korea, since she was there all her life.[3] We will probably spend the night and come back here to Haifa very early Wednesday morning.

Much love,

Marjorie

P.S. The news in this part of the world is certainly sad these days. It is really a critical situation. I hope we are not in a full scale war by the time you get this. Night before last there was a big battle down in the Negev and last night there was another one.…The newspaper reports and radio reports are really bad. Trust and pray the situation improves rather than goes the other way. You know Ben Gurion is back in as Prime Minister [of Israel]. Some think that is good and some think not. Don't know.

In the following letter Marjorie Rowden writes about Hanukkah (also spelled Chanukah). It celebrates the victory of the Maccabees, a Jewish rebel group, who fought to regain the temple in Jerusalem in 164 B.C. When the Jews rededicated the temple, oil was supposed to burn throughout the night every night. There was only enough oil to burn for one day. Miraculously, it burned for 8 days—the time needed to prepare a fresh supply of oil. The menorah has eight main branches for candles plus a ninth branch in the middle used to start the other lights.

Aerogramme To:
Coles
1546 Richland Rd. SW
Atlanta, Ga. USA

Marjorie Rowden

Box 6096
Haifa, Israel

Sunday afternoon, December 11, 1955

Dearest Folks:

On December 20th we are all invited to the American Consul's home [Leonard Cowles] for a big Christmas dinner, children and all. The consul's three kids are real cute and come often to visit Becky and Robin, so they are looking forward to the party.

This week is *Hanukkah*, the Jewish [festival] of lights. Friday was the last day of school for 8 days of holidays. Thursday afternoon we went to Robin's kindergarten to the program put on by the children for the parents. The place was all decorated and colored lights were everywhere. The children sang and danced and acted the parts of the brave Maccabees who rescued the Temple from the Greeks...

...Then Friday A.M. we went to Becky's school to see their program. It was pretty much the same but on a more complicated level. Becky made a nice little speech in Hebrew and introduced a whole bunch of kids who came up and joined her and they did a Hebrew folk dance. She was all dressed up and thought she was Lana Turner[4] or somebody. She practiced her speech so much that even Robin knew it by heart. Then Friday afternoon our neighbor upstairs took Becky and Robin to another Hanukkah program at the school where her daughter is teaching. They came home from all the parties loaded with bags of candy, doughnuts, trinkets etc. They both have 8-branch candlesticks, which they light each night during the 8-day holiday. Every night an additional candle is lit until on the 8th night they all burn brightly.

They have had such a good time with the other children celebrating Hanukkah that I'm afraid Christmas will be just an anti-climax to them. Yesterday afternoon was Shabbat so we drove up to Acre to have supper with Bill and Roberta Channel. They are working with the Quakers, and are from Ohio. They have a little girl exactly Becky's age named Meridith. They had invited Becky and Robin to spend the night and today, so about 10 last night Paul and I left the gals and came home alone...

Much love,

Marjorie

In the following letter Marjorie Rowden writes of visiting with Mr. and Mrs. Donald Branyon. Donald L. Branyon Sr. was an agronomist and soils specialist in the School of Agriculture at the University of Georgia and worked with county agricultural agents. His academic thesis was on the topic of "cotton." Don Branyon joined a group of American agricultural specialists sponsored by the State University of New York, to travel to Israel and share expertise with the Israeli farmers. Jessie Branyon taught English. The Branyons lived in Tel Aviv, Israel from 1954 to mid 1956. The Branyons and Rowdens were on the same boat returning to the U.S. the summer of 1956 and remained friends. Donald Branyon Sr. and his wife Jessie were Baptist lay leaders and members of the First Baptist Church of Athens, Georgia, where he served as Chairman of the Deacons and she taught Sunday school. Don Branyon retired from the University of Georgia in the early sixties.[5]

Aerogramme To:
Coles
1546 Richland Rd SW
Atlanta, Ga. USA

Marjorie Rowden
Box 6096
Haifa, Israel

Monday, December 19, 1955

Dearest Folks:

...We took a tour all over Galilee [with the Smiths]. It rained most of the day but we enjoyed it anyway. We took them to lots of places where they hadn't been before. We hastened back, however, because we were driving through territory that was pretty close to the Syrian border where there has been trouble lately. Don't think we'll go back around there any more until things calm down. Guess you read about the battle on the opposite side of the Sea of Galilee. The Syrians have been shooting the Israeli fishing boats for years and causing much damage. Finally the Israelis got tired of it and went over and knocked out their shooting stations...

Then Thursday A.M. early we drove to Jerusalem. Paul and I and Jim and Betty [Smith] and Herman [Petty] had to go to the American Consul and register to cross over into Jordan on January 6th. Then that night we all drove back down to Tel Aviv and had a big Christmas dinner at the home of Mr. and Mrs. [Donald] Branyon from Athens, Georgia. He is on the faculty of the University of Georgia and has been here in Israel a year helping the cotton industry. They are very sweet people and really put on a feast for all of us.

Yesterday, Sunday, we finally got around to getting a Christmas tree and we decorated it all up and the kids are thrilled to death. They brought all the little neighbors in to look at it. I made a red brick (paper) fireplace and we have a table size tree on top. It looks real cute. We have a red light in the fireplace and it makes us think we have a real fire.

This Tuesday (tomorrow) we are all invited to the American Consul's house here in Haifa for a Christmas dinner. The children are looking forward to it. Then Thursday we drive to the farm for our mission Christmas dinner and the exchange of gifts…Sunday we will spend Christmas Day with the Smiths and Pettys in Nazareth…

Much love,

Marjorie and all

Aerogramme To:
Coles
1546 Richland Rd. SW
Atlanta, Ga. USA

From:
Rowdens
Box 6096
Haifa, Israel

December 27, 1955

Dearest Folks:

We celebrated Christmas Eve and Christmas Day on Friday night and

Saturday (a day early) because we knew Sunday would be so busy in Nazareth and the children wanted all day Saturday to play with their new toys. So Friday night Santa came and he really did a bang up job! Robin had a fit over her new doll and Becky absolutely was thrilled to death with her camera. She took everybody's picture coming and going…

And then yesterday, [the women in a] "Marjorie Rowden Circle," from Roanoke, Virginia sent us the nicest Christmas box you have ever seen…Oh, they also sent the girls two big boxes of 4th of July sparklers, so last night the girls and Paul went out front and lit the whole place up. Becky and Robin thought they were the most wonderful things...

Our dinner at the American Consul last Tuesday night was wonderful. There were 8 of us plus 7 children, who ate in another room. I never saw so much food. Mrs. [Leonard] Cowles had made large red stockings for each child just chunked full of gifts and candy and apples.

The neighbors have all been wonderful and have brought in little gifts to Becky and Robin and sent beautiful flowers from the florist to us. We are so thankful for their friendship and interest. On Christmas Eve we had a living room just packed with people and children. In fact, it turned into a party and we played games with all the neighborhood kids…

…We feel very humble when we think of all that people do for us. I don't think we deserve it. Well, I must close. Write soon.

Much love,

Marjorie and all

45

LETTERS

JANUARY 1956

Aerogramme To:
Coles
1546 Richland Rd. SW
Atlanta, Ga. USA

Marjorie Rowden
Box 6096
Haifa, Israel

January 3, 1956

Dearest Folks:

Well, three days of 1956 has already gone by. In just 4 months and 17 days we will be leaving here for home. It almost frightens me when I think how much I have to do in that length of time. We do not yet know what to do with most of our furniture and with our apartment. We won't have our annual mission meeting until April and it won't be until then that we decide what to do...

This week has been busy like all the rest. Last Thursday we drove over to Nazareth for the mid-week service. Afterwards we had a reception and farewell gathering for Dr. [William] Bathgate of the [EMMS] Hospital. He is leaving (retiring) next week. We will all miss him so very much. He is 71 years old now and very white-haired but very active and beloved by all. He has built the hospital practically by himself and has worked there for 35 years. Next Monday John and Odette Tester are coming back from furlough and Dr. Bathgate is turning over the hospital to John...

The farewell party we had was very nice. Paul spoke in honor of Dr. Bathgate for about 30 minutes. His topic was "Dr. Luke, the Beloved Physician"[1] and he compared Dr. Bathgate to [Luke]. I thought it was very well done and the whole hospital appreciated it. Also it was a farewell affair for Lynn and Helen Davis and Murph's [Milton Murphey's] mother. They will leave together on Feb. 14. However, we will probably have something else later on in honor of them. One of the Arab men in our church spoke on what Lynn and Helen had meant to the church and it was so sweet. Both of them just broke down trying to speak afterwards...Herman spoke in behalf of Mrs. Murphey Sr. and told how she had been a mother and grandmother to us all during these past 10 months. She has worked so hard with the new Home and everyone appreciates all she has done.

Saturday night we all went to the annual New Year's Eve dinner and party at the [EMMS] Hospital. It was lots of fun as usual. Friday night Paul and I went to have the Sabbath-Eve meal with some Jewish friends here in Haifa. They have a lovely home and we enjoyed the evening so much. Friday evening is usually family night for the Jewish people and we appreciated their sharing it with us. They had the Hebrew prayers and blessings between the courses of food.

We are going to Jerusalem Friday A.M. early and see about crossing into Jordan. They were having some anti-American riots over there last week and we were wondering whether it would be safe to go or not. But all seems quiet now...

Much love,

Marjorie

Aerogramme To:
Coles
1546 Richland Rd SW
Atlanta, Ga. USA

Marjorie Rowden
Box 6096
Haifa, Israel

January 9, 1956
Dearest Folks:

...These are mighty tense times we are living in these days...About three weeks ago they had some bad anti-Western (particularly anti-American) riots [in Jordan], but things seem to be calmed down. So bright and early last Friday A.M. Paul and I, Jim and Betty [Smith], Herman and [his son] David [Petty] and Becky all headed for Jerusalem...We got to Jerusalem about 10 A.M. and crossed at Mandelbaum Gate into Jordan. It was raining and we got a taxi straight to the National Hotel. We were practically the only guests in the hotel because everyone had been scared off by the troubles...

...We had a good supper at the hotel and several of our Arab friends from Nazareth, who are now living in Jordan or in Lebanon, came to the hotel and visited us in the evening. It was nice seeing them. Early Saturday morning we got a taxi for Bethlehem. We made pictures at Shepherd's Field and in Bethlehem. At 10 we were back in Jerusalem, (the part still in Jordan) and I got out of the taxi and decided to go shopping. All the rest [of the group] took the taxi and drove to Jericho to be gone until 4 P.M. I walked all through the old City just looking and having a big time. The Lindsey family was [in Jordan] so I was with them part of the time... [A]t noon I went to the YMCA and had lunch with them.

...Margaret [Lindsey] and I decided to go out and shop some more. I was to meet Paul and the others at 4 P.M. Well...Margaret and I got two blocks down the street and saw a mob forming with sticks and stones. We watched for a minute and then retreated back to the YMCA, which is right next door to the American Consulate building. The mob grew larger and was around a thousand people headed straight up the road for our [American] consul. It was awfully scary. I did not have any of my papers, passport, etc., because they were with Paul. I kept praying that [Paul and the others] would hurry back from Jericho. Also I was scared that they had gotten stopped by other rioters on the highway. The whole country was rioting.

Margaret and I took all 5 of her kids up on the roof of the YMCA...Bob [Lindsey] was running around madly trying to get his car battery out of the garage not far away, which was being recharged. He never did get the battery, so he got some men to help him move the car off the street into the YMCA fenced-in yard. The American consul next door was crawling with American Marines and Arab Legionnaires. The women and children of the [American] consul had been driven over into Israel territory.

Well, the Lord certainly was with us, because two minutes before the mob reached the YMCA the taxi drove up with Paul and all in it. We turned the taxi around in the face of the mob, I jumped in and he rushed us straight around the corner to Mandelbaum Gate. We got out and walked through the Arab check-post, through no-man's land and into the little wooden Israel check-post house. As soon as we stepped into the Israel side the gun shots and tear gas bombs exploded all over the area we had just that minute left. The mob tore down the American flag and broke all the windows in the consul building. The wounded rioters were brought into the YMCA, although none were badly hurt. [N]o American personnel [were] hurt.

Margaret [Lindsey] took her kids inside and Bob [Lindsey] watched from the roof. They stayed there until the next morning, because they couldn't have gotten to Mandelbaum Gate. We were the last ones to pass [through] until after the riot was over. But we called [the Baptist house in] Jerusalem [Israel] last night and talked to Bob. He said that the next morning as soon as possible they got the car battery and crossed into Israel, but the rioters were still going strong. There is a heavy censorship on news coming out now, so we don't know how bad the situation is.

In Amman, the capital of Jordan, yesterday several American and British buildings were on fire, including the Point-4 office.[2] ...We were only gone two days and one night, but it seemed like years...

Much love,

Marjorie and all

46

TENSION IN THE MIDDLE EAST
1955–1956

The riots in Jordan were orchestrated and related to a mutual security agreement signed by Great Britain, Turkey, Iran, Iraq and Pakistan in 1955 (the Baghdad Pact). The main purpose of the pact was to block possible expansion by the Soviet Union into the Middle East. On one side Iraq was pressing Jordan to side with the West. On the other side Egypt, Syria and Saudi Arabia were pressing Jordan not to join the pact. *Time* magazine reported: "These three countries, out to frustrate the West, aroused anti-western passions with inflammatory broadcasts. Demonstrations began outside Jerusalem's mosques [in Jordan] and spread all across the country. In U.N. refugee camps, 450,000 dispossessed Palestine refugees were idle and restless. With the encouragement of Egyptian agitators and Saudi Arabian bribes, they challenged Britain's position."[1] About the riots, *Time* magazine reported:

> Communists, though small in number, know how to guide mobs. In Jericho, 20,000 Arab refugees from Israel poured out of their dismally squalid camps and rampaged through a model-farm school, established for their benefit by U.S. and Middle Eastern philanthropists, smashing incubators and killing or stealing 10,000 chickens...Next the mob burned down a warehouse containing $60,000 worth of clothing which an American Mennonite mission had planned to distribute to the refugees as gifts. In the little town of Bethlehem, usually host to thousands of Christian pilgrims at this season, another mob stormed a police station...The U.S. consulate in the Jordanian half of Jerusalem

was attacked for a second time in a week. The American
flag was hauled down from a 30-ft. pole and trampled in
the streets...But by week's end, the furor had abated...the
toll: at least 16 dead, more than 100 injured. [2]

At the Baptist Hospital in Ajloun, Jordan, Alta Lee Lovegren noticed that
anti-American tension had been building for several weeks. One day she
saw a crowd coming toward the Baptist Hospital. A riot broke out. "The
crowd burned and destroyed the building containing the Baptist hospital
outpatient clinic, the pharmacy, dispensary and the home of the Arab business manager of the hospital, Jerius Ashkar, who, since the founding of the
hospital, had served the people of Ajloun most generously," she said. "Also
damage was done to the boys' dormitory, the home of the mission school-
teachers and a new residence under construction. The rioters did not, however, enter the hospital."[3]

Dr. August Lovegren was the only doctor on the premises at the time and
was in the operating room delivering a baby when the riots began. Alta Lee
Lovegren gathered all the women and children in the compound and went
upstairs to a nurse's room. At a certain point, she noticed the mob just seemed
to dissipate. One Arab man involved with the riots sustained a bad injury due
to a motorcycle accident and was brought to the hospital for treatment. Medical service had to be provided without anesthesia because all the pharma-
ceutical supplies had been destroyed. Another Arab man was very
anti-American and would not allow his daughter to go to the Baptist Hospital to obtain assistance with a difficult labor. The daughter and baby died. In
both cases local Arabs said that it was "God's revenge" on those who participated in the riot.[4] Arabs from about eight surrounding villages were thought
to have participated.[5] By the end of the week the British Arab Legion regained
control. Leaders of the attack against the Baptist Hospital compound were
sought out, but the Baptist hospital administrator refused to press charges
against them. Damaged buildings were repaired and the hospital staff determined to manifest the mind of Christ toward their persecutors.[6]

The *Atlanta Constitution* reported that the United States protested to
Jordan regarding the inadequacy of police protection against mobs that
damaged U.S. property, endangered American lives and subjected the
American flag to indignities. Although the United States supported the
Baghdad Pact with economic and military aid for its members, the U.S had
not joined in the pact because it was opposed by Egypt, with whom the U.S.
was negotiating construction of the high dam at Aswan on the Nile River.[7]

The FMB minutes reflected that damage in Ajloun, Jordan to the Baptist property was estimated to be somewhere between $25,000 and $50,000. The Executive Secretary of the FMB said, "Missionaries remained at their post throughout the rioting and met this situation in the same spirit which characterizes God's servants ministering in His name in many parts of a troubled world."[8]

47

LETTERS

FEBRUARY–MAY 1956

Aerogramme To:
Coles
1546 Richland Rd SW
Atlanta, Ga. USA

Marjorie Rowden
Box 6096
Haifa, Israel

Friday, February 25, 1956 –
Petah Tikva, Israel

Dearest Folks:

It certainly is a lovely day down here in Petah Tikva today. The girls and I drove down yesterday afternoon with Paul to stay until tomorrow noon. The place seems to be getting along O.K. with the Murpheys gone [on vacation].[1] All the kids are well. The "help" are all fighting between themselves, but that is their usual procedure. Bob and Margaret [Lindsey] come tomorrow at noon and relieve us, then Herman [Petty] comes on Tuesday to relieve them. Then Paul again next Thursday…

It really is a rest to be down here [in Petah Tikva on the farm] and get all our meals in the [dining] room and not have to worry over a thing. Becky and Robin are playing so hard they can hardly stop to speak. The weather is still cool, but not uncomfortable without heat. We have a small fire up here in the Murphey's apartment in the open fireplace. Then at night after all the children are in bed we light the big fireplace downstairs in the playroom. We had lots of fun down there until 11 last night playing ping pong and scrabble. There are 4 workers here for the farm and 5 for the Home…

…I took two of my *uplan* lady friends [from Haifa] over to Nazareth last Tuesday for the morning. I had called June and Herman [Petty] ahead of time so they had a lovely tea party waiting. The two friends are lovely women and were so impressed with our work there. I was so glad we took them. I want to bring them down here to the farm someday. In Nazareth, we visited our school and sat in one of the Hebrew classes and they thought the Arab boys and girls were doing remarkably well in Hebrew…

Much love,

Marjorie

Aerogramme To:
Coles
1546 Richland Rd SW
Atlanta, Ga. USA

Marjorie Rowden
Box 6096
Haifa, Israel

Saturday, March 17, 1956

Dearest Folks:

…Paul is working night and day these days to finish up all the treasurer's reports and get the books in good order for the poor soul that gets elected treasurer at our meeting April 2-4. It is a hard job…

It is Shabbat and the weather is beautiful. All the people are out promenading up the street in their "Saturday best." A few go out to the synagogue but by far the majority just use it as a day of rest and recreation and visiting. They seem to enjoy it very much, especially on warm sunny days. All the children are dressed up.

The sixth fleet is in this week. A U.S. destroyer is here in [Haifa] port making a courtesy call. The consul [Leonard Cowles] gave us passes to go aboard today so we are taking the children at 3 P.M. to have a tour of the boat. Tomorrow night we are invited to a reception for the whole crew...

...Thursday was Becky's last day at school for 2 ½ weeks holiday for Passover. They had a nice program and Becky sang one of the main Passover songs by herself for the audience. They had a small Passover meal at the school and the children enjoyed it. Then on Friday morning they had the same thing at Robin's kindergarten...

The situation in this part of the world is not very pretty these days. We had a mock air raid this week and it was almost too realistic with explosions and anti-aircraft guns and low-flying planes. Everyone had to clear the streets and get into shelters. I really don't think actual war will come but there seems to be more danger right now than anytime since Israel came into being. There is constant war on the borders, two and three incidents every night. People are killed practically every day along the borders, and Israel is just one big border!

Cyprus is also in a big mess. It seems awful to think that the peaceful little village of Kyrenia where we spent two lovely vacations is practically under siege. Troops patrol the streets and prisoners are being kept in the ancient medieval castle there. I guess the hotel must be occupied by the troops. All of it makes you wonder how long the world can go on without an explosion...

Well, I guess I had better stop and cook some dinner. I think Jim [Smith] is coming over to go on board the destroyer with us...We are having a time trying to decide what to do with each little item we have—sell it, give it away, take it home, or store it. What a job! I feel like just leaving the whole place just sitting here as is. Paul is real good at throwing away things so maybe that will solve the problem!

Much love,

Marjorie and all

Aerogramme To:
Coles
1546 Richland Rd SW
Atlanta, Ga. USA

Marjorie Rowden
Box 6096
Haifa, Israel

April 5, 1956, Thursday

Dearest Folks:

...Passover came and we had a wonderful evening with some friends. I believe we enjoyed it even more than last year...That afternoon Becky and I drove out to a *kibbutz* (settlement) where the people all gathered together to celebrate the cutting of the first grain of the season as is done in the Old Testament. It was a beautiful and thrilling ceremony and we enjoyed it so much. The little kibbutz children did colorful dances in the fields of grain.[2]

Easter Sunday we spent in Nazareth. Jim [Smith] preached a wonderful Easter message and we enjoyed being together. I had a program planning meeting with all the Auxiliary [women] leaders after dinner and then after that we had a small Easter egg hunt for all our children.

...Monday A.M. we got up and drove down below Tel Aviv to *Kibbutz Menahem* where Mr. [Charles Cowen] is buried. He was the man who came over on the boat with us. We had dinner at the *kibbutz* and toured the whole settlement seeing all the things they have accomplished there. It was really wonderful to see what a group of settlers have accomplished by working together and pooling their resources. They received us most cordially and invited us back again. Mrs. [Ida] Cowen is retiring from teaching in New York this year and is coming back here to settle in that *kibbutz* for the rest of her life. We hope to see her briefly in New York.

Monday afternoon we left the *kibbutz* and drove to our farm. We spent the night with Marty and Murph [Murphey] and the next morning all the other "dudes" arrived and we had our 5th annual mission meeting...It was the Smiths' first meeting and they were real interested to see how it worked. All day Tuesday and Wednesday we read reports and discussed the future. It looks like everybody is going to have to do a "fruit-basket turn-over" and move. For one time we were grateful it isn't us moving again.

Much love,

Marjorie

Kibbutz members and guests gather to celebrate the cutting and harvesting of the first grain of the season, c. 1956.

Aerogramme To:
Coles
1546 Richland Rd SW
Atlanta, Ga. USA

Marjorie Rowden
Box 6096
Haifa, Israel

May 14, 1956
Haifa

Dear Folks:

Well, here I am with a million things to do and don't know where to start. The living room is bare, the bedroom suite will go to Nazareth day after tomorrow when we go, and the children's room is also bare. The kitchen stuff goes Wednesday also. The washing machine goes tomorrow.

Everyone has been so wonderful to us and we have been fed half to death. Also we have received many nice going away gifts. We have enjoyed this year in Haifa and have made so many nice friends. Last Saturday Betty [Smith] and June [Petty] gave a tea for us in Nazareth and 35 people from here drove over for it…It was an all-Jewish get-together. Then this Thursday night the Nazareth church people are having a farewell party [for us]. It will be our last night here. Becky's school friends…made a book for her, each one writing a page. The teacher sent us candy for the trip. Robin's kindergarten honored her today and they all nearly wept…

Some of my *Ulpan* friends called and said they were coming over for tea tomorrow even if they had to sit on the floor and bring the tea along themselves, which they will do, of course. It is hard to leave people like these…The door just opened and Nava (Becky's best friend) came in car-

From (L-R) are Paul Rowden, Becky Rowden, Bob Lindsey, Penina Nehama and David Lindsey at a baptismal service at the Sea of Galilee in May 1956.

rying her pajamas. She says she is going to spend the night. She is a darling little girl and she and Becky weep on each other's shoulder when they talk about parting.

Paul is in Nazareth tonight. He is preaching a revival this last week that we are here. It is a wonderful way to end it all. He will be there without us tonight and tomorrow night. But Wednesday we move over to Nazareth and will be there the last two nights.

We had a thrilling day yesterday (Sunday). We all drove to the Sea of Galilee and had a beautiful baptismal service. It was the loveliest Mother's Day gift I could have received because Becky was the first one baptized [by Paul Rowden]. David Lindsey and [Penina Nehama] were also baptized [by Bob Lindsey].

Our plane leaves this Friday at 11:15 Israel time...We stop in Athens very briefly and on to Rome by 5:30 in the afternoon. I don't know any more news. We will call you from New York when we get there. We are scheduled to leave N.Y. for Atlanta by Eastern Air Lines on June 8th about one or two P.M.. We will tell you later when we get to N.Y. the definite arrival time. This will be my last letter, but we will be mailing you cards along the way.

Much love,

Marjorie

48

SUMMER 1956 to July 1957

For a couple of weeks during the summer of 1956, the Rowdens went on a whirlwind trip through Europe and then boarded the *S.S. United States* for home. In Atlanta, there was a joyous celebration as Paul and Marjorie were reunited with their families. Marjorie's parents turned their home on Richland Road into a duplex and the Rowdens lived on one side. Cascade Baptist Church members, friends and relatives came and went. Marjorie enjoyed visiting while sitting on the glider on the front porch. Paul's parents lived nearby with a screened-in porch filled with rocking chairs where Paul rocked and visited with his parents.

The summer was busy with speaking engagements, revivals, and mission retreats. In September, Paul departed for Philadelphia to begin work on his doctorate at Dropsie Hebrew College, returning to Atlanta as often as he could. Dropsie College was founded in Philadelphia in 1907 under Jewish auspices but was not affiliated with any religious denomination or with any American university. It offered the world's first accredited doctoral program in Jewish Studies and taught both Arabic and Hebrew.[1]

In February of 1957, Marjorie gave birth to a son—Richard Wayne Rowden. The Rowdens would now go back to the Middle East with prestige. They were officially *Abu* (father of) Richard and *Im* (mother of) Richard, taking on the Arab custom of additionally being known by the name of their first son.

Dr. August Lovegren and wife, Alta Lee, arrived in Atlanta in May of 1957 from Jordan for an extended furlough and the Rowdens visited with them—no longer separated by the Israeli-Jordanian border. Dr. August Lovegren began a residency at Emory University Hospital.

Soon after the Rowdens left Israel in June of 1956, the Israel mission carried out a turnover. Every mission household loaded up a truck full of goods and headed out to a new destination. When Dwight Baker returned from furlough to take up his duties as pastor of the Nazareth Baptist Church, Jim

Smith, who had served as pastor for a year, moved to Jerusalem to become pastor of the Jerusalem Baptist Church, thus allowing Bob Lindsey and his family to move from Jerusalem to the farm in Petah Tikva to take over the work from Milton and Marty Murphey who moved from the farm in Petah Tikva to the Rowden's apartment in Haifa for a year of language study. The Pettys moved to a different house in Nazareth.

Jim Smith's Israeli visa indicated that he had traveled to Israel to be the pastor of the Nazareth Baptist Church. He was replacing Dwight Baker, who returned to the States for furlough. The Israeli visa office noted that Dwight Baker had returned to Nazareth, and had resumed the pastorate. Therefore, Jim and Betty Smith's visa was not renewed. At one point the Smiths were issued an order to leave the country within two weeks. Bob Lindsey, with assistance from the FMB, finally straightened out the problem and obtained a visa for the Smiths from the Israeli authorities. Although Baptists were recognized as an established Christian religious group in Israel, each mission member had to fight a battle anew for extension of visas. This experience served as a guide for the mission and other Christian groups working in Israel as well.[2] In time the visa restrictions eased for Baptists and the Smiths never had another visa extension denied. A number of years later, the Israeli Government office in Ashkelon, where the Smiths were living, issued them permanent residency visas until they retired and left Israel in 1989.

In Nazareth, Dwight Baker finally received official legal authority from the Israeli Ministry for Religious Affairs to perform marriages. Baptist pastors in Nazareth had been performing marriages within the Baptist congregation since the days of the British Mandate. However, this right was revoked without explanation following the establishment of the State of Israel. Although Dwight continued to marry couples in his congregation, each case had to be taken up with the Israeli Ministry for Religious Affairs in Jerusalem before the marriage was officially registered. Baptists retained counsel and challenged the revocation of their official right to perform marriages. After a year of legal representation and just prior to taking the case to court, Dwight Baker was told that an official book of marriage certificates was being mailed to him, thus ending the dispute. Dwight wrote, "There were times when both sides felt the strain of the conflict, but after the matter was settled, a feeling of mutual respect was established between the Baptist Convention in Israel and the Ministry for Religious Affairs and we have found that we now work closely on numerous occasions."[3]

Since the Israeli-Arab war of 1948, tension on the Israel-Jordan frontier had resulted in small raids. However, in 1955 and 1956 the main center of danger shifted to the Israel-Egyptian frontier along the Gaza strip with almost continuous small-scale acts of aggression interspersed with acts of retaliation between Israel and Egypt. Relations deteriorated between Israeli representatives and some of the UN truce observation staff. The Negev remained an area of insecurity. As Jim and Betty Smith settled in to the Baptist House in Jerusalem, war loomed on the horizon. Written notices were passed out to every household telling the occupant to prepare for war. Following directions, the Smiths taped up their windows, put up blackout curtains, painted the headlights on their vehicles blue for night traveling and kept their ears tuned to their radios for the latest news bulletin.[4]

On July 26, 1956, President Gamal Abdel Nasser announced Egypt's nationalization of the Suez Canal, most of whose shares were held by Britain and France.[5] The Suez Crisis (the Sinai Campaign) began on October 29, 1956 as a result of Egypt closing the Suez Canal to Israeli shipping. Britain and France joined Israel in the battle against Egypt. By November 1st the Gaza Strip was cut off from Egypt and fell completely into Israeli hands the following day.

While the prolonged political struggle over the outcome of the war was taking place, Baptists were already going to the aid of the Baptist church and hospital in Gaza City. The Baptist Convention in Israel was assisting by providing needed medical supplies. Bob Lindsey traveled to Gaza to check on colleagues.[6] Jim Smith filled in as pastor of the Gaza Baptist Church for the pastor, whose return from furlough had been delayed due to the Suez Crisis. Over several months members of the Baptist Mission in Israel invited members of the Gaza Baptist church and hospital staff to visit them and took them on trips across Israel to acquaint them with biblical sites that they had never been able to visit due to the closed border.[7]

On March 16, 1957, Israel withdrew her troops from the Sinai and Gaza Strip after receiving international reassurances that Israel's vital waterways would remain open. Three thousand United Nations troops replaced Israeli soldiers.[8] The Gaza Strip was once again closed off from Israel—separating the Baptist missions in Israel and the Gaza Strip.

During 1956, Jim Smith was invited to join the Jerusalem Rotary Club, where he met a large number of outstanding citizens. He also inherited the job of treasurer from Paul Rowden and this job kept him busy working with an auditor and a lawyer. Baptists were offered several opportunities to have the Jerusalem Baptist Church worship services recorded for re-broadcast on Israel Radio. Jim brought in various instrumental musicians and choirs to the church. Betty organized the Saturday morning Bible study period to include a class for children of attendees. The Smiths set up an outdoor con-cert hall of sorts they created by turning an old unused tennis court in the back of the Baptist mission property into an attractive outdoor hall with a stage and amplified band shell. "We invited musicians to perform and could easily seat up to 200 guests," said Betty.[9] "The long dry summer evenings permitted use of our new facility. Most of the people who attended had in-vitations, but those who just wandered in were also seated in our garden."[10]

Jim and Betty were getting acquainted with their Jewish neighbors and with Jewish religious expression. They visited a variety of synagogues. Jim became a "*Shabbas Goy*," a non-Jew who is willing to do tasks that the Or-thodox Jews were forbidden to do themselves on the Sabbath. Jim went to the Jewish home of a friend upon request to re-light the stove so the fam-ily's Sabbath meal could be warmed. One neighbor brought his watch on Saturday mornings for Jim to wind and set. However, not all visits were for duties such as these. "Many came with problems and asked for help in solv-ing them," said Jim. "Most of these involved money, mercy and matrimony! Others wanted answers to spiritual questions which were troubling them."[11]

The Lindsey family moved to the farm in Petah Tikva—and stayed for two years taking charge while the Murpheys lived in Haifa for a year of lan-guage study followed by a year of furlough in the States. The Home chil-dren, who spoke Arabic and English, were also becoming fluent in Hebrew. At Christmas a huge Christmas tree and lights were placed atop the build-ing and the kids put on a play that was attended by the local populace. The Home children also traveled to Nazareth to present the play. There was an Open House for guests and friends in the area.

All the older children, including the older Lindsey children, worked two hours a day in the fields under the supervision of the men who lived in worker's cottages and farmed the acreage. Vegetables, meat and dairy prod-ucts consumed at the center were often produced right on the farm. The children also were assigned chores and received weekly allowances. The money was placed in bank accounts and the children learned how to bal-ance their checkbooks.[12]

In Tel Aviv, Baptists finally secured a building permit to enclose the ground floor in the same building where rooms had earlier been torn down. The fact that Baptists could and did get such a permit indicated a change of attitude on the part of local officials toward the presence of evangelicals in Israel's largest metropolis. The project gave Baptists in Tel Aviv a meeting place for Christian activities as well as a cultural center. The center also pro-vided office and working space for Dugith Publishers, the Israel Baptist

Convention Press, from which a steady stream of Hebrew and English books and publications flowed.[13] Bob Lindsey conceived the idea of a Baptist art gallery and located suitable property in Tel Aviv. He led in opening the art gallery, named *Dugith* (later transliterated *Dugit*) a Hebrew word meaning "little fishing boat." The exhibits always drew an appreciative crowd. The popular gallery sold art, books and Christian literature.[14]

In the summer of 1957, the last Sunday before departing Atlanta for Israel, Paul Rowden sent a letter to be published in the Cascade Baptist Church Bulletin.

> Dear Friends in Christ: Last Sunday night I purposely stood outside the church as the evening hour began, and in the encircling darkness listened to the singing of gospel hymns, to prayer, and to the Scripture being read. I wanted to store this memory up for the days ahead....Now the time has come to return to the field. We are grateful to each of you for your kindnesses to us. Often we have been concerned and embarrassed at the recognition and attention given us as missionaries, because our job is no more important than any other Spirit-led member of Cascade. Perhaps it is because we have no other missionaries to give attention to, and this is the burden of our hearts—that after 35 years Cascade has produced only one missionary couple. Let us pray that God shall mightily work among us and that we shall be willing to dedicate our children to God's will, whatever it might be.[15]

Paul and Marjorie and the children, Becky, Robin and Richard (Ric) left Atlanta from the Terminal Station to travel by rail to New York Harbor where they boarded the S.S. Israel *to sail back to Israel.*

49
Letters
JULY to SEPTEMBER 1, 1957

Rowdens
Box 6096
Mt. Carmel
Haifa, Israel.

Sunday, July 28, 1957

Dear Friends:

This is a hurried farewell note. By the time you receive this we will have sailed out of New York harbor aboard the *S.S. Israel*...Our ship leaves at 2 P.M. August 1 and is scheduled to arrive in Haifa, Israel, our own city of residence, on August 15.

This has been a wonderful furlough year. Often we have stood amazed at the speed with which it was flying past, but we have managed to cram each day full with activities. During the year we have spoken over 200 times, Paul has completed a year of graduate study at Dropsie Hebrew College in Philadelphia, and we have welcomed a baby son into our family...

There is naturally sorrow in our hearts as we part from our family and friends for another 5-year period, but there is also joy as we anticipate seeing our...friends in Israel again soon. Having already served one term in the Middle East, we are returning with no illusions as to the easiness nor the overwhelming results of our work. We realize, more than ever, what our Lord meant when He said, "Apart from me you can do nothing." Only God can bring victory for Himself in Israel. Our task is to be found faithful to the task He has given us.

We [covet] your prayers and would appreciate your letters. Encouragement from the "home base" means much. May God bless each of you. In Hebrew we say *"Shalom"* when we say good-bye. *Shalom* means peace. We sincerely pray that peace may reign in the Middle East so that the Gospel of Christ might go forth.

In Christian love,

Paul and Marjorie Rowden

Aerogramme To:
Coles
1546 Richland Rd SW
Atlanta, Ga. USA

Marjorie Rowden
Box 6096
Haifa, Israel

Saturday, August 24, 1957

Dearest Folks:

Well, we have been here [in Haifa, Israel] 10 days and have accomplished a lot. We still have much to do to get completely settled but we feel at home again. It was wonderful to be able to come right straight to our apartment and get started unpacking immediately…
…After we left home we drove to the [Atlanta] Terminal Station and there was Charlie Brown[1] and Alta Lee Lovegren…Alta Lee had corsages for all three of us girls [Becky, Robin and me]. Charlie had two big boxes of candy and took the girls riding on the horses in the Terminal. We had a real nice compartment and slept pretty good. We got to NY about 9 and got a cab to the hotel…We got a telegram from Dr. [Baker James] Cauthen[2] assuring us of his prayers, which I thought was very thoughtful. Paul stayed busy [in New York] the whole time rounding up last minute items. He and Becky had box seats to hear Billy Graham one night and both girls and I went the second night. It was a thrilling experience to see that sight in Madison Square Garden.

We got a cab Thursday about 2:30 for the port…We didn't actually sail until about 7 P.M. It was just getting to be sunset as we sailed behind Manhattan Island, on out past the Statute of Liberty. We were pulled out of dock by two tug boats.

After all the visitors went ashore, we found out who were passengers…and met some lovely people. I think I told you there were 350 passengers and 150 crew and we were the only Gentiles. But having been in Israel 5 years we felt right at home…Our waiter was former head waiter at the King David Hotel in Jerusalem. We learned to know him and like him very much. We also had tea at 4 in the Tel Aviv Lounge each day.

…The Captain was especially nice to us… One …evening he especially called us up to see a real comet through his binoculars. It was beautiful with a tail of fire and everything. He said it was the first one he had ever seen in his career.

…We passed several Greek Islands and Crete before getting to Israel Thursday A.M. Everyone was up early to see the first sight of Mt. Carmel and Haifa Bay. Most of our fellow first class passengers were American Jews coming for their first visit, although most of the tourists [class passengers] were Israeli people returning from visiting the States.

…There was Bob Lindsey at the bottom of the gangplank, naturally. All the rest [of the mission and friends] were behind the fence but we could see them peeping through and shouting at us. Everyone and their brother were there—even all the children…Penina [Nehama] was there and also Yusef Qupti from Nazareth…Then they all came up to our apartment for lunch.

It looked so nice and clean. Herman and June [Petty] had worked hard cleaning out most of the Murphey's stuff and having the apartment done over. But by the time we all got in and ate lunch here it was a grand mess. But it was like old times again…

…We are going to Jerusalem Monday afternoon late and stay until early Thursday. Betty and Jim [Smith] are having a reception for us to meet all our Jerusalem friends again. I think that is real nice. We will come back Thursday by the farm [in Petah Tikva] and spend the day. The girls are dying to see the children at the Home…

Lots of love,

Marjorie and all.

341

Aerogramme To:
Coles
1546 Richland Rd SW
Atlanta, Ga. USA

Marjorie Rowden
Box 6096
Haifa, Israel

Sunday, September 1, 1957

Dearest Folks:

...Becky and Robin start to school tomorrow and from now on they will be in school on Sunday through Friday each week [and off on the Sabbath]. We have had a time getting them enrolled. They had to take entrance tests and we had to make umpteen trips to the *[Reali]* school office down town, but at least they are in. It is by far the best school in Israel and is very expensive and hard to get in.

Last Monday evening we drove to Jerusalem. Left here about 4:30 and got there at 7:30. It is a nice drive especially at that time of day. [Ric] sat in his car seat and slept in my lap all the way. Betty and Jim [Smith] and Miss Fenderson were waiting with supper and we had the thrill of being back in Jerusalem again. There is just something exciting about that city. Seeing it in the distance on the mountaintop as we drove up was thrilling...

...Tuesday the regular monthly city-wide prayer service was held at our Jerusalem church, next door, and Paul spoke to the group...Wednesday A.M. Paul and I drove out to the new Hebrew University campus (the old one is in Jordan territory now) and we had a private tour of the 14 new buildings. I have never seen such progress. The campus is going to be huge and beautiful. All the buildings are very modernistic and lovely.

Early Thursday A.M. we left and drove to the farm. We were all dying to see the 19 [Home] kids. They have grown a foot each and looked so good and seemed happy helping with all the cattle and chickens, etc. Bob and Margaret [Lindsey] seem to be carrying on real well there although it has nearly killed Margaret. Their little year-old-baby girl, Debbie, is precious. We had lunch with them and then drove on into Haifa.

Night before last Kathy and Leonard Cowles (the American Consul and his wife) [in Haifa] came to see us. They had a baby girl last year while we were gone. They already had 3. They are leaving in October for two months in the States and then they have been assigned to Bolivia. We are sorry to see them go.

Yesterday Paul went to Nazareth [Baptist School] for a faculty meeting. He seems to think all will go well in the school this year. Herman [Petty] is still there even though he will be studying language this year, so he can help out. Also we are expecting [a] young couple from Georgetown College who are to help teach this year. They should arrive this week sometime…

Much—much love,

Marjorie and all.

P.S. Got a letter from Alta Lee [Lovegren] saying their baby girl had arrived. We were so happy everything was OK.

50

THE UCCI, VOLUNTEERS, and BIBLE LAND SEMINARS

In a letter dated September 1, 1957, Marjorie wrote of a city-wide prayer service held at the Jerusalem Baptist Church. Ministers of a growing number of evangelical churches had been meeting together once a week for prayer and fellowship. Gradually the ministers felt that a wider fellowship of evangelical Christian groups was urgently needed. They arranged several exploratory meetings in Jerusalem. The first annual conference of the group was held at the Baptist Center at Petah Tikva on October 24, 1957. Seven groups formed the United Christian Council in Israel (UCCI). This organization grew to include 17 member bodies from Norway, Finland, Great Britain and America, and included agencies such as the Edinburgh Medical Missionary Society, the British and Foreign Bible Society, and indigenous churches such as the Messianic Assemblies and the Evangelical Episcopal Community. They met for mutual advice and encouragement as well as to cooperate on projects such as organizing educational conferences, publishing brochures for Christian tourists and pilgrims, publishing a glossary of Christian terms in Hebrew from a Protestant perspective with equivalents in Arabic, French and English for newspaper reporters, and publication of Bible study books in Arabic. The Baptist ministers in Israel enjoyed good ecumenical relations with other ministers of evangelical churches and congregations.[1] The translation into Hebrew of 400 traditional hymns, worship songs, spirituals and choruses based on Bible texts of the Christian churches was the joint effort of several of the evangelical churches in Israel. The dedication of the hymnbook took place in the garden of the Baptist property in Jerusalem on July 9, 1957. Distribution for use in the local churches began immediately.[2] Today the UCCI encompasses a multitude of Christian churches, organizations, charitable trusts, assemblies and congregations.[3]

Paul Rowden once again took over the administration of the Nazareth Baptist School, driving back and forth between Nazareth and the family's home in Haifa. During the summer of 1957, Bob Lindsey had asked Dr. Leo Eddleman, President of Georgetown College in Kentucky and former Baptist missionary to Palestine (1936–1941), to recommend a young couple who could travel to Nazareth to teach for a year at the school. The Baptist Convention in Israel offered to provide room and board. Dr. Eddleman talked with Bill Marshall and Alice Lee Gardner, who volunteered to go. They had both just graduated from Georgetown College and planned to marry. Bill Marshall planned to enter the ministry, but was willing to defer seminary for a year. "On August 10, 1957, one day after our wedding," said Alice, "we began our journey abroad—financed with donations from friends."[4] The Marshalls traveled by freighter to Italy and then took another freighter to Lebanon. They finally completed their long journey as they crossed from Lebanon into Israel. "We were eager to cross into Israel because we were down to twenty five dollars!" she said.[5] The Baptists of Nazareth welcomed them. The Marshalls attended a reception for Paul and Marjorie Rowden hosted by the school and the members of the Nazareth Baptist Church. Bill and Alice both taught English during the school year. Bill led the music in chapel and also played his trumpet—adding a new dimension to the music program.

While living in Nazareth, the Marshalls recalled two challenging encounters with chickens. Roosters roamed freely outside many Arab homes. All across Nazareth, roosters could be heard crowing at the break of dawn. One day as Alice left the house to walk down the hill to the Nazareth Baptist School, a rooster came out of nowhere—jumping at her and frightening her. Yelling for help, she climbed up on a limb of a mulberry tree. Bill came to her rescue and she cautiously avoided roosters from then on. Chickens were available for purchase in the Nazareth market. Live chickens were preferred so that they could be cooked and eaten right after they were killed. Bill brought a live chicken home from the market one day and tried to kill it. He wasn't successful in cutting its neck off completely—so when he dropped the chicken to the ground, it began flopping and kicking and running around—until finally it died. The Marshalls then boiled the chicken thinking that it would be easier to pull the feathers out. Alice said, "We either boiled it too long or not enough, because we couldn't get the feathers out and finally Bill had to use *pliers* to pluck out the feathers."[6] After this experience, Bill and Alice decided they would forego buying live chickens. The summer before they returned to the United States, the Marshalls lived at *Kibbutz Mizra* in the Jezreel Valley, where they studied Hebrew along with *kibbutz* members.

Upon their return to the United States, Bill Marshall completed a degree at the Southern Baptist Theological Seminary in Louisville, Kentucky. He served as pastor of churches in Kentucky and Virginia before being asked to join the Personnel staff at the FMB in Richmond, Virginia. Young mission volunteers, such as the Marshalls, served as forerunners of the Journeyman Program of the FMB. The Journeyman Program was born partly from the "experiment" of soliciting Georgetown College couples after graduation to serve as year-long volunteers to Israel. By the time the Journeyman Program was officially begun in 1965, six student couples (five from Georgetown College and one couple from Oklahoma Baptist University) had served successfully in Israel. Of the six couples that served as volunteers, four couples ultimately returned as career missionaries—with three couples returning to the Middle East. Bill Marshall's experience as a volunteer in Israel at the Nazareth Baptist School, coupled with his position at the FMB, enabled him to play an important role in designing and implementing the Journeyman Program.[7] The program enabled young college graduates to serve on the mission field for one or two years and gain valuable experience.

With daily responsibilities, the Baptist workers rarely stopped long enough to visit biblical sites or study biblical topics in depth. Therefore, when Bob Lindsey decided to initiate the *Bible Lands Seminar* in Petah Tikva, everyone wanted to participate. The group initially was composed of leaders in the congregations, mission members, visiting teachers and the older children on the farm. Topics included Judaism, Eastern Orthodox Christianity, Islam and historical geography of Bible lands. Trips were added so the participants could see the historical sites, such as the Dead Sea, Shephelah (Philistine country), Ashkelon, Mount Tabor, Jezreel Valley, Safed, Caesarea and the Gulf of Aqaba at Eilat.[8] Alice Marshall recalled that she and Bill would travel to Petah Tikva for the weekend and join in when Bob Lindsey taught the Seminar. The group visited numerous Biblical sites of importance in the Old Testament. "Many of the sites," she said, "were then, nothing more than mounds of earth and potsherds…We visited Masada, En Gedi, Beersheva, East Jerusalem and Petra in Jordan and traveled to places in the Negev Desert."[9] Some sites had no access roads. The Marshalls remember "those rich, unique seminar experiences," not only for educational purposes, but also because it enhanced their understanding of the unique aspects of their Jewish and Christian heritage.[10]

51

LETTERS

SEPTEMBER 1957

Aerogramme To:
Coles
1546 Richland Rd SW
Atlanta, Ga. USA

Marjorie Rowden
Box 6096
Haifa, Israel

Saturday, September 7, 1957

Dearest Mother and Daddy:

It is hard to believe that this is already our 4th *Shabbat* (Sabbath day) in Israel. Time sure goes by in a hurry. This has been a busy week. I have been working all week trying to get the girls settled in school. Becky started last Monday and is in 4th grade… One night she had 20 pages of Hebrew assigned to read. I'm just glad it is she and not I who have to do it…I have hired a private tutor, a recent high school graduate from this same [*Reali*] school, to come each afternoon for an hour and help her with her homework. I'm so thankful that she adjusts to situations as well as she does.

Robin started Thursday. She was scared to death and was almost white with fear. I went with her. She has forgotten almost all her Hebrew but Becky's has returned quickly. Robin cried and didn't want to stay but her teacher was real sweet and spoke English to her the first few minutes. Yesterday was her second day. She cried again and they had to call Becky from her class to come and sit with Robin for 15 minutes. I think she will be better tomorrow. She went with me yesterday to buy all of her supplies and she feels real proud of her book satchel and everything…

Thursday, Fida [Ateek] and her sister, Selma, came over from Nazareth and spent the night. Paul and I wanted to go to Nazareth for the service and for a reception the Nazareth church was giving for us. [Ric] just loved Fida from the first moment. We surely do appreciate all these affairs everyone is having in honor of our return. We can't help but think over and over how different this arrival has been. We had the regular mid-week service and afterwards the church gave a huge reception out on the lighted basketball court by the school. I think everyone in Nazareth came and Dwight [Baker] made the nicest, most complimentary speech you ever heard.

Alice and Bill Marshall have arrived. They are the young couple that have just graduated from Leo Eddleman's school and have just gotten married.[1] They will teach in the [Nazareth Baptist] school until June and then return for seminary work. They are…volunteers. They will live in a little apartment across from Dwight and Emma's house. We like them very much and I'm sure they will be a big help to Paul in the school. Another couple, Max and Velma Stitts, from the same school came along to help Bob and Margaret at the farm by teaching the [Children's Home kids] this year. They will return to the States in June also. They all four arrived together, having taken in the Arab countries briefly first, and they came with upset tummies as usual.

It is 5:30 and *Shabbat* is almost over. At sunset the new week starts and everyone and their family will be out parading up the streets. It is hot here today. As soon as [Ric] wakes up we will join the rest and go for a walk.

Marjorie

The following letter references a visit to Israel by Fon Scofield, who worked for the Foreign Mission Board as Associate Secretary in the Department of Communications from approximately 1948–1977. He traveled the world documenting and photographing Baptist work and taking pictures of the countries in which the missionaries lived and worked. He also produced mission films. The missionaries and the Foreign Mission Board staff used the visual aids in presentations at churches and conferences. Scofield saw the 16mm motion picture come into being as a basic tool of communication. He worked with colleagues in the Radio and Television Commission and with Broadman Products. His name endures in awards of excellence in communications.[1] His

slides, pictures and films are housed in the LifeWay buildings in Nashville, Tennessee.

Aerogramme To:
Coles
1546 Richland Rd SW
Atlanta, Ga. USA

Marjorie Rowden
Box 6096
Haifa, Israel

Saturday, September 14, 1957

Dearest Folks:

Another week has passed. The weather is a little cooler now and really just perfect. We still love our view [of the Mediterranean Sea] and have enjoyed eating out on our porch. Last Sunday morning Paul went down to the Anglican church here in Haifa for the service. He wants to get to know all the Christian workers and groups in the city better. Sunday afternoon Robin was invited to the [Leonard] Cowles (American Consul) for a birthday party for their little 5-year-old son. I went with her and we had a nice time….Robin hasn't cried anymore in first grade and is learning Hebrew so fast that she doesn't even realize it. She is so funny. All the children in her class fight over who is going to play with her at recess and everywhere I go up the streets and in the shops all the women come up to me and say [in Hebrew], "*At eema shell* Robin?" (Are you Robin's mother?) Then they tell me how their children come home each day talking about her…

…Last Monday Bob [Lindsey] started teaching a seminar on Biblical Places in Israel to the two new couples who have arrived to help us out this year. All the rest of us said we'd like to study it along with them so about half were there at the farm for it last Monday.

Tuesday Fon Scofield, Visual Aids head of the Foreign Mission Board and Dr. Pearce (pastor in Deland, Florida) were here for lunch. They had been in the country 3 days. They were very impressed with all of our work and we enjoyed having them. Fon Scofield is a real funny soul. He had just come from Africa and Indonesia and Hawaii and he said he was so mixed up with the time that he was waking up at midnight ready to get up. Then, he said, he got to Israel and had to go to church 3 days in a row, which further mixed him up. [Through translators] they preached in Jerusalem [on] Friday night and Saturday A.M. and then in Nazareth both services on Sunday. Fon said by Sunday night he was holding on to huckleberry bushes to keep from being translated into Heaven.

Fida [Ateek] came over for two days and nights. She will come each week and give us a chance to get out a little. She is so good with the children. Penina [Nehama], from Jerusalem, has been on a week's vacation here in Haifa this week and has been over three times to see us. She had supper here Wednesday night. And came back this morning for our Saturday morning Bible study. I'll close now. We surely do appreciate your letters and look forward to them all the time…

Lots of love,

Marjorie and all.

52
THE JOURNEY HOME

The following letter is written by Rev. Ernest E. Brown, Pastor of the Cascade Baptist Church in Atlanta, Georgia to the members of the church referencing a letter written by Paul Rowden.

Cascade Baptist Church
Alvarado Terrace at West Haven Drive
Atlanta, Georgia

Ernest E. Brown, Pastor

September 24, 1957

Dear Christian Friends,

As Paul and Marjorie Rowden's pastor, I am writing to inform you that they have returned to Atlanta from Israel. They arrived by TWA flight on Saturday, September 21, at 2:00 P.M. and Paul immediately entered the Georgia Baptist Hospital. The following is an excerpt from a letter, which he wrote me at dawn of the day they arrived:

> A few weeks ago I had a swelling in a thigh gland, which would not respond to treatment and drugs. Doctors said that it must be removed, which it was, in Haifa. Pathological examination proved it to be quite malignant, but the source of the infection could not be found. The surgeon felt that expert treatment in America was immediately advisable, as Israel is limited in this respect—hence our locking our apartment door and returning.

Our hearts are not rebellious, nor do we question why. God knows in our hearts that we live for one purpose only—to glorify Him, and we are sure that He had a purpose in letting us return to Israel, only to have to return to America so soon. We trust that treatment shall be only a matter of weeks and that we might return to Israel and the needy work—if God wills.

… [O]ur hearts are heavy for the work we left—our field is so short of workers, our missionaries so overworked and tired. Yet we know that all things are working out to glorify God and we are content to say, "Not my will, but Thine be done."

In the last few days before leaving Haifa we had opportunities opened up to witness for God like we had never had before. May we count on your prayers that His perfect will might be done in us—that in everything we might glorify Him, whose we are and whom we serve.

I am sure you recognize that his condition is serious; you are conscious, too, that God hears and answers prayer. So let me urge you to pray earnestly for him and for Marjorie as she ministers to him and cares for the children…

Earnestly yours in Christ,
Ernest E. Brown (John 3:30)

Following a second operation, the prognosis was optimistic. Paul regained his strength and was eager to return to Israel. However the FMB recommended that he stay in the United States for observation and continue working on his doctorate. Paul spoke at numerous churches in Atlanta and served a few months as interim pastor at the First Baptist Church of Chattahoochee, Atlanta.

The family moved to Philadelphia in February 1958 and lived in seminary housing at the Eastern Theological Baptist Seminary. Paul attended classes at Dropsie College for Hebrew and Cognate Learning continuing to work on his doctorate. Marjorie took a class at the seminary. In March 1959, the Rowdens celebrated the birth of a daughter, Paige Allison. The family went on picnics, visited interesting sites in Philadelphia and learned how to maneuver during snowfalls. Becky and Robin tried ice-skating on a frozen lake with instructions from friends. At a nearby Baptist church Paul led an adult Sunday school class called, "The Kitchen Class." The members met in the church's kitchen and made a big pot of coffee every Sunday morning. They brought doughnuts to eat while Paul engaged everyone in spirited discussions of the scriptures. Paul and Marjorie were asked to speak at mission conferences in the area. They corresponded with the missionaries in Israel, visited with those on furlough and looked forward to a return. Paul worked toward his doctoral degree in Hebrew and Arabic and completed his dissertation, "A Century of American Protestantism in the Arab Middle East: 1820–1920." On June 2, 1959, the Doctor of Philosophy degree was conferred upon him by Dropsie College.[1]

At the end of the school year, the Rowdens headed back to Atlanta. They rented a small house a block from the Cascade Baptist Church. The family enjoyed seeing friends and family again and attended services. One Sunday night, Paul baptized Robin at the Cascade Baptist Church. Plans were made to travel back to Israel in August 1959 and tickets for passage were purchased. Then another medical test showed that the cancer had returned and spread to the lungs. On October 3, 1959, Marjorie wrote:

The hospital corridor was quiet except for the rapid efficient actions of the nurses on duty. It was Saturday afternoon. A few visitors sat in the lounge speaking in undertones.

A green tank of oxygen was rolled into Room 412. Through the door, as it was opened and closed again quickly, one could see the Resident Physician and several nurses bending over the unconscious form.

A few minutes passed. I walked several steps away, and then turned. I glanced back at the door just as it was opened again noiselessly and the Resident stepped out.

"May I see my husband?" I asked hesitatingly.
"I'm sorry," he said simply, "he just passed away."[2]

In the Cascade Baptist Church bulletin for October 18, 1959, Marjorie wrote, "Our hearts are broken and our home is lonely, but God is good and His mercies are new each day. He [Paul] was more prepared for Heaven than anyone I ever knew. He was an inspiration to all who knew him. He loved his Bible and his prayer life was deep and powerful. He was the best Christian I ever knew, and I knew him best."

"Paul was generous in giving his love, interest and genuine concern for all the people of Israel," said Jim Smith. "He loved equally the believer and the non-believer. He did not flinch before danger and trouble. During his sickness he once said, 'I do not know how long I will live in this world, but I do know that I want to live for the glory of God while I am here.'"[3]

In addition to the funeral service in Atlanta, a memorial service was held at the Nazareth Baptist Church and at the Baptist Center in Petah Tikva, where the mission members, Home children and folks who knew Paul gathered. Marty Murphey sang a solo and said it was the hardest solo she ever had to sing.[4] Many shared their memories of Paul or "Uncle Paul," as the children knew him. A telegram came from the Nazareth Baptist School and simply said, "Entire school grieved—Mr. Rowden's memory blessed among us—may God's peace be yours."[5]

As summer approached Marjorie decided to further her education and was accepted at the New Orleans Baptist Theological Seminary. In the fall of 1960, she began a two-year program of course work toward completion of a Master's Degree in Religious Education. The family lived in seminary housing on the campus.

From Nazareth came word that Baptists dedicated a new building for the primary division of the Nazareth Baptist School and named it the "Paul D. Rowden Primary School." As principal of the school, Paul Rowden had written: "The basic aim of the school is to reach the students for the kingdom of God, which includes not only the salvation of *souls* but also the salvation of *lives*."[6] Dwight Baker stated, "As headmaster, Paul Rowden needed boundless energy to keep the growing school going…He was never too busy to talk with someone about a problem, or with someone who just wanted to talk. He tried to speak individually with each student about being a Christian, and about what Christ meant in his own life."[7] "No one has outlined the basic aims of this school so clearly, nor pursued their fulfillment as intently as did the one after whom we name this school."[8]

In the summer of 1962, the family moved to Hattiesburg, Mississippi where Marjorie began teaching and working in the Office of Public Relations at William Carey College, (now William Carey University), a Baptist college named after William Carey, an English Baptist missionary to India (1793–1834). Church members and college staff stopped by the house and showered us with southern hospitality. The friendships we made in Hattiesburg enriched our lives. For the next seventeen years, my mother served as Associate Professor of Religion and eventually as Vice President for College Relations at William Carey College. She wrote several Baptist mission books.[9] Dr. Ralph Noonkester, President of the college (1956–1989) once said, "It was fitting that Marjorie, who had a vision for missions—if anyone did—should be associated with a former woman's college named for the proverbial "Father of Modern Missions."[10]

During the years my mother worked at William Carey College, she frequently led tours to Europe, Asia, South America and the Middle East—enlisting students, faculty and church friends. My brother, sisters and I often traveled with her. She loved to travel and inspired her students to think about missions.

In 1979, Marjorie married Dr. Earl Kelly, Executive Director-Treasurer of the Mississippi Baptist Convention. Dr. Kelly's wife had died after several years of illness. Marjorie retired from her position at William Carey College

Students mingle at the Paul D. Rowden Primary School. To the right is the first Nazareth Baptist School building on the site, Nazareth, c. 1961.

and the couple made their home in Jackson, Mississippi. Following Dr. Kelly's retirement, they traveled extensively. They both taught classes at the Baptist Seminary in Bagio, Philippines and spent a year in Okinawa where Dr. Kelly filled in for a pastor on furlough.

In 1994, my sister Paige planned and carried out a surprise 70th birthday party for *Marge*, as everyone called mother. It was held in Hattiesburg, Mississippi at the home of my mother's dear friend, Ollie Thomas. Friends and family gathered from far and wide. A map of the world was placed on the wall and guests, many of whom had traveled with my mother on tours abroad, were challenged to name a country in the world that Marge had *not* visited. My mother died in 2002 at the age of 78. A scholarship fund named in her honor was set up at William Carey University.

53

EPILOGUE

I received an invitation to the June 2004 Fifty-Year-Jubilee Graduation at the Nazareth Baptist School, the school I attended as a young child. The Jubilee celebration commemorated the 50th year since the first graduation of the twelfth grade class. My husband and I traveled to Israel to attend the event and met up with Bill Baker, my childhood friend, who volunteered to drive us around to see the sites.[1] Bill is the son of Dwight and Emma Baker, who faithfully served in the Baptist Convention in Israel among the Arab communities for 27 years and then served in India for 10 years—retiring in 1986. Bill speaks Hebrew and Arabic like a native, and knew all the local hole-in-the-wall eateries where we could gorge ourselves on schawarma— slow cooking lamb sizzled on a rack—sliced and put in pita with toppings of our choice—tahini sauce, eggplant, peppers, cabbages, cucumbers, tomatoes, yogurt, herbs and spices. It was a rare treat for me to taste genuine Middle Eastern food again. As we traveled around the country I became reacquainted with family friends and saw many of the places that remain a vivid part of my childhood.

Asa Farrah, former Children's Home kid and a childhood playmate, now a grandfather, invited us to his home in Jaffa where we reminisced, looked at pictures from our childhood and caught up on news. Asa called me "the lost and found." Our lives diverged for many years; we were "lost" to each other, and now, he concluded, I had been "found." His wife and two daughters prepared a multitude of Arab dishes and we had a true feast.

We drove into Nazareth to see the Baptist church and school. Over the past fifty years the Nazareth Baptist School has expanded enormously. The buildings making up the school are now three stories tall and occupy three sides of the lot. Enrollment is limited to about 1,000 because there is no further room for expansion in the cramped and noisy downtown area. I saw the primary school building named after my father and remembered fondly the years I attended the school.

Next to the school is the Nazareth Baptist Church where we attended a service. The church building has been enlarged to accommodate the growing number of worshipers. The painting by Bill's grandmother of the Jordan River still hangs over the baptistery. After the service, I visited with Rhadia Shurrush Qubti, who was the first child accepted in the George W. Truett Children's Home. As children, we routinely marched down the hill from the Children's Home to the Nazareth Baptist School and Church. Rhadia had the opportunity, not only to be part of the Truett Children's Home, but to also enjoy gatherings with her father, Abu George, her stepmother Soriya, and her brothers and sisters. Rhadia traveled to the United States in the late nineteen sixties to further her education. She received a B.A. from Iowa Wesleyan College and a Master's Degree in Social Work from Michigan State University. Rhadia was determined to return to her home community in an attempt to make a difference. In Israel she worked for three years in a project that resulted in the establishment of a Comprehensive Health Rehabilitation Center for the disabled in Jewish and Arab villages. She also worked toward establishing a social service department at the Edinburgh Medical Mission Society (EMMS) Hospital in Nazareth, now called the "Nazareth Hospital," and accredited by the Israel Ministry of Health.[2] Rhadia married Elia Qubti, a teacher at the Nazareth Baptist School, who obtained his teaching degree at Haifa University. They raised a houseful of children. Rhadia participates in an international peace movement initiated by Palestinian Christians. In 2008 she represented the group at a conference in the Netherlands where she gave a presentation on the complexity of being a Christian Arab and a Palestinian Israeli.[3]

In the nineteen sixties, the Baptist congregations in Nazareth, Jerusalem and Petah Tikva joined forces to promote mutual cooperation and fellowship. They formed the Association of Baptist Churches in Israel.[4] Over the years there has been an increase in the number of Baptist churches resulting in a community of approximately 3,000 believers making up approximately 20 churches and assemblies in Galilee and Central Israel.

As Baptist congregations in Israel began to experience growth, local lay pastors, deacons and teachers had a need for theological training. The lay pastors in Israel, being Arab-Israelis, could not get a visa to go to the Baptist Theological Seminary in nearby Beirut, Lebanon. In 1964, Dwight and Emma Baker moved to Haifa, and Dwight Baker began a Christian Service Training Center, later called Theological Education by Extension. It was the beginning of a program of theology.[5] Dwight Baker's tireless efforts, alongside Arab leaders he trained, laid a foundation for many Baptist ministries in Galilee.[6] In 2007, a major step toward achieving training for local ministers was met with the opening of the Nazareth Evangelical Theological Seminary. The seminary is a Baptist initiative and has a website.[7] Other protestant groups are invited to participate. Bader Mansour, Secretary of the Association of Baptist Churches in Israel, states the difficulty of finding qualified ministers to meet the needs of churches. He writes, "Although the number of churches in Israel is growing, pastors are often untrained and some have to work more than one job in order to survive. Many churches do not own a church building and meet in rented apartments, which limit their activities."[8] The Nazareth Seminary is serving the needs of lay pastors, teachers and a diverse student body. Funds are solicited from around the world to help the program succeed. Visiting theological professors contribute to the program.

Near Nazareth is the town of Tur'an. Fida Ateek Ramadan and her husband Suhail Ramadan lived in Tur'an above the Baptist church in an apartment. Suhail was retired from his position as pastor of the Tur'an Baptist Church where he had served since 1971.[9] Fida played a significant role in raising and nurturing the Home children and served as a mother figure to all the mission kids. She remained a stabilizing force for many of the Home children as they became adults, married, began careers and in many cases, traveled to distant shores. They often visited Fida upon their return to the Galilee area, and she was "The One" to see in order to get updates on everyone. We sat around her table eating watermelon and talking while her grandchildren sat playing on the tile-covered porch.

From Tur'an we drove on to the Sea of Galilee and stayed in the guesthouse of the YMCA Harte House, just north of Tiberias. The Harte House sits on a rock outcrop that juts out into the water. Its exterior is made of dark basaltic rock found in the Tiberias area.[10] As a child I knew it as the "black" house on the grounds where we had our picnics, swam about in cool waters and where Baptists and other Christian groups held baptismal services. Eucalyptus and palm trees lined the rocky shore where fishermen hung their nets to dry. We dined in Tiberias by the Sea of Galilee mesmerized by the still water and beautiful scenery.

Nearby was the house where Bob Lindsey and his family lived for a while as he began his many years translating the Gospels into Modern Hebrew. In his book, *A Translation of the Gospel of Mark,*[11] Dr. Lindsey concluded that there was proof of Hebraic literary sources behind the Gospels.[12] Lindsey struggled over many years to discover the earliest form of words attributed to Jesus in order to find an authentic picture of Jesus interacting with the people of Jerusalem and Galilee. He collaborated with David Flusser, professor at the Hebrew University, to examine Jesus' sayings from a Judaic and Hebraic perspective and published his findings in a book, *Jesus Rabbi & Lord*.[13]

We next headed south to Jerusalem. In 1967, during the Six Day War, the area called "East Jerusalem," in Jordan, was captured by Israel. The Jerusalem Baptist Church has expanded its ministry over the years. Eventually it changed its name to "Narkis Street Baptist Congregation," and is now know as the "Narkis Street Congregation." It is located on the corner of Narkis and Hagidem Streets in downtown Jerusalem. A Hebrew speaking congregation grew out of the Narkis Street Baptist Congregation. In 1994, a Russian speaking congregation was established.[14] When arsonists burned the church down in 1982, Jews in Jerusalem expressed their overwhelming support of the congregation's right to worship, without victimization by hate crimes. Bob Lindsey, the pastor at the time, was invited to speak at a nearby synagogue and presented with a Hebrew pulpit Bible with an inscription that said, "This Hebrew Bible is presented to the Baptist congregation of West Jerusalem by your neighbor, Congregation Har-El of Jerusalem (Israel Movement for Progressive Judaism) as a token of friendship and encouragement after the fire which destroyed your house of prayer."[15] Israelis from all parts of society contributed money to the Narkis Street Baptist Congregation—from Jerusalem's Mayor, Teddy Kollek, to workers at a nearby butcher shop, as well as school children.[16]A new and larger church building now stands on the site of the old one. Services are held in several languages. "The congregation is an open door for all followers of Jesus from every nation, language and denomination."[17] Also in Jerusalem is the Jerusalem Prayer Center (JPC) located in an historic building that was once part of the American Colony of Jerusalem. Baptists have owned the building since the late sixties. Located on Nablus Road, the JPC is positioned on the dividing line between East and West Jerusalem. This location places it on a strategic site to facilitate prayer for all people in the Holy Land and beyond. Believers living in Israel, as well as pilgrims and tourists from around the world, can visit and pray.[18] Dale and Anita Thorne with the Baptist Convention in Israel, serve as hosts.[19]

Gaza is southwest of Jerusalem. When the Gaza Strip fell to Israel in 1967, Jim Smith served for a few years as liaison between the Baptist Mission in Israel and the Gaza Baptist Mission. He traveled back and forth from his home in Ashkelon, Israel. Jim served as the business manager of the hospital operated by Baptists in Gaza and as pastor of the English language section of the Gaza Baptist Church. He later served as chaplain to the American military stationed at the Israeli Ramon Air Base south of Beersheba. Betty Smith served as press representative for the Baptist Mission in Israel for 12 years and was editor of publications for several civic and ecumenical groups. Jim and Betty Smith used their home in Ashkelon as a base from which to reach out to believers in *kibbutzim* and towns in the large area south of Tel Aviv. Both were active in fostering interfaith dialogue among Jews, Muslims and Christians.

From the time of the establishment of the State of Israel, the number of Messianic Jews has grown and is now anywhere between 6,000 and 15,000. They meet in congregations and house-churches. The leaders gather their congregations together to celebrate Jewish holidays. In 1997, more than 1,500 Jewish believers and their families met for a national day of prayer and fasting at Baptist Village in Petah Tikva during the Jewish New Year. They hesitate to be officially linked to any Christian mission group, partly because of harassment by anti-mission groups in the country.[20] However, some Messianic communities participate in educational forums with Christian groups. They have a united commitment to developing faith-based education and to celebrating diversity.

The highlight of the trip for me was the Jubilee Graduation in Nazareth. It was held up on one of the hills under a huge tent set up beside a modern high-rise hotel. The General Director of the Nazareth Baptist School, Fuad Haddad and his wife Abla, along with staff and faculty, welcomed us graciously.[21] As evening came, hundreds of guests—families of graduates—dignitaries and alumni—all gathered for the celebration. On one row sat ladies who had been in the first secondary school graduating class fifty years before. They were recognized and everyone applauded. The music began. Elementary school girls marched in and stood on either side of the middle isle holding up arches made of flowers. Eighty or so graduates in their robes and mortarboards filed in under the arches. Everyone clapped in time with the festive music. The young men and women were bright and attractive. Their faces held so much promise for the future.

A huge cake in the shape of an open Bible was rolled in on a cart. Above the dais where the graduates sat was a big sign that read, "Nazareth Baptist School – 50 Years." As each diploma was handed out, a Bible was also given. At the end of the celebration the mortarboards went flying into the air—students cheered—parents cried and guests were exuberant. I thought of my parents, who had attended the first secondary school graduation fifty years earlier, and imagined, had they been at this huge celebration, they simply

Becky Rowden, center, is pictured at the Jubilee Graduation in Nazareth, June, 2004, with ladies from the first Nazareth Baptist School-secondary school graduating class.

would have been amazed and humbled. Numerous people—too many to count—have committed themselves to the development and growth of the school over the decades. Hundreds of alumni have become influential professionals. Honors are bestowed yearly on students and faculty alike. For the school year 2007–2008 the Israeli Education Ministry announced that the Baptist Secondary School in Nazareth ranked fourth in the country in percentage of students who received an "outstanding" grade on their matriculation exams.[22] About 85 percent of all graduates of the school go on to study at the country's top universities. Although the FMB (now the International Mission Board) no longer provides financial support for the school's administration, there is continuing interest in support of the school. The school, (it now has its own web site),[23] continues to value and rely on the financial contributions of Baptists and other Christian denominations and fellowships around the world as it struggles to grow and seek a new campus. Only time will tell if the school will survive and continue to educate Christian leaders for the next fifty years.

"There is no greater thrill," wrote Paul Rowden, "than to watch believers grow in the knowledge of the Lord and demonstrate the change that has come into their lives by witnessing among their people. This is the goal of Christian missions."[24]

NOTES

INTRODUCTION

[1] Paul Rowden, letter to James Smith, July 10, 1953.
[2] Hannah Belle Scoggin, "Home on the Farm," *Commission* (June 1952).

BAPTISTS IN NAZARETH 1911–1952

[1] Jean Said Makdisi, *Teta, Mother, and Me—Three Generations of Arab Women*, (New York: W.W. Norton & Company, 2006), 218.
[2] Velora Griffin Hanna, "Questing in Galilee," in *Questing in Galilee*, (Richmond: Foreign Mission Board of the Southern Baptist Convention, 1937), 29-31.
[3] Makdisi, *Teta, Mother, and Me—Three Generations of Arab Women*, 219.
[4] I am indebted to Julia Hagood Graham for her mimeographed history, "Entrance of the Foreign Mission Board of the Southern Baptist Convention into the Middle East," in "Baptist Beginnings in Lebanon 1893–1956" (1986).
[5] Mrs. J. W. Watts, "Palestine and Syrian Mission," in *Report of the Foreign Mission Board of the Southern Baptist Convention*, May 14, 1924, (Accession Number 2717, International Mission Board Archives and Records Services, Solomon Database) http://archives.imb.org/solomon.asp (accessed December 21, 2009).
[6] Makdisi, *Teta, Mother, and Me—Three Generations of Arab Women*, 170.
[7] Ibid. 171.
[8] Roswell E. Owens, "Two Timothies in Haifa," in *Questing in Galilee*, (Richmond: Foreign Mission Board of the Southern Baptist Convention, 1937), 47-48.
[9] Hanna, *Questing in Galilee*, 34-36.
[10] Hanna, *Questing in Galilee*, 32-33.
[11] Betty Jane Bailey & J. Martin Bailey, *Who Are the Christians in the Middle East?* (Grand Rapids: Wm. B. Eerdmans Publishing Co., 2003) 97.

12 Hanna, *Questing in Galilee,* 36-38.

13 BibleWalks.com, "Christ Church," http://www.biblewalks.com/Sites/ ChristChurch.html (accessed December 21, 2009).

14 Mrs. J.W. Watts, *Report of the Foreign Mission Board, Southern Baptist Convention,* May 14, 1924, (Accession Number 2717), http://archives. imb.org/solomon.asp

15 Ibid.

16 Ibid.

17 J. Wash. Watts, "Palestine and Syrian Mission," in *Report of the Foreign Mission Board of the Southern Baptist Convention,* May 13, 1925, (Accession Number 2715, International Mission Board Archives and Records Services, Solomon Database), http://archives.imb.org/solomon.asp, (accessed December 21, 2009).

18 Ibid.

19 Ibid. Also, Graham, "Entrance of the Foreign Mission Board of the Southern Baptist Convention into the Middle East," in "Baptist Beginnings in Lebanon 1893–1956," (1986).

20 Betty Jane West, (daughter of Dr. & Mrs. Washington Watts), in conversation with author, October 10, 2009.

21 I am indebted to Dwight L. Baker for his mimeographed history, "Baptists' Golden Jubilee, 50 Years In Palestine-Israel, 1911–1961, A Short Commemorative History" (1961).

22 J. Wash Watts, *Report of the Foreign Mission Board of the Southern Baptist Convention,* (1925).

23 Ibid.

24 "Jureidini": See Mrs. J. Wash Watts, *Palestinian Tapestries,* 2nd ed. (Richmond: Foreign Mission Board of the Southern Baptist Convention, 1936) 55-57. Also see, Jane Carroll McRae, *Photographer in Lebanon, the Story of Said Jureidini.* (Nashville: Broadman Press, 1969).

25 Graham, "1926," in "Baptist Beginnings in Lebanon 1893–1956," (1986).

26 J. Wash Watts, "Palestine and Syrian Mission," in *Report of the Foreign Mission Board of the Southern Baptist Convention,* May 16-20, 1928, (Accession number 2712, International Mission Board Archives and Records Services, Solomon Database), http://archives.imb.org/solomon.asp (accessed December 22, 2009).

27 Ibid. Also see Watts, *Palestinian Tapestries,* 2nd ed., 66.

28 Watts, *Report of the Foreign Mission Board of the Southern Baptist Convention,* May 16-20, 1928.

29 Roswell E. Owens, "Palestine," *Report of the Foreign Mission Board of the*

Southern Baptist Convention, May 9-12, 1929, (Accession Number 2720, International Mission Board Archives and Records Services, Solomon Database) http://archives.imb.org/solomon.asp, (accessed December 22, 2009).

[30] Roswell E Owens, "Palestine," *Report of the Foreign Mission Board Southern Baptist Convention*, May 13, 1931, (Accession Number 2728, International Mission Board Archives and Records Services, Solomon Database), http://archives.imb.org/solomon.asp, (accessed December 22, 2009).

[31]*Encyclopedia of Southern Baptists*, s.v. "Watts, James Washington," (Nashville: Broadman Press, 1982). In 1931, Dr. Watts became professor of Old Testament and Hebrew at the Baptist Bible Institute (now New Orleans Baptist Theological Seminary). He launched a career of scholarly teaching and writing, interim administrative responsibilities, and leadership in theological education, continuing with the institution for 36 years.

[32] Also known as Rev. Hanna Beshoti. See "The History of the Nazareth Baptist School," http://www.nbs.org.il/en (accessed December 14, 2009).

[33] Baker, "Baptists' Golden Jubilee."

[34] Roswell E. Owens, "Two Timothies in Haifa," in *Questing in Galilee* (Richmond: Foreign Mission Board of the Southern Baptist Convention, 1937).

[35] Hanna, *Questing in Galilee*, 44. See also, Watts, *Palestinian Tapestries*, 69.

[36] Makdisi, *Teta, Mother, and Me—Three Generations of Arab Women*, 220.

[37]"Presidents of Georgetown College," "Leo Eddleman, 1954–1958," http://library.georgetowncollege.edu/Special_Collections/Leo_Eddleman.htm, (accessed December 22, 2009).

[38] Baker, "Baptists' Golden Jubilee."

[39]"Presidents of Georgetown College," s.v. "Leo Eddleman, 1954–1958." Dr. Leo Eddleman taught Old Testament and Hebrew at New Orleans Baptist Theological Seminary for a year, and was pastor of Parkland Baptist Church in Louisville, Kentucky for ten years. In 1954, he accepted the position of president of Georgetown College. In 1959, he accepted the presidency of New Orleans Baptist Theological Seminary where he remained until his retirement in 1970. He returned to Louisville where he died in July 1995.

[40]"Kate Ellen Gruver," Papers, Foreign Mission Board Missionary Correspondence Collection, Southern Baptist Historical Library and Archives, Nashville, Tennessee. Kate Ellen Gruver was born in the Panama Canal Zone, the daughter of a U.S. Public Health Service medical doctor working in the quarantine camps. The family later lived in Mexico and then moved back to the United States. Gruver received an undergraduate ed-

ucation from Vanderbilt University in Nashville and at Tennessee College. She also completed a Master of Religion Education at the WMU Training School in Louisville, Kentucky.

[41] George Sadler, "Europe, Africa and The Near East," *Report to the Foreign Mission Board of the Southern Baptist Convention*, February 24, 1943, (Accession Number 2734, International Mission Board Archives and Records Services, Solomon Database), http://archives.imb.org/ solomon.asp, (accessed December 22, 2009).

[42] Baker, "Baptists' Golden Jubilee."

[43] Ibid.

[44] Rhadia Shurrush Qubti, email to author, September 10, 2008. Also, Julia Haygood Graham, in telephone conversation with author, August 25, 2008.

[45] Graham, "Entrance of the Foreign Mission Board of the Southern Baptist Convention into the Middle East," in "Baptist Beginnings in Lebanon 1893–1956," (1986). Graham states that during this period of time, one of the missionaries stated that Graham was "more interested in changing diapers than in saving souls."

[46] "Scots Hospital": For an early history see W. P. Livingstone, *A Galilee Doctor, Being a Sketch of the Career of Dr. D. W. Torrence of Tiberias*, (London: Hodder and Stoughton Limited, 1923). Dr. David Watt Torrance, a Scottish doctor and head of the Church of Scotland mission, founded the Scots Hospital in Tiberias in 1894. His son, Dr. Herbert Torrance, later joined his father and continued operating the hospital until retirement in 1953.

[47] Elizabeth Holt Lee, Papers, Foreign Mission Board, Missionary Correspondence Collection, Southern Baptist Historical Library and Archives, Nashville, Tennessee.

[48] Graham, "Baptist History in Palestine-Israel-Lebanon," (speech before a Middle East Baptist mission group, Waco, Texas, July 2, 2007).

[49] Children were admitted to the Children's Home in Nazareth during the upheaval of the partition of Palestine when families were separated. Some of the children were left at the Edinburgh Medical Missionary Society Hospital in Nazareth and later brought to the Children's Home. Some were orphans. A few of the children had lost one parent—usually the mother. The father, unable to both work and care for the children, brought the siblings to the Children's Home. The reference in the letters is generally to the "orphans" in the Children's Home, although some of the children had one or both parents living at the time they entered the Home. Some of the children had a parent living in an Arab country outside of Israel.

[50] Graham, "1947," in "Entrance of the Foreign Mission Board of the Southern Baptist Convention into the Middle East," in "Baptist Beginnings in Lebanon 1893–1956," (1986).

[51] Tom Segev, *1949 The First Israelis,* (New York: Henry Holt and Company, Inc., 1986), 22.

[52] Anna Cowan, in conversation with the author, July 2, 2005.

[53] Kate Ellen Gruver, "Baptist Children's Home in Nazareth Favored by State of Israel Government," *Commission,* (July 1949).

[54] Marjorie Moore Armstrong, "They Want a Home Too!" *Commission,* (July 1952).

[55] Kate Ellen Gruver, "Nazareth, Israel," *Minutes of the Foreign Mission Board of the Southern Baptist Convention,* May 9, 1950, (Accession Number 2741, International Mission Board Archives and Records Services, Solomon Database), http://archives.imb.org/solomon.asp, (accessed December 22, 2009).

[56] Ibid.

[57] Ibid.

[58] Ibid.

[59] Ibid.

[60] Dwight Leonard Baker, interview by David Stricklin, April 27–May 9, 1989, "Oral Memoirs of Dwight Leonard Baker," Institute for Oral History, Baylor University, Waco, Texas, 1994. Also see, "Dwight Baker," Papers, Foreign Mission Board Missionary Correspondence Collection, Southern Baptist Historical Library & Archives, Nashville, Tennessee.

[61] Emma Baker, "New Appointees," *Commission,*" May 1950. Also see, "Emma Baker," Papers, Foreign Mission Board Missionary Correspondence Collection, Southern Baptist Historical Library & Archives, Nashville, Tennessee.

[62] Dwight Leonard Baker, interview by David Stricklin, April 27–May 9, 1989.

[63] H. Leo Eddleman, *Mandelbaum Gate,* (Nashville: Convention Press, 1963), 82. Also see Dwight Baker, "Religious Liberty in Israel, A Study Covering a Period of Fifteen Years From the Founding of the State in 1948 until 1963," (doctoral dissertation, Hartford Seminary Foundation, Hartford, Connecticut, May, 1963).

[64] "Israel," American Jewish Year Book Vol. 54 (1953), http://www. ajarchives. org. (accessed December 22, 2009).

[65] Bailey & Bailey, *Who Are the Christians in the Middle East?,* 52.

[66] Baker, "Religious Liberty in Israel, A Study Covering a Period of Fifteen

Years From the Founding of the State, 1948–1963."

[67] Herbert Weiner, quoting Dwight Baker in *The Wild Goats of Ein Gedi, A Journal of Religious Encounters in the Holy Land,* (Cleveland: The World Publishing Company; Philadelphia: The Jewish Publication Society of America, 1954, (reprinted 1961 by arrangement with Doubleday & Company, Inc.), 39. Citations are to the Doubleday edition.

[68] Eddleman, *Mandelbaum Gate,* 84.

[69] Weiner, quoting Dwight Baker in *The Wild Goats of Ein Gedi, A Journal of Religious Encounters in the Holy Land,* 39.

[70] Baker, interview by David Stricklin, April 27–May 9, 1989.

[71] Ibid.

[72] Ibid.

PAUL AND MARJORIE ROWDEN

[1] The Cascade Baptist Church members worshiped in their first church home on Beecher Street from 1923 until 1940. In 1941 the church moved to the corner of Westhaven Drive and South Alvarado Terrace. *Silver Anniversary, of the Cascade Baptist Church, The History and Growth, March 11, 1923—March 7, 1948,* 12, privately printed, n.d., [ca. 1948]. The church disbanded in 1970 and the building was sold to a black congregation. Charlie Brown, *Charlie Brown Remembers Atlanta, Memoirs of a Public Man,* as told to James C. Bryant, (Columbia: The R. L. Bryan Company 1982), 111.

[2] Winston Crawley, *Global Mission, A Story to Tell,* (Nashville: Broadman Press, 1985), 30.

[3] Paul Harvey, "Saints but Not Subordinates: The Woman's Missionary Union of the Southern Baptist Convention," in *Women and Twentieth-Century Protestantism,* ed. Margaret Lamberts Bendroth and Virginia Lieson Brereton, (Urbana: University of Illinois Press, 2002), 5.

[4] WMU (Women's Missionary Union) Library, "Women's Missionary Union Emblem and Colors," http://old.wmu.com/resources/library/history_emblem.asp, (accessed January 4, 2010.)

[5] Louie D. Newton, "Atlanta Prepares for the Alliance," *Commission,* (May 1938).

[6] *Atlanta Constitution,* July 24, 1939.

[7] *Atlanta Constitution,* July 16, 1939.

[8] Richard V. Pierard, "History of the Baptist World Alliance: Blacks and the

Baptist World Alliance," *Baptist Studies Bulletin,* 4, no. 4, (2005), http://www.centerforbaptiststudies.org/bulletin/2005/april.htm, (accessed November 5, 2009).

9 *New Georgia Encyclopedia,* 2007, s.v. "Louie D. Newton (1892–1986)," http://www.georgiaencyclopedia. org/nge/Article.jsp?id=h-1613, (accessed November 5, 2009).

10 "Baptist Leaders Arrive in City," *Atlanta Constitution,* July 16, 1939.

11 *Atlanta Constitution,* July 23, 1939.

12 Ibid.

13 "Text of Presidential Address Delivered by Dr. George Truett," *Atlanta Constitution,* July 24, 1939.

14 *Atlanta Constitution,* July 23, 1939.

15 Ibid.

16 "The National Baptist Convention, USA, Inc.", http://www.nationalbaptist.com/Index.cfm?FuseAction=Page&PageID-1000008, (accessed November 5, 2009).

17 *Atlanta Constitution,* July 23, 1939.

18 Byron Hunt Cole to Marjorie Ann Cole, September 23, 1941.

19 Paul Rowden Jr., sermon, First Baptist Church Chattahoochee, Atlanta, Georgia, December 1957, (transcribed from an audio cassette copy of a reel-to-reel audio recording in author's private collection.)

20 Dr. & Mrs. Howard Taylor, *Hudson Taylor and the China Inland Mission,* (London: The China Inland Mission, 1918), Litho Printed in U.S.A. (Ann Arbor: Edwards Brothers, Inc., 1943)

21 Paul Rowden, Papers, Foreign Mission Board Missionary Correspondence Collection, Southern Baptist Historical Library and Archives, Nashville, Tennessee.

22 Henry C. Herge Sr., *Navy V-12,* (Paducah, KY: Turner Publishing Company, 1997), 23.

23 Paul Rowden, to parents, April, 1945.

24 Paul Rowden, to parents, June 8, 1945.

25 Samuel Maddox, "Personnel Department Report of the Foreign Mission Board," *Minutes of the Foreign Mission Board of the Southern Baptist Convention,* April 10, 1951, (Accession Number 1944, International Mission Board Archives and Records Services, Solomon Database) http:// archives.imb.org/solomon.asp.

26 Crawley, *Global Mission, A Story to Tell,*162-163

27 Crawley, *Global Mission, A Story to Tell,* 165

28 Paul Rowden, Papers, Foreign Mission Board Missionary Correspon-

dence Collection, Southern Baptist Historical Library and Archives, Nashville, Tennessee.

[29] *Minutes of the Foreign Mission Board of the Southern Baptist Convention*, January 11, 1951, (Accession Number 1904, International Mission Board Archives and Records Services, Solomon Database), http:// archives. imb.org/solomon.asp (accessed December 22, 2009).

[30] Samuel E. Maddox, to Paul and Marjorie Rowden, May 23, 1951.

[31] Ione Gray, "Three Georgians Among Eight Appointed For Foreign Fields," *Christian Index*, October 18, 1951.

[32] "Missionary Family," *Atlanta Constitution*, November 30, 1951.

[33] "Atlantic Storm Hero Clings to Battered Ship 3rd Day," *Atlanta Constitution*, January 2, 1952.

[34] "Captain Carlsen, Mate Swim To Safety, Watch Enterprise Plunge Beneath Stormy Ocean," *Atlanta Constitution*, January 11, 1952.

[35] "We Will Sink or Swim Together," Editorial, *Atlanta Constitution*, January 10, 1952.

LETTERS FEBRUARY–MARCH 1952

[1] "Cities of Paul's time": refers to the travels of the Apostle Paul as set out in the New Testament of the Bible.

[2] The young people were living within the Baptist compound with the Bakers and working to pay for their tuition as students at the Nazareth Baptist School. The two Jewish youth had come with their family from Egypt. Although they spoke several languages, they didn't speak Hebrew. The Nazareth Baptist School was taught in English and Arabic. Also see Marjorie Cole Rowden, "A Modern Rachel in a New Israel," *Commission*, December 1954.

[3] "American Pace Too Fast, 3 Arab Students Admit," *Atlanta Constitution*, January 3, 1952.

[4] "Dr. [Gus] Stegar owned and operated Stegar's Drug Store, a popular gathering place at the end of the streetcar line at Cascade and Beecher." *Charlie Brown Remembers Atlanta, Memoirs of a Public Man*, as told to James C. Bryant, (Columbia, S.C.: The R. L. Bryan Company, 1982) 112. Dr. Stegar and his wife, Mary, were members of the Cascade Baptist Church in Atlanta.

[5] Also called, *Mahshi Malfouf*, stuffed cabbage leaves.

[6] For a transcript of an interview with Wilbur P. Chase, see http://memory.loc.gov/cgi-bin/query/, (accessed November 10, 2009), Library of Congress, The Foreign Affairs Oral History Collection of the Association

for Diplomatic Studies and Training, "Interview with Wilbur P. Chase," 1990, interviewer, Charles Stuart Kennedy. Wilbur Chase, U.S. State Department, Consul in Haifa, Israel, was the principal officer over four or five officers and about eighteen trained locals from 1951–1955. In the interview Mr. Chase states, "I was the main officer for reporting on Arab affairs in Israel. I would go up to the Arab communities and talk with them about their problems, trying to find out what was happening…The Israelis were very cordial to me, very open."

7 "Hannah Scoggin," Papers, Foreign Mission Board Missionary Correspondence Collection, Southern Baptist Historical Library and Archives, Southern Baptist Convention Building, Nashville, Tennessee. Also see, "Blainard Elmo Scoggin," Papers, Foreign Mission Board Missionary Correspondence Collection, Southern Baptist Historical Library and Archives, Nashville, Tennessee. Hannah Belle [Pearlman] Scoggin earned an A.B. from the University of Louisville, Kentucky and began work toward the M.A. degree in sociology while Elmo Scoggin was attending Southern Baptist Theological Seminary in Louisville. Elmo continued in graduate school as a fellow in Hebrew Old Testament. In March 1948 he received the Th.D. degree. Elmo and Hannah Scoggin were appointed to the Baptist Convention in Israel on October 11, 1949 and sailed for Israel in December 1949. They later adopted Scarlett, a child at the George W. Truett Children's Home in Nazareth, Israel.

LIFE IN ISRAEL–1952

1 Tom Segev, *1949 The First Israelis*, (New York: Henry Holt and Company, Inc., 1986), 95.

2 "Population of Israel-General Trends and Indicator," Israel Ministry of Foreign Affairs, December 24, 1998, http://www.jafi.org.il/MFA/ Archive/ Communiques/1998/POPULATION%20OF%20ISR (accessed November 18, 2009).

3 Baker, interview by David Stricklin, April 27–May 9, 1989.

4 "34,000 Immigrants Arrived in 1951/52," *Jerusalem Post*, October 2, 1952.

5 R. L. Lindsey, "Israel," *Minutes of the Foreign Mission Board of the Southern Baptist Convention*, June 20, 1951, (Accession Number 2742, International Mission Board Archives and Records Services, Solomon Database), http://archives.imb.org/solomon.asp, (accessed December 22, 2009).

6 "Readers Letters—Preventing Disease," *Jerusalem Post*, April 1, 1952.

[7] Segev, *1949 The First Israelis*, 314.

[8] "History Lesson: Israel's Economy, 23–May-96," Israel Ministry of Foreign Affairs, http://www.mfa.gov.il/MFA (accessed December 22, 2009).

[9] "Care History," http://www.care.org/about/history.asp, (accessed January 13, 2009). The mission began in 1945 when 22 American organizations came together to rush lifesaving CARE packages to survivors of World War II. In the 1950's, CARE expanded into emerging nations.

[10] Segev, Tom, *1949 The First Israelis*, 300.

[11] Alan Dowty, "Civil Liberties under Pressure," in *The Jewish State: A Century Later*, (Berkeley: University of California Press, 1998) http://ark.cdlib.org/ark:13030/ft709nb49x/, (accessed December 22, 2009).

[12] *American Jewish Year Book*, 54, s.v. "Foreign Countries: Israel," (1953), 447, http://www.ajcarchives.org, (accessed on January 4, 2010).

[13] "Easter Services Today Climax Holy Week in Jerusalem," *Jerusalem Post*, April 13, 1952.

[14] "Easter Sunday Services at Holy Sepulchre," *Jerusalem Post*, April 14, 1952.

[15] The Garden Tomb was maintained by Anglicans. It is now owned and administered by a charitable trust in the United Kingdom. See http://www.gardentomb.com.

[16] William G. Baker, *The Cultural Heritage of Arabs, Islam and the Middle East*, (Dallas: Brown Books Publishing Group, 2003), 109.

LETTERS APRIL–JUNE 1952

[1] Easter in the Orthodox Church is often celebrated on a different date to that of the Western Churches.

[2] In the letter, dated April 13, 1952, Marjorie Rowden mentions Herbert Pollock and Harold Campbell, serving with the American Friends Service Committee, the service arm of the Quakers. They were Co-Directors of the Village Development Project in Tur'an, Israel. Tur'an was an Arab village about eight miles northeast of Nazareth. The American Friends Service Committee entered into an agreement with the newly established Israeli government to initiate a pilot agricultural project in the Arab village of Tur'an. For two years the men lived in Tur'an, which had no electricity, telephones, running water or sewage system. They assisted the farmers in learning new techniques in agricultural development with the goal of improving the yield, quality and variety of the crops. I am indebted to Herbert Pollock who furnished me with a mimeographed copy of

Harold Campbell's historical memoirs, "Mid-East Memoirs," (August 4, 1951–August 10, 1953).

3 See *My Mission in Israel 1948–1951*, (New York: Simon and Schuster, 1951). James G. McDonald, the first Ambassador to Israel, was appointed by President Harry S. Truman and lived in Israel from 1948–1950.

4 The Dionne Quintuplets were born in 1934 in Corbeil, Ontario. They were the first known surviving quintuplets and received worldwide publicity.

5 Dr. M. Theron Rankin became Executive Secretary of the Southern Baptist Convention Foreign Mission Board in 1945. The administrative offices were in Richmond, Virginia.

6 The name was spelled in the letter as it sounded phonetically. It can also be spelled, "Manseur," or "Mansour."

7 Rev. & Mrs. Alvin Martin left the U.S. in October 1947, and traveled to Palestine as missionaries with the Christian Missionary Alliance (CMA). The Martins were from Minneapolis, Minnesota and graduated from the St. Paul and Nyack Missionary Training Institute. *Alliance Weekly*, Vol. 82, No 45, 717.

8 The museum on Mount Zion had relics of the Holocaust on display. In 1953 a center for reflection of the Holocaust, called *Yad Vashem*, began construction. Located in Jerusalem, it is the memorial of martyrs and heroes and preserves the memory of six million victims.

9 "Stegar's drug store": located in Atlanta, was a small, narrow building approximately 20' wide and 60' long.

10 "tied up properly": Marjorie's brother Bill was planning his wedding.

11 The names of the children were spelled phonetically by Marjorie Rowden as they sounded to her in Arabic. Phonetic spellings of the names of some of the children appearing in various Baptist mission articles over the years include: "Bascillius, Basilious, Bacilla, Hadiyeh, Hediyeh, Hadiya, Ann, Easa, Terese, Therese, Rema, Rahdia, Raufe, Milady, Meladeh, Aly, Affaf, Dalal, Lorice."

12 Two small churches in south Alabama where Paul Rowden served as pastor.

13 Hannah Scoggin, email to author, August 20, 2004.

14 "Uncle Paul": The children in the Children's Home and the children of the Baptist missionaries called all the adult missionaries "Aunt" or "Uncle" followed by their first name.

15 "advanced to kindergarten": an expression of humor because kindergarten was the lowest level of education for children; therefore, Paul's knowledge of Arabic was still that of a young child.

[16] "spic and span": refers to a U.S. brand of household cleaning products and is an expression that means "very clean."

DR. THERON RANKIN VISITS THE MIDDLE EAST

[1] *Minutes of the Foreign Mission Board of the Southern Baptist Convention*, October 13, 1953, (Accession Number 1879, International Mission Board Archives and Records Services, Solomon Database, http://archives.imb.org/solomon.asp (accessed December 22, 2009).

[2] Ibid.

[3] Ione Gray, "He Carried a World in His Heart," *Commission*, September 1953, 2-3.

[4] Ibid.

[5] Ione Gray, "He Carried a World in His Heart," 2-4.

[6] Ione Gray, "He Carried a World in His Heart," 2.

[7] Theron Rankin, "Foreign Mission Board," *Report of the Southern Baptist Convention*, May 6, 1953, (Accession Number 2744, International Mission Board Archives and Records Services, Solomon Database), http://archives.imb.org/solomon.asp, (accessed December 22, 2009).

[8] Marjorie Rowden, to parents, July 1, 1952.

[9] See Johnnie Human, *Finlay and Julia Graham: Missionary Partners*, (Nashville: Broadman Press, 1986); also see Finlay M. Graham, *Sons of Ishmael, How Shall They Hear?*, (Nashville: Convention Press, 1969).

[10] Finlay Graham, *Sons of Ishmael, How Shall They Hear?* (Nashville: Convention Press, 1969) 105: "Missionary Mabel Summers [was] leading in a welfare ministry in the Karantine area of Beirut."

[11] Mrs. George R. Martin, "Conversation of Our Hearts," *Royal Service*, December 1952.

[12] Finlay Graham, "Opportunity is Great in Lebanon," *Minutes of the Foreign Mission Board of the Southern Baptist Convention*, May 6, 1953, (Accession Number 2744, International Mission Board Archives and Records Services, Solomon Database), http://archives.imb.org/solomon.asp, (accessed December 22, 2009).

[13] Lorne E. Brown, "Jordan," *Annual [Report] of the Foreign Mission Board of the Southern Baptist Convention*, May 14, 1952, (Accession Number 2743, International Mission Board Archives and Records Services, Solomon Database), http://archives.imb.org/solomon.asp, (accessed December 22, 2009).

[14] Ibid.
[15] Hereditary title of an Arab tribal chieftain or a leader of an Arab family or village. Also spelled *sheikh*.
[16] Martin, "Conversations of Our Hearts."
[17] Ibid.

LETTERS JULY TO MID-SEPTEMBER 1952

[1] Haifa is the international headquarters for the Baha'i Faith.
[2] See *The New Georgia Encyclopedia*, s.v. "William Ragsdale Cannon (1916–1997)," www.georgiaencyclopedia.org/nge/Article.jsp?id=h-1602&hl=y (accessed on January 4, 2010). Dr. Cannon joined Candler School of Theology, Emory University in 1943. From 1953–1968 Dr. Cannon was dean of Emory University's Candler School of Theology in Atlanta. Dr. Cannon wrote sixteen published books focusing on church history, theology and ecumenicalism. He was a United Methodist Bishop, educator and scholar.
[3] The Roman Catholic Church built the Church of the Annunciation over the site where they believe the Virgin Mary received the news from Gabriel that she would give birth to Jesus. The Greek Orthodox built St. Gabriel's Church over a spring where Mary would have drawn water and believe that it is the place where she received the news from Gabriel that she would give birth to Jesus. Both churches are in Nazareth.
[4] Ein-Dor is mentioned three times in the Old Testament; Joshua 17:11; 1 Samuel 28:7; and in Psalms 83:11.

FUNDING FOR THE FARM

[1] "Near East," *Minutes of the Foreign Mission Board of the Southern Baptist Convention*, October 14, 1952, (Accession Number 1890, International Mission Board Archives and Records Services, Solomon Database), http://archives.imb.org/solomon.asp (accessed December 22, 2009).
[2] Ibid.
[3] Ibid.

LETTERS MID-SEPTEMBER TO DECEMBER 1952

[1] "cool-aide" or "Kool-Aid" contained packets with different powder fla-

vors that could be mixed with water to produce a fruity drink.

[2] "Nushcor Allah," means, "We thank Allah," but also generally, "We thank God," or "Thank God."

[3] "Churchill: World Lost a Distinguished Citizen," *Jerusalem Post*, November 19, 1952.

[4] "Susan B. Anthony": (1820–1906) A woman who struggled to gain voting rights for women and equal rights for all in America.

[5] Martha Murphey, (Mrs. Milton Murphey), in conversation with author, February 2006.

LETTERS JANUARY TO MID-FEBRUARY 1953

[1] See Kenneth R. Mullican, Jr. and Loren C. Turnage, *One Foot in Heaven, The Story of Bob Lindsey of Jerusalem*, (Baltimore: Publish America 2005), 104-105, regarding Mandelbaum Gate and "no-man's land."

[2] See Ione Gray, "Within Him There Is More!" *Commission*, December 1952, 6-7.

[3] "S.S. class": Paul Rowden taught a Sunday school class on Saturdays for young men who worked on Sunday.

WE GO WAY BACK

LETTERS MID-FEBRUARY to APRIL 1953

[1] Job 23:3 King James Version.

[2] For the history of the American Colony, see, Bertha Spafford Vester, *Our Jerusalem, An American Family in the Holy City, 1881–1949*, (Jerusalem: American Colony, 1950), reference is to a facsimile edition of the book published in 1988 by The American Colony and Ariel Publishing House, Jerusalem.

[3] "Good Samaritan Inn": reference is to the Parable of the Good Samaritan in the New Testament, Luke 10:25-37.

MEDICAL MISSIONS

[1] Michael Marten, *Attempting to Bring the Gospel Home, Scottish Missions to*

Palestine, 1839–1917, (London: Tauris Academic Studies), 41, referencing C. Peter Williams, (1982) 'Healing and evangelism': the place of medicine in later Victorian missionary thinking,' in *The Church and Healing (Papers read at the twentieth summer meeting and the twenty-first winter meeting of the Ecclesiastical Historical Society),* ed. W J Shiels Oxford, 271-285: 281.

[2] Dr. Herbert W. Torrance, *2000 Years After Christ the Healer, The Beloved Hakeem of Nazareth,* ed. Edgar L. Farrow, (Edinburgh: Macdonald Printers, 1967), 15.

[3] See "The Nazareth Trust," http://www.emms-nazareth.org, (accessed January 4, 2010). Medical services began in 1861 when Dr. Kaloost Vartan arrived. He set up a dispensary. Dr. Frederick Scrimgeour followed and saw the first building completed in 1912. During World War I the hospital buildings were confiscated for use as a military hospital under the Ottoman government. After the war the hospital was returned to EMMS. Dr. Bathgate arrived in 1921 and oversaw continued repair to the buildings and the construction of new buildings. In 1935 the hospital welcomed the arrival of electricity and a school of nursing was established.

[4] "History," The Nazareth Hospital E.M.M.S., http:www.nazhosp.com /ENGWEB/history.htm, (accessed on November 10, 2009).

[5] Edgar L. Farrow, *2000 Years After Christ the Healer, The Beloved Hakeem of Nazareth,* (Edinburgh: Macdonald Printers, 1967), 8.

[6] Farrow, *2000 Years After Christ the Healer, The Beloved Hakeem of Nazareth,* 14.

[7] Dr. Herbert W. Torrance, *2000 Years After Christ the Healer, The Beloved Hakeem of Nazareth,* ed. Edgar L. Farrow, (Edinburgh: Macdonald Printers, 1967), 19-20.

[8] Ibid. 21.

[9] Ibid. 23.

[10] Ibid. 24.

[11] Dr. W. D. Bathgate, "Up the Hill in Nazareth," *Royal Service,* December 1950.

[12] Torrance, *2000 Years After Christ the Healer, The Beloved Hakeem of Nazareth,* 19.

[13] Mrs. Paul D. Rowden, "A Baby Really Special," *Royal Service,* 1952.

[14] "Board Actions and Reports," *Commission,* June 1953. Also see, *Minutes of the Foreign Mission Board of the Southern Baptist Convention,* April 14, 1953, (Accession Number 1943, International Mission Board, Archives and Records Services, Solomon Database), http://archives.imb.org/

solomon.asp. Also, in a letter written to Jim and Betty Smith, dated February 27, 1955, Marjorie Rowden states that Dr. George Sadler, Foreign Mission Board Area Secretary, "was so appreciative of their [EMMS] services to all of us [missionaries] that he recommended that the Foreign Mission Board give [EMMS] $2,000 for a new hospital car. And [the FMB] did. And it is the only car they have."

[15] Alta Lee Lovegren, "Waiting for You," *Commission,* February 1954, 4-5.

[16] Alta Lee Lovegren, telephone conversation with the author, January 13, 2008.

[17] J. T. McRae, M.D., *Mission Doctor,* (Nashville: Convention Press, 1955), 38. Alta Lee Lovegren, telephone conversation with the author, January 13, 2008.

LETTERS JULY–DECEMBER 1953

[1] "Ridgecrest": A Baptist assembly, retreat and conference center now administered by LifeWay and located in the North Carolina mountains. The campus has housing, a cafeteria, auditorium and multiple buildings for meetings and gatherings. Ridgecrest sponsors meeting venues for various Baptist organizations. One week each year the focus is on foreign or international missions. Missionaries who are retired or on furlough gather and share experiences. The Executive Secretary and staff of the Foreign Mission Board (now International Mission Board) also attend and talk with those interested in missions.

NAZARETH NATIONAL BAPTISTS

[1] Baker, "Baptists' Golden Jubilee."

[2] Ibid.

[3] Ibid.

[4] Ibid.

[5] Emma Baker, note to author, June 15, 2005.

[6] Dwight L. Baker, email to author, May 14, 2005.

[7] Dwight L. Baker, "Issa Saba and Jareer Tabari," *Accent,* (January 1973).

[8] Dwight L. Baker, email to author, May, 14 2005.

[9] Laurella Owens, *Shalom,* (Richmond: Convention Press, 1961), 52-54.

[10] Dwight L. Baker, email to author, February 2, 2005.

[11] John Allen Moore, "An International Seminary Is Born," *Commission,*

October, 1949, 4-5. In September 1949 Baptist leaders established an International Baptist Theological Seminary in Switzerland. A large estate in a suburb of Zurich (Ruschlikon) was acquired to house the institution. Switzerland was selected because of its neutral position in Europe. Also see Mrs. John D.W. Watts, "International Life at Zurich," *Commission,* October 1957. At that time the seminary averaged about forty students a year representing approximately fifteen different countries from points as far away as Norway, South Africa, Canada, Israel and Indonesia.

[12] Baker, "Baptists' Golden Jubilee."

[13] Nazareth Baptist School, "Beginnings," http://www.nbs.org.il/ en/nbs_history.php (accessed on October 1, 2009).

[14] Baker, "Baptists' Golden Jubilee."

[15] Nazareth Baptist School, "Beginnings," http://www.nbs.org.il/en/ nbs_history.php (accessed on October 1, 2009).

[16] Nazareth Baptist School, "Home Page," www.nbs.org.il/en (accessed on 2/7/2008).

[17] Owens, *Shalom,* 56.

[18] Dwight L. Baker, email to author, January 14, 2008.

[19] Naim Stifan Ateek, *Justice and Only Justice,* (Maryknoll, NY: Orbis Books, 1989), 7-13. Naim Stifan Ateek, brother of Fida and Naomi Ateek, became Canon of St. George's Cathedral in Jerusalem and was pastor of its Arabic-speaking congregation.

[20] Owens, *Shalom,* 42-43.

[21] United Christian Council in Israel, http://www.ucci.net, (accessed on November 18, 2009).

[22] Owens, *Shalom,* 56.

[23] See, Ray Register, *Back to Jerusalem, Church Planting Movements in the Holy Land,* (Enumclaw, WA: WinePress Publishing 2000).

LETTERS JANUARY 1954

[1] Juliette Mather was Editorial Secretary of the Women's Missionary Union from 1948–1957.

RACIAL SEGREGATION, QUAKERS AND ARTIST

[1] "Mid-East Reading Ability Lags, Calvary Club Hears," *Atlanta Constitu-*

tion, January 20, 1954.

[2] "Supreme Court Weighs Segregation Decision," *Atlanta Constitution,* December 10, 1953.

[3] See "Herman Talmadge, Georgia Senator and Governor, Dies at 88," *New York Times,* March 22, 2002. Herman E. Talmadge (1913–2002), a Democrat, was elected governor of Georgia twice and served four terms in the U.S. Senate. He boasted that he never carried a county with a streetcar line because he concentrated on rural areas. Talmadge was a Southern populist who built schools as governor of Georgia and then called for stopping desegregation by closing them. While he denounced the 1954 Supreme Court decision on school desegregation—saying "there aren't enough troops in the whole United States to make the white people of this state send their children to school with colored children,"—he also saw to it that black teachers' salaries were made equal to those of whites, a step for which there was no political support.

[4] "Legislators Hail Segregation Plan," *Atlanta Constitution,* November 18, 1953.

[5] William R. Miner, telephone conversation with author, January 17, 2005.

[6] Ibid.

[7] Ibid.

[8] Martha Murphey, telephone conversation with the author, May 3, 2008.

[9] William R. Miner, telephone conversation with the author, January 17, 2005.

[10] Marjorie Cole Rowden, "Grandmother Comes to Visit," *Royal Service,* January 1955, 8-9.

[11] Ibid.

[12] Ibid.

LETTERS FEBRUARY–EARLY-APRIL 1954

[1] "two young fellows": William R. Miner and Don Rosedale, with the American Service Friends Committee (Quakers) were working in the Arab farming village of Tur'an.

[2] "first grade course": Marjorie Rowden was home schooling using the Calvert Course. By the 1950s, more than 85 tons of Calvert materials were being shipped every year all over the world. See www.calvertschool.org/education-services/home-history/, (accessed on 1/1/2009).

[3] See William G. Baker, *The Cultural Heritage of Arabs, Islam and the Middle East,* (Dallas: Brown Books Publishing Group, 2003), 47. "At funerals, both Arab men and women cry, wail, beat their chests, yell, scream, pull

at their hair and clothes, kiss the face of the deceased, shout promises of vengeance to the deceased (if appropriate), and throw their bodies over the casket…They are expressing to the community how much they will miss the departed and how much the deceased meant to them…"

BAPTISTS FROM THE UNITED STATES EMBASSY IN ISRAEL

[1] Marjorie Cole Rowden, "Double Commission," *Commission,* June 1955, 4-5.
[2] Ibid.
[3] Lynn Davis, in conversation with the author, October 2004.
[4] Ibid.

LETTERS APRIL 1954

CORONATION OF QUEEN ELIZABETH II

[1] "Elizabeth II To Ascend in Triple Rites," *Atlanta Constitution,* June 2, 1953.
[2] "Largest TV Audience Will Watch Crowning," *Atlanta Constitution,* May 29, 1953.
[3] "Misty-Eyed Atlantans Toast Queen; Thrill to Pageantry by Radio, TV," *Atlanta Constitution,* June 3, 1953.
[4] "Garden Party in Ramat Gan," *Jerusalem Post,* Tuesday, June 2, 1953.

LETTERS JUNE 1954

[1] Paul Rowden, letter to parents, May 31, 1954: "We had a nice trip over—uneventful, and landed in Nicosia, Cyprus, and especially Kyrenia, is a very nice place, and very inexpensive. Three meals a day, two of which we have two meats such as fish, lamb chops or steaks; tea and 2 rooms (one for the children) cost only $12.00 daily. Food would cost us this much or more in the States. Our room has a balcony overlooking the water."

BAPTISTS IN JERUSALEM 1923–1954

[1] Watts, *Palestinian Tapestries,* 14-18.

[2] Ibid.

[3] Ibid. 43

[4] "Palestine and Syrian Mission," *Annual [Report] of the Foreign Mission Board of the Southern Baptist Convention*, May 12, 1926, (Accession Number 2710, International Mission Board Archives and Record Services, Solomon Database), http://archives.imb.org/solomon.asp, (accessed December 22, 2009).

[5] Ibid.

[6] Watts, *Palestinian Tapestries*, 45.

[7] Watts, *Palestinian Tapestries*, 44. Also see "Palestine and Syrian Mission," *Annual Report of the Southern Baptist Convention*, May 16-20, 1928, (Accession Number 2712), http://archives.imb.org/solomon.asp (accessed December 22, 2009).

[8] Mrs. J. Wash Watts, "Burning Lights in Jerusalem," in *Questing in Galilee*, (Richmond: Foreign Mission Board of the Southern Baptist Convention, 1937), 73.

[9] Watts, *Palestinian Tapestries*, 50-51.

[10] Mullican, Jr. and Turnage, *One Foot in Heaven*, 257.

[11] Watts, *Palestinian Tapestries*, 51. For additional information about the Jerusalem Good Will Center run by Miss Elsie Clor, see Kate Ellen Gruver, "The Good Will Center, An Instrument of Missions in Developing Native Christian Leaders in Palestine," (Master of Religious Education Thesis, Department of Missions, Baptist Women's Missionary Union Training School, April 1938), 16. The dissertation was accessed in the James P. Boyce Centennial Library, Southern Baptist Theological Seminary, Louisville, KY.

[12] Margaret Lindsey, "Paralyze the Powers of Darkness," *Royal Service*, October 1955.

[13] Baker, "Baptists' Golden Jubilee."

[14] Watts, *Palestinian Tapestries*, 5.

[15] Leo H. Eddleman, "The Palestine Ferment," *Commission*, January 1947, 10.

[16] H. Leo Eddleman, "Our Hearts Desire is that Palestine and Syria Be Saved," *Minutes of the Foreign Mission Board, Southern Baptist Convention*, May 13, 1937, (Accession Number 2724, International Mission Board Archives and Records, Solomon Database) http://archives.imb.org/solomon.asp, (accessed December 22, 2009).

[17] "The Gospel in the Near East," *Annual Report of the Foreign Mission Board of the Southern Baptist Convention*, May 16, 1944, (Accession Number

2735, International Mission Board Archives and Records, Solomon Database) http://archives.imb.org/solomon.asp. (accessed December 22, 2009).

[18] A book documents the prolific work of Robert and Margaret Lindsey during the years 1945–1987. See Kenneth R. Mullican, Jr. and Loren C. Turnage, *One Foot in Heaven, The Story of Bob Lindsey of Jerusalem*, (Baltimore: PublishAmerica, LLLP, 2005).

[19] Mullican Jr. & Turnage, *One Foot in Heaven*, 77.

[20] Ibid. 83-85.

[21] Ibid. 89.

[22] Ibid. 102.

[23] "Near East," *Minutes of the Foreign Mission Board, Southern Baptist Convention*, May 9, 1950, (Accession Number 2741, International Mission Board Archives and Records, Solomon Database) http://archives.imb.org/solomon.asp, (accessed December 22, 2009).

[24] Ibid.

[25] Baker, "Baptists' Golden Jubilee."

[26] Ibid.

[27] "Near East," *Minutes of the Foreign Mission Board, Southern Baptist Convention*, May 9, 1950, (Accession Number 2741, International Mission Board Archives and Records, Solomon Database).

[28] R. L. Lindsey, "Israel Mission," *Annual Report of the Foreign Mission Board of the Southern Baptist Convention*, May 28-31, 1957, Southern Baptist Historical Library and Archives, Nashville, Tennessee.

[29] Baker, "Baptists' Golden Jubilee."

[30] Roy H. Kreider, *Land of Revelation*, (Scottdale, Pennsylvania: Herald Press, 2004), published in cooperation with Mennonite Mission Network, 70.

[31] Mullican Jr. & Turnage, *One Foot in Heaven*, 137-138. Also see, Robert L. Lindsey, *The Jesus Sources*, (Tulsa: Academic Series, HaKesher, Inc., 1990) and Robert L. Lindsey, *Jesus Rabbi & Lord*, (Oak Creek, WI: Cornerstone Publishing, 1990).

[32] R. L. Lindsey, "Israel," *Minutes of the Foreign Mission Board of the Southern Baptist Convention*, June 20, 1951, (Accession Number 2742, International Mission Board Archives and Records, Solomon Database) http://archives.imb.org/solomon.asp, (accessed December 22, 2009).

[33] Baker, "Baptists' Golden Jubilee."

[34] Mullican Jr. & Turnage, *One Foot in Heaven*, 110.

[35] Robert Lindsey, "Israel in Christendom: The Problem of Jewish Identity"

(doctoral dissertation, Southern Baptist Theological Seminary, Louisville, Kentucky, n.d., ca 1954) (bound copy located in James P. Boyce Centennial Library, Southern Baptist Theological Seminary, Louisville, Kentucky).

[36] Robert Lindsey, "Israel's Coming Crisis over Jewishness," *Commentary*, July 1954.

[37] Also spelled "Bar Kokhba." Shortly after the destruction of the Second Temple, the Jewish warrior Bar Cochba led a short-lived rebellion against the Roman occupation of Israel (80-83 CE). Maimonides describes Bar Cochba as "a great king whom all Israel, including the great sages, were convinced was the messiah." See www.templeinstitute.org/messiah_temple.htm.

[38] Robert Lindsey, "Israel in Christendom: The Problem of Jewish Identity," 8.

[39] Ibid. 337.

[40] Ibid. 340-341.

[41] Weiner, *The Wild Goats of Ein Gedi*, 310-311.

[42] Dwight Baker, "Near East, New Challenge to Israel," *Minutes of the Foreign Mission Board of the Southern Baptist Convention*, May 6, 1953, (Accession Number 2744, International Mission Board Archives and Records, Solomon Database) http://archives.imb.org/solomon.asp, (accessed December 22, 2009).

[43] Mullican Jr. & Turnage, *One Foot in Heaven,* 112.

LETTERS - JULY–AUGUST 1954

[1] The communists waived red flags when they paraded through Nazareth.

[2] Georgette Jeries Campbell, a native of Nazareth, taught at the Nazareth Baptist School. She taught herself English by correspondence course. One summer she lived in the Jerusalem Baptist House with Elmo and Hannah Scoggin and attended *ulpan* classes where she learned Hebrew. On a visit to Israel, Dr. Leo Eddleman, former missionary to Palestine-Israel and President of Georgetown College, met Georgette, who impressed him with her linguistic skills. He assisted her in obtaining a scholarship to attend college in America. Georgette Jeries Campbell, telephone call with author, October 29, 2009.

[3] The Baptist World Congress was scheduled to meet in London in 1955. Many Baptist tourists planned to extend their travels to other countries

in Europe and the Middle East, including Israel.

[4] *"Gan"* is Hebrew for "preschool." It means "garden." Thus preschool is a garden for children, or in Hebrew, *"Gan Yeladim."*

[5] The Anglican Mission Hospice in Jerusalem was turned over to Israel's Hadassah Hospital to operate as a medical clinic in 1948 after the war when the Hadassah Hospital on the Mt. Scopus campus fell within Jordanian Jerusalem.

ULPAN

[1] Paul Rowden, sermon, First Baptist Church of Chattahoochee, Atlanta, December 1957, transcribed from an audio cassette copy of a reel to reel audio tape in author's private collection.

[2] Bob Lindsey, letter to Dr. John Carter, June 28, 1968.

[3] Marjorie Rowden, Letters, September, 1954.

LETTERS - SEPTEMBER 1954

[1] *"Shabbat"*: the Sabbath Day

[2] *"Yom Kippur"*: a day set aside by Jews to atone for the sins of the past year. Leviticus 23:26-32.

[3] *"Shavu'ot"*: a Jewish festival that commemorates the revelation of the Torah to Moses on Mount Sinai.

PENINA

[1] Paul D. Rowden, "Jesus in her Heart," *Commission,* October 1955. In this article, Rowden substituted the name "Rebekah" for "Penina" in order to protect her from negative publicity.

[2] See Owens, *Shalom,* 87. Penina died in 1961 before *Shalom* was published.

[3] I am indebted to Elizabeth (Betty) Smith, for her mimeographed copy of "Penina," located in her private writings, 1961.

[4] Ibid.

[5] Ibid.

[6] Paul D. Rowden, "Jesus in her Heart," *Commission,* October 1955.

[7] Elizabeth (Betty) Smith, "Penina."

[8] Rowden, "Jesus in her Heart."

[9] Ibid.

[10] Elizabeth (Betty) Smith, "Penina."

[11] Ibid.

[12] Owens, *Shalom*, 91.

[13] Ibid., 90.

[14] Elizabeth (Betty) Smith, "Penina."

[15] A 1977 anti-proselytizing law prohibits any person from offering or receiving material benefits as an inducement to conversion. "Israel and the occupied territories," Bureau of Democracy, Human Rights and Labor, U.S. Department of State, 2001, http://www.state.gov/g/drl/rls/irf/2001/5697.htm, (accessed January 8, 2010).

[16] John Carter, *Witness in Israel, The Story of Paul Rowden*, (Nashville: Broadman Press, 1969), 48.

[17] See http://www.tikvatenu.org.il/innerE.asp?id=1641. *Keren Yaldenu* was established in 1953 to empower immigrant children living in poverty-stricken conditions. The first *Keren Yaldenu* center was established in the disadvantaged *Morasha* neighborhood of Jerusalem.

[18] "Anti-Mission Group Opens Appeal," *Jerusalem Post* (February 4, 1954).

[19] "French Rabbinate Denounces Catholic Church on Finaly Case," *Jerusalem Post* (June 7, 1953).

[20] "Finaly Boys Returned Under Catholic-Jewish Agreement," *Jerusalem Post* (June 28, 1953).

[21] "Gedera Children Greet Finaly Boys," *Jerusalem Post* (July 27, 1953).

[22] Paul Rowden, "The Religious Situation in Israel," *Christianity Today*, December 22, 1958, 7.

[23] Uri Bailer, *Cross on the Star of David, The Christian World in Israel's Foreign Policy, 1948–1967*, (Bloomington: Indiana University Press, 2005), 191.

[24] Ibid. 93.

[25] Mark 15:16 (King James Version).

[26] Mullican Jr. & Turnage, *One Foot in Heaven*, 74.

[27] James Willis Smith, Jr., Papers, Foreign Mission Board Missionary Correspondence Collection, Southern Baptist Historical Library and Archives, Nashville, Tennessee.

[28] Ray Register, *Back To Jerusalem, Church Planting Movements in the Holy Land*, (Enumclaw WA: WinePress Publishing, 2000), 34.

[29] *American Jewish Year Book*, 55, "Israel," (1954), 346.

LETTERS OCTOBER–NOVEMBER 1954

[1] In 1931, Dr. Washington Watts, former Baptist missionary to Palestine-Syria (1923–1929), became professor of Old Testament and Hebrew at

the Baptist Bible Institute (now New Orleans Baptist Theological Seminary).

[2] See Mullican Jr. & Turnage, *One Foot in Heaven*, 106. A picture of the car Bob Lindsey built is also included in the book.

THANKSGIVING IN JERUSALEM 1954

[1] William R. Miner, in telephone conversation with author, November 15, 2005.

[2] "Sholem Asch," see http://www.encyclopedia.com/topic/Sholem_ Asch. aspx, (accessed January 5, 2009).

[3] "Sholem Asch," see http://www.britannica.com/EBchecked/topic/ 37900 Sholem-Asch, (accessed January 5, 2009).

[4] Chaim Lieberman, *The Christianity of Sholem Asch, An Appraisal From the Jewish Viewpoint*, (New York: Polyglot Press 1953), 1.

LETTER OF NOVEMBER 28, 1954

THE SPIRIT OF THE SEASON

[1] Hugh Park, "Around Town," "Telephone Call to Jerusalem Carries the Spirit of Christmas," *Atlanta Journal/Constitution*, December 22, 1954.

[2] Ibid.

[3] Ibid.

LETTERS DECEMBER 1954

[1] "Put on the dog": an idiom that generally means to appear more important than you are.

[2] "The Robe": The first Cinema Scope feature film, 20th Century-Fox's *The Robe*, stars Richard Burton as the Roman tribune who is assigned by Pontius Pilate to supervise the crucifixion of Christ. He wins the robe in a dice game. Gradually, the mystical influence of the holy garment transforms Burton from a roistering cynic into a true believer—at the cost of his own life, which he willingly gives up in the service of his Lord.

[3] Reference to the Bible, Galatians 3:28 (King James Version), "There is nei-

ther Jew nor Greek, there is neither bond nor free, there is neither male nor female: for ye are all one in Christ Jesus.

[4] "the investment": Cascade Baptist Church in Atlanta was providing financial support for Paul and Marjorie Rowden.

[5] Reference is to the New Testament, Gal 6:9 (King James Version) "And let us not be weary in well doing: for in due season we shall reap, if we faint not."

[6] *New Georgia Encyclopedia*, s. v. "Walter F. George (1878–1957)," http://www.georgiaencyclopedia.org.

[7] "Konrad Adenaurer": (1876–1967), German statesman and first Chancellor of the Federal Republic of Germany 1949–1963.

THE BROCHURE

[1] *Christmas Greetings, The Baptist Convention in Israel, Pictorial Report, 1954*, ed. Marjorie Rowden (Jerusalem, Israel: 1954).

[2] Elizabeth (Betty) Smith, note to author, September 19, 2000.

[3] James Willis Smith, Jr., "IMB Archives – Emeritus Survey," February–March 2009, Papers, Foreign Mission Board Missionary Correspondence Collection, Southern Baptist Historical Library and Archives, Nashville, Tennessee.

LETTERS - JANUARY–FEBRUARY 1955

[1] See Roy H. Kreider, *Land of Revelation*, (Scottdale, Pennsylvania: Herald Press, 2004), published in cooperation with Mennonite Mission Network. Roy Kreider and his wife were commissioned to Israel by the Mennonite Board of Missions, and arrived in 1953. They were living in Jerusalem.

[2] "Yarkon River": in the Sharon Plain, flows on the property of the farm and Baptist Center at Petah Tikva.

BAPTISTS IN TEL AVIV

[1] J. Wash Watts, "Palestine and Syria," in *Annual Report of the Foreign Mission Board of the Southern Baptist Convention*, May 6, 1928, (Accession Number 2712, International Mission Board Archives and Records Serv-

ices, Solomon Database), http://archives.imb.org/solomon.asp, (accessed December 22, 2009).

[2] Roswell E. Owens, "Palestine and Syria," in *Annual Report of the Foreign Mission Board of the Southern Baptist Convention*, May 13-16, 1932, (Accession Number 2729, International Mission Board Archives and Records Services, Solomon Database), http://archives.imb.org/solomon.asp, (accessed December 22, 2009).

[3] H. Leo Eddleman, "The Near East Faces Divers[e] Demands," in *Annual Report of the Foreign Mission Board of the Southern Baptist Convention*, 1938, Southern Baptist Historical Library and Archives, Nashville, TN.

[4] " Petah Tikva," in *Minutes of the Foreign Mission Board of the Southern Baptist Convention*, May 9, 1950, (Accession Number 2741, International Mission Board Archives and Records Services, Solomon Database), http://archives.imb.org/solomon.asp, (accessed December 22, 2009).

[5] Baker, "Baptists' Golden Jubilee."

[6] Ibid.

[7] R.L. Lindsey, "Israel Mission," in *Report of the Foreign Mission Board of the Southern Baptist Convention*, May 30–June 2, 1956, Southern Baptist Historical Library and Archives, Nashville, TN.

LETTERS - MARCH–MAY 1955

[1] Bob Lindsey wrote informally in a letter about Paul Rowden's role as treasurer: "We were a small mission and the rules for the use of funds were not always clearly spelled out. Paul tried to be fair, more than anything, and was as honest as a man can be in Israel…Paul had a keen conscience and he tried desperately to be…right about everything and sometimes he referred to himself as a bit over conscientious. But this was just the kind of a person we appreciated in that delicate job of treasurer on the field where it is easy to be accused of being inconsistent in one way or another in the disbursement of funds. I never heard a word of criticism about Paul's handling of the funds. That is really quite unusual…" Robert Lindsey, letter to Dr. John Carter, June 28, 1968.

[2] *American Jewish Year Book*, vol. 57, s.v. "Foreign Countries: Israel, Middle East" (1956), http://www.ajcarchives.org, (accessed December 29, 2009). The demand for introduction of civil marriage was frequently voiced by Israelis, and stubbornly resisted by the parliament. The non-Orthodox public in general complained about "Orthodox encroachment" and there

was much criticism of the religious courts in the debates on the law for the appointment of Religious Court judges.

[3] See "Mixed Marriages in Israel," *Time* (April 4, 1955). Moshe Barak, 27, an Israeli of Rumanian parentage who was wounded four times in the Arab-Israeli war, staged a hunger strike to force the Knesset, Israel's Parliament, to repeal its rabbinical ban on civil marriages. Barak met his fiancée, Oriah, a Christian, soon after she arrived from Yugoslavia in 1951. Israel's religious parties feared that mixed marriages may dilute or destroy the separate racial identity of the Jewish people. Also see Dwight Baker, "Religious Liberty in Israel 1948–1963," (doctoral thesis, Hartford Seminary Foundation, May 1963), 251, 252. "The hunger strike ended fifteen days after it began when the Speaker of the Knesset indicated that the Knesset would discuss the Marriage and Divorce Law. In the end Barak was unsuccessful in his attempt either to change the law or to marry his fiancée in Israel. They chose to leave the country and to establish their home in Europe."

[4] See *Eleanor and Harry*, ed. and with commentary by Steve Neal, (New York: A Lisa Drew Book, Scribner, New York, 2002), for correspondence between Eleanor Roosevelt and Harry Truman beginning in 1945. In 1945, following the death of her husband, President Franklin D. Roosevelt, Eleanor Roosevelt was designated by Harry Truman as the "First Lady of the World." From 1946 through 1953, she would be the most influential and highest-ranking woman in the Truman administration as a member of the U.S. delegation to the United National General Assembly.

[5] "Roy Sewell": Roy Brown Sewell Jr. and Paul Rowden were both students at Emory University. W.H. Heard, First Baptist Church, Bremen, Georgia was Sewell's pastor in 1956. Roy's father, Roy Brown Sewell 1898–1988, was one of America's largest manufacturers of men's clothing. He operated several plants in Georgia and Alabama. (http://www.lib.auburn.edu/arch/buildings/images/sewellpcx.jpg) (accessed December 29, 2009). Paul Rowden received a new suit as a gift from Roy Brown Sewell Jr. when his pastor traveled through Israel on tour.

THE FIRST NAZARETH BAPTIST
SECONDARY SCHOOL GRADUATION

[1] Marjorie Cole Rowden, "They Grew up with the Baptist School," *Commission*, November 1955.

[2] Ibid.
[3] Ibid.

LETTERS JUNE 1955

[1] Dwight and Emma Baker and their four children left for a year of furlough in the United States.

BAPTIST TOURISTS VISIT THE MIDDLE EAST 1955

[1] In 2004, the Southern Baptist Convention voted to remove itself as a member of the Baptist World Alliance.

[2] "Israel is 1955 Mecca for Baptists," *Christian Century,* September 21, 1955, 1534–1535.

[3] "Catholics Apply Pressure To Stop Excavations; Fear Dogma Mary's Ascension Be Disproved," *Charity and Children,* 68, no. 50, July 7, 1955. *Charity and Children* is the monthly publication of the Baptist Children's Home of North Carolina.

[4] "Notes of My Tour of Israel," (Jerusalem: Baptist Convention in Israel, Summer 1955).

[5] Alta Lee Lovegren, "Welcome to the Middle East," *Commission,* June 1955.

[6] Ibid.

[7] Alta Lee Lovegren, "Waiting for You," *Commission,* February 1954, 4-5.

[8] Ibid.

[9] "Baptist Work in Israel Rigorous," *Christian Century,* September 21, 1955, 1535.

[10] "Israel is 1955 Mecca For Baptists," *Christian Century,* September 21, 1955, 1534–1535.

[11] "Baptist Church In the Land of Jewish People," *Charity and Children,* 68, no. 50, July 7, 1955.

[12] Ibid.

[13] "Catholics Apply Pressure," *Charity and Children,* 68, no. 50, July 7, 1955, 4.

LETTERS JULY 1955

[1] "Roland Q. Leavell": President of the New Orleans Southern Baptist Theological Seminary.

[2] "Billy Graham": Billy Graham traveled to Israel in 1960 and preached in several locations. Robert (Bob) Lindsey was one of the people selected to translate. Milton Murphey and James (Jim) Smith helped to locate venues for the services. See Mullican, Jr. & Turnage, *One Foot in Heaven,* 220-226.

[3] "Dick Hall": Pastor of the First Baptist Church, Decatur, Georgia.

[4] See *Charlie Brown Remembers Atlanta, Memoirs of a Public Man,* as told to James C. Bryant, (Columbia: The R.L. Bryan Company, 1982). "Back in the 1920's, two families moved into the Cascade-Beecher community who were destined to make a profound impact on the Cascade Baptist Church as well as the entire area. One family was Dr. and Mrs. Ward Beecher Du-Vall…a physician from South Georgia and a graduate of the University of Georgia Medical College in Augusta…They had a particular interest in the growth of Cascade Baptist Church because Dr. DuVall's brother W.O. DuVall was a member there."

[5] "Monroe Swilley": Pastor, Second-Ponce de Leon Baptist Church, Atlanta, Georgia

[6] "Courts Redford": Executive Director, Home Mission Board, Atlanta, Georgia. Courts Redford became Executive Director of the Home Mission Board in 1954.

[7] "Searcy S. Garrison": Executive Secretary-Treasurer, Baptist Convention in Georgia.

BAPTISTS IN HAIFA

[1] Watts, *Palestine Tapestries,* 2nd ed.

[2] Baker, "Baptists' Golden Jubilee."

[3] Roswell Owens, "Palestine and Syria," in *Annual[Report] of the Foreign Mission Board of the Southern Baptist Convention,* May 13-16, 1932, (Accession Number 2729, International Mission Board Archives and Records Services, Solomon Database), http://archives.imb.org/solomon.asp.

[4] See Doreen Hosford Owens, *The Camel Bell,* (Richmond: Foreign Mission Board of the Southern Baptist Convention, 1937). Robert S. Hosford, Doreen's father, was ordained by Southern Baptist missionaries that traveled to Argentina in the early 1900's. Doreen's mother was from a large family of missionaries that went to Liberia, West Africa. In December 1922, Doreen Hosford came to America for the first time. She entered Bethel Women's College in Hopkinsville, Kentucky and graduated in 1927. Roswell and Doreen married on December 27, 1927 in Providence,

Kentucky. Rev. and Mrs. Owens served a church field in West Baden, Indiana, where he held the pastorate for more than four years, until April 1929 when they sailed for Palestine. The Owens had two daughters, Laurella and Rosalind.

[5] Watts, *Palestine Tapestries,* 2nd ed.

[6] Ibid.

[7] "The Near East Will Not Forget Thy Word, Palestine and Syria," in *Annual Report to the Southern Baptist Convention,* 1934, Southern Baptist Historical Library and Archives, Nashville, Tennessee.

[8] Rev. Roswell E. Owens, "Two Timothies in Haifa," in *Questing in Galilee,* (Richmond: Foreign Mission Board of the Southern Baptist Convention, 1937), 47-57.

[9] Watts, *Palestine Tapestries,* 2nd ed.

[10] Also spelled "Saleeby."

[11] Owens, "Two Timothies in Haifa," in *Questing in Galilee,* 58-61. Also, Graham, "Elias Saleeby," in "Baptist Beginnings in Lebanon 1893–1956," 26, 37.

[12] Watts, *Palestinian Tapestries,* 2nd ed., 65-66.

[13] Ibid.

[14] Graham, "Early 1940's," in "Baptist Beginnings in Lebanon 1893–1956," 40, 50.

[15] H. Leo Eddleman, "Middle East," *Commission,* May 1945.

[16] *Minutes of the Foreign Mission Board of the Southern Baptist Convention,* May 14-18, 1941 and June 12, 1941, (Accession Nubers 2732 and 2079, International Mission Board Archives, Records and Services, Solomon Database), http://archives.imb.org/solomon.asp.

[17] Graham, "Early 1940's," in "Baptist Beginnings in Lebanon 1893–1956," 40.

LETTERS AUGUST–MID-SEPTEMBER 1955

[1] Camp was held on the pine forested hillside of the Edinburgh Medical Mission Society Hospital grounds in Nazareth.

THE BEGINNING OF BAPTIST VILLAGE IN PETAH TIKVA

[1] Mullican, Jr. & Turnage, *One Foot in Heaven,* 114.

[2] Martha (Marty) Murphey, telephone conversation with the author, April 23, 2008.

[3] Ibid.

[4] Ibid.
[5] Marjorie Cole Rowden, "On Holy Ground," *Commission,* March 1956, 12-13, 29.
[6] Owens, *Shalom,* 86.
[7] Owens, *Shalom,* 72-86.
[8] Martha (Marty) Murphey, in conversation with the author, February, 2006.

LETTERS LATE-SEPTEMBER–DECEMBER 1955

[1] See Saul Paul Colbi, *Christianity in the Holy Land, Past and Present,* (Tel Aviv: Am Hassefer 1969). Biographical information is on the jacket of the cover to the book.
[2] "Baptist Work in Israel Rigorous," *Christian Century,* September 21, 1955.
[3] Margaret Lindsey's parents were Mr. & Mrs. Dexter Lutz, who served with the Presbyterian mission in Pyongyang, Korea. Dexter Lutz had a PhD in agriculture and helped farmers raise better crops. He also taught in Korean mission schools. Mrs. Lutz taught voice at the mission school. See Mullican, Jr. & Turnage, *One Foot in Heaven,* 32.
[4] "Lana Turner": a well known glamorous American actress who appeared in numerous films.
[5] Dr. Donald L. Branyon Jr., (son of Dr. Donald L. Branyon), in telephone conversation with author, January 10, 2008.

LETTERS JANUARY 1956

[1] "Luke," described in the New Testament as "the beloved physician." Col. 4:14 (King James Version).
[2] President Harry Truman's Point Four Cooperative Program included aid for world economic recovery.

TENSION IN THE MIDDLE EAST 1955–1956

[1] *Time,* January 23, 1956, 23.
[2] *Time,* January 23, 1956, 23. Also, *Time,* January 2, 1956, 22.
[3] Alta Lee Lovegren, telephone conversation with author, January 13, 2008.
[4] Dr. August Lovegren and wife, Alta Lee Lovegren, in conversation with author, January 13, 2008. Alta Lee Lovegren stated that a *Time* magazine article in the January 23, 1956 issue is incorrect insofar as stating that Dr.

Lovegren met the mob and talked them out of burning the hospital. She does not know where that story originated. Dr. August Lovegren was in the operating room when the riots occurred. Dr. August Lovegren concurred stating that he was delivering a baby during the riots.

5 *Minutes of the Foreign Mission Board of the Southern Baptist Convention*, Executive Secretary, February 9, 1956, (Accession Number 1864, International Mission Board Archives and Records Services, Solomon Database), http://archives.imb.org/solomon.asp.

6 Graham, *Sons of Ishmael, How Shall They Hear?* 80-81.

7 "Halt Anti-U.S. Mobs, Dulles Warns Jordan, Demands Protection for Flag; Britain's Pact Role Criticized," *Atlanta Constitution*, January 9, 1956, 6.

8 *Minutes of the Foreign Mission Board of the Southern Baptist Convention*, Executive Secretary, February 9, 1956, (Accession Number 1864, International Mission Board Archives and Records Services, Solomon Database), http://archives.imb.org/solomon.asp.

LETTERS FEBRUARY–MAY 1956

1 Milton and Martha (Marty) Murphey traveled through parts of Europe on a holiday. They were accompanied by Lynn and Helen Davis. Lynn Davis had completed his assignment with the military working as a US Army attaché in the American Embassy in Tel Aviv. Lynn and Helen Davis returned to America after traveling through Europe and the Murpheys returned to Israel.

2 The first fruits, including the first grains to ripen each season were to be brought as an offering to God. (Ex. 23:19; 34:26, Num. 15:17-21; 18:12-13; Deut. 26:1-11).

SUMMER 1956–JULY 1957

1 Aaron Kiron, "The Professionalization of Wisdom: The Legacy of Dropsie College and its Library," www.library.upenn.edu/exhibits/rbm/at250/dropsie/ak.pdf, (accessed January 8, 2009). Dropsie College merged with the University of Pennsylvania in 1993.

2 Elizabeth (Betty) Smith, referencing notes in her diary, in conversation with the author in March 2008.

3 Dwight Baker, "Baptists' Golden Jubilee."

4 Elizabeth (Betty) Smith, referencing notes in her diary, in conversation with the author in March 2008.

[5] The Jewish Agency for Israel, "The Sinai Campaign 1956," www.jafi.org.il/education/100/maps/sinai.html, (accessed January 8, 2009).

[6] See Mullican, Jr. & Turnage, *One Foot in Heaven,* 174.

[7] Elizabeth (Betty) Smith, referencing notes in her diary, in conversation with the author in March 2008.

[8] The Jewish Agency for Israel, "The Sinai Campaign 1956."

[9] Elizabeth (Betty) Smith, referencing notes in her diary, in conversation with the author in March 2008.

[10] Ibid.

[11] James (Jim) and Elizabeth (Betty) Smith served with the Baptist Convention in Israel for 34 years. The Smiths were supported by Kirkwood Baptist Church in Atlanta, Georgia, now the Rainbow Park Baptist Church in Decatur, Georgia. Jim acted as Director of the Nazareth Baptist School for a number of years in the sixties. They then moved to Ashkelon. The Ashkelon Municipality in Israel awarded Jim a certificate of recognition for his voluntary work through the Ashkelon Rotary Club having served as a member in Jerusalem, Nazareth and Ashkelon for thirty years. Betty received a certificate of merit from the Ashkelon Municipality for her 12 years of volunteer work at the Government Hospital and from the Israel Government Ministry of Tourism for her aid to tourists and pilgrims.

[12] Mullican, Jr., & Turnage, *One Foot in Heaven,* 119-120.

[13] Baker, "Baptists' Golden Jubilee."

[14] Mullican, Jr., & Turnage, *One Foot in Heaven,* 123.

[15] Paul D. Rowden, Jr., Cascade Baptist Church Bulletin, (n.d., circa end of July 1957).

LETTERS - JULY–SEPTEMBER 1, 1957

[1] Charlie Brown was one of the founders of the Cascade Baptist Church and a friend of the family. Active in politics, Charlie Brown lost in a race for Mayor of Atlanta against William B. Hartsfield in 1949 and 1953, but won the 1956 election for State Senator from Fulton County. See *Charlie Brown Remembers Atlanta, Memoirs of a Public Man* as told to James C. Bryant.

[2] Dr. Baker James Cauthen, Executive Director of the Southern Baptist Foreign Mission Board, Richmond, Virginia.

THE UCCI, VOLUNTEERS & BIBLE LAND SEMINARS

[1] Elizabeth (Betty) Smith, notes from her diary, in conversation with the author in March 2008.

[2] Ibid.

[3] "United Christian Council in Israel," http://www.ucci.net, (accessed December 30, 2009).

[4] Alice Marshall, in conversation with the author September 28, 2009. Also, Alice Marshall, emails to author, September 30, 2009 & October 2, 2009.

[5] Ibid.

[6] Ibid.

[7] Ibid.

[8] Owens, *Shalom,* 96-99.

[9] Alice Marshall in interview with the author, September 28, 2009. Also, Alice Marshall, emails to author, September 30, 2009 & October 2, 2009.

[10] Ibid.

LETTERS - SEPTEMBER 1957

[1] In 1969, Bill and Alice Marshall were appointed by the Foreign Mission Board to the Middle East. They and their three children moved to Cyprus where Bill served as Field Representative for North Africa, the Western Orient and the Near East until his return to the Foreign Mission Board as Director of the Furlough Ministries Department and later as Vice President of the Mission Support Division. In 1983, Bill became the Executive Director of the Kentucky Baptist Convention. He retired in 1997.

[2] *Minutes of the Foreign Mission Board of the Southern Baptist Convention,* May 10, 1977, (Accession Number 815, International Mission Board Archives and Records Services, Solomon Database), http://archives.imb.org/solomon.asp.

THE JOURNEY HOME

[1] "Program of The Dropsie College For Hebrew and Cognate Learning, The College, Conferring of Degrees," June 2, 1959, Broad and York Streets, Philadelphia, Pennsylvania.

[2] Marjorie Rowden, n.d. in author's private collection.

[3] James Smith, letter to Dr. John Carter, August 21, 1968, in author's private collection. Dr. John Carter was in the School of Education, Samford Uni-

versity, Birmingham, Alabama. He wrote a Baptist mission book for young people about Paul Rowden entitled, *Witness in Israel,* (Nashville: Broadman Press, 1969).

[4] Martha (Marty) Murphey, telephone conversation with author, April 23, 2008.

[5] Western Union Telegram, October 11, 1959, in private collection of author.

[6] Owens, *Shalom,* 59.

[7] Dwight Baker, "Paul D. Rowden Primary School," *Accent,* (January 1973).

[8] Dwight Baker, "Remarks at the Dedication Service of the Paul D. Rowden Primary School, Nazareth," from clipping of unknown Baptist magazine, March 1961.

[9] Marjorie Rowden, *The Three Davids,* (Nashville: Convention Press 1963); *The Flying Dragon,* (Nashville: Convention Press, 1966); Marjorie Rowden Kelly, *The Gifted Woman I Am,* Birmingham: Women's Missionary Union, 1981).

[10] Dr. Ralph Noonkester, former President of William Carey College, speech at Memorial Service for Marjorie Rowden Kelly, Jackson, Mississippi, March 2, 2002.

EPILOGUE

[1] Bill Baker lived most of his life in Israel, beginning in 1950 when he moved with his family to Nazareth, until 1967, when he left Israel to complete high school and attend Baylor University in the United States, graduating with a degree in Foreign Service and then obtaining a Master's degree in Political Science from Southwest Texas State University. He was commissioned a Second Lieutenant in the United States Air Force and served twenty-seven years, retiring in 2000 as a Lieutenant Colonel. His overseas assignments included embassy tours of duty as an Assistant Air Attaché in Tel Aviv, Israel; acting Air Attaché in Riyadh, Saudi Arabia and Defense and Air Attaché in Doha, Qatar. He had served as Senior Middle East Intelligence Analyst at the Pentagon, Adjunct Lecturer in International Affairs at the Air Force Special Operations School and as Assistant Professor of Arabic at the United States Air Force Academy. Bill Baker is Senior Lecturer in Arabic and Middle Eastern Studies at Baylor University, Waco, Texas. He wrote a book assisting Americans in understanding the Arab culture. See Baker, William G., *Arabs, Islam and the Middle East,* (Dallas: Brown Books Publishing Group, 2003).

2 "Nazareth Hospital," http://www.nazhosp.com/ENGWEB/about-us.htm, (accessed on November 10, 2009).

3 "Rhadia Qubti—a complex identity of a Palestinian Israeli," in *Come and See*, www.comeandsee.com, the Christian website from Nazareth, April 30, 2008.

4 See "Association of Baptist Churches in Israel," www.baptist.org.il, (accessed January 8, 2010).

5 Baker, A Series of Interviews Conducted 27 April 27–May 9, 1989.

6 Register, *Back To Jerusalem, Church Planting Movements in the Holy Land*, 20-21.

7 See "Nazareth Seminary," www.nazarethseminary.org, (accessed January 8, 2010).

8 Bader Mansour, "Baptists in Israel, to Mark 100 years of Baptist Witness in 2011," "Latest News," http://www.baptist.org.il, (accessed January 8, 2010).

9 Suhail Ramadan died in 2009 at the age of 74. A funeral was held April 23, 2009.

10 "Harte House": The YMCA owned a hostel and shoreline property on the Sea of Galilee (Lake Kinneret) just north of Tiberias and shared it with Christian groups. "The YMCA seaside hostel was built as a residence for Dr. Archibald Harte, the General Secretary of the Jerusalem YMCA in the 1920s. After his death it became a guesthouse." See http://www.ymca-galilee.co.il/about.html, (accessed January 8, 2010).

11 Robert Lyle Lindsey, *A Hebrew Translation of the Gospel of Mark*, (Jerusalem: Dugith Publishers Baptist House, n.d. ca. 1970, with foreword by David Flusser, Hebrew University, Introduction in English).

12 See also, David Flusser, *The Sage from Galilee, Rediscovering Jesus' Genius*, (Grand Rapids, Michigan: William B. Eerdmans Publishing Company, 2007) 3.

13 Robert L. Lindsey, *Jesus Rabbi & Lord* (Oak Creek, Wisconsin: Cornerstone Publishing 1990).

14 "House of Prayer for all Nations, Narkis Street Congregation," http://www.narkis.org/whoweare.htm, (accessed January 8, 2010).

15 Har-El in Jerusalem is the founding congregation of the Reform Movement in Israel. See "Kehillot B'Yachad," (KBY) Congregations Together, http://www.kharel.org.il, (accessed December 19, 2009).

16 Elizabeth F. Smith, "Jews Show Concern in Wake of Jerusalem Church Fire," *California Southern Baptist*, March 10, 1983.

17 "House of Prayer for All Nations, Narkis Street Congregation in

Jerusalem," http://www.narkis.org/whoweare.htm, (accessed January 8, 2010).

[18] "Baptist Convention in Israel," http://www.bcisrael.com, (accessed December 30, 2009).

[19] Dr. Dale Thorne served in Nazareth for 17 years (1966–1983) as a member of the Baptist Convention in Israel and served as General Director of the Nazareth Baptist School. After leaving Nazareth, Dale and Anita moved to Haifa where Dr. Thorne served as Secretary of the Middle East and North African Region (1984–1997) for the International Mission Board of the Southern Baptist Convention. The Thornes returned to the U.S. and from 1999–2007, Dale served as pastor of the Sonrise Community Church in Cincinnati, Ohio. In 2008, the Thornes moved to Jerusalem to start the prayer center. See "Nazareth Educational Ministries Association," "Board of Directors," http://www.nazarethedu.org, (accessed January 8, 2010).

[20] Register, *Back To Jerusalem, Church Planting Movements in the Holy Land*, 20-21.

[21] Botrus Mansour became the General Director of the Nazareth Baptist School taking over from Fuad Haddad in 2005.

[22] Or Kashti, "One-third of outstanding Israeli schools are from Arab sector," *HARRETZ.com*, August 24, 2009, http://www.haaretz.com/hasen/spages/ 1109607.html (accessed September 21, 2009).

[23] "Nazareth Baptist School," http://www.nbs.org.il/en, (accessed January 8, 2010).

[24] Paul Rowden, letter to Ione Gray, April 8, 1954, in author's private collection.

Selected Bibliography

Allen, Catherine B. *The New Lottie Moon Story.* Nashville: Broadman Press, 1960.

Armstrong, Marjorie Moore. "They Want a Home Too!" *Commission,* July 1952.

Ateek, Naim Stifan. *Justice and Only Justice.* Maryknoll, NY: Orbis Books, 1989.

Bailer, Uri. *Cross on the Star of David, The Christian World in Israel's Foreign Policy 1948-1967.* Bloomington: Indiana University Press, 2005.

Bailey, Betty Jane & J. Martin Bailey. *Who Are the Christians in the Middle East?* Grand Rapids: William B. Eerdmans Publishing Company, 2003.

Baker, Dwight. "Religious Liberty in Israel, A Study Covering a Period of Fifteen Years from the Founding of the State until 1963." doctoral dissertation, Hartford Seminary Foundation, Hartford, Connecticut, May 1963.

Baker, Dwight. "Paul D. Rowden Primary School." *Accent,* January 1973.

Baker, Emma. "New Appointees." *Commission,* May 1950.

Baker, William G. *The Cultural Heritage of Arabs, Islam and the Middle East.* Dallas: Brown Books Publishing Group, 2003.

"Baptist Church in the Land of Jewish People." *Charity and Children,* 68, no. 50, July 7, 1955. *Charity and Children* is the monthly publication of the Baptist Children's Home of North Carolina.

"Baptist Work in Israel Rigorous." *Christian Century,* September 21, 1955.

Bathgate, Dr. W.D. "Up the Hill in Nazareth." *Royal Service,* December 1950.

Brown, Charlie. *Charlie Brown Remembers Atlanta, Memoirs of a Public Man,* as told to James C. Bryant. Columbia: The R.L. Bryan Company, 1982.

Carter, John T. *Witness in Israel, The Story of Paul Rowden.* Nashville: Broadman Press 1969.

Colbi, Saul, Paul. *Christianity in the Holy Land, Past and Present.* Tel Aviv: Am Hassefer, 1969. Biographical information is on the jacket of the cover.

Crawley, Winston. *Global Mission, A Story to Tell.* Nashville: Broadman Press, 1985.

Dowty Alan. "Civil Liberties under Pressure." In *The Jewish State: A Century*

Later. Berkeley: The University of California Press, 1998. http://openlibrary.org/b/OL661171M/Jewish_state (accessed February 1, 2010).

Eddleman, H. Leo. *Mandelbaum Gate.* Nashville: Convention Press, 1963.

———. "The Palestine Ferment." *Commission,* January 1947.

———. "Middle East." *Commission,* May 1945.

Eleanor and Harry. ed. and with commentary by Steve Neal. New York: A Lisa Drew Book, Scribner, New York, 2002.

Farrow, Edgar L. *2000 Years After Christ the Healer, The Beloved Hakeem of Nazareth.* Edinburgh: Macdonald Printers, 1967.

Flusser, David. *The Sage from Galilee, Rediscovering Jesus' Genius.* Grand Rapids: William B. Eerdmans Publishing Company, 2007.

Graham, Finlay M. *Sons of Ishmael, How Shall They Hear?* Nashville: Convention Press 1969.

Gray, Ione. "He Carried a World in His Heart," *Commission,* September 1953.

———. "Within Him There is More!" *Commission,* December 1952.

———. "Three Georgians Among Eight Appointed for Foreign Fields." *The Christian Index,* October 18, 1951.

Gruver, Kate Ellen. "Baptist Children's Home in Nazareth Favored by State of Israel Government." *Commission,* July 1949.

Hanna, Velora Griffin. "Questing in Galilee," in Chapter 1 *Questing in Galilee.* Richmond: Foreign Mission Board of the Southern Baptist Convention, 1937.

Harvey, Paul. "Saints but Not Subordinates: The Woman's Missionary Union of the Southern Baptist Convention." In *Women and Twentieth-Century Protestantism,* edited by M.L. Bendroth and V.L. Brereton. Chicago: University of Illinois Press, 2002.

Herge, Henry C. *Navy V-12.* Paducah, KY: Turner Publishing Company, 1997.

Human, Johnnie. *Finlay and Julia Graham: Missionary Partners.* Nashville: Broadman Press, 1986.

"Israel is 1955 Mecca for Baptists." *Christian Century,* September 21, 1955.

Kelly, Marjorie Rowden. *The Gifted Woman I Am.* Birmingham: Women's Missionary Union, 1981.

Kreider, Roy H. *Land of Revelation.* Scottdale, Pennsylvania: Herald Press, 2004.

Lieberman, Chaim. *The Christianity of Sholem Asch, An Appraisal From the Jewish Viewpoint.* New York: Polyglot Press, 1953.

Lindsey, Margaret. "Paralyze the Powers of Darkness." *Royal Service,* October 1955.

Lindsey, Robert Lyle. *A Hebrew Translation of the Gospel of Mark.* Jerusalem: Dugith Publishers, 1970.

Lindsey, Robert L. *Jesus Rabbi & Lord.* Oak Creek, Wisconsin: Cornerstone Publishing, 1990.

Lindsey, Robert. "Israel in Christendom: The Problem of Jewish Identity," doctoral dissertation, Southern Baptist Theological Seminary, Louisville, Kentucky, ca 1954 (bound copy located in James P. Boyce Centennial Library, Southern Baptist Theological Seminary.

——— "Israel's Coming Crisis over Jewishness." *Commentary,* July 1954.

Lindsey, Robert L. *The Jesus Sources.* Tulsa: Academic Series, HaKesher, Inc., 1990.

Livingston, W. P. *A Galilee Doctor, Being a Sketch of the Career of Dr. D.W. Torrence of Tiberias.* London: Hodder and Stoughton Limited, 1923.

Lovegren, Alta Lee. "Waiting for You." *Commission,* February 1954.

———. "Welcome to the Middle East." *Commission,* June 1955.

Makdisi, Jean Said. *Three Generations of Arab Women.* New York: W.W. Norton & Company, 2006.

Marten, Michael, *Attempting to Bring the Gospel Home, Scottish Missions to Palestine 1839-1917.* London: Tauris Academic Studies 2006.

Martin, Mrs. George R. "Conversation of Our Hearts," *Royal Service,* December 1952.

McDonald, James G. *My Mission in Israel 1948–1951.* New York: Simon and Schuster 1951.

McRae J. T. *Mission Doctor.* Nashville: Convention Press, 1955.

McRae, Jane Carroll. *Photographer in Lebanon, the Story of Said Jureidini.* Nashville: Broadman Press, 1969.

Moore, John Allen. "An International Seminary is Born." *Commission,* October 1949.

Mullican, Kenneth R. Jr. and Loren C. Turnage. *One Foot in Heaven, The Story of Bob Lindsey of Jerusalem.* Baltimore: Publish America, 2005.

Newton, Louie D. "Atlanta Prepares for the Alliance." *Commission,* May 1938.

Owens, Doreen Hosford. *The Camel Bell.* Richmond: Foreign Mission Board of the Southern Baptist Convention, 1937.

Owens, Laurella. *Shalom.* Richmond: Convention Press, 1961.

Owens, Roswell E. "Two Timothies in Haifa." Chapter 2 in *Questing in Galilee.* Richmond: Foreign Mission Board of the Southern Baptist Convention, 1937.

Register, Ray. *Back To Jerusalem, Church Planting Movements in the Holy Land.* Enumclaw, WA: Winepress Publishing 2002.

Rowden, Marjorie Cole. "Double Commission." *Commission,* June 1955.

———. "On Holy Ground." *Commission,* March 1956.

Rowden, Marjorie. *The Three Davids.* Nashville: Convention Press, 1963.

Rowden, Mrs. Paul D. "A Baby Really Special." *Royal Service,* 1952.

Rowden, Marjorie Cole. "They Grew up with the Baptist School." *Commission,* November 1955.

Rowden, Paul D. "Jesus in her Heart." *Commission,* October 1955.

Rowden, Paul. "The Religious Situation in Israel." *Christianity Today,* December 22, 1958.

Scoggin, Hannah Belle. "Home on the Farm." *Commission,* June 1952.

Segev, Tom. *1949 The First Israelis.* New York: Henry Holt and Company, Inc., 1986.

Silver Anniversary of the Cascade Baptist Church, The History and Growth, March 11, 1923-March 7, 1948. Privately printed, n.d. [ca.1948].

Smith, Elizabeth F. "Jews Show Concern in Wake of Jerusalem Church Fire." *California Southern Baptist,* March 10, 1983.

Taylor, Dr. & Mrs. Howard. *Hudson Taylor and the China Inland Mission.* London: The China Inland Mission, 1918. Litho printed in U.S.A. Ann Arbor: Edwards Brothers, Inc., 1943.

Torrance, Dr. Herbert W. in *2000 Years After Christ the Healer, The Beloved Hakeem of Nazareth.* Edgar L. Farrow, ed. Edinburgh: Macdonald Printers, 1967.

Vester, Bertha Spafford. *Our Jerusalem, An American Family in the Holy City, 1881-1949.* Jerusalem: American Colony, 1950. Reference is to a facsimile edition of the book, *The American Colony.* Jerusalem: Ariel Publishing House, 1988.

Watts, Mrs. J. Wash. *Palestinian Tapestries.* 2nd ed. Richmond: Foreign Mission Board of the Southern Baptist Convention, 1936.

———. "Burning Lights in Jerusalem." In Chapter 3, *Questing in Galilee.* Richmond: Foreign Mission Board of the Southern Baptist Convention, 1937.

Watts, Mrs. John D. "International Life at Zurich." *Commission,* October 1957.

Weiner, Herbert. *The Wild Goats of Ein Gedi, A Journal of Religious Encounters in the Holy Land.* Cleveland: The World Publishing Company; Philadelphia: The Jewish Publication Society of America, 1954. Reprinted 1961 by arrangement with Doubleday & Company, Inc. Page references are to the Doubleday edition.

ACKNOWLEDGMENTS

While working on this book, I had an opportunity to talk with most of the retired members of the Baptist Convention who lived in Israel in the fifties. I shared work-in-progress drafts with them and greatly valued their comments. I visited Dwight and Emma Baker several times at their home in Texas. Between visits I frequently called and emailed asking specific questions about people and events referenced in the letters. I relied heavily on Dwight as a resource for details about the history of the Baptist ministry in Nazareth and in the Galilee area. His contribution was invaluable. William (Bill) Baker, son of Dwight and Emma, is Associate Director of Middle East Studies at Baylor University. He assisted me with Arabic words. In correspondence, my parents spelled Arabic words as they sounded phonetically in English. Bill reviewed the correspondence and suggested more precise and generally accepted spellings in English of Arabic words. He also explained the common usage of the words. *Shukran*—thanks, Bill.

One afternoon when I was visiting Marty Murphey at her home in Kentucky, she served me afternoon tea with cinnamon bread as we talked and watched a beautiful snowfall. Marty's husband, Milton Murphey, had died a few years earlier and we spent most of the weekend looking at his Israel slide collection and talking about the pictures. Marty was most helpful in providing information about the beginnings of Baptist Village in Petah Tivka. Listening to Marty as she tells a story and laughs, with her wonderful way of finding humor in almost everything, reminded me why she and my mother took easily to one another. Three of Bob and Margaret Lindsey's children attended William Carey College (now University) in Hattiesburg, Mississippi where my mother worked, and were in and out of our house as a home-away-from-home. Bob and Margaret Lindsey dropped in for a visit from time to time. Bob Lindsey died before I began work on this book, but *One Foot in Heaven*, a book about his life, documents his work beautifully. Bob Lindsey was one of a kind and everyone I talked to had a funny story about him. Bob's daughter, Lenore Lindsey Mullican, who teaches Modern Hebrew at Oral Roberts University and Biblical Hebrew in the ORU Graduate School of Theology, was my translator. When I came across a word in Hebrew, either in a letter or picture, she would translate. *Toda*—thanks, Lenore. Although I had a good command of Hebrew and Arabic as a child living in Israel, it faded over the years from lack of use. Ken Mullican, Lenore's husband, graciously read not one, but two drafts of my book and his comments about Bob Lindsey and his work were most helpful.

James (Jim) Smith and my father were friends beginning with high school days in Atlanta. I have spent long hours enjoying Jim and Betty's company. One day we watched old 16mm movies from the fifties filmed by various Baptist mission members in Israel. Betty provided me with information about Penina Nehama, who is the subject of one chapter. She also provided information from her diary about Baptist work and events in Israel the summer of 1956 to the summer of 1957, when my family was in America for a year of furlough. Jim and Betty not only read drafts of the book but also shared stories and wonderful memories. I would like to thank Elmo and Hannah Scoggin who read a draft of the book and commented. Hannah graciously provided me with information about her relatives, the Biebergal family members living in Haifa during the fifties, who entertained my parents in their homes on several occasions. Their generosity enabled the Children's Home and mission children to attend their cinema in Haifa at no cost. I spent an afternoon with Lynn Davis who filled in details about his job as U.S. Army Attaché at the U.S. Embassy in Tel Aviv. The Baptist mission members "adopted" Lynn and Helen Davis as their own, considering their dedicated contribution to the ministry of the Nazareth Baptist Church. Alta Lee Lovegren read a draft of the book and was very helpful in explaining events at the Baptist Hospital in Ajloun, Jordan during the 1956 riots, a topic my mother addressed in her letters. Both August and Alta Lee Lovegren were exceptionally helpful in clarifying, and providing additional information about Baptist work in Jordan in the fifties.

Bill and Alice Marshall read a draft of the book and shared stories of their experiences in Nazareth during the school year 1957–1958. They also shared information about the Journeyman Program and their memory of the Bible Land Seminars led by Bob Lindsey. Georgette Jeries Campbell, native to Nazareth, taught me and my parents Hebrew one summer in Jerusalem and her sister, Nahil, taught Arabic to my parents in Nazareth. Georgette made several suggestions about the format of the book that I incorporated. I located William (Bill) Miner through Dwight Baker and I have thoroughly enjoyed our conversations over the past few years. Bill Miner, who worked with the American Friends Service Committee in Tur'an, a village near Nazareth, talked with me about his friendships with the Baptist mission members and the musical concerts in which he and Marty Murphey performed to enthusiastic audiences. Bill was especially helpful in recalling events at the Thanksgiving gathering for Americans at the YMCA in Jerusalem, 1954, where he served as Master of Ceremonies. Dr. John Tester, former director of the Edinburgh Medical Mission Society (EMMS) Hospital in Nazareth, corresponded with me regarding Dr. William Bathgate and directed me to the EMMS office staff in Edinburgh, Scotland, who provided me a booklet about Dr. Bathgate's life and work in Nazareth. Dr. Donald L. Branyon Jr. spoke with me about his parents. His father served as an American agrarian consultant to Israel. The Branyons were from Georgia, as were my parents, and they struck up an immediate and lasting friendship. Betsy Watts (Mrs. Elmer) West read a draft of the book and talked with me by phone. It was wonderful to talk with the daughter of the first Baptist mission members appointed by the FMB to Palestine in 1923, (Dr. and Mrs. Washington Watts), and her encouragement was especially meaningful. Of all the storytellers I spoke with over the course of compiling this book, Julia Hagood Graham has to be the most remarkable. Her recall of dates and events that transpired in Palestine in the forties was amazing and transported me to a time before my family arrived in Israel.

I would like to thank Bill Summers at the Southern Baptist Historical Library and Archives in Nashville, Tennessee for helping me locate material written by Baptist missionaries to Palestine-Israel from 1923–1957 located in mission magazines, books, papers and with locating volumes of Annual Reports of the Foreign Mission Board to the Southern Baptist Convention. I would also like to thank Eddie Jeter at the International Mission Board & Archives for her encouragement and suggestion of people who had an interest in reading a draft of the book. The library staff at the James P. Boyce Centennial Library, Southern Baptist Theological Seminary in Louisville, Kentucky assisted me with location of several dissertations and books. I am indebted to the library staff at Baylor University in Waco, Texas for providing me the transcribed Oral Memoirs of Dwight Baker. Emory University library staff assisted me in locating information about William Ragsdale Cannon, former head of the Candler School of Theology, who traveled to Israel and visited with my parents. I am thankful to the staff of the Chatham County, Georgia, Live Oak Public Libraries, who obtained copies of the *Jerusalem Post* for me through interlibrary loan. I also thank the staff at the Tarver Library at Mercer University in Macon, Georgia, who provided assistance locating documents in the special historical archives.

My friends, Harry and Jo Hickson, listened often to my ramblings about research for the book and encouraged me to keep going. Jo contributed significantly when she suggested that I use the Epilogue to describe my return to Israel in 2004 to attend the Jubilee Graduation of the Nazareth Baptist School. I would like to thank former members of the Cascade Baptist Church in Atlanta who provided me with historical church booklets, pictures and bulletins and who shared memories of the church family.

This book would not have stood a chance for survival if it were not for my husband, Dan, who has knowledge of all things having to do with computers and computer programs. Dan scanned pictures and set up computer programs. When my computer crashed one day, and when I was ready to forget that I ever wanted to compile this book, he brought home a new computer, retrieved the hardware from my old one and installed my old files in the new computer. Thanks Dan. Let me say in closing that any shortcomings or mistakes in this book are entirely my own.

INDEX

About the Author

Rebecca Rowden was born in Atlanta, Georgia and at age four, traveled with her parents and sister to Israel arriving in March 1952. She spent most of her childhood in Israel where she attended the Nazareth Baptist School in Nazareth, a British Anglican school in Jerusalem and Beit Hasefer Hareali (the Hebrew Reali School) in Haifa. Upon returning to America, she lived with her family in Atlanta, Philadelphia, New Orleans and Hattiesburg. Rebecca received a Bachelor's degree from Samford University and a J.D. from the University of Richmond. She practiced law in Franklin, Tennessee and then moved to Savannah, Georgia where, for over twenty years, she specialized in environmental law. She is retired from public service and lives with her husband on the Georgia coast.

Rebecca Rowden